Coming Into Being

Mothers on Finding and Realizing Feminism

Edited by Andrea O'Reilly,
Fiona Joy Green, and Victoria Bailey

DEMETER

Coming into Being
Mothers on Finding and Realizing Feminism
Edited by Andrea O'Reilly, Fiona Joy Green, and Victoria Bailey

Copyright © 2023 Demeter Press

Individual copyright to their work is retained by the authors. All rights reserved. No part of this book may be reproduced or transmitted in any form by any means without permission in writing from the publisher.

Demeter Press
PO Box 197
Coe Hill, Ontario
Canada
K0L 1P0
Tel: 289-383-0134
Email: info@demeterpress.org
Website: www.demeterpress.org

Demeter Press logo based on the sculpture "Demeter" by Maria-Luise Bodirsky www.keramik-atelier.bodirsky.de

Printed and Bound in Canada

Cover image: *Emerge* by Lianne Milton, in collaboration with Fábio Erdos
Cover design and typesetting: Michelle Pirovich
Proof reading: Jena Woodhouse

Library and Archives Canada Cataloguing in Publication
Title: Coming into being: mothers on finding and realizing feminism / edited by Andrea O'Reilly, Fiona Joy Green, and Victoria Bailey.
Names: O'Reilly, Andrea, 1961- editor. | Green, Fiona J., editor. | Bailey, Victoria (Victoria Jane), editor.
Description: Includes bibliographical references.
Identifiers: Canadiana 2023015736X | ISBN 9781772584493 (softcover)
Subjects: LCSH: Motherhood. | LCSH: Feminism.
Classification: LCC HQ759.C66 2023 | DDC 306.874/3-dc23

 The publisher gratefully acknowledges the support of the Government of Canada

In memory of Christina Cudahy
May 24, 1961 – February 2, 2023

In *Of Woman Born: Motherhood as Experience and Institution* Adrienne Rich emphasized that "daughters need mothers who want their own freedom and ours....The quality of the mother's life—however embattled and unprotected—is her primary bequest to her daughter, because a woman who can believe in herself, who is a fighter, and who continues to struggle to create livable space around her, is demonstrating to her daughter that these possibilities exist" (247). I suggest all women need mothers who abundantly, assiduously, and adamantly model and mentor this struggle for and possibilities of empowered womanhood. This collection is dedicated to Christina, the original mother outlaw who with outrage, irreverence, defiance, and hilarity showed us that indeed Eve was framed, and Mary lied.

Acknowledgements

Creating a collection takes the inspiration, energy, commitment, and labour of many. We greatly appreciate each of the contributors, who have generously and courageously shared their insights and experiences of combining mothering and feminism in their meticulous pieces. We would especially like to thank Lianne Milton whose photo appears on the front cover—for the inspirational visual representation of the collection's theme of coming into being in her moving photograph that graces the cover of the collection.

A deep and distinct thanks to the exceptional team at Demeter Press—copy editor Jesse O'Reilly-Conlin, proof reader Jena Woodhouse, administrator Tracey Carlyle and type setter and designer Michelle Pirovich—for their hours of work ensuring the publication of this collection. Thank you also to the reviewers of the manuscript for their close reading and insightful suggestions.

Contents

Introduction
Coming into Being: Mothers on Finding and
Realizing Feminism
Andrea O'Reilly, Fiona Joy Green, and Victoria Bailey
11

Section One
Losing and Finding
29

1.
Journeying through Feminist Motherhood:
Reflections on Identity and Practice
Heather E. Dillaway
31

2.
Sunrise
Lianne Milton
49

3.
Single Teen Motherhood and the Good Mother:
Feminist Responses
Natasha Steer
57

4.
Discovering Feminist Motherhood through Art Practice
Jen McGowan
75

5.
Holding and Being Held
Eve Darwood
83

6.
Colostrum
Victoria Bailey
97

7.
We Are Mothers
Rachel O'Donnell
103

Section Two
Challenging and Critiquing
115

8.
Coming into Motherhood: An Anishinaabeg Feminist View on Birth and Motherhood in Hospital Spaces
Renée E. Mazinegiizhigoo-kwe Bédard
117

9.
Meandering through the Intersections: Feminist Mothering as a Transnational Migrant Academic Mom
Lili Shi
141

CONTENTS

10.
Coming Home to Myself: On Single Black Motherhood
Kahaema Byer
161

11.
Reflections from a Settler and an Immigrant Mother of Colour: How Motherhood Helped Me Develop My Feminist Politics over the Last Decade
Shruti Raji-Kalyanaraman
181

12.
I Am Never Sleeping with You Again: Reflections on Mothering, Community Building, and Unstable Allyship
Zaje A.T. Harrell
197

13.
The "Wildness of Motherhood": Transforming Maternal Rage and Transgressing Patriarchal Motherhood to Realize Maternal Empowerment: A Reading of Rachel Yoder's *Nightbitch*
Andrea O'Reilly
215

Section Three
Connecting and Conversing
237

14.
Becoming a (Better) Feminist: Autoethnographic Lessons I Learned about Feminism by Becoming a Mother
Molly Wiant Cummins
239

15.
Recognizing Their Feminist Selves through the Journey of Mothering: Reflections of Urban Indian Mothers
Ketoki Mazumdar, Sneha Parekh Gupta, and Isha Sen
253

16.
A Conversation: A Mother and Daughter Discuss Feminism
Tara Carpenter Estrada and Emily Rae Robertson
273

17.
Motherhood, Art, and a Revolution
Jillayna Adamson
287

18.
Between Mothers: Dialogically Exploring the Mother-Scholar Relationship
Rachel E. Stough and Elizabeth A. Bennett
309

19.
The COVID-19 Pandemic as a Catalyst for Feminist Thought
Lisa H. Rosen and Linda J. Rubin
325

20.
Feminist Representations of Maternity in Caryl Churchill's *Top Girls* and Sarah Daniels's *Neaptide*
Tuğrul Can Sümen
339

Notes on Contributors
361

Introduction

Coming into Being: Mothers on Finding and Realizing Feminism

Andrea O'Reilly, Fiona Joy Green, and Victoria Bailey

As many projects tend to do, this book began with a question. Near the end of 2020, Victoria Bailey interviewed Andrea O'Reilly for an article that was later included in the 2021 spring issue of the feminist magazine *Herizons*. The article, entitled "Why I am a Feminist: Seeing the World Anew," and the interview opened with Victoria asking Andrea: "Why are you a feminist?" In the ensuing discussion, and article, Andrea shared that as a teenager, she had the outlook and behaviours of a feminist, but that on reflection, she likely would not have had "the language for it or the community" (qtd. in Bailey 12). Andrea went on to describe how this language developed along with a more concrete understanding of, and connection to, feminism through studying women's and feminist literature. However, for Andrea, it was when she became a mother that "feminism became very real" for her (qtd. in Bailey 12). Andrea elaborated: "Many people think becoming a mother is a conservatizing influence on women, but I would say the absolute opposite; for most mothers it is the most radicalizing moment of their life" (qtd. in Bailey 12). Indeed, as Adrienne Rich similarly and powerfully shares in her 1982 text "Split at the Root": "The experience of motherhood was eventually to radicalize me" (212). Victoria also identified with Andrea's insights, as her experiences of becoming a mother, and being an immigrant mother and at one time a single mother, resulted in an awareness of the inequalities specific to mothers. Victoria also desired a feminist mother community, especially in her early years of mothering, and longed for the support of other mothers. These experiences set Victoria on a path to motherhood studies. Andrea similarly shared:

> I experienced significant discrimination as a mother when a graduate student. That's when I turned to matricentric feminism but again, at that time I didn't have that language or the feminist allies to support me as a mother; I felt let down by and became disillusioned with feminism. However, I think feminism gave me the power to fight, so I'm not minimizing the importance of and need for feminism in my life, but at the time I did not have the feminist community, language or theory to empower me as a mother (qtd. in Bailey 12).

Andrea's citing of her desire for community was also echoed by Victoria during their discussion. As Jacqueline Rose shares in *Mothers: An Essay on Love and Cruelty*, "After all, it is indeed true that, if your vision of being in the world is one of untrammelled self-realisation, motherhood is a bit of a shock, to say the least" (133). For both Andrea and Victoria, their experiences of mothering made them aware of the inequalities mothers experience and the need for a feminist maternal community to support and empower mothers.

The initial question that sparked this collection led Andrea and Victoria to ask subsequent questions, such as: Why is motherhood seen as a conservatizing experience when for most, it is not? What does motherhood have to offer feminism? How can feminism support mothers and those who work with them or aim to support them? Why is motherhood a feminist issue? They decided to create an edited collection to explore this topic and invited Fiona Joy Green, a leading scholar in feminist mothering, to join them. Fiona agreed without hesitation, as her own doctoral research into the interconnected nature and influence of feminism and mothering in the lives of feminist mothers was based upon her own trajectory and relationship with feminism and mothering analogous to those of Andrea and Victoria, albeit three decades earlier. The call for submission abstracts was sent out soon thereafter.

The process of becoming and being a mother is often shaped by, and interconnected with, how mothers realize feminism and/or become feminists. For example, what might have been tolerated, overlooked, or dismissed before becoming a mother can become intolerable, acutely apparent, in dire need of addressing, and downright unacceptable once one becomes a mother. Motherhood often brings with it specific and unique discriminations and oppressions, along with new challenges and possibilities. For instance, mothers in the paid labour force find themselves "mommy tracked." Canadian mothers with at least one child under the age of 18 in 2015 earned eighty-five cents for every dollar earned by full-time fathers (Moyser). As first theorized by Sara Ruddick, subsequent to becoming a mother and engaging in maternal practice, mothers often experience different identifications with feminism as they negotiate and navigate new challenges on behalf of their children. Becoming a mother may also cause one to question current feminist priorities and practices and to demand and realize a mother-centred mode of feminism. Andrea O'Reilly has argued that "many of the problems mothers face—social, economic, political, cultural, psychological, and so forth—are specific to women's role and identity as mothers. A mother-centred feminism is needed because mothers—arguably more so than women in general—remain disempowered despite [fifty] years of feminism" (*Matricentric Feminism* 42).

The aim of this collection is to create space for reflecting on, contextualizing, reframing, discussing, inciting, and facilitating a sense of community and connection for feminist mothering and feminist mothers. This collection offers a broad range of voices and experiences, insights, and observations and presents them in a diverse range of formats and styles concerning the many meanings and practices of mothers finding and realizing feminism. The collection is organized by way of three interconnected sections: Losing and Finding, Challenging and Critiquing, and Connecting and Conversing. This introduction will first introduce the central concepts of feminist mothering and will then introduce each chapter under the three sections.

Feminist Mothers and Mothering: Central Concepts

Feminist mothering entails the distinct approach of combining one's feminism with one's parenting. As such, the convergence and interaction of feminism and mothering are fundamental to the lives and praxis of feminist mothers. It is important to note that the term "mother" refers to any individual who engages in motherwork; it is not limited to cisgender women; rather, it includes anyone who takes upon the work of mothering as a central part of their life. Building on Ruddick's concept of maternal practice, matricentric feminism positions the word "mother" as a verb, as something one does—a practice. For Ruddick, as Sarah LaChance Adams notes, "It is the practice of mothering that makes one a mother, not a biological or social imperative [and] therefore, the title of 'mother' is not strictly limited to biological mothers, or even women" (727). She continues: "Maternal commitment is voluntary and conscious; it is not inevitable, nor is it dictated by nature" (727). Repositioning mother from a noun to a verb degenders mothering and divests care of biology to dislodge the gender essentialism that grounds and structures normative motherhood. Defining mother in this way counters biological essentialist concepts of who women and mothers are and can be. Hence, mothers are not limited to a narrow group of cisgender people, assigned female at birth. While there may be as many understandings and definitions of feminism as there are feminists, the feminism of these coeditors honours the existence and legitimacy of trans and nonbinary people's knowledge, experiences, and voices, including within feminism and mothering.

Feminism and mothering are vital to the lived experiences of feminist mothers—as feminists, as mothers, and to their parenting practices. Drawing on six prevailing themes within the experiences of feminist mothering, feminist mothering is understood to 1) interrupt and negate the master narrative/ideology of patriarchal motherhood. As such, it 2) is a resistant and an empowered mode of mothering that is 3) a political act. Furthermore, feminist mothering 4) engages in matroreform by claiming power in motherhood through engaging in new mothering rules and practices and by 5) creating feminist motherlines to name and support feminist mothering, which 6) actively resists patriarchal patterns of gender acculturation through feminist parenting practices. The power of an intersectional analytic framework, which is foundational to feminist theorizing, offers further insight to understanding and acknowledging the work and empowerment of feminist mothers and feminist mothering. It is also central to addressing the significant need of disrupting the dualistic and binary social structures that divide people into categories of either/or related to mothering.

1) Feminist Mothering Interrupts and Negates the Master Narrative/Ideology of Patriarchal Motherhood

Feminist mothering and mothers provide an oppositional feminist discourse as well as mothering practices that challenge patriarchal motherhood. Feminist mothers understand the distinction made between motherhood and mothering—an insight first made by Adrienne Rich. Rich sees a separation between the experience of motherhood—that is "the *potential relationship* of any woman to her powers of reproduction and to children"—and "the *institution*" of motherhood, described as "ensuring that that potential—and all women—shall remain under male control" (*Of Woman Born* 13). Motherhood is an oppressive patriarchal institution that is defined and controlled by male-dominated societies, whereas mothering entails the potentially empowering experiences that mothers have when they are engaged in relationships with their children and with the work of parenting.

In *Of Woman Born*, Rich writes, "We do not think of the power stolen from us and the power withheld from us in the name of the institution of motherhood" (275). The aim of empowered mothering is to reclaim that power for mothers and to imagine and implement a mode of mothering that mitigates the many ways that patriarchal motherhood, both discursively and materially, regulates and restrains mothers and their mothering. However, empowered mothering, or what may be termed "mothering against motherhood," has yet to be fully defined, documented, or dramatized in feminist scholarship on motherhood. Rather, empowered mothering is understood for what it is not—namely patriarchal motherhood. Indeed, as Fiona Joy Green notes, what is still missing from discussions on motherhood is "Rich's monumental contention that even when restrained by patriarchy, motherhood can be a site of empowerment and political activism" ("Feminist Mothers" 31). A theory of empowered mothering begins by positioning mothers as "outlaws from the institution of motherhood" (Rich, *Of Woman Born* 195) and seeks to imagine and implement a maternal identity and practice that empowers mothers.

2) Feminist Mothering Is a Resistant and Empowered Mode of Mothering

Wanda Thomas Bernard and Candace Bernard offer a definition of empowerment that is useful when thinking about empowerment within the context of feminist mothering. They understand empowerment to include naming, analyzing, and challenging oppression through the development of critical consciousness with the aim of gaining control, exercising choices, and engaging in collective social action. Feminist mothering both meets and respects a number of criteria for empowered mothering outlined by various feminist theorists. For instance, feminist mothering follows O'Reilly's theory of empowered mothering as it: 1) functions as an oppositional discourse to patriarchal mothering; 2) challenges the dominant discourse and practices of motherhood; 3) transforms the various ways that the lived experience of patriarchal motherhood is limiting or oppressive to mothers/parents. Feminist mothering also meets the seven characteristics of empowered mothering identified by Erica Horwitz i.e., that Feminist mothers recognize 1) the importance of challenging mainstream parenting practices. They 2) acknowledge that mothers must meet their own needs and that 3) being a mother does not fulfill all of one's needs. Feminist mothers believe 4) that mothers are not solely responsible for how kids turn out, and they 5) challenge the idea that the only emotion mothers feel for kids is love. Furthermore, they value 6) involving others in their children's upbringing and 7) actively question the expectations society places on mothers.

Feminist mothers also observe O'Reilly's five organizing aims of empowered mothering that are denied to mothers in patriarchal motherhood. As feminists and as mothers, they value and practice: 1) agency: the ability to influence and control one's life and mothering; 2) authority and 3) autonomy: the conviction, determination, and ability to define one's life and practices of self and mothering; 4) authenticity: being true to one's self and to one's values as feminists and mothers; and 5) advocacy/activism: making visible and challenging the political and social dimensions of motherwork.

Feminist mothering refers to an oppositional discourse of motherhood—one that is constructed as a negation of patriarchal motherhood. A feminist practice of mothering, therefore, functions as a counternarrative to normative motherhood: It seeks to interrupt the master narrative of motherhood to imagine and implement a view of mothering that is empowering to mothers. Feminist mothering is, thus, determined more by what it is not (i.e., patriarchal motherhood) rather than by what it is. Feminist mothering may refer to any practice of mothering that seeks to challenge and change various aspects of patriarchal motherhood that cause mothering to be limiting or oppressive to women. Rich uses the word "courageous" to define a nonpatriarchal practice of mothering, whereas Baba Copper calls such a practice "radical mothering." Susan Douglas and Meredith Michaels use the word "rebellious" to describe outlaw mothering, and "hip" is Ariel Gore's term for transgressive mothering. For this collection, the term "feminist" is used to signify maternal practices that resist and refuse patriarchal motherhood to create the practice of feminist mothering.

Feminist mothering differs from empowered mothering in so far as the mother identifies as a feminist and practices mothering from a feminist perspective or consciousness. A feminist mother, in other words, is a parent whose mothering, in theory and practice, is shaped and influenced by feminism. Thus, although there is much overlap between empowered and feminist mothering, the latter is informed by a particular philosophy and politic—namely, feminism. Although empowered mothers may demand more support, they do not originate specifically from a feminist desire to dismantle a patriarchal institution. In contrast, feminist mothers resist because they recognize that gender inequity, in particular male privilege and power, is produced, maintained, and perpetuated in patriarchal motherhood. As feminists, feminist mothers reject an institution founded on gender inequity, and as mothers, they refuse to raise children in such a sexist environment (Green, *Practicing*). Thus, although in practice the two seem similar (i.e., demanding more involvement from fathers and insisting on a life outside of motherhood), only feminist mothering involves a larger awareness of, and challenge to, the gender (among other) inequities of patriarchal culture. The distinction between empowered mothering and feminist mothering is that feminist mothers identify as feminist; they bring their feminist theory and practice to their everyday motherwork of parenting to challenge the patriarchal institution of motherhood through their relationships with their children, matroreform, and feminist motherlines. Whereas feminist mothering entails empowered mothering, empowered mothering does not always include feminist maternal practice.

3) Feminist Mothering Is a Political Act

Feminist mothers see their parenting as no different from other parts of their lives; their feminism informs and influences everything. Mothering is shaped and informed by feminism in both theory and practice.

Feminist mothers and feminist mothering regard motherhood as a site of power wherein mothers can affect political social change through maternal activism within and outside of the family (Green, *Practicing*). A feminist standpoint on mothering affords people a life, a purpose, and an identity outside and beyond motherhood, and it does not limit childrearing to the biological mother. Likewise, from this standpoint, a person's gender, race, age, sexuality, or marital status does not determine their capacity to mother. A feminist theory on motherhood also foregrounds maternal power and confers value to mothering. Mothering from a feminist perspective and practice redefines motherwork as a social and political act. In contrast to patriarchal motherhood, which limits mothering to privatized care undertaken in the domestic sphere by cisgender women, feminist mothering, more so than empowered mothering, regards mothering as explicitly and profoundly political and social.

Feminist mothering is an essential strategy for contributing to positive political social change that has cultural significance and political purpose (O'Reilly 7). Evidence of the power of feminist mothering is seen in the ways in which family structures and dynamics continue to be shaped and reformed by feminist parents and the ways in which children are being raised and coming into their own through their relationships with their mothers that are based upon their mother's agency, authority, autonomy, authenticity, and acts of advocacy and activism.

4) Feminist Mothering Engages in Matroreform

Closely related to the feminist understanding of motherhood as institution and mothering as experience is matroreform, which is a feminist term and transformative maternal practice coined by Gina Wong. Matroreform is a psychological, spiritual, cognitive, and emotional reformation of mothering that takes place at both an intrapersonal and an interpersonal level. It is a process by which mothers reproduce a new way of mothering for themselves and their families and holds potential for a holistic, sociocultural revolution of motherhood at a global level. As a transformative maternal practice of claiming motherhood power, this progressive movement to mothering includes new and empowering motherhood ethos, ideologies, rules, and views; it involves practices that challenge and are separate from dominant and normative discourses of the sacrificial and good mother.

Feminist mothering consciously disrupts the concept and practice of patriarchal motherhood in an effort to recognize and dispute current patriarchal systems of power (Green, *Practicing*). This action may include subversive and overt practices that challenge cis/heteronormativity, sexism, queer/homo/transphobia, or other forms of discrimination levied against mothers, families, and individuals. Feminist mothers parent in ways that do not follow the narrow definition and model of the nuclear family. For example, they may engage in othermothering, co-parenting, queer, nonbinary, or trans mothering practices, whether alone or with others. Believing that mothering is not the sole identity of mothers, feminist mothers model how mothers are complex, whole human beings with rich lives beyond their mother identities and their relationships with children. They consciously and actively reveal negative biases, attitudes, beliefs, and discriminatory practices in social, political, educational, and judicial systems regarding lesbian, comother, queer, nonbinary, trans, and othermothering practices. Feminist mothers uphold the rights of mothers to parent, to custody, to access, to child support, and to make choices for their children.

5) Feminist Mothers and Mothering Generate Feminist Motherlines

Feminist mothers create feminist motherlines to name and support feminist mothering. The theory of the motherline is credited to Naomi Ruth Lowinsky. The motherline provides a life-cycle perspective and the knowledge of female ancestors who have shared struggles of mothering in different historical times. According to Lowinsky, it offers mothers a heritage founded on the biological, psychological, and cultural link among generations of women to rediscover their own feminine identities. However, Lowinsky argues that most women "are cut off from their motherline and [have] paid a terrible price for cutting [them]selves off from [their] feminine roots" (31). By disconnecting themselves from their motherline, these daughters have lost the authenticity and authority of their womanhood. Women may reclaim that authority and authenticity by reconnecting to the motherline. When a woman comes to understand her life story as a story from the motherline, she gains female authority in a number of ways. First, her motherline grounds her in aspects of her femininity, as she struggles with the many options now open to women. Second, she reclaims carnal knowledge of her own body, its blood mysteries, and their power. Third, as she makes the journey back to her female roots, she will encounter ancestors who struggled with similar difficulties in different historical times. This provides her with a life-cycle perspective that softens her immediate situation. Fourth, she uncovers her connection to the archetypal mother and to the wisdom of the ancient worldview, which holds that body and soul are open and all life is interconnected. And, finally, she reclaims her female perspective, from which to consider how men are similar and how they are different (Lowinsky 13).

Moving beyond an essentialist understanding of the motherline, the expanded feminist motherline recognizes personal and collective struggles for maternal empowerment through connection with others and by (re)framing expectations placed upon them by society or family. Feminist motherlines, in conjunction with matroreform, validate the multiplicity of maternal experiences and identities (Green, "Motherline"). For instance, this may include the intricacies of raising kids; the convoluted labour and experience of seeking, obtaining, and maintaining one's sense of authority, authenticity, autonomy, agency, and activism while mothering; developing and practising authentic and nonjudgmental connections with others who engage in primary work associated with childrearing; and centring maternal knowledge in critical feminist understandings of imperialist/colonialist, white supremacist, capitalist cis-hetero patriarchy related to challenging the ideology and the institution of motherhood.

6) Feminist Mothers Actively Resist Patriarchal Patterns of Gender Acculturation in Their Parenting

Feminist mothers believe it is their responsibility to raise the next generation to be consciously aware of patriarchal and other discriminatory cultural and social systems (Green, *Practicing*). This is crucial to feminism and to political change. Feminist mothers willfully encourage their children to develop a worldview that is critical of interlocking systems— such as patriarchy, white supremacy, colonialism, capitalism, ableism, and cis/heteronormativity—which privilege some and oppress many others. Feminist mothers engage their kids in conversations about the restrictive and oppressive messages and values held, told, and perpetuated about people and society. They may spend time addressing these perspectives when reading books, watching videos and films, listening to and using language, and engaging with family, friends, the media, and popular culture. Their discussions are both critical and supportive, as they teach their children about age-appropriate understandings and realities of the world around them. Together, they explore their interests and discover ways to be curious and supportive. Feminist mothers also support their kids in exploring and developing their own sense of self; they provide role modelling of how to approach and live in the world from a place of empowered feminist curiosity. They encourage their children to be true to themselves and to be who they are without necessarily adhering to sex, gender, and sexuality binaries and stereotypes. Feminist mothers value agency, authority, autonomy, and authenticity in themselves and in their children. By being active advocates of feminism and feminist mothering, they foster these same values in their kids through their parenting practices.

The theory of intersectionality, which has contributed significantly to feminist theory and feminist mothering, is central to feminist mothering to address the significant need of disrupting the dualistic and binary social structures that divide people into either/or categories related to gender, sex, and mothering. Intersectionality, coined by Kimberlé Crenshaw in 1989, is an analytical framework for understanding how aspects of a person's social and political identities intersect to produce specific and different modes of discrimination and privilege in people's lives. It recognizes that social identities—such as ability, age, class, ethnicity/race, gender, religion, sexual orientation, and social class—simultaneously overlap with one another and with systems of power that oppress and advantage people (OED). By integrating an awareness of intersectionality in their parenting, feminist mothers become more conscious of the ways in which families and the lives of parents, mothers, and children are more complex and diverse than ever before. They are more apt to trouble and contest gender essentialism in mothering identities and childcare practices. And they are becoming more open to considering questions regarding who and what is included in the practice of feminist mothering.

Intersectionality values the lived experiences of mothers located at various intersectional locations (including but not limited to age, class, culture, ethnicity, familial status, gender, geography, ideology, physical ability, race), which are often ignored, underrepresented, misrepresented, and misunderstood within imperialist/colonialist, white supremacist, capitalist cisheteropatriarchy (Cox; hooks). Including the perspectives of men and masculinities, two spirit (2S), trans and nonbinary folx continues to facilitate the disruption of gender-essentialist beliefs about mothering and norms about care.

Section One: Losing and Finding

The first section of the book explores the role of feminism, understandings of feminism, and feminist maternal theory in helping mothers find their way in relation to various points in their experiences of mothering. In chapter one, "Journeying through Feminist Mothering: Reflections on Identity and Practice," Heather E. Dillaway explores how the pursuit and practice of feminist mothering becomes a never-ending journey and how the journey necessarily changes over time. Dillaway details how she attempts to reach two separate yet intertwined goals in her feminist mothering: maintaining her own identity while mothering and raising children who understand and support gender equality. Although these goals may stay the same over a mother's life course, daily tactics and focus may evolve. Photographer Lianne Milton never wanted to be a mother for fear of losing her identity as a visual artist and agency as a woman. However, in chapter two, entitled "Sunrise," Milton describes her reconnection to feminism as she became a mother as a fluid experience in an extended artist statement and autobiographical photography. The third chapter, "Single Teen Motherhood and the 'Good' Mother: Feminist Responses" by Natasha Steer, examines conflicting cultural and media messaging to suggest that resistance and empowerment are difficult yet possible when one's motherhood journey does not fit the societally preferred two-parent, heterosexual, and cisgender family structure. The following chapter, "Discovering Feminist Motherhood through Art Practice" by Jen McGowan, explores making art as a way to understand and integrate motherhood as a feminist. Support and validation from connecting with the artist-mother community and other feminist texts on motherhood help to identify and disrupt the internalization of patriarchal notions of what a mother is. The fifth chapter, "Holding and Being Held" by Eve Darwood, explores the role of the body in the performance of motherhood, and the tension between changing perspectives on bodily autonomy which arise in light of a physical disability. In this chapter, fragments of scenes narrate experiences of early motherhood and the development of multiple sclerosis to show that responses to the question of to whom the female body belongs are complex and ever changing. In chapter six's short collection of poetry, entitled "Colostrum," Victoria Bailey reflects upon her personal memories and perceptions of the interconnectedness of the beginnings of her mothering and its relation to her understandings of feminism. She meditates upon her experiences, observations, and challenges of becoming and being a mother and her ensuing pursuit of finding her way guided by feminism, feminist mothers, and feminist mothering. The final chapter of section one, "We Are Mothers" by Rachel O'Donnell, explores complicated mother-daughter relationships to argue that it is possible to become a "good mother" even when one does not have a good mothering relationship to draw from. Here, the author must figure out how to love as a mother and how it intersects with how she was denied true mothering, arguing for compassion for one's children and for oneself.

Section Two: Challenging and Critiquing

The second section of the book shares the challenges specific to becoming and being a feminist mother and considers how the potentiality of feminist mothering may be realized. Chapter eight, "Coming into Motherhood: An Anishinaabeg Feminist View on Birth and Motherhood in Hospital Spaces" by Renée E. Mazinegiizhigoo-kwe Bédard, explores aspects of maternal feminism from an Anishinaabeg perspective. Here, Bédard delves into how she uses Indigenous based maternal-centred feminism to navigate the historical and contemporary complexities of medical colonialism that Indigenous women experience in Canada. Using traditional Anishinaabeg knowledge and traditions, Bédard shares her personal narratives as a way to articulate an Anishinaabeg feminist standpoint centred on the challenges of entering Indigenous motherhood in hospital spaces. Lili Shi's chapter, "Meandering through the Intersections: Feminist Mothering as a Transnational Migrant Academic Mom," is a reflection on how the author translates her transnational and intersectional feminist consciousness as an immigrant Chinese academic mom into her everyday mothering experiences with her biracial children in different sociocultural and geopolitical contexts. She centralizes issues of race, identity, positionality, belonging, language, and global gender inequality in this exploration. The next chapter, "Coming Home to Myself: On Single Black Motherhood" by Kahaema Byer, explores matricentric feminist praxis through the lens of a Black single mother. It begins with a personal narrative (from pregnancy to the postpartum period) to crucially situate the context of Black single motherhood within an imperialist, white supremacist, capitalist, and patriarchal context. The chapter later examines how race relations in online mothering communities that centre whiteness became a catalyst for the author's Black feminist homecoming. She concludes with reflections on her mothering practice as a Black mother primarily in relation to whiteness. Chapter eleven, "Reflections from a Settler and an Immigrant Mother of Colour: How Motherhood Helped Me Develop My Feminist Politics over the Last Decade" by Shruti Raji-Kalyanaraman, explores how any realization of gender disempowerment, as a feminist, is incomplete without acknowledging one's privileges and complicities. As a researcher and maternal activist, she reads together the concepts of normative motherhood principles, caste privilege, and Indigenous-immigrant relationalities to bring about an intersectional understanding of realizing feminism in racialized mothering. The following chapter, "I Am Never Sleeping with You Again: Reflections on Mothering, Community Building, and Unstable Allyship" by Zaje A.T. Harrell, explores motherhood through her involvement in natural parenting and breastfeeding-support communities. The analysis offers a Black feminist lens on how these spaces fill an important need while also suppressing the role of social identity and position in women's lives. Harrell also found that regressive values related to the role of women in society were held by some community members. Within the context of her own evolving Black feminist motherhood, she explores the complexity and implications of building mothering communities without centring feminist principles. In the final chapter of this section, "The 'Wildness of Motherhood': Transforming Maternal Rage and Transgressing Patriarchal Motherhood to Realize Maternal Empowerment: A Reading of Rachel Yoder's *Nightbitch*," Andrea O'Reilly considers how maternal power may be reclaimed and how the potentiality of empowered mothering may be realized. More specifically the chapter explores how the mother in *Nightbitch*, through claiming and harnessing maternal rage, moves from motherhood to mothering to achieve maternal empowerment and become Rich's outlaw from the institution of motherhood.

Section Three: Connecting and Conversing

The last section of the book focusses upon the importance of connection, community, and conversation in the realization of feminist mothering. In "Becoming a (Better) Feminist: Autoethnographic Lessons I Learned about Feminism by Becoming a Mother," Molly Wiant Cummins explores lessons she learned about feminism after becoming a mother. She uses autoethnographic letters in the form of emails written to her two children assigned female at birth to investigate how her investment in intersectional feminism compels her to recognize some of the responsibilities she has to create a better world for all of them. Chapter fifteen, "Recognizing Their Feminist Selves through the Journey of Mothering: Reflections of Urban Indian Mothers" by Ketoki Mazumdar, Sneha Parekh Gupta, and Isha Sen, explores how a cohort of urban Indian mothers with children below the age of ten years are recognizing their feminist selves and breaking away from their traditional mothering practices in the twenty-first century. The chapter, "A Conversation: A Mother and Daughter Discuss Feminism" by Tara Carpenter Estrada and Emily Rae Robertson, investigates how views about feminism are shaped by family and social contexts. Through a candid conversation between mother and daughter, the chapter argues that feminism can allow women to see a greater range of options for themselves and to make more conscious choices about how to shape their lives. Chapter seventeen, "Motherhood, Art, and a Revolution" by Jillayna Adamson, uses artistry and in-depth personal narratives to argue that the shortcomings of current feminisms are not fully realized until one enters the motherhood experience. The increasingly candid expressive arts and narratives on motherhood are assessed and further utilized to serve as a marker of the eagerness of women mothers to further propel matricentric feminism into practice. In the chapter, "Between Mothers: Dialogically Exploring the Mother-Scholar Relationship," Rachel E. Stough and Elizabeth A. Bennett collaboratively examine the nuances of their matricentric feminist mentoring relationship via the letter poem, a creative, autoethnographic medium. As professor and doctoral student in the same graduate program, the authors enjoy a rich and subversive mentoring relationship, which exists in opposition to traditional expectations of mentoring in academe. Their letter poems, written in dialogue, enable fertile consideration of the ways in which their maternity has deepened their feminisms, and vice versa. They conclude the chapter with considerations of different ways to do and experience academic mentoring. Chapter nineteen, "The COVID-19 Pandemic as a Catalyst for Feminist Thought" by Lisa H. Rosen and Linda J. Rubin, explores how mothers' experiences of acute stress and significant duress during the pandemic highlighted the need for feminism in their lives and the larger society. Qualitative accounts from working mothers are presented, which argue for the importance of building back better from the challenges of the pandemic to create a more equitable future for these mothers and their children. The concluding chapter, "Feminist Representations of Maternity in Caryl Churchill's *Top Girls* and Sarah Daniels's *Neaptide*" by Tuğrul Can Sümen, examines the antifeminist political climate of Margaret Thatcher's era, which witnessed discrimination against mothers, and argues that Churchill's and Daniels's respective plays advocate for the unification of mothers and feminism to resist patriarchal oppression.

Conclusion

In *Matricentric Feminism: Theory, Activism, and Practice*, O'Reilly outlines how matricentric feminism "works from one particular assumption: mothering matters, and it is central to the lives of women who are mothers" (41). Although the same can be said of this collection, one may also add that feminism matters and is central to the lives of many women and others who mother and that mothering should matter in feminism. Decades ago, Rich observed in *Of Woman Born* that "The words are being spoken now, are being written down; the taboos are being broken, the masks of motherhood are cracking through" (24-5). However, as this collection exemplifies, there is still much work to do to support and empower mothers as feminists. As O'Reilly asserts in *Matricentric Feminism*: "Motherhood, it could be said, is the unfinished business of feminism" (42). There is an ongoing need for feminist mothers' stories to be shared and connections to be made, to know, reclaim, and enact empowered feminist mothering. For, as Rich explains in her essay "When We Dead Awaken," "Re-vision—the act of looking back, of seeing with fresh eyes, of entering an old text from a new critical direction—is for women more than a chapter in cultural history: it is an act of survival. Until we can understand the assumptions in which we are drenched we cannot know ourselves" (35).

This collection was completed as a long pandemic drew to an end, when the stresses and expectations placed upon mothers were made undeniably acute and apparent—as captured in the collection *Mothers, Mothering and COVID-19: Reflections from a Pandemic* (O'Reilly and Green). As you read through this collection, we invite you to reflect upon how feminist mothering—the interconnectedness of becoming a mother and a feminist—has been and may be realized, how feminism may empower mothers, and how mothering may enrich feminism.

Works Cited

Bailey, Victoria. "Why I am a Feminist: Seeing the World Anew." *Herizons*, Spring 2021, vol. 35, no. 1, pp. 12-13.

Bernard, Wanda Thomas, and Candace Bernard. "Passing the Torch: A Mother and Daughter Reflect on Their Experience across Generations." *Canadian Women's Studies Journal/cahier de la femme,* vol. 18, no. 2-3, summer-fall 1998, pp. 46-50.

Benincasa, Sara. "Laverne Cox Spills On Self-Acceptance, Finding Love & Battling The Patriarchy." *Bust,* https://bust.com/entertainment/14200-laverne-cox-spills-on-self-acceptance-finding-love-battling-the-patriachy-bust-exclusive.html. Accessed 24 Mar. 2023.

Crenshaw, Kimberlé. "Mapping the Margins: Intersectionality, Identity Politics, and Violence against Women of Color." *Stanford Law Review*, vol. 43, no. 6, 1991, pp. 1241-99.

Green, Fiona Joy. "The Motherline." *Maternal Theory: Essential Readings*. 2nd edition, edited by Andrea O'Reilly, Demeter Press, 2021, pp. 643-662.

Green, Fiona Joy. *Practicing Feminist Mothering*. Arbeiter Ring Publishing, 2011.

Green, Fiona Joy. "Feminist Mothers: Successfully negotiating the tension between Motherhood as 'institution' and 'experience'." *Mother Outlaws: Theories and Practices of Empowered Mothering*, edited by Andrea O'Reilly. Women's Press, 2004, pp. 31-42.

hooks, bell. *Teaching to Transgress: Education as the Practice of Freedom*. Routledge, 1994.

Horwitz, Erika. "Resistance as a Site of Empowerment: The Journey Away From Maternal Sacrifice." *Mother Outlaws: Theories and*

Practices of Empowered Mothering, edited by Andrea O'Reilly, Women's Press, 2004, pp. 43-58.

"Intersectionality." *Oxford Educational Dictionary*. https://www.oed.com/view/Entry/429843. Accessed 24 Mar. 2023.

LaChance, Sarah Adam. "Maternal Thinking." *The Encyclopedia of Motherhood*, edited by Andrea O'Reilly, Sage Press, 2010, pp. 726-27.

Lowinsky, Naiomi Ruth. *Stories from the Motherline: Reclaiming the Mother-Daughter Bond, Finding our Feminine Souls*. Jeremy P. Tarcher Inc., 1992.

Moyser, Melissa. "Women and Paid Work." Statistics Canada. https://www150.statcan.gc.ca/nl/pub/89-503-x/2015001/article/14694-eng.htm Accessed 8 Apr. 2023.

O'Reilly, Andrea. *Matricentric Feminism: Theory, Activism and Practice*. 2nd Edition. Demeter Press, 2021.

O'Reilly, Andrea. "Introduction." *Feminist Mothering*, edited by Andrea O'Reilly, SUNY Press, 2008, pp. 1-20.

Rich, Adrienne. "When We Dead Awaken: Writing As Re-Vision." in *On Lies, Secrets, and Silence: Selected Prose*, by Adrienne Rich, 1979, W. W. Norton and Company, Inc., 1995, pp. 33-49.

Rich, Adrienne. *Of Woman Born: Motherhood as Experience and Institution*. W. W. Norton and Co. 1986.

Rich, Adrienne. "Split at the Root: An Essay on Jewish Identity (1982)." *Essential Essays: Culture, Politics, and the Art of Poetry*, edited by Sandra M. Gilbert, W. W. Norton & Company Inc., 2018, pp. 198-217.

Rose, Jacqueline. *Mothers: An Essay on Love and Cruelty*. Farrar, Straus and Giroux, 2018.

Wong-Wylie, G. "Images and Echoes in Matroreform: A Cultural Feminist Perspective". *Journal of the Motherhood Initiative for Research and Community Involvement*, vol. 8, no. 1, Nov. 2006, https://jarm.journals.yorku.ca/index.php/jarm/article/view/5020. Accessed 24 Mar. 2023.

Wong-Wylie, Gina. "Matroreform." *Encyclopedia of Motherhood*, edited by Andrea O'Reilly, SAGE Publications, Inc., 2010, p. 740.

Section One

Losing and Finding

Chapter 1.

Journeying through Feminist Motherhood: Reflections on Identity and Practice

Heather E. Dillaway

Introduction

I have engaged in feminist mothering since at least 2004, when I became pregnant with my first child. I now have two teenagers, ages fourteen and seventeen, and they help me make sense of both my feminism and my mothering. As I reflect on my time as a mother, it is clear to me that my pursuit of feminist mothering is as much a journey to become myself as it is to mother in a particular way. This journey is never ending, as both my feminism and my mothering represent life-long pursuits.

In *Practicing Feminist Mothering*, Fiona Green describes how mothering can become a "site of feminist praxis" (21), and this is definitely the case for me. Feminism has shaped my decisions and actions as well as my identity over time. Until writing this chapter, however, I had not reflected fully on exactly how I personally perceive and carry out my mothering, or how it might be a "feminist act" (Green). Upon reflection, I find that I am attempting to reach two intertwined goals: maintaining my own personhood while mothering and raising children who understand and support gender equality. As I learn more about myself over time and as my children and I meet with new life stages, my feminist mothering necessarily transforms—that is, although my primary goals may stay intact over time, my daily tactics and foci evolve.

This chapter is constructed around reflections on moments that exemplify my attempts at feminist mothering. These reflections demonstrate that feminism not only becomes a guidebook for me as I engage in a range of mothering decisions and actions but also allows me to see myself. I use this chapter to highlight the long-term nature of the pursuit of feminist mothering as well and how the practice of feminist mothering can transform over time. Because my perceptions of feminism, mothering, and the life course inevitably inform my narrations, I describe these conceptual lenses before sharing my stories.

Framing the Pursuit and Practice of Feminist Mothering

I take seriously feminist writer Marie Shear's famous quote that "Feminism is the radical notion that women are people" ("Feminism 101"). Several decades ago, my brother painted a wooden sign for me with a version of this quote, accidentally altering it to read: "Feminism is the radical notion that women have the right to be themselves." I still have that sign hanging in my office at work. and its unique rendition of Shear's quote means a lot to me. Adrienne Rich also proclaims that as a woman, I should be able to "exist as myself" and define my own personhood (12). Furthermore, I should have the right to "return to [a self] that is [my] own" even if I prioritize others' needs at times (Rich 19). I want to be myself, and I want others around me—regardless of gender—to be able to be themselves too.

Taking a broad perspective, feminism is the belief that all women and men—indeed, all genders—should have equal access to rights, choices, and opportunities. Feminist literature makes it clear, however, that a system of inequality exists whereby all women (and some groups of men) have been blocked from what and who we want to be because of culturally prescribed ideologies about gender (West and Zimmerman). Practising feminism, then, not only includes growing into one's own power, opportunities, and self as much as one can[1] but also actively engaging in work to contest cultural norms and dismantle gender inequality. Candace West and Don Zimmerman suggest that if "we view gender as an accomplishment [or] achieved property" (126), then we begin to understand that every decision, action, and interaction either upholds or challenges an unequal and gendered status quo. Consequently, we must act purposefully and consciously to confront and defy existing ideas about feminine and masculine roles to redefine the possibilities for ourselves and others. As we adopt this perspective "our attention shifts from matters internal to the individual and focuses on the interactional and, ultimately, institutional" reproduction of gender inequalities (West and Zimmerman 126).

In thinking about my own pursuit of feminist mothering, I am also guided by feminist scholars who write about mothering and motherhood. In her book, *Matricentric Feminism: Theory, Activism, Practice*, Andrea O'Reilly explains that essentialist perspectives "[position] maternity as the basis of female identity" (10). Nancy Russo also suggests that motherhood is culturally mandated; therefore, women are supposed to desire motherhood and make motherhood a primary identity and role. As a result, women's lives are "defined by motherhood whether or not [women] have children" (Bliss xiv). In *Of Woman Born*, Adrienne Rich clarifies that the institution of motherhood is the root cause of these cultural expectations. The institution of motherhood is a "set of laws, traditions, religious practices, and economic structures" (Bliss xv) that defines women as having a natural propensity to be the primary caregivers of children because of their reproductive function. Within patriarchal societies, women therefore become a category of invisible, unpaid workers who raise the next generation of workers for others' economic benefit (Rich). Within this context mothers' rights, choices and opportunities are often curtailed. Mothers have not been recognized for the economic contributions they make to society. Mothers have been unable to define their personhood as separate from motherhood and have been blocked from accessing a full range of opportunities outside of the home (Rich). Cultural ideologies that support the equation of women with motherhood bolster this larger system of inequality.

Nonetheless, feminist scholars explain that if we analyze mothering as a set of daily behaviours and practices—and, thus, motherhood as a potential site of power and resistance—we can understand better the identities and experiences of women and mothers. In other words, if we concentrate on the behavioural aspects of mothering (rather than on motherhood as an inflexible institution), we can see the forces acting upon mothers and observe how women uphold, challenge, and redefine this institution on a daily basis (Green; O'Reilly; Rich; Ruddick). Mothering can even be a feminist act—that is, a way that women "invent and live their feminism" (Green 21). As Rich also proposes, we must pay attention to the "process of mothering" so that we can realize the potential relationships of any woman to her own powers. Women can claim back their personhood, the contours of their labour, and their choices and opportunities through daily acts of mothering. From an interactionist perspective, then, the practice of both feminism and mothering allows us to challenge existing norms and inequalities for ourselves and others.

As a person who studies women's aging, I am also attuned to the importance of a life-course perspective. A life-course lens enables us to observe and contextualize how individuals navigate a particular experience within one single moment as well as consider how individuals go through sequential life stages and negotiate a particular experience over time. This perspective means understanding the importance of paying attention to transitions, stages, sequencing, and changes in identity and behaviour as women traverse motherhood and interact with their feminism. For example, Rich shares how the actions she took during the first decade of her mothering were less resistant than in subsequent decades. During her children's younger years, she struggled to "bring her life into focus" (8), but as her sons grew older, she "began changing her own life" and felt more "equal" to them (13). Rich's retrospective reflections therefore highlight how women sometimes "return" to themselves as their children age (19). Women may reshape their relationships with mothering and implement their feminism differently as they travel through various life phases. Practising feminist mothering with infants or toddlers is definitely different than carrying out feminist mothering while caring for tweens and teenagers. Career opportunities and health events can also impact how one practises feminist mothering over time. Inevitably, my identity and practice changes as I encounter new life stages and decision points. I am not the same feminist mother I was five, ten, or fifteen years ago, nor will I be the same in another five, ten, or fifteen years. I move along a continuum of mostly conscious and purposeful action, encouraging both myself and my children to reach for opportunity, support gender equality, be resilient in the face of burden, and be who we want to be.

Episodes in Coming into Being

As I reflect on particular episodes or chapters in my mother years, I can understand better the ways in which I have tried to engage in or practise feminist mothering. In different moments, my focus and tactics may vary, but I perceive myself as trying to accomplish two main goals over time: maintain my own identity as both a mother and more than a mother and raise children who understand and support gender equality. I organize my discussion around these goals, and I share my narrations chronologically to help readers see how feminist mothering can shift over time.

Both Mother and More than Mother: Finding Myself

As a child, I already understood that women are more than mothers even when motherhood is a central part of their identity. Every year, when we had to fill out forms for elementary school, my mother would always make sure to tell us that she was "a farmer and homesteader, not just a homemaker and mother." We had to write her occupation in particular ways on those forms, for she would not stand for being called "just a stay-at-home mother." I also saw her struggle to go back to school, earn a master's degree, become certified to teach, and then finally become a full-time teacher. I'd make dinner and put my siblings to bed while she studied for exams, wrote papers, and then worked for pay. She felt badly when my youngest brother resisted her help in going to bed on the nights when she was home and asked for me instead. I was a stand-in mother for him during my later middle school and high school years, and he was closer to me than her simply because of our daily routines. In seeing my mother struggle to prioritize mothering while also maintaining the rest of herself, it was crystal clear to me that women might want to be both mothers and more than mothers and that they had the right to be both. Thus, my understanding of women's potentially complicated relationship with motherhood came early. Seeing how hard it was for women like my mother to get a credit card in their name, get a divorce, or work for pay, I saw the unjust impact of gender inequality. Several decades later, I am well versed in feminist literature and know that my mother's experiences are widely shared (Green; Hays; O'Reilly; Rich; Ruddick).

When pregnant with my first child, I remember my mother wishing me a happy Mother's Day. My response was that "I was not yet a mother," and she was both saddened and hurt by my response. From her point of view, I was coming into motherhood and should value that transition. Even with her own complicated relationship with motherhood, she still felt I should be valuing the transition to this status. From my vantage point, I was not yet holding a baby in my arms and needed to focus on the other aspects of my life before becoming a mother. While I was happy to be entering into motherhood, it was important to me to maintain my whole self at the same time—not unlike my mother had done before me. I worked hard for the career I held and wanted to maintain my reputation as a hard-working, productive, collaborative, and involved academic. After the birth of my daughter, and then my son a few years later, I strived to make sure that my mothering activity never lowered my productivity or lessened my presence on campus. I still attended the same number of academic conferences out of town, often carrying breast pumps in tow. I never questioned my own attempts to maintain a paid work identity or a research agenda, although others around me sometimes did try to remind me of the importance of my motherhood role while I was engaging in paid work. When my kids were young, some of the most progressive of colleagues asked "who watched my kids" while I taught night classes or attended conferences, when most knew I had a partner and that they were a perfectly capable coparent. Green, O'Reilly and Rich all note that cultural norms about the primacy of the mother role are reinforced in mothers' interactions with others, and that even mothers police other mothers using these norms.

I felt the stigma and guilt of being away from my young children at times. I was in New York City when my almost two-year-old daughter broke her leg (a mishap on a metal slide about which my partner will forever feel guilty). I also returned from a conference in Montreal when my daughter was just twelve months old, and she acted like she didn't remember me or want to be around me. I knew right away that I had been gone too many days; it took her about twenty-four hours to warm up to me again. I started both of my children in full-time daycare around four months of age. I would sometimes stay home from campus to write or to grade student assignments while they were at daycare. I was privileged enough to be able to pay for this childcare and redefine my home as a place for paid work on selected days, but I still felt guilty that I was physically in the home, and they were not. If I were at home, I knew neighbours would expect to see my children there as well, but their presence would undermine my ability to be more than a mother and to get paid work done. When they were older, I also enrolled them in camps during spring break or winter break when they did not have full-day school. I felt guilt about this as well, as I saw other mothers take the day off from paid work to spend time mothering. In these moments of guilt, I recognized my own internalization of the cultural expectations surrounding mothers, especially those with young children.

The guilt of not always being around and/or prioritizing myself in those early days was intense at times, even if I was around more often than not. I did want to be around my children, and I was an involved mother, but I wanted to have other responsibilities and purposes, too. As I look back, there were so many moments during which I struggled to make sure that motherhood was not my only identity and role—especially in their toddler and preschool years. Now I understand that the transition to motherhood, and those early mother years, taught me as much about myself as it taught me about motherhood or mothering. My feminism—in particular, my understanding that women have the right to be people, to be themselves, even while mothering—informed my perspectives and actions. In moments, I did define my career as equal in priority to my children. I wanted to be a multifaceted person, both a mother and more than a mother.

To be clear, though, I did, and do, want to be present in my children's lives and teach them how to be strong, thoughtful, and feminist themselves. When I'm around my children and not engaging in paid work, I value the time spent with them. I wouldn't trade that time for anything. To protect time with my children, especially when they were under age five, I often juggled time so that I could be both mother and more than a mother. I'd get up early, often at four a.m., to get paid work hours in before my kids woke up—protecting the mother time that would come later in the morning. I'd also work late at night instead of during active family hours. I knew how important it was to protect mother time, but I refused to give up paid work time. I struggled to maintain the boundaries between my two types of time and failed to get the balance right on many days.

Weekends were extremely hard during my children's younger years because I needed to grade student assignments or work on publishing papers, and it was easy to be mentally preoccupied by work demands. But I also needed to be physically and mentally present for my family on

Saturdays and Sundays. I always felt the tug of normative good mother expectations, which meant that I felt pressure to allow childrearing to become all-encompassing when they were not in school or daycare. I knew others might think I should prioritize my children above myself on weekends (Hays; Dillaway and Pare; Dillaway, Haskin, and Velding). I witnessed the same struggle in my friends and colleagues with younger children, even if they didn't talk about it much. All mothers who want to be more than mothers struggle against these cultural expectations (Green; Hays; O'Reilly; Rich; Ruddick). The daily tussles between mothering and paid work can affect our moods and the ways we converse with others. I know I've allowed my daily struggles to affect how I communicate with my partner and children. On many days I've been snappier than I wanted to be.

This struggle to be both mother and more than mother continues over time, even if it is less intense as children age. Over time, I have watched other mothers participate in more school-related functions than me as an extension of their mothering work. I did not extend my mothering in this way, and for that reason, I have never been more than a marginal member of the mother networks at my children's schools. I did not feel like I was missing out, nor did I feel that my mothering was less complete, but I have been more removed from my children's school life than other mothers, especially during their elementary and middle-school years, as I took on leadership roles at paid work. There were years during which my children's teachers knew my husband more than me; the parents of my children's friends would text my husband to set up playdates because they knew he was more likely than me to answer in a timely fashion. This sometimes bothered me and made me question my actions, but I knew that my attempts to fulfill my expanding paid-work responsibilities did not mean that I was a bad mother. I came to the important school and sporting events and was as present as I could be when I was around them. I have always valued my identity as more than a mother while also a mother. I can and want to be both.

More recently, as my children have aged into their teenage years, my prioritization of paid work rarely causes me guilt. They are self-sufficient and do not need me to be an active mother in all moments, which means that I can step back from being involved in the minute details of their lives. I don't need to preserve mothering time the way I used to because they are independent and busy with their own lives now. Instead, I see them when they are free or when they need my assistance, and I have become more of a chauffeur, sounding board, and curfew setter. Parallel to the changes in daily mothering work, I have a growing sense that they need me to model what it means to work hard and be successful in one's pursuits, which means I can invest additional energies in showing them that women are not only mothers but also more than mothers. I've been showing them this all along, but it seems even more important now. I recently had a conversation with my daughter about how it is okay to procrastinate at times, but that then buckling down and getting big projects done is critical. She sees me do this in my paid work, and I'm therefore exhibiting this behaviour for her. In addition, last winter, I went to visit a graduate-school friend by myself for a long weekend, and I think my kids were as happy as I was that I did that. My daughter also just helped me purchase a new purse and more work clothes; allowing her to help me prioritize myself has been an interesting new development in mothering time. Thus, my recent work to be more than a mother is, in some ways, also turning out to be how I mother in part. I am not sidelining myself anymore when I am engaged in mothering, and they can see me better now, I think. They see me as a full-fledged person as well as their mother. Rich's reflections on being more "equal" to her children as they age resonates with me.

    I'm still in the process of coming into being and defining myself as more than a mother but also a mother. I've just accepted a job out of state, and it is exciting because it opens up a new career chapter for me. I am ready to embark on this next adventure, as it allows me to come into being differently than before. Yet this career move could impact my motherhood in significant ways, and I will have to be careful about how it does. My kids are older and do not need me as much as they used to, but I realize that I sneak in my mothering in moments now—in the mornings before school, at night after dinner, and in random conversations after sports or before bedtime. I will move to start this new job ahead of my children and partner, therefore separating myself from the day-to-day routines of my family. I won't be there to make sure my daughter gets out of bed in the morning. I won't be there for late night herbal tea, chips, popcorn, or ice cream. I won't be there to take them to the doctor or to soccer practice. That means I'll also miss the unplanned conversations in which I might guide them as they continue to formulate their own perspectives on the world. I'll have to put effort into having purposeful conversations via phone calls, texts, and video chats, and I'll need to make sure to commute back to see them regularly—to catch as many in-person mothering moments as possible. I will need to make sure I stay connected in ways that I have not had to before making this move and that will involve forethought. I can no longer count on my physical presence garnering me the chances to mother.

I could have waited to apply for new jobs, but I had already done that for several years. I have not prioritized myself in major decision-making moments in the past, and it is time that I do so. I'm forty-nine years old and presumably at midlife, but good physical health and longevity are not guaranteed. I have been underemployed for several years, and I am beyond ready to take the next step in shaping my own career. In this new stage I can be a leader for others and for this family. This will be a test of my feminist mothering as much as it is a test of my abilities at paid work. It is up to me to figure out how to be a mother as well as more than a mother in this new phase.

Actively Mothering in Feminist Ways

I've purposely discussed my attempts to find myself as a feminist mother first, before discussing how I mother actively in feminist ways. In addition, how I mother on a daily basis is informed by my own personal project to be both a mother and more than a mother. Yet how I mother is also informed by my understanding of structural gender inequalities and how important it is that we attempt to interrupt the reproduction of inequalities on a daily basis. I've engaged in mothering in very specific ways to undo gender or prop up my children to understand and engage with our gendered world. Of course, I did not realize how much I would need to actively interact with heteronormative gender expectations in the process or rather how much trial and error there is in this work. In my children's younger years, I played out my feminist mothering in action-based ways and did this work day in and day out. Over time, however, I have realized how individual moments matter less than the long-term arc of what I am trying to do. Endurance matters in this life-long game of attempting to undo, reshape, and resist gender expectations and inequalities.

Rich makes it clear that feminist mothering should include claiming (back) and owning our own bodies. Accordingly, being body positive has always been important to my feminism and therefore my mothering.

I've made it a priority to talk about physical bodies with both of my children on a regular basis. Early on, I talked about menstrual periods as the "good blood" to begin shaping my daughter's perspective on menstruation and make her see that it is a normal and healthy bodily process. I talked about it so positively that it also affected my son, and he was disappointed to know that he would never get the good blood (Dillaway). This was a critical moment for me, as I learned that I have to be careful in feminist parenting—to not glorify women's processes to the detriment of those around them. Advocating for girls and women should not mean denigrating boys and men. I had to change the way in which I discussed menstruation with both children so that they understood that bodies are different and that there are great things about all bodies. As they both entered puberty, I consciously tried to talk about changing bodies as normal and healthy and gave them books about their changing bodies. We have talked about how everyone has their own body stories and that no one's body is perfect. We've talked about the body-related norms that kids might call upon to bully others. One of my daughter's so-called friends paid another girl to talk about my daughter behind her back, simply because my daughter is skinnier than her. This became a great moment to teach about how much we have ingrained gendered body norms into our psyches and how harmful these norms are to individuals' wellbeing. Being body positive and open to discussion about bodily changes does not mean that your teenagers want to talk to you about their bodies at every turn. I am learning as I go and coming into being along with my children about what it means to be supportive of a gender-equal and body-positive world. Part of my feminist mothering project is to make sure that they are aware of their bodies and know how to talk about and negotiate them and know that everyone has a perspective that is rooted in their bodies. It is also important to me now that they are teenagers that they understand what consent is and know that they are in charge of their bodies. This is an ongoing conversation with both my son and daughter. They may roll their eyes at me when I bring it up yet one more time, but I'm still going to bring it up again.

As a feminist mother I've also invested effort in understanding and attempting to resist the expectations surrounding gendered appearances. When my daughter was little, I made a point of never dressing her in pink, believing that it was important to challenge gendered appearance norms. I thought about this every morning when I dressed her until it became clear that she desired pink clothing and princess dresses a few years later. I had to come to terms with how stereotypically feminine she wanted to be during her preschool years and tried to make sense of how to interact with her and her gendered preschool environment. It became clear that to make friends with others, she needed to understand and participate in stereotypically gendered behaviour. I acquiesced in many moments, as I would drive all the way back home from daycare to pick up a forgotten princess costume and take it back to her one morning. I eventually realized that in itself gendered clothing was not the enemy. As I've told my students all along, gender difference is not the problem until we attach values to those differences. My strong reactions to clothing were gendered at their core because, for me, clothing represented the values attached to heteronormative gender locations and, thus, the precursor to gender inequality. I eventually became conscious of the fact that I could zoom out and work to change the ways in which she understood or placed value on gender. Subsequently, I changed my tactics and focus, making sure to attack gender norms from other angles while she went through her princess phase. For instance, I made a concerted effort to buy children's books with feminist themes and made sure she watched television shows and movies that covered more than just heteronormative themes.

Later on, I prioritized making my son feel comfortable when he wanted to dress up in ballet costumes and princess dresses and loved the colour pink. (He still does as a teenager.) He often wore a pink Sleeping-Beauty headband to daycare, until the security guard at the daycare teased him enough that he decided, unprompted, to leave it in his car seat every morning (so that it would be waiting for him each evening when I picked him up). I talked to the security guard about how he had made my son feel, but it didn't matter: My son had received the message loud and clear. He still loved to play dress up at home but adjusted his activities at daycare. Ultimately, I didn't want to dress my daughter in pink but then caved, and then I supported my son's choice to adopt feminine clothing and accessories but acquiesced to his curtailing of his own choices. Across many action-filled and gender-tangible moments, I realized that there were a lot of different ways to fight gender norms and that struggling over a particular set of gendered choices was not productive. I could teach my children to be strong and thoughtful about gender in a multitude of ways. Yet I didn't completely give up. I still bought my daughter blue bikes and red scooters and steered away from pink winter coats and hats. Supporting my son's love of bright pastels and a pink laundry basket also helped me limit our range of stereotypically gendered purchases. Even in their Easter baskets, I'd purposely mix up the colours of candies and toys to make sure that my son got more pink-foiled chocolates and my daughter blue ones. This continued to be conscious behaviour for me as they progressed through elementary school. I wanted to play with gender rules and did try as much as possible to show them that they did not have to be boxed in by gender.

If I am being honest, though, this work to undo and redefine gender felt like work at the margins, since the weight and power of gender norms were crystal clear as my children interacted with the rest of the world. For example, even if I purchased gender-neutral birthday presents, they received stereotypically gendered presents from almost everyone else (especially from their peers). Thus, my gender-neutral action could always be negated by others' normative behaviours. Interacting with a gendered world was a daily slog, and there was always a new negotiation on the horizon. At the time, I felt like every one of those negotiations was important, partially because I was also trying to come into being myself as a new feminist mother.

Now that my children are teenagers, I see them choose to realize appearances that both align and play with gender in different moments. For instance, my son recently bought himself a sweatshirt with butterflies and flowers and happily wears it in public. As I watch them now, and try not to comment on their appearances, I believe that some of the actions I took early on may have paid off—more so in creating their identities, perspectives, and their relationships with a gendered world rather than their exact appearance preferences or daily behaviour choices. Maybe it was not the action-filled moments when they were little as much as the way in which we talked about gender over time or the fact that they saw me at paid work more than my husband and how he cooks all of our dinners. It makes me happy when I see them challenge gender norms, but I also understand on the days when they strictly adhere to what they know is normal. Even with more fluid gender identities and tolerance these days, there still is a gendered normal, and they are both clear about that reference point, which means I must accept that my daughter gets her nails done and wears makeup. They are allowed to engage in trial and error just like I do, playing with gender performances as they feel comfortable. I've learned over time that feminist mothering is less about how one necessarily performs gender or mothers on a particular day; it is more about the change and growth that one is effecting over time. In mothering for almost eighteen years now, I understand that to be feminist while mothering means questioning a gendered system alongside my children on a daily basis. I also realize that negotiating with our gendered world is a long-term endeavour that is not always won in specific moments. They are starting to understand that as much as I do now.

I've also come to realize that much of what I do as a feminist while mothering is to teach my kids to be thoughtful and critical of the world around them and to be strong in as many moments as they can be. Now that they are teenagers, I see that the most important lessons that I have taught them are perspectives and ways of seeing the world. They don't gain those perspectives in moments. They come to understand and adopt those perspectives over time. Having conversations about gender, race, human rights, politics, pandemics, and how to navigate personal situations is crucial right now in their teenager years. When I see my daughter explain to her friend that she does not have to wear skimpy clothing to attract others or hear my son critique his friends for how much they bully each other in conversation, I know they are present in the conversations we've been having all along. When I see my daughter give the finger to a body shamer in the audience while playing varsity basketball or see my son, unprompted, decide to avoid a certain clothing company because of its misogynist practices, I am proud to know I have succeeded in raising strong advocates for gender equality. It's a work in progress though, and we are all still coming into being on how to do this.

Finally, while we tango with our gendered worlds, I know that I must model strength for them as well. Personal fortitude is part of what gets us through trying situations. Sometimes I take being strong too far, and I have to dial it back. I was diagnosed with breast cancer several years ago and embarked on a six-month period of treatment that included two surgeries and five weeks of radiation. Until that moment, I had always been extremely healthy. My only contact with the healthcare system was to recover from a car accident while a teenager, to deal with acid reflux in my early thirties, and to have my two babies. I have prided myself in not needing doctors and being healthy. But a breast cancer diagnosis meant a reality shift, as happens with all who receive a health-altering diagnosis. Since that time, I have learned to shift how I think about being strong and resilient, even though I still stubbornly try to stay strong in all moments. Throughout the treatment and recovery process, I tried to maintain all parts of my life as if nothing were wrong. I told almost no one at my job that I was going through treatments, and I believed at the time that I did not need much support from others. What my kids saw was me still trying to do everything I did prediagnosis and not asking for much in the way of help. What I know now is that I was mistaken and that I did need more support. In fact, I needed both emotional and physical support during that time, and I only realized the toll that the diagnosis and treatment had taken after the fact. Priding myself in being strong, independent, and tough in the face of hard times, and capable of leading my own life, led me to portray a hollow kind of strength for my children. They probably knew I was suffering more than I did at times, but neither they, nor I, knew how to handle it. In retrospect, I know I have to teach them that the strength I showed in that moment was actually a misguided type of strength. We need support from others, and we can and should show our vulnerabilities. It is only now, several years later, that I realize that I need to adjust how I frame women's strength. One of my colleagues alerted me to a wonderful article by Leslie Anderson about resilience and its burdens, and it has renewed my interest in revising how I think about women's strength and struggles. Resilience seems wholly positive on the surface until we realize what a burden it is to have to be strong in every moment. Anderson therefore highlights how African American families are often resilient out of necessity, as they face everyday racism, and this resilience takes a serious toll. Much of what has been written about mothers during the COVID-19 pandemic makes a similar point (O'Reilly and Green): Since March 2020, mothers have had no choice but to brace themselves against changing family and paid work situations. Mothers' resilience, however, comes at a cost in the form of serious damage to mental health and wellbeing and a constriction of women's choices to work for pay. I want my children to learn resilience and strength but not to their own detriment. I want them to learn that resilience and strength are more nuanced than people make them out to be. My job is not only to teach them to be strong to a point but also to view strength through a critical lens no matter where they see it. This is an important recalibration of my feminist mothering in recent years.

Overall, I find that the practice of feminist mothering involves stops, starts, and wrong moves as much as it includes daily successes. I find myself second guessing my mothering as much as I am satisfied with it. As illustrated by many of the stories I have told here, feminist mothering is a constant work in progress. I am doing my best to broaden their perspectives on gender as well as my own. This work is ongoing. I'm also trying to model particular identities and behaviours for them at the same time, and sometimes I am not even sure of my own identity or stance. What I do realize again and again, though, is that feminist mothering has to be purposeful and active practice if we have particular goals that we desire to achieve.

Reflecting on Feminist Mothering

The journey through feminist mothering is not linear, nor is my search for identity, method, or focus. I realize that some of my daily behaviours are my attempts to protect and maintain my personhood, and other actions represent my aim to raise children who understand gender and support gender equality. Some of my behaviours achieve both goals. In the end, all of my actions shape me and my children and hone my version of feminist mothering. Some days I make missteps, but other days I feel myself accomplishing my goals. I will not achieve or reach feminist mothering perfectly in any moment or life stage. Engaging in active efforts to mother in feminist ways involves much trial and error, and the long-term pursuit is what is important.

Feminist mothering is chaptered, performative labour that continues across the life span. Every new phase, opportunity, and hurdle on this maternal journey means realizing both feminism and mothering in new, different, or recursive ways. The personal reflections above represent moments, both rewarding and challenging, in a sustained journey to practise feminist mothering. Although it is cliché to suggest that one should enjoy the journey, I'm not sure we have anything else. I am engaging in feminist mothering every day, and I am conscious about feminism, mothering practice, and the life stages in which my children and I reside. I am not sure how I will rethink and revise my feminist mothering in future life stages, but I know it will transform. Ultimately, my mothering will not wane, nor will my feminism. I am committed to my goals and to an ideal of feminist mothering. This is a worthwhile pursuit—for me, my children, and broader society.

Works Cited

Anderson, Leslie A. "Rethinking Resilience Theory in African American Families: Fostering Positive Adaptations and Transformative Social Justice." *Journal of Family Theory Review*, vol. 11, 2019, pp. 385-97.

Bliss, Eula. "Of Institution Born." *Of Woman Born*, edited by Adrienne Rich. W. W. Norton & Company, 1986, pp. xi-xx.

Dillaway, Heather. "Sorry, You'll Never Get the Good Blood." *Society for Menstrual Cycle Research*, 21 June 2012, https://www.menstruationresearch.org/2012/06/21/sorry-you%E2%80%99ll-never-get-the-good-blood%E2%80%A6/. Accessed 30 Mar. 2023.

Dillaway, Heather, Jennifer Haskin, and Victoria Velding. "Getting Past the Dream of a Bounded Life? An Analysis of Advertisements in *Working Mother* Magazine." *International Journal of Gender & Women's Studies*, vol. 3, no. 22, 2015, pp. 20-27.

Dillaway, Heather, and Elizabeth Paré. "Locating Mothers: How Cultural Debates about Stay-at-Home and Working Mothers Define Women and Home." *Journal of Family Issues*, vol. 29, no. 4, 2008: pp. 437-64.

"Feminism 101." *Red Letter Press*, 27 Aug. 2007, http://www.redletterpress.org/feminism101.html. Accessed 30 Mar. 2022.

Green, Fiona. *Practicing Feminist Mothering*. Arbeiter Ring Publishing, 2011.

Hays, Sharon. *The Cultural Contradictions of Motherhood*. Yale University Press, 1996.

O'Reilly, Andrea. *Matricentric Feminism: Theory, Activism, Practice*. Demeter Press, 2021.

O'Reilly, Andrea, and Fiona Green, editors. *Mothers, Mothering, and COVID-19: Dispatches from a Pandemic*. Demeter Press, 2021.

Rich, Adrienne. *Of Woman Born*. W. W. Norton & Company, 1986.

Ruddick, Sara. *Maternal Thinking: Towards a Politics of Peace*. Beacon Press, 1989.

Russo, Nancy Felipe. "The Motherhood Mandate." *Journal of Social Issues*, vol. 32, no.3, 1976, pp. 143-53.

West, Candace, and Don H. Zimmerman. "Doing Gender." *Gender & Society*, vol. 1, no. 2, 1987, pp. 125-51.

Chapter 2.

Sunrise

Lianne Milton

Throughout my adult life, I never wanted to be a mom. I didn't want to contend with the pursuit of my demanding career as a photojournalist while attending to children at home. I felt committed to my photography and believed the two could not coexist. I had plenty of anecdotal evidence to draw from: Pregnant journalists are deferred from photography fellowships and see their residency awards retracted and assignments cancelled. I certainly did not want to be another victim to motherhood—losing my career for having a child.

The censoring, judging, and misperception of the maternal body occur with such regularity that it becomes normalized. I did not view mothering as an empowering experience; in fact, it looked to me like a punishment. This perspective diminished my identity as a woman, a photographer, and an artist. In becoming a mother, I gave birth to a new kind of feminism—an embrace of my maternal power as an act of defiance. I vowed to maintain the same agency as a mother-artist that I had before having a baby.

When I finally became pregnant—intentionally, through fertility-assisted IVF—I did what most women photographers and journalists do in my field: I hid my pregnancy so that editors wouldn't think I was suddenly incapable. I also rejected the idea of creatively exploring or documenting the pregnancy—the biggest transformation of my life—because I viewed it as a cliché. An artist friend and professor, who raised two daughters as a single mother while in graduate school, pointed out that such thinking was the patriarchy speaking. Those words cracked the wall I had built around myself in which I viewed motherhood as an oppressive identity. I observed how discrimination and the lack of social support affected the women I know. I realized that to dismantle the patriarchy, I first had to dismantle my own bias. Although I had always thought of myself as a feminist, it wasn't until I became a mother that I understood what this truly meant.

What would it look like if we perceived childbirth, and the transition into motherhood, as a sacred transformation? The physical act of giving birth is an experiential power that comes with a profound psychological experience. In the same way becoming a mother marked a real identity shift in my life, so did the vulnerable experience of photographing my pregnancy. For me, it inherently became a political act. To photograph myself meant that I wanted this transformation to be seen, felt, and realized. I wanted to shatter the barriers set up by men (and women) to retain their privilege and fragility—to let its energy seep through the cracks in our walls.

When I embarked on this photographic project, I finally connected to something larger than life. It was through the act of photographing that I began to process how transformational and emotional these changes had been. I knew this transformation would be fleeting and evolving. For me, these biological changes were a tidal force of a love that was both giving yet depleting. I grappled with moments of trying to preserve memory and remain present while running the marathon of daily domestic baby labour. The joys and sadness of milestones, both past and present, clash and exist together.

The photography project that accompanies this essay, *Between Dark & Dawn*, is an autobiographical project about the maternal temporality of becoming a mother. In the photo *Shifting*—a triptych that depicts depletion and exhaustion within the first year of having a baby—I use self-portraiture to document my own experience. I also photographed my family in our small apartment in *Cocoon* to convey a place of not only refuge but also confinement during the pandemic. In contemporary landscapes, I drew metaphorical references to connect both my transformation as a mother and my Chinese American family lineage with the natural world of ocean and trees. In some of those landscapes, I immersed myself as a part of that environment—the maternal body as an extension of nature. In *Birth Canal*, for example, there are subtle rings of water surrounding me as I slowly submerge into the ocean and then a gradual surge pressure and a pause. My son emerged into the light in a gush of water.

Buddhist monk Thich Nhat Hanh has said: "The wave does not need to die to become water. She is already water" (97). For me, this quote symbolizes resilience. It represents the ocean as the womb of life and its transformative depths from which mothers emerge. I carry forth the layers of ancestral maternal experience while navigating the systemic issues of patriarchy and misogyny rooted within our culture and our artistic communities.

As I strive for a more fluid mothering experience, I make space for raising a child to be a part of the everyday. Instead of finding balance, I intentionally try to nourish the main relationships of my life: my son, my creative work, and my marriage. My mothering practice, much like my creative practice, needs its own devotion for my son and me to develop and flourish. I was not born a mother overnight. It was not intuitive as the social constructs of motherhood imply it to be. I am learning, the same way I learn how to guide him through life. I carry that practice with me into the classroom, too, as a newcomer to academia. With time, I imagine these roles and identities will eventually merge into a process of feminist growth for me.

Most of all, I hope our intersectional approach to parenting will be reflected in our son as my husband and I teach him to be a kind and sensitive person who engages his surroundings with confidence and courage. We recognize that histories of violence and systematic discrimination infringe on the progress of an equal society. Our multiracial son —who carries these overlapping cultural, ethnic, and economic experiences—represents an expansive and compassionate form of a feminist son.

Images in order:
1. *Shifting*
2. *Birth Canal*
3. *Emerge*
4. *Son*
5. *Family Tree*
6. *Sunrise*
7. *Family Lineage II*
8. *Cocoon*
9. *Reflection*
10. *Morning*

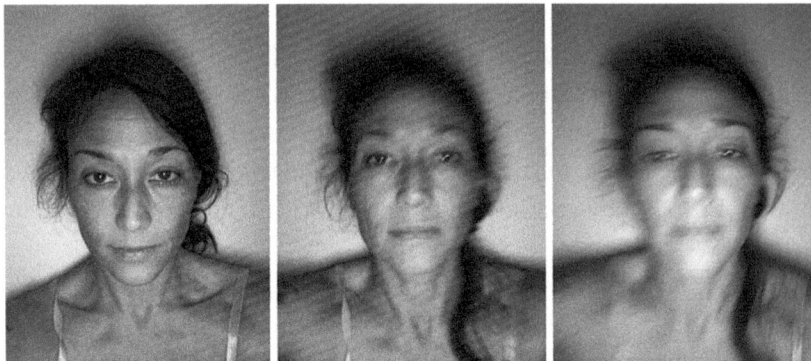

Shifting. 2021. A self-portrait triptych of myself to convey my identity shift while becoming a mother.

Birth Canal. 2021. Just before I submerge underwater, my hair floats atop the surface of the ocean, Miami Beach, Fl. Water is an important element for representing my connection to the ocean. The photo highlights how all life is born in water as well as the transformation that occurs when becoming a mother.

Emerge. 2021. As an ocean swimmer and surfer, I have always felt connected to the ocean. Here, I am submerged, a place where I float. I let the water blanket me, releasing the weight of the stress and anxiety of the pandemic.

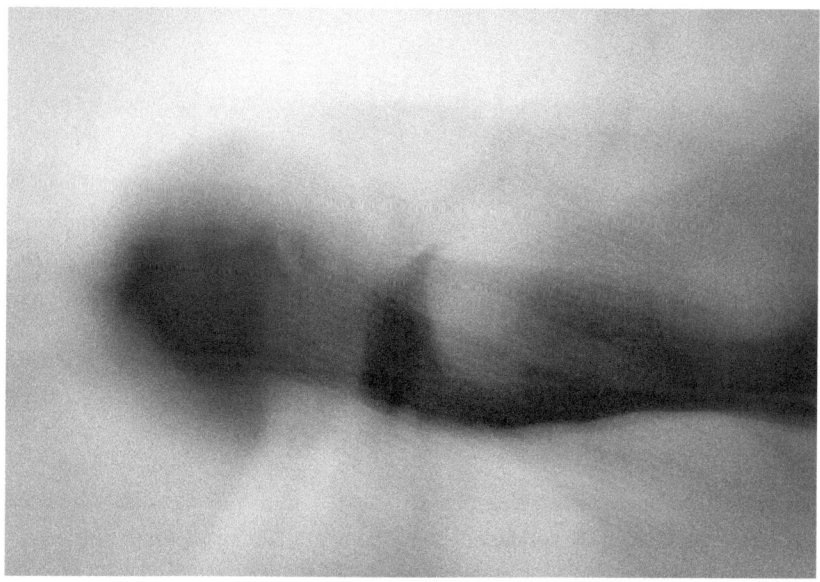

Son. 2021. My son plays under a sheet. The photo represents his movements in my belly when I was pregnant.

 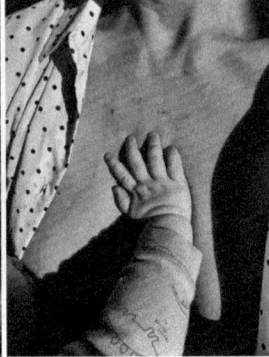 

(Left) *Family Tree.* 2021. Roots of a strangler fig tree intertwine with each other in a symbiotic process of engulfing the host tree, in Miami Beach, Fl. (Center) *Sunrise.* 2021. As my son nurses, he digs his sharp nails into my chest. He often picks and pinches my skin, leaving scabs on my chest. For me, breastfeeding is the only moment when my son and I are one again. But the feeling of emptiness in my belly still lingers after his birth. I never thought how strong this feeling of attachment would be. (Right) *Family Lineage II.* 2020. A patch of bamboo trees surrounds a local tree in northern Virginia. The photo references my mixed racial identity and motherhood.

Cocoon. 2021. During the pandemic, every moment that I've been a mother has been defined by deep isolation and physical distancing. Our small apartment became a cocoon—a place of not only refuge but also confinement. It is where I wrestle with my existence, surrender to time and impermanence, and oscillate between moments of fragility and fortitude.

Reflection. 2021. I am holding my son during a sunrise in Miami Beach, Fl. We left northern Virginia to spend a couple of months in Florida during the winter. The escape was a mental health retreat to spend time at the beach and in the warmth of the sun.

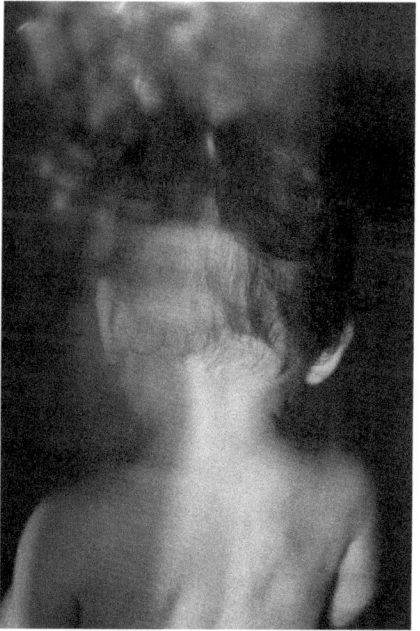

Morning. 2021. The morning sunlight reflects off the window, highlighting my son.

Works Cited

Hanh, Thich Nhat. *Heart of the Buddha's Teaching: Transforming Suffering into Peace, Joy, and Liberation.* Rider Books, 1999. p. 97.

Chapter 3.

Single Teen Motherhood and the Good Mother: Feminist Responses

Natasha Steer

Mrs. Richardson had, her entire existence, lived an orderly and regimented life.... She had had a plan, from girlhood on, and had followed it scrupulously: high school, college, boyfriend, marriage, job, mortgage, children.... She had, in short, done everything right.

—Celeste Ng, *Little Fires Everywhere* 69

I found out I was pregnant two days after my nineteenth birthday. I'd legally gone out for drinks for the first time, and the hangover was beyond anything I'd ever experienced. Two days later, I realized it wasn't the hangover from hell.

It was morning sickness.

It was January 2003. I was still attending high school, and motherhood at nineteen wasn't the plan—my own, or society's.

I became instantly reminded of classroom lectures that doggedly insisted that teen pregnancy was to be avoided at all costs. Unlike an older, more responsible mother, a teen mother didn't yet have financial stability, not to mention any lived adult experience. Teen pregnancy was something to prevent because our culture sees teen moms as a dangerous risk to themselves, their child, and society at large.

To become pregnant as a teenager was to have failed. Teen moms begin their motherhood journey knowing they've already gotten it wrong.

As a single teen mom, I was instantly flawed—incapable and delinquent, a careless and immoral teen. Nonetheless, the world told me that if I wanted to, and if I tried very, very hard, I could transform. I could, quite possibly, become a "good" mother.

As a young single mother, I felt twice the pressure to be everything my child needed. In part, this pressure was doubled because I was a single parent in a society that deemed two parents the "correct" number of parents to have. But I also felt double the pressure because there were two conflicting motherhood narratives pushing and pulling at me: the incapable single teen mom and the idealized good mother who could do it all.

Though the latter seemed the more appealing of the two, Susan Douglas and Meredith Michaels note that "to be a remotely decent mother, a woman has to devote her entire physical, psychological, emotional, intellectual being, 24/7, to her children.... [This] is a highly romanticized view of motherhood in which the standards for success are impossible to meet" (4). And as Andrea O'Reilly notes in *Mother Outlaws*, "The patriarchal ideology of motherhood makes mothering deeply oppressive to women because sacrificial motherhood ... requires the repression or denial of the mother's own selfhood" (11). Although I responded to such messaging with painful perfectionism, I also rejected many notions of what good motherhood looked like and who society told me I should be striving to be. Through the lens of feminism, I crafted my own version of empowered motherhood.

I raised my son through the lens of feminism by consistently having conversations about gender roles in the media, examining forms of oppression through children's books, and encouraging him to resist patriarchal ideals for both himself and for others. Feminism empowered me in my decision not to partner up and to instead craft caring, intentional communities for my son and me. It also allowed me to shun many motherhood norms and embrace a playful approach to my parenting style. Lastly, feminism allowed me to embrace the freedom that came with my single-lone mother status, which led to my son, Zac, and I living and travelling abroad. We travelled to our fiftieth country by the time he was fifteen years old.

All the while, I straddled these two narratives of motherhood—the incapable single teen mom and the good mother—trying my best to navigate the one while attempting to disrupt the stereotypes of the other. As I did so, I navigated the reality of cultural expectations, systemic discrimination, chronic stress, and complex trauma.

> Too many in this society are entrenched in the devout belief that there is something magically awesome for children about the heterosexual two-parent household.
> —Rebecca Solnit, *The Mother of All Questions* 7

"Where's your dad?"

"I don't have one," Zac responded off-handily, as he always did, still gazing at the jerseys in front of him. We were strolling through stores along La Ramblas before the FC Barcelona match we were heading to—a surprise for my son. The man, a stranger, looked up at me in surprise from behind the counter of the store.

"Everyone has a father," he insisted.

His words were a match that lit me on fire. My son had come up with his own response to this question he was asked by nosy strangers—usually men—too many times to count.

"Some people don't," I replied. Taking Zac's hand, we left the store.

In my mind, every time we were asked this question—or an assumed variation of it, aimed at me: "Where's your husband?"—it told my son that we were incomplete as we were. It was a notion I knew the world was pushing on my son at every opportunity, right down to the anime cartoons that revolved around the father-son bond and relegated the mother to a nagging, whining side character. A child, especially a boy, we were told, needed a father.

Although we were happy and complete as we were, our life was constantly scrutinized.

Families with single mothers at the head of the household are continuously seen as a second-hand, less-than-ideal option. As Elizabeth Bruno notes in "Her Cape is at the Cleaners", "Our society is deeply in [favour] of two-parent families. While the notion of *who* constitutes a 'nuclear family' has shifted since the 1950s—we now include interracial families, gay and lesbian parents, unwed parents, etc.—the two-partner nuclear family remains the acceptable narrative" (395). One reason for this viewpoint is the perceived detriment single mothers are seen to inflict: It is believed that single-mother households are not good for children's well-being. "Whether being linked to gun violence or criticized for being overly independent, real single mothers face the seemingly endless stream of using the phrase 'single mother' as a short hand for social problems" (Bruno, "Her Cape" 387).

I knew that absent fathers didn't need to navigate the line of questioning we were constantly subjected to. I wondered what that would be like, for a man who had abandoned his child to be so visible, and to be asked so frequently, "Where is your child?" Of course, an absent father wouldn't know the answer. He'd have no idea.

It's well documented that in two-parent heterosexual households, mothers are still the ones providing the bulk of support to children. Why, then, does society push the idea that kids are somehow automatically better off if they have a father in the home? There are partnered women who are doing it all. So why does being unpartnered cause such outrage?

> You are not crazy. You are a goddamn cheetah.
>
> —Glennon Doyle, *Untamed* xvi

When my son was one and a half, he began to get ear infections, one after the other. Then he was diagnosed with asthma and began to develop rashes and severe allergic reactions, although we couldn't figure out what in response to.

Early on, I asked the doctors what would cause this onset of allergic reactions in my son and expected them to answer. I found instead that they simply brought out their prescription pads and carried on. When I asked what would cause my son to develop asthma so rapidly—I always want to know the why—I was told that it just, simply, was.

The rashes quickly escalated, and a few weeks later, my son's skin was peeling off, revealing oozing pus and a sheen of redness lying below. However, his skin was constantly changing, which meant that by the time I got my son into his appointment, his skin sometimes looked differently than the way I had described it, either days or only hours prior.

I asked our family doctor for referral after referral—another paediatrician, dermatologist, paediatric dermatologist. Doctor after doctor told me the same thing: "It's just eczema." Then they'd grab their prescription pad and start writing yet another prescription for cortisone cream.

I knew they were wrong. I knew they were missing something. No matter how hard I tried to explain that my son's skin got worse, not better, with traditional eczema treatment, it didn't seem to matter. Every time I pushed for more, I tempered my voice. I didn't want to personify the stereotype of an overly emotional, overprotective mother—but I didn't want to come across as the inexperienced, too young mother who didn't know what she was talking about either. I don't know what good it did. My advocacy didn't seem to get us anywhere.

As my son's skin continued to get worse, not better—no matter how many prescriptions I filled—I tried my best to distract my baby from his inflamed, painful, and itchy skin. Sometimes, no matter how much I tried, there was no escaping it. He alternated between pain and constant irritation, and it was devastating to see him in such a condition. Although I explained repeatedly that sometimes my son's skin was missing, making the cortisone cream useless, I was told simply to do my best to apply it. Once, uncertainly, I dabbed some of the cream on his vibrantly red, wet flesh, and as he screamed and wailed, I knew I'd never do it again, no matter how many doctors told me otherwise. I tried to become the doctor Zac didn't yet have: I researched the internet and communicated constantly with our family doctor (who supported me enough to continue referring me to specialists), labouring to learn all I could to advocate for my son.

A couple of months of trying doctor after doctor, my hopes rose. We had an appointment with a highly regarded paediatrician who specialized in skin conditions. The doctor walked into the room, glanced at my son, and reached for her prescription pad, saying, "Oh, this is eczema." Tears flooded my eyes instantly, devastated that even this specialist was letting us down, letting my son down. I explained that this was more than eczema. Perhaps it was also eczema, but something else was going on, too. She gave me a sympathetic smile that felt like a pat on the head, handed me the prescription, and left the room. I felt like I was being treated like a child myself, and that this, more than anything, was what was hurting my son's chances at having his health taken seriously.

Then came the day when my attempts to distract Zac from his open, oozing neck were pointless. As he screamed in agony, I sobbed in solidarity, the two of us at our breaking point. My mom returned home from work, and we immediately drove downtown to Sick Kids Hospital in Toronto.

When the nurse got her first look at my son, she put us straight into a quarantine room. Four doctors—all immersed in protective body suits and headgear—came in, one at a time, to inspect Zac. It took me a while to process that my son's health was finally being treated with the respect he deserved. Several tests and hours later revealed two blood infections and one skin infection. All three infections were so serious that they needed to be treated with the highest antibiotics legally available in Canada. My son spent about two weeks in the hospital, me by his side for all of it. I was infinitely grateful that my persistence and advocacy had finally resulted in Zac recciving the help he needed.

I knew that wasn't always the case.

> Asking single mothers to be self-sufficient ... is [asking] them to accept unfair social structures and to assume responsibility for maintaining the illusion that self-sufficiency is possible.
> —Elizabeth Bruno, "Her Cape Is at the Cleaners" 390

When my son was fourteen years old, I went to a sleep study. When I went back to get my results, the doctor stared at me, aghast. "You don't know this, but you wake up about fourteen times an hour. We really only see that in people who have experienced complex trauma or have PTSD." He stared at me, waiting. I paused, thinking, just in case I had blocked out some specific traumatic event. I didn't yet know what complex trauma was—or that I was, indeed, living with it. I shook my head and shrugged. "Well, I don't have PTSD. I do have chronic neck and shoulder pain though. That's where I hold my stress." He frowned and referred me to a psychologist.

I sat in front of the psychologist a few weeks later. "Tell me about yourself," he invited. As I spoke about my life, he nodded knowingly. "Ah. So, you're a perfectionist." I laughed out loud as I pictured the days-old pile of laundry in our living room and the general disarray of our home.

"No! Absolutely not. Come to my home and see. It's a mess. Nothing is perfect in my life!"

"Not everything, no. But when I hear you talk about work, school, and especially your son, I hear very clearly the pressure to be perfect. Everything cannot be perfect, though. The rest, you let slide. The rest, you have no energy for."

I thought about my mom's insomnia. She'd told me just the week before, "I can't turn my thoughts off. But you, you can sleep anywhere." Except that, it turns out, I wasn't actually sleeping. Was I thinking, too? Worrying, planning, trying, even in my sleep? I stared back at this man, amazed that someone who had known me for such a short period of time could suddenly seem to know me so intimately.

> [T]here are...many rewards and possibilities that make this [single mother] family status desirable and rich with possibilities.
> —Jennifer Ajandi, *Single Mothers by Choice* 410

I was navigating two competing forms of expectations—that as a mom I should do it all, and that as a young single mom, I would never be enough. It was exhausting. In response, I found empowerment in choosing how to raise my son. Being a feminist was at the heart of my parenting philosophy. As O'Reilly notes,

> The overall aim of empowered mothering is the redefinition of patriarchal motherhood to make mothering less oppressive and more empowering for mothers. Or, more specifically, feminist mothers seek to fashion a mode of mothering that affords and affirms maternal agency, authority, autonomy, and authenticity and confers and confirms power to and for mothers. (*Mother* 15)

As an intersectional feminist, I understand that my identity is complex and made up of a variety of aspects. I navigate the world as a biracial, single-lone mom who began her motherhood journey as a single teen mother. I'm also privileged through my nationality, language, education, ability, sexuality, gender identification, and profession.

Feminism was the lens through which I was introduced to all oppressions, and I learned how feminism could be intimately connected to help support the dismantling of such oppressions. With this knowledge, I ensured my son learned about, noticed, and had the tools to speak out against oppression. I also raised him to resist the patriarchy and how it directly impacted him. I felt empowered to carefully craft my son's communities and the people around him, and I chose to actively pursue authentic, engaged, and playful parenting. Feminism also empowered me to live and travel abroad with my son, which fit in with the spirit of freedom and playfulness with which I was embracing motherhood.

It's important to note that my resistance to patriarchal motherhood wasn't entirely successful—can it ever be? Raising my son in a patriarchal society consistently told me that I needed to do all of the things for my son and that I alone would be the marker of success for him—but that I better not overdo it either, lest I become a dreaded helicopter mom. This is what led to the chronic neck and shoulder pain; this is, in part, what led to the impact on my sleep.

I was trying desperately to do all I could for my son's well-being. I just didn't believe having a nine-to-five job, a partner, and a pristine clean house was the only way to do it. I wanted to make choices that felt more authentic to our family values: social justice, community, playfulness, and adventure.

I found feminism in university when my son was a toddler. Zac's existence helped fuel my drive to do well, and he followed me, sometimes literally, into every classroom. I decided my child wouldn't have to wait until university (should he choose to go) to learn about inequality and oppression. The feminism I found in the classroom followed me outside of it and connected intimately to how I decided to raise my son. As O'Reilly notes, "[F]eminist mothering positions mothers in the public realm by way of activism and views childrearing as a social-political act" (*Feminist* 19). I learned from scholars and artists such as bell hooks, Paulo Freire, and W.E.B. Du Bois. From childhood through to his teens, my son discussed and read about many of the issues I studied in an age-appropriate way.

It was important to me that Zac understood that as an individual, he had the power and ability to contribute to important change for so many who are marginalized and oppressed. It was also important that he learned to critically analyze media messaging and that he understood that such messaging directly related to the treatment of those same groups of people in real life.

It's still a source of amusement to others at how frequently I utilized the pause button while watching a movie: "Do you notice how she's wearing a bathing suit while he wears a business suit? Why do you think that is?" Zac knew the drill, and complaints at these interruptions weren't an issue, simply because this was how we watched movies. After we talked, we'd resume watching, sometimes only to pause again a few minutes later.

I wanted to lay bare to Zac how the patriarchy worked. I wanted to show him how women were constantly undermined and undervalued, whether that was through stereotyped media portrayals or descriptions of women that used sexist and gendered language. In examining media forms with my son—from movies to TV shows to magazines to advertisements—we identified how often women were deemed less capable, less intelligent, and less athletic. This was ongoing work, but I was rewarded by our constant conversations and analysis of media consumption every time Zac whispered loudly in a movie theatre that it wasn't fair that only the mom was cleaning the house, or that there were no women present in an office meeting. Other times, evidence of his learning came during real life interactions, as with the time Zac ran away from his grandfather, visibly upset as he yelled, "Grandpa said I kick like a girl, and that's sexist!"

Feminism also allowed me to disrupt constructs of gender when it came to household tasks. As Bruno argues, "Is it possible that single motherhood is partly offensive because it rejects certain beliefs? The threat of single mothers is not simply the threat of children without fathers; it is the threat of dirty dishes in the sink and dirty clothes in the schoolyard. It is a threat to our system of meaning" ("Her Cape" 394). I was never much of a cook or cleaner, and as an often exhausted single-lone mom, this was amplified. But I pushed Zac to develop these skills more than I had them because I knew that in heterosexual relationships, men statistically don't participate in equal amounts of work in childrearing and household tasks. I wanted to lay the groundwork for Zac to break the cycle and do better.

While women and gender non-conforming humans are primary targets of the patriarchy and therefore hurt the most, this system of inequality hurts everyone, including boys and men. I wanted Zac to understand how the patriarchy worked so that it would be limited in its ability to confine and hurt him. As O'Reilly states, "Feminist mothers seek to dismantle, destabilize, and deconstruct normative patterns of male socialization and traditional definitions of masculinity" (*Mother* 15).

When Zac was a child, I blurred gender constructions. I gifted him dolls and painted his nails; I also played cars and built Lego towers with him. I shared with my son the importance of sharing his feelings and crying, since all humans cry, because they're, well, human. It felt authentic and empowering to share my knowledge with my son about what I'd learned and use that knowledge to push against the messaging he was receiving—from friends, teachers, and, of course, the media—about who he should be as a boy. I loved that I gave him access to this information as a toddler and that he had critical thinking and questioning skills modelled to him throughout his entire childhood.

Still, it was all consuming work that never ended. And it was all up to me.

> [E]mpowered mothering recognizes that both mothers and children benefit when the mother lives her life and practices mothering from a position of agency, authority, authenticity, and autonomy.
> —Andrea O'Reilly, *Mother Outlaws* 12

For much of Zac's childhood, I chose to remain unpartnered. I knew someone who'd told me, in no uncertain terms, that her life had been easier as a single mother before her marriage. "I still have to do everything," I remember her telling me after her wedding. "But before, I'd known that would be the case. Now, I have to deal with disappointment and unmet expectations on top of that." As Jennifer Ajandi notes, many women feel privileged to be single mothers because it gives them the freedom to be the sole decision maker for the family. They're able to raise their children with their own values and don't need to negotiate decisions with a partner. As Ajandi explains: "Some women felt that even though they experienced barriers and being a single mother student was a 24-hour job, not having the other partner to take care of reduced their burden significantly" (418).

I knew there was a chance I could find a partner who took on their equitable share of housework and childrearing. I also knew the odds were against me and that it would take time and effort away from parenting my son in order to search that out. Besides, I was content with my life. I didn't feel like I needed a partner to complete it.

Just as intentional as my decision to not partner up was my decision to carefully craft positive communities for my son. As O'Reilly notes, "Feminist mothers transform the meaning of family to include...

matrifocal, communal, and extended families" (*Feminist* 12).

From the moment my son was born, I pulled my current friends closer, and they were eager responders. My closest friends became Zac's godmothers, and other core friends turned from friends into family friends—people we celebrated Christmas and birthdays with, alongside other days throughout the year. Crafting communities of loving humans around Zac was something I did every time we moved—from Wuhan, to Shanghai, to back home again. Although this took active and ongoing work on my part, it inevitably meant that I was unintentionally crafting supportive communities for my own wellbeing, too.

> Play ... is a fundamentally human way to create meaningful, complex social structures: a way in which not just children, but adults experiment, process, communicate, and respond to the world around them.
> —Elizabeth Bruno, "I Play" 310

Being a young single mom intimately affected our dynamic and how I parented Zac. In *Of Woman Born*, Adrienne Rich discusses how different her experiences were with her children when her husband was away for several weeks for work:

> Without a male adult in the house, without any reason for schedules, naps, regular mealtimes, or early bedtimes so the two parents could talk, we fell into what I felt to be a delicious and sinful rhythm.... We lived like castaways on some island of mothers and children ... I felt wide awake, elated; we had broken together all the rules of bedtime, the night rules, rules I myself thought I had to observe ... or become a "bad mother." We were conspirators, outlaws from the institution of motherhood; I felt enormously in charge of my life. (195-96)

Of course, this temporary escape into solo mothering is not the same as constantly navigating the difficulties that society impresses upon single lone mothers. And stereotypically, in heterosexual relationships, mothers tend to do much of the work while fathers have the freedom to play with their children.

I did both.

Nonetheless, there is truth in Rich's account. The freedom of existing only with your child means that you can choose to throw a lot of so-called rules out the window. I can only agree with Bruno, who notes the following in "I Play, Therefore, I Am": "Addressing single parent play ... is rooted in my own observation of the stark contrast between my joyful daily experiences and the cold and broken visions of single motherhood that society has offered me ... the robust play life that I experience exists not despite a missing spouse but, perhaps, because of it" (289-290).

As Catherine Price notes in "The Power of Fun," fun is the intersection of playfulness, connection, and flow. With the demands placed on single-lone mothers—never mind those beginning the process of mothering straight out of high school—it's a miracle that I was able to intuitively prioritize fun and ease for my son and myself. This was in direct resistance to the narratives that said I was already a failure for being a single teen mom and that I'd have to work really, really hard to—possibly—change that. As already noted, I was working hard—it's impossible not to as a lone mom—but I was learning not to allow that to overshadow our relationship and experiences.

In my first year of teaching, I brought marking home to our Wuhan apartment each night. As I navigated an immense workload and being a solo mother, more than once I found myself "watching" a movie with Zac while I attempted to mark a never-ending pile of essays.

I felt in tune enough, however, to feel discomfort at not being fully present with Zac, and I understood that this was not authentic parenting. I put up stronger boundaries around working outside of set work hours, and once my contract was up, I left the school for another with a much more manageable workload in Shanghai. In these ways, I actively pursued authentic and playful parenting. As I did, it was in direct resistance to the stereotype of the good mother—the overextended mom trying to juggle all of the responsibilities and duties that patriarchal motherhood tries to impose.

According to Price, "Playfulness refers to the ability to let down your guard, shed formality, not care too much about outcomes, and open yourself to—indeed, proactively seek out—opportunities for humour and lighthearted connection" (90). I relaxed and let my relationship with Zac guide me as to how I thought he should be engaged with and parented.

There were, inevitably, pangs of envy when I saw put-together moms who were taken more seriously than I was. The ones who sipped coffee and watched their children play from afar while I crawled through the jungle gym, pursuing my son as he squealed in delight. The ones who lounged on beach chairs watching their children swim while my own son threw heaps of sand on my body before beginning a massive water fight.

Nonetheless, my parenting experiences were incredibly rewarding. Sometimes society's gaze was less so, as evidenced by the looks we received while playing hide-and-seek in grocery stores, or by the stares I endured while sitting neck-deep in a ball pit, whipping little plastic balls in my son's general direction.

My engagement with my son, my parenting style, was decidedly more relaxed than others I had seen modelled for me, both in real life and on the screen. In choosing to parent authentically, I was rejecting patriarchal norms that said I needed to look and act a certain way to be a good mother. Despite the pressure that was hardening my neck and shoulder muscles, we were happy. We laughed, played hide and seek, and chatted while strolling through different neighbourhoods. We were playful and adventurous. We had so much fun.

I took pride in how I chose to raise my son, and that feeling was reinforced whenever other people noticed the care I took in, and my prioritization of, my role as Zac's mom. Sometimes, it was with amusement, when, for example, Zac and I were mid-tickle fight and I tried to carry on a conversation with other adults. Once, in Wuhan, after breakfast with some old and new friends, I finally had my son in a strong hold from our latest tickle fight when I saw that a man we'd just met was smiling at us. "I love your relationship," he confided, his eyes twinkling.

Years later, at a friend's gathering, I saw a young adult wrestling with his sister and started laughing. "This is what we look like to everyone else," I told Zac. "No wonder everyone thinks I'm your sister." He laughed.

As I think about this, I wonder how negative narratives of single-lone mothers contributed to how others initially viewed us. I like to think that our very existence helped push against stories that suggested a single mom, especially a single teen mom, was detrimental to her child.

When on our road trip through New Zealand, we came across a chalkboard sign by the beach that asked, "What do you want to do before you die?" Zac promptly wrote down, "Explore the world."

—Natasha Steer, *Great Lakes to Great Walls* 175

After years of not finding a job in my field, I decided to relocate Zac and myself to Wuhan, China. I carefully selected a location that had everything we needed in one place: the international high school I'd teach at, the international elementary school for Zac, and our apartment would all be on one campus.

As we settled into another way of living, I embraced it as an opportunity to explore the world. While living in China, my son and I were able to travel during the Mid-Autumn Festival, Chinese New Year, the Qingming Festival, and Chinese Labour Day. It was during the summer—and some Christmases—that we returned to Canada to spend time with our family.

It was empowering living and solo parenting abroad. I was mothering in a completely different way than the narratives of single-lone moms I'd seen. I did have to navigate opinions and judgments from friends and family about travelling with my son through underdeveloped countries; many of these judgments insinuated that I was irresponsible for bringing my son to such places, and that I alone wasn't capable of keeping us both safe. For me, resistance to these notions lay in research that dug beyond characterizing developing countries as dangerous and trusting that I was the best person to know what was safe for my son and me. Feminism— an ideology that constantly reminds me that I, a woman, am capable and intelligent—underlined my navigation of all of these moments.

There was a real sense of freedom in being able to decide where we were travelling without having to consult a partner (though decisions about where to travel to were always made with Zac's input). Choosing to live abroad and to travel to over fifty countries allowed for an unencumbered freedom in a way I'd previously never realized was possible for a single mom. I'd seen no examples for this type of life. As my life itself became an active resistance to the teen mom stereotypes I'd previously felt chasing me, I revelled in living in a way that actively disrupted mainstream portrayals of single-lone motherhood.

Travelling multiple times a year allowed me to further extend the playfulness with which I was consciously choosing to raise Zac. Our first Christmas away from home, Zac and I flew to Hong Kong and went to Disneyland. Thus began our intention to visit every Disney Resort. Less than four years later, we visited Shanghai Disneyland just before it officially opened, meaning we'd officially been to all of the Disney resorts in the world, and all of the Universal Studios, too.

Whenever we travelled, we sought out theme parks, carnivals, and fun events. Travel, for us, was another type of play. We splashed with elephants in Thailand and rode camels in the Moroccan desert. We played with our food, taking cooking classes in several of the countries we visited. We jumped waves on island beaches and bantered back and forth while trekking through the oldest rainforest in the world.

We ditched boring walking tours for a segway tour in Manila and a moped tour in Ho Chi Minh City. We whizzed down the streets of Ljubljana on electric scooters and strolled on foot through the streets of Prague.

My son and I were privileged in these experiences, although we experienced them on a shoestring budget that ensured life was still more affordable than owning or renting a home back in Canada. Such a budget brought with it its own anxieties and burdens. Our travel always necessitated copious amounts of planning time and effort on my part. There was never any escaping that; as a lone mother, it would always be true. Nonetheless, it was absolutely worth the labour that rested on my shoulders alone.

Living and travelling abroad empowered me and made me come alive. It was counter to the patriarchal expectations of motherhood that said I should instead be spending my time cooking, cleaning, and bringing my son to all of his extracurricular activities, and said that parents needed to wait until their children were older to practically travel with them because it was too much work otherwise (not true). Travel took us out of the mundane day to day and allowed us to reconnect with ourselves, with other people, and with the world.

> Only an empowered mother can empower children, and children can only be empowered by an empowered mother.
> —Andrea O'Reilly, *Mother Outlaws* 13

Rebecca Solnit notes that "We are consistently given one-size-fits-all formulas, but those formulas fail, often and hard ... we are given a single story about what makes a good life" (6). Navigating motherhood as a single-lone mother in a patriarchal society has been so hard for so many reasons. Remaining empowered in my mothering journey is a constant navigation, something I must choose to do over and over again.

Choosing to resist many of the narratives that surround me— narratives that almost don't even feel constructed, though I know they are—is exhausting. Being empowered in my motherhood journey requires a great deal of ongoing effort on my part. But the work is so important. One of its greatest gifts has been my relationship with my son, as well as an empowered self-image for myself in a society that suggests I shouldn't have one.

Raising my son consciously as a feminist, living unpartnered while crafting intentional communities, mothering authentically and playfully, and bringing my son to live abroad and to travel have all led to increased freedom in my motherhood journey. These were the ways in which I resisted the patriarchy and found empowerment in being a single-lone mother. My greatest hope is that all mothers may find their own sources of resistance and empowerment—whatever that may look like for them.

Works Cited

Ajandi, Jennifer. "Single Mothers by Choice: Disrupting Dominant Discourses of the Family through Social Justice Alternatives." *International Journal of Child, Youth and Family Studies,* vol. 43, no. 4, 2011, pp. 410-31.

Bruno, Elizabeth. "Her Cape Is at the Cleaners: Searching for Single Motherhood in a Culture of Self Sufficiency." *Mothers, Mothering and Motherhood across Cultural Differences,* edited by Andrea O'Reilly, Demeter Press, 2014, pp. 385-412.

Bruno, Elizabeth. "I Play, Therefore, I Am." *Motherhood and Single-Lone Parenting,* edited by Maki Motapanyane, Demeter Press, 2016, pp. 155-76.

Bzostek, Sarah H., Sara S. McLanahan, and Marcia J. Carlson. "Mothers' Repartnering after a Nonmarital Birth." *Social Forces,* vol. 90, no. 3, 2012, pp. 817-41.

Douglas, Susan. J, and Meredith W. Michaels. *The Mommy Myth: The Idealization of Motherhood and How It Has Undermined Women.* Free Press, 2004.

Ng, Celeste. *Little Fires Everywhere.* Penguin Books, 2019.

Price, Catherine. "The Power of Fun." The Dial Press, 2021.

O'Reilly, Andrea. "Introduction" *Feminist Mothering,* edited by Andrea O'Reilly, State University of New York Press, 2008, pp. 1-20.

O'Reilly, Andrea. "Introduction." *Mother Outlaws: Theories and Practices of Empowered Mothering,* edited by Andrea O'Reilly, Women's Press, 2004, pp. 1-28.

Rich, Adrienne. *Of Woman Born: Motherhood As Experience and Institution.* Norton, 2021.

Solnit, Rebecca. *The Mother of All Questions.* Haymarket Books, 2017.

Steer, Natasha. "Great Lakes to Great Walls: Reflections of a Single Mom on Young Motherhood and Living Overseas." *Motherhood and Single-Lone Parenting,* edited by Maki Motapanyane. Demeter Press, 2016, pp. 155-76.

Chapter 4.

Discovering Feminist Motherhood through Art Practice

Jen McGowan

At art school at Concordia in the late 1990s, I was profoundly affected by a class called Feminism in Art History. It was pedagogically feminist, as it honoured each individual's ways of learning and was inclusive of the intersecting identities and experiences of the students. We read texts like Linda Nochlin's, "Why Have There Been No Great Women Artists?" and studied artists like the Guerrilla Girls, Cindy Sherman, Adrian Piper, and Judy Chicago. We learned about feminist movements, from essentialist feminism to postcolonial Feminism. It had a big impact on me both as a young student—it was where I first felt safe to speak out in an academic classroom as opposed to a studio-based class—and as an artist. It also helped me to understand how patriarchal norms and policies had affected my own life and the lives of the women in my family. My artwork has always come from my own experience and included feminist themes, although I didn't necessarily recognize them as such when starting out. But it was through learning about the bigger context of feminism and seeing how artists had confronted confining aspects of being a woman in a patriarchal society that my work gained greater meaning and purpose. After art school in Montreal, I returned to Vancouver—back into my mom's house—and the feminist worldview gained in art school got a bit lost. The focus of my life was on finding a profession that would allow me some freedom for creativity and that would enable me to afford a life in Vancouver. I became a high-school art teacher and for the next few years focused on getting a permanent position and developing my teaching career. Around that time, I met and later married an exceptionally supportive and caring man. We then had children.

As I think it does for most women, to a greater or lesser degree, motherhood blew everything apart. Now that my life is coming back together—amid a pandemic—things look fundamentally different. I didn't have an easy time with the early years of mothering. Such factors as a traumatic birth, postpartum anxiety, secondary infertility, and processing childhood trauma all contributed to a challenging introduction to motherhood. I continue to feel maternal ambivalence, but I hadn't made art about it or understood the larger feminist implications of the difficulties I was having until the pandemic hit.

One day during lockdown, I felt like a good mother. I had been down on myself because my normally passable mothering skills had been overcome by rising panic and complete paralyzing fear when the world came to a halt. But this day, I felt victorious: I cleaned the kitchen, did laundry, and even vacuumed the stairs. After some reflection, I was appalled that I only congratulated myself in my caretaking role when I performed domestic tasks. Where had my education spanning essentialist feminism to postcolonial Feminism gone? Why had I set the barometer of a good mother to the ideal of a 1950s housewife?

Through the constraints of the pandemic, the problematic disconnect between my feminist education and worldview and the way I perceived and enacted motherhood became evident. I have been wrestling with this cognitive dissonance in my artwork. For example, in the performative self-portrait series *MILF MOUTH MADNESS*, clichéd sexy red lips are stuffed with domestic objects and food—where neither sexual nor maternal identity has agency as they push up against each other. It was the claustrophobia and imbalance of labour amid the pandemic, felt by me and legions of other mothers, that reminded me that these limiting expectations of what a good mother is are not specific to my own family history but are learned and have been internalized from the patriarchal society we are mothering within. Through my work, I am deliberately calling this out.

The exhibitions I have been in, such as *IF NOT NOW, WHEN?* hosted by the artist-mother supporting Spilt Milk Gallery, are a rallying cry from artist-mothers. The pandemic has been the tipping point for our collective reckoning with unquestionable imbalances of power in society. Motherhood has been the lens through which I have been reminded of how oppressive forces systematically disenfranchise and disempower women so that we doubt our own ability to create meaningful change.

I have become braver in my thinking and in my art because of the artist-mother community. Through another organization called the Artist/Mother podcast, I was in the exhibition *You are not wonderful just because you are a Mother*. It was impactful to show with peers whose art reflected my experience of motherhood. In Sally Butcher's *Infertile Platitudes of Embodied Emptiness*, a series of white relief prints of her stomach appear like sonograms on black paper, with text below that states empty platitudes you hear when you are trying to get pregnant, and it isn't working. In another work that resonates with me, *Child's Blanket*, Jill Saxton Smith hangs a child's pink security blanket from the ceiling pulled taut by its heavy, concrete-dipped bottom. The piece speaks to the resurfacing of childhood trauma that often happens when we become mothers. Although the show doesn't overtly call itself feminist, it celebrates the full complexity of the female experience without a predetermined idea of what is appropriate for a woman to be. The feminist-thinking artist-mother community has disrupted my internalization of the patriarchal notions of what a mother is. It has been revolutionary in my life.

In the next couple of years, I plan to study historically relevant feminist artists, such as Mary Kelley, and dive deep into my experience of feminist motherhood through my art. It feels like such an exciting time to be focused on this subject. The well-deserved popularity of books such as *Nightbitch* and films such as *The Lost Daughter* is indicative that maternal ambivalence is becoming socially acceptable in a deeply considered way. My own experience is that the pressures and unrealistic idealization of motherhood is the unfinished work of feminism. But I feel optimistic about the conversations we artist-mothers are having, buoyed by the support of our communities. When we support one another's courageous thinking, we will be more likely to feel deserving of, and therefore demand, something better.

Image list:

1. *Perfect Mother.* Digital Photography, 17" x 32", 2020. Performative self-portrait of a Perfect Mother.
2. *Runaway.* Digital Collage, 13" x 19", 2021. Collage of mother running away from children and dishes.
3. *MILF.* Digital Photo with found image, 10" x 10", 2020. Pin-up torso stuck in milk bottle.
4. *Cookies MILF.* Digital Photo with found image, 8" x 8", 2020. Pulp fiction torso with Fruit Crème breasts.
5. *Mommy Mouth* (MILF MOUTH MADNESS series). Digital Photo, 5" x 5", 2021. Performative self-portrait close-up of mouth with alphagetti.

1. *Perfect Mother*

DISCOVERING FEMINIST MOTHERHOOD THROUGH ART PRACTICE

2. *Runaway*

3. *MILF*

DISCOVERING FEMINIST MOTHERHOOD THROUGH ART PRACTICE

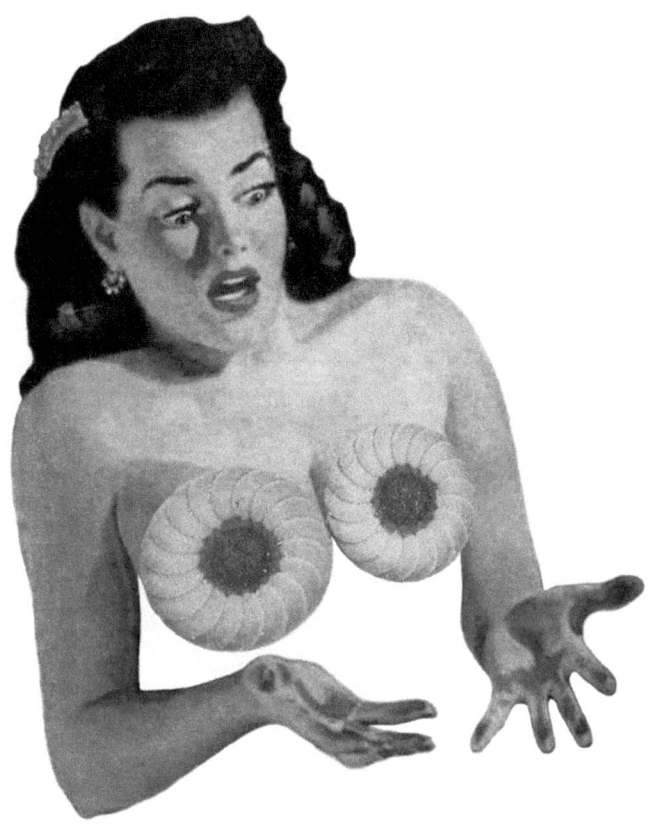

4. *Cookies MILF*

5. *Mommy Mouth* (MILF MOUTH MADNESS series)

Works Cited

Gyllenhall, Maggie, director. *The Lost Daughter*. Netflix, 2021.

Nochlin, Linda. "Why Have There Been No Great Women Artists?" *ArtNews*, 1971.

If not now, when? March 8, 2021–April 11, 2021, www.spiltmilkgallery.com. Accessed 17 Apr. 2023.

Yoder, Rachel. *Nightbitch*. Random House, 2022.

You are not wonderful just because you are a Mother. December 14, 2020–February 14, 2021, www.artistmotherpodcast.com. Accessed 17 Apr. 2023.

Chapter 5.

Holding and Being Held

Eve Darwood

Each of us is a combination of multiple facets, parts of ourselves, and those parts come to feminism from different perspectives, each approaching at a slightly different angle. For me, the moments of increasing awareness are underpinned by the same fundamental question: What is the role of my female body in the world?

As a teacher of religious studies, one of my favourite lessons each academic year is the one where we tackle the ethical issues of bodily autonomy. "To whom does your body belong?" I ask my year-nine pupils, in preparation for dealing with questions about abortion, euthanasia, animal testing, and war. Every academic year, I am surprised by how much my own perspectives have changed since the last time I taught the topic. In my professional life, I have always considered my views aligned with a version of feminism, even if I was unclear about which version this might be at any one time. I have always believed the question of female bodily autonomy was a simple one. My body belongs to me, and to me alone. I hold this to be true, but every year I teach this topic raises more questions than it answers.

As a mother of three children, now all grown into teenagers and young adults, I notice how my own responses to the questions of the role of the female body have shifted over time. I have become aware of my increasing frustration at the way society offers me, my son, and my two daughters different answers to the question of our bodies and the roles they must perform out in the world. And we do perform.[1] Therefore, I find myself revisiting the question considering my mothering experiences. Although I have always claimed ownership of my own body, did motherhood support my own premise?

As a woman diagnosed with multiple sclerosis (MS)—a degenerative neurological condition—in my mid-thirties, the performance of my female body in the world has been forced to change. This forced shifting has manifested in myriad ways over time as the disease progresses and changes my relationship to my body, to the people in my life, and to society. As I move through the world, and as this movement evolves, I constantly question what my body does and how it does it. More and more, I question the relationship between motherhood, disability, and being female, as I am forced to reevaluate my previously held claims about autonomy and what it may signify.

My awareness of these questions, and their relationship to my constantly evolving feminist perspective, develops in fragments. Each piece of me offers a different answer. In adolescence and early adulthood, I had felt that the question of my body was resolved: It belonged to me and me alone. In early motherhood, I felt the certainty of this position crumble; there was now no space in the world that was my own. My body became the property of others and was overwhelmed by obligatory duties to be performed.

In these early days after the birth of my third child, it feels like I have simultaneously shrunk and expanded. In giving birth, I have both reclaimed my body and lost it to another, all at once. I look down at my alien body noting the vacated cavity, now sagging, a void, which once held what is now this other, this person, this version of me which is both part of me and also not me. I feel my border control is all off kilter. I no longer know where I begin and where I end. I wonder now if it's different this time. Did my eldest, a boy, make me question my body in this way? Is there something about creating girls, another woman in the world, who may decide to follow down this path with her own body one day? In mothering girls, I feel a sense of being part of a machine, a turning wheel of reproducing, handing batons to the next generation of producers. My body is a vessel, and these two new girls who will one day be women—the older one beside me handing me the baby wipes—they move through me into the world and beyond. One day, new women may move through them, too. I don't recall this sense of reproductive potential when my son was born. I also realize with irritation, although he is the oldest of them all at eleven and his first sister is only six, that he never passes me the wipes. I begin to question whether this is my own doing. Have I allowed his body to remain his own but claimed my daughters' bodies for service? Am I becoming the very embodiment of the patriarchal society in which these girls will always feel their bodies subjected to the gaze of others?

Without me, without these breasts, which feel like an appendage—bolted on—this other life cannot be. This suckling child takes from me, and I give willingly, exhaustedly, abandoning all sense of myself. In the early hours, I ask, was I ever a self? To whom did I belong before this time? Will I ever be my own again?

All day and all night, I hold my child. This is, of course, not true. Others come and take her from my tired arms, tell me to rest and sleep while she sleeps. Now she's been alive for six weeks, I have employed a pumping machine, which invades my space, but allows me to reclaim my body for more than two hours at a time. Every morning while she suckles from one breast, the yellow pump squeezes the other, filling the bottle in a spluttering stream, ready for the early evening feed. When I first attach the pump, it holds to my skin, the suction cup like an enormous leech. After just a few minutes of whirring from the motor, the weight of the milk in the bottle becomes too heavy. I have to somehow juggle the wriggling, hungry baby and the motorized filling bottle to stop it all collapsing onto my still-sagging stomach. I can't hold the weight of it all. I feel like I am holding someone or something all the time, and I must not let them fall.

My husband brings me a pint of cold water, boils the kettle for a cup of tea, and I thank him for his kindness, which I realize is optional. I am angry at his freedom to choose whether to leave or to stay and be kind and bring me water.

"Anything you need. You only have to ask," he tells me. But no one asks me these days. It's assumed that no one needs to ask. I will just do what I should do. I don't meet his eye as he passes by me getting dressed in the bedroom. I'm convinced there is nothing for him to see here. I can't hold it all in long enough—my stomach, the combined weight of all these items in my hands and in my head, and my frustration at the feeling that it is all mine to carry.

The work a mother's body must carry out is partly that of holding and carrying. This begins in pregnancy but doesn't end when we give birth. This holding (or holding in) extends to our own interior emotional states. We keep our sighs and groans to ourselves. Our body, our selves, and even our feelings are now claimed by—or rather controlled by—the world. Mothers are handed a script, and I felt I had failed to learn my lines, to speak them with meaning. Or perhaps I mean to say that someone had taken my lines from me and silenced me. I became an extra to this new star performer, this tiny human. Every maternal action and comment are scrutinized to check if it fits the mould carved out by society, as represented by the women with whom I interact: the woman behind the post office counter, my mother-in-law, our grandmothers, and all my friends with babies of their own. I wonder now which lines did they not speak aloud? Did they feel silenced too? Do they still?

The world is not a willing audience for the truth of motherhood. And my truth is that it is hard. It hurt to wake so many times in the night, my eyes stinging and my head pounding. It hurt to attach a human to my raw skin, smeared in lanolin, the thinnest film of a barrier. It hurt to hold this in while my silence choked me. I would tell friends, "I am tired, but all is good; of course it is, she's beautiful. I can't imagine life without her." But I could, and I did sometimes. And then came the shame. My body, my emotions, should have been playing the role of the glowing mother, and I couldn't keep it up, couldn't hold up my end.

People ask how I am. I play along and recite their own lines in this script. I talk of glowing, of a type of love I never thought possible. I put on foundation and a slick of mascara to shield the world from my drawn cheeks, my greyed eye sockets. I cannot disappoint the world by telling the lady in the post office, "My God, I'm knackered." An old lady in a blue hat puts her hand on my arm and reminds me to "treasure this time; it's so special," and I want to weep at her sincerity. I am letting her down. I am letting everyone down.

We cannot show the world the truth. Our job in motherhood is to pretend. To keep up the pretence of appearances. Yet I cannot shake the feeling of complicity. I want to run to all the mothers, all the other women I know, and ask them to speak up, to drop the heavy loads they're carrying—no, to fling them all above their heads and scream—and tell the world that we will not be silenced, not be shamed, and not be laden down with all this weight. But I don't. Of course, I don't because to do so is to break role and go off script. I'm beginning to see through the scripts and the roles and to question their validity. They were written by those whom it serves well to keep us silent. If the world knows how hard motherhood is and how much labour it requires, then its value would rise above its allotted lowly status. No, this work must remain unspoken, hidden. Society tells us that if we complain about how hard it is, we must be doing it wrong. So we continue to perform. To whom does my body belong? To those who write the lines.

The bright red pushchair we'd chosen is rear facing. I'd wanted to keep my daughter looking towards my face for as long as possible—to withhold her gaze from the world. All you need is here, I'd think. But of course this isn't true. She gazes at strangers who peer beneath the rain hood; her eyes are wide, and her lashes curl towards the skies. "Oh, she's a beauty, isn't she? What a pretty girl," the strangers say while they gaze at her. I want to tell them not to comment on her face. I want to tell them to wait a year or two and then comment on her kindness, on her humour, or her ability to read, to paint, or to build a tower of bricks. I want to turn her face away. My son, at eleven years old, towers over her pushchair and is congratulated for being such a help to his mum. My older daughter stands and smiles sweetly. She's learning already: The world is watching, and there is a right way to be a good girl.

I push her up and down the streets. The contact of the pushchair's wheels on tarmac is like white noise to my frazzled mind. Like a long sigh. Like a quiet groan. On sunny mornings and wet afternoons, when I don't know what else to do to hold back her babyish fretfulness, her frustrated slamming of board books onto the carpet or her launching of her two-handled beaker across the table of her highchair, I push her through the village, longing for the day when she can, finally, make her own journey on foot. Her journey towards independence and taking her place in the world, one step at a time.

From early girlhood, even before they walk, our daughters are performing; they are moulded by the gaze of strangers and family. Smiles are rewarded; tears elicit frowns of concern or disapproval. As girls begin their first steps in the world, we hover beside them, around them, mediating and modifying the point where body meets world. We discourage them from making a mark, from leaving a trace. I begin to anger at the messaging that says making a mess is boys' domain, whereas cleaning it up the work of girls and women. Must our bodies always be in service of this work?

It's called cruising, this in-between state when my baby's legs can hold her weight, but she is not yet stable enough to move around without being held up by something or by someone. Her tiny hands grip my fingers, and I shuffle backwards, inching her forwards towards my face as she wobbles, on tiptoes, on stomping heels, on one foot while the other forms a clumsy pirouette. She pulls herself up and leans on the sofa, on the edge of the coffee table, while I hold my fist around its corner, just in case. She presses her knuckles into the piano stool and grasps the door jamb, holding on tight to these landmarks in her tiny world. I hover, never far behind. Her body is my responsibility for now. Another thing for me to hold up.

In the evenings when she is in bed, I take a dampened cloth to the sticky fingerprints she's left in her wake and wipe away the smears of the day in case we have visitors tomorrow. My husband beckons from the sofa, tells me to rest, but doesn't offer to wipe the smears while I sleep. He tells me they don't matter, seemingly unaware of the threat of the gaze of others.

For women, the way we move through the world and the choices we make in presenting our bodies to the world are a statement. This should not be the case, and I desperately want not to believe this. And yet.

A young shoe-store employee presses his fingers into the sides of my older daughter's feet in the measuring device. She obeys the instructions with the pleasant demeanour of a middle child. I wonder if this would be the case if she were a boy.

"That's it now, nice and tall for me."

Nice. For me. I bristle but stay silent, lips pursed, purse at the ready.

"Size 13F. Lovely. Have you seen anything you like the look of?"

My daughter points at kitten heels, its black patent like a mirror shining out from the downlit shelves.

"Mummy, can I have those ones? For parties, maybe?"

"Absolutely not. They're ridiculous. How can any child walk in those? Why do you even stock those in small sizes? Surely children shouldn't ..."

He avoids my stare, waves his hand towards the display.

"Well, they are really more occasional wear..."

"That's a no, sweetheart."

She frowns, her lip forming a pout of indignation.

"Not fair. Everyone else..."

"I don't care about everyone else's feet, but I do care about yours. You need shoes that will do their job—keeping your feet protected and letting them grow."

What I do not say: The job of shoes is not to make you pretty or to make you feel pretty. And I believe this, logically. The voices of the feminist *writers I've read lately speak loudly in my head, and I try to believe their words as I speak them aloud.*

I disappoint myself by wondering silently, if not shoes, then what? Clothes, heels, red lipstick, sparkle, the gaze of strangers, or well-meaning grandparents who compliment the dresses of the girls while turning to the boys to say how big and strong they're getting?

We select a pair of flat, wide shoes, with sturdy Velcro straps. The fit is checked, her heels pressed and pinched, her toes wiggled into the growing space.

"Would you like the matte black or the patent?"

As she meets my eye, we both know I will concede.

"We will take the shiny ones, please."

The trainee history teacher in my department—early twenties, keen as a puppy—brings her other shoes in a canvas bag. I watch her pad through the staff room door in flat, smart pumps, offer her a cup of tea, and ask which class she is teaching first today.

"Year eleven." Her face contorts into a wince.

"Okay, well, I'll be right next door, but I'm sure they'll be fine. You had them in the palm of your hand yesterday."

"Hmmm. I'm not sure that's true. I think Jack D wrote two lines all lesson. If I could get him to stop asking me about my favourite foods, we might get more work done. He's just so easily distracted."

She opens her canvas tote as she talks, removes her flat black slip-on shoes, and stands to step into the three-inch heels she's pulled from the bag. I recognise them from when I observed her teaching a lesson yesterday. As she rises the few inches beside me, I hand her the cup of tea and gaze downwards to her feet. She catches me looking.

"Confidence shoes. Heels for GCSE groups, flats for Key Stage Three.[1] I don't think I could deal with year eleven in flat shoes." She snorts a giggle, sips her tea, and turns towards her classroom.

For women, presentation is a statement, and movement is a performance. All of these are to some extent matters of choice, but with the onset of my MS, my body began to restrict my options. My own kitten heels became impractical, and so I reverted to flat shoes. My clicking, swaying walk down the school corridors became a slower, silent shuffle. I appeared an inch or two smaller. In the gaze of others, I felt smaller, too.

I am flat on my back in the MRI's tube. Cold and naked, except for the hospital gown and the blanket the nurse offered when she noticed me shivering. No one is looking at my exterior here, yet I feel vulnerable and naked, despite the coverings. Exposed. My body is here for inspection, for scrutiny. Not just the exterior but all of me. It feels like I have no choice in this.

In MS, there is a breaching of the blood-brain barrier. Another failure of border control. In this form of disability, as in motherhood, one territory is invaded, penetrated. Antibodies insert themselves into the central nervous system and wage war, stripping the protective coating from the nerves. Messages cannot get through. Movement, feeling, and signals are all lost in there somewhere as though they never existed.

The trouble is that from the outside, it all looks the same. The mantra I repeated to my own children and to all the teenagers I've ever taught—"What matters is what's on the inside"—rings in my ears. You can't trust what you see. But I also, paradoxically, know how much it matters: what is visible and seen.

At lunch time, I walk to the staffroom, and a colleague points down at my feet, his eyebrows raised in a question. I am wearing two different shoes. Not a pair. At no point this morning have my feet communicated this difference in style and shape to my brain. It takes a man's gaze to make me aware, and I can't get past my anger at this fact. My face burns red with shame.

I'm also beginning to walk wobbly, and this matters. I have a permanent bruise on my thigh at the height of the desks in my classroom. I seem unstable. I'm constantly aware that others might think I am unstable. I cannot allow this.

My body is the manifestation of who I am. It is to how it looks that matters, I insist (to whom?), but, rather, what it does. My actions in the world are watched and interpreted constantly, I am realizing. To my students, my body acts as a visible symbol of control, certainty, and security. As I tour the room, stride down the corridors, and stand in the front of an assembly hall, my presence means something. My body is seen, and the world attaches meaning to it, whether I allow this or not. To my own family, my body is supposed to serve as a source of their comfort, sustenance, and guidance. My body and I belong to others, and the world is changed by this; it depends on what I say and how I act and move. I walk straight. I click my heels. Until I don't.

As I'm getting a new back door key cut, I spot the walking sticks in a stand by the counter. A frame holds them all upright. Like soldiers. Not like soldiers but rather like wounded veterans. Being held.

I wonder for a moment why they're not lain out horizontally to make them easier to see. The thoughts move back and forth in my head like the kind of playfully argumentative conversations I might have with my best friend on the drive to work: "Well, that wouldn't work. They display them vertically because that's how you use them." "No, it's not that. It's because no one wants to see them; they're ugly." "What, even the flowery ones? The more modern ones?" Those in particular, I imagine myself replying, ugly. Too much. Or maybe whatever design, they wouldn't be welcome. A symbol of all that could happen to you. A caution. Like illness, like all disability. There but for the grace, and all that.

Eventually my internal dialogue with an imagined adversary settles on what I deem the cynical truth. It's an issue of space. Upright things take up less space, and in retail, space is capital.

Anything that cannot hold itself up needs to be held. As a mother, I was doing the holding up. Now, as a disabled woman, I feel the shift as it takes place: I am moving from holder to held. There is tension here; this does not fit with my own ideas of what a woman does. My body lets me down and prevents me from performing womanhood in the ways I have been taught. With the stick in my hand, and my increasingly wobbly gait, I take up too much space. I feel my body's boundaries expanding; the line of my walk is no longer slim and streamlined. Women are taught to take up less space. Close your legs. Stop slouching. Thigh gaps: good. Muffin tops: bad. Please sit nicely. Ladylike. Be a good girl.

The walking stick I buy has a white background. Pure, innocent, clean. All the others are black, and despite all my adolescent years of Doc Martens and baggy black jumpers, this takes my mind these days too quickly to death. I must portray this cheerily, hopefully—must not project my negativity onto the world. It is emblazoned with printed daisies, each with six petals, symmetrical but imperfect. The first time I take it into school, I have my nails painted to match.

Now that I am carrying this visible sign of my condition, people must be told, and I rehearse my pitch for days. How to inform but not upset people. How to make it easier on everyone else.

I sketch a simple outline of a neuron on my classroom whiteboard, draw a border of myelin around its edges, and practise rubbing it away to show the damage inflicted when MS attacks the nerve cells. I list the symptoms, selecting only the most innocuous to share in my explanation: numbness, slightly blurry vision, fatigue. (These are not innocuous at all, but I decide that they might sound less shocking, less repulsive than the bladder or bowel issues, problems with swallowing, searing pain.) I edit carefully.

I'm learning that the trick is to always be ready to lighten the mood. Once the explanation has been served—not too long-winded, as I don't want to bore anyone—I finish with a garnish of humour: "So, you see, I am literally getting on my own nerves!" Nervous giggle. I move on swiftly and ask them a question about themselves. Deflect. No one wants to stay there for too long in that crevasse of awkwardness, of negative thoughts of an uncertain future.

My main role in telling people about my diagnosis is to make it easy. So I do.

What is the work of my body? To comfort, to coddle, to appease, and to soothe. The feelings of others weigh heavy on my shoulders, one more thing for me to carry. Always outwards facing, I find myself performing being disabled to make it more palatable to those around me—to my audience. As it was in early motherhood, the truth and pain of this experience are not for me to share. My script does not allow for this. Like my morning face before make-up is applied, this will not do for the world. It must be coloured, filtered, and edited to be ready for presentation.

When I was first diagnosed, I'd asked my consultant if I would end up using a wheelchair. He had treated my question with scorn, told me he couldn't predict whether this would be the case, and left me feeling ashamed of having dared to ask.

Now, my body has decided it cannot live with this unanswered question indefinitely. For the sake of certitude, my legs are beginning to stop working. Except it's not my legs that are failing in their defence; it is the nerves to and from my legs. The muscles, bones, and ligaments are, I'm told, in full working order. They are just no longer receiving the commands about what this entails.

I can no longer hold the weight of it all, of myself.

Stand on your own two feet. Stand up for yourself. Put your foot down. Make a stand.

I will live the next few months down at crotch level.

Problem: my legs don't move me around.
Solution: get wheels.
One wheelchair.
Model: electric blue. Self-propelling. Lightweight.
Delivery: priority two-day service.

From my armchair, I watch the white van pull up outside, and I wave through the front window, leaning on two walking sticks to prop up my movement towards the door. The box is the size of a large dining table, and the delivery guy looks me up and down before offering to lift it into the hall. It leans against the wall, promising everything. I use the car key hanging from the peg to saw through a length of the packing tape and open a cardboard flap to peer into the box. I know it will remain here until my husband and my son are both home to assemble its parts, but I just want a glimpse. The contents of this enormous box represent freedom, motion, hope. After so much stasis, I need to peer inside to see the way forwards that is contained within.

    I deliberately ordered the electric blue because it meant clear skies and cheerful optimism. It shouted, "Look, this is in fact okay. I need to wheel but I can do it brightly coloured, so you don't need to feel bad for me. Don't tilt your head, don't look away embarrassed. This is fine. My chair is blue, and all is good."

    I pull a flap of cardboard, revealing a section of the frame.

    It's hospital grey. Dark, utilitarian, storm-skies grey.

    I pound a fist down on the box, double stick back to my armchair station, and pick up the phone. The man on the end is apologetic but offers no solution. I tell him that I need to go to work. I need to go to school tomorrow, and he says, "Just use the grey one. They're the same model." I can hear him shrug. But no, he's wrong. They're not the same.

    My husband arrives home to find me sobbing.

    "Hey, you okay?"

    "They sent the wrong chair! It's wrong."

    He strokes my hair, goes towards the box, and peers inside.

    "What's wrong with it? Do they come in different sizes?"

How can I explain that yes, this chair in our hallway works fine, but it doesn't do what I need it to? I ordered the sky blue, not the grey. No one wants to look at the grey.

It was meant to be bright blue, like the sky.

Here is what I think of when I think of blue. Growth. Springtime. Blossom. Flowers in full bloom. The summer, ahead of me. Exam halls, waiting for results. Free periods. Longer evenings, longer walks. Fields of oil-seed rape in sunshine yellow set against the sky. Only going home when hunger sets in. Timeless, unrestricted days. Cloudless, rainless, hazy mornings. Reading books. The sea, the endless sea.

When I think of blue, I think of the absence of negativity—no clouds, no time, no ending. Blue is the backdrop to what's possible. Blue makes it seem better for everyone. I must make it better for everyone.

I move around the house propped on two sticks, no longer caring that they don't match. Symmetry is less important than motion. I must move myself. My husband stirs when I wake to go to the bathroom in the early hours, but I flap my hands to dismiss his offers of help. Instead, I raise the two walking sticks up from their spot, leaning against the bedside cabinet, frustrated at the clatter they make as I wiggle them apart. I concentrate on moving silently along the bedroom carpet. Don't wake anyone. Don't be a bother.

My relapse begins to subside, allowing me to hope that the damage to my nerves might be temporary, this time. The commands are starting to get through from brain to body. My legs can bear my weight with just one stick, then no stick at all at some points in the day as long as I don't overdo it too early. I move myself around by leaning on the walls, the door handles; there is a smear of handprints forming on the low wall at the top of the landing, on the sideboard where I keep a stack of books. I notice greying patches like cloudy smears along the middle of the hallway wall, at hand height. I'm in my own cruising phase. My female body is again learning how to interact with the physical world, and I am relearning the rules I taught to my toddlers: don't make a mess, be tidy, leave only positive traces of your existence. This is the job of your body.

The aisles of the supermarket are whizzing past me. I know this isn't the reality. I know I am, in fact, slowly wheeling past these aisles, but from where I'm sitting, it feels like I'm static, and it is, instead, the world, as represented by these high-stacked aisles, that's in active motion. I'm amazed by the movement of the world, past my shoulders, up above my line of vision. By how high it all seems. How low I feel.

This passivity is not my natural state. I keep reaching down to the rims of the wheels beneath me and trying to find the momentum to make me move forwards. But instead I keep catching the tips of my fingers on razorlike spokes.

I felt sure this would be easy. It looks easy when other people do it. Have I seen other people do it? Have I watched, really watched? I don't see why I would. Until six months ago this was not something I ever thought of needing to notice. Even after my diagnosis, wheelchairs might—might—bring on a subtle sense of sinking for a moment. Then I'd push the thought away. Later. Worry about that later, if at all. Yes, much later.

Yet here I am, being wheeled along the soup aisle. Wheeling. Being wheeled. All my verbs are in the passive form now. I am being pushed. I am being driven. Being helped. Being cared for. Caring used to be a mutual relationship, fully reciprocal, albeit in ebbs and flows of balance, one way during a friend's difficult time, the other way when I needed the favour returned. I cared for my husband in miniscule moments of thoughtfulness, tiny kindnesses. His favourite meal, cooked on a Friday night. A cup of coffee delivered to his desk in the study when he was still on the line giving on-call tech support service on a Saturday morning. In turn, he would wake me with a cup of tea on a Sunday or replace the bed linen, fresh from the washing line while I was reading, so the freshly made bed was a pleasant surprise. Now, caring is a one-way process. Like my hands on these wheelrims, concentrating hard on pushing forwards, clumsy, awkward, grasping.

I take myself along the village streets, determined to go alone, then realize the arrangement of the dropped kerbs, the parked cars, the roots of trees, which form distorted spines beneath the path, all render solitude impossible. To whom does my body belong? To those who push me, who lift me and hold me. To those who see me take up yet more space, my body extended to include this movement machine.

Once again, wheels on tarmac. Once again, someone being pushed. Once again, the question of what my body is doing, to whom it belongs, and what is its role in the world. The contact of the wheelchair's tires on the path is, again, like a long sigh. Like a quiet groan.

And so I arrive here, where I break the silence, go off script. My groans and sighs are no longer quiet here. I acknowledge the friction between the beliefs I had held onto and the experiences that force me to question them. These questions I can no longer hold alone, so I hand them to you on the page. I offer with them some answers of my own. As a teacher, I am an embodiment of the very questions my students are wrestling with. As a mother, I move from holding to being held and back again, a constant dance of renegotiation of the performance of motherhood. My certainty about ownership of my body is shattered by the realization that rearing children makes my body a public servant. As a disabled woman, I begin to hand over control of my body even as I reclaim its place. As a feminist, I may find myself frustrated by the patterns that the fabric of society is weaving, but as a disabled teacher and mother of three, I recognize that I am stitched into this very fabric, and my relationship to my body is inevitably shaped by it. To whom does my body belong? In coming to feminism, in motherhood, in disability, somewhere along the way, I realise the answer is complex, cannot be reduced to the false dichotomy of answering either "to the world" or "to myself": It is, and always has been, to both.

Endnotes

1. Key Stage Three is the first phase of secondary school in the UK, for pupils aged eleven to fourteen; GCSE is the two year phase, which follows for fourteen- to sixteen-year-olds.

Chapter 6.

Colostrum

Victoria Bailey

Birth

I had never had
such a love before they came,
nor felt so betrayed.

Losing Track

Days passed and I began losing track.
I had not expected what was expected of me.

Wanted

They were all wanted
but I never said that they
were all I wanted.

Bonding

All my babies cried
while I roared right beside them
calling for mothers.

Lost and Found

I once was lost
in a state of motherhood
disconnected
jarred and barred
all sense of self
drained away with my bathwater
while each baby
multiplied my aloneness
powerless I struggled
but could not shake
my trappings
ensnared
my pain made worse
by attempts at freedom
until I found them
the feminist mothers
those wonderful others
in books
in stories
in poems
in pictures
in films
in paintings
in sculptures
and songs
I sat down with them
listened to their voices
and felt reclaimed
and so set my compass by their light
and carried on my way again.

Recovery

When my children were moulded
every part of me melted
the pain the pain the pain the pain
then I learned to swaddle myself
in anointed words
until I rose again.

Chapter 7.

We Are Mothers

Rachel O'Donnell

Inception

My mother told me recently, now that I am a mother myself, that she was so tired when I was a baby that she would come downstairs first thing in the morning, lie down on the couch, and let me crawl around the living room as she dozed off and on, trying to catch up on sleep as I played. To anyone reading this, especially parents with young children, this doesn't sound like anything out of the ordinary. But for some reason, I find this image disturbing. If a friend told me this about her young child, I would say, "Of course you lied back down on the couch! You were tired!" Caring for young children is exhausting. But in my context—the childhood context in which my mother spent a lot of time on the couch, isolated herself from friends and family, and struggled with depression, fear, and paranoia—this image is profoundly disturbing. Now, as a mother, I can see my childhood through the lens of my own parenting beliefs. Was I left alone to cry? Was I held enough? Did anyone ever reassure me?

I have clear memories of the violence of my childhood home, though not too many of my childhood itself, meaning that the memories I do have are extremely violent. They are of hitting or punching, of shouting or of being hit, and when I yell at my children, I remember this. Am I that mother when I yell? Am I damaging my children? Will they feel loved and supported? Will they doubt their abilities? For all their successes, will they remain wanting to please their parents, like I do, consumed with thoughts about being a profound disappointment?

The first time I recognized how much I wanted my mothering to be different from the way I was mothered was when my mother visited when my daughter was just a few weeks old. I told her that the most helpful thing for me would be for her to hold the baby so I could take care of a few things for myself, and I watched, from the kitchen, as she kept trying to put the baby down in a tiny bassinet we had in the corner. She seemed full of anxiety and frustration with the infant, who just wanted to be held, whereas my mother wanted to do laundry or things around the house instead. "Babies just want to be held," I said. "Can you hold her while I take a shower?" Any new mother remembers this desire. All you want is someone to hold the baby—to know the baby is safe while you do things for yourself. "Oh," she said. "She will be okay." And off my mother went to take care of something else.

My mother's lack of ability to sit still and hold the baby stirred up unpleasant memories and realizations about my childhood. Not only was she unsympathetic to what I was feeling as a new mother, but she was also dismissive of my feelings. She couldn't relate to what I was experiencing: the need to know the baby was safe and held so I could take care of myself. More than any other time in my adult life, I needed a mother, but she refused to act like one. Perhaps, I thought, she just didn't have it in her and never had.

When I was pregnant, I was afraid I wouldn't be able to do it either. I had always felt disconnected from my own mother. When I was younger, if people asked, I would explain, "My mother and I aren't close." What I really meant was that I hadn't been mothered. I wasn't sure how I would manage the maternal role. Would I be able to love a child adequately and unconditionally? Maybe I wouldn't be able to hack it, the whole unconditional love thing. Maybe I would be angry at the child or jealous and resentful, as my mother was with me. I had never really spent time with children, although I had a strong desire for a family of my own. I started attending La Leche meetings, and here is what I learned: All mothers feel self-doubt. Images of motherhood don't often match reality. We muddle through with little social support, desiring someone to safely hold the baby so we can care for ourselves.

My mother has always been unable to care for herself as well as she could. Her ruminations of things she has done wrong in the past or things I had potentially done wrong as a child stay with her, and when she is with me, this is often all she can talk about. She tells my husband that I have lied to her. She accuses me of blaming others for my own problems in front of my family. In a moment of self-protection, I did not invite her for Christmas. Alice Walker asks, when did our "overworked mothers have time to know or care about feeding the creative spirit?" (406). I needed the space away from my mother, especially during the holiday. The familial violence my mother faced affected her mothering practice. Weighed down by untreated mental illness, guilt, and rumination, she had limited choices. Poverty left her lonely and likely scared. One memory I have is of packing vegetables from my father's garden into my red wagon and walking them to the wealthy neighborhood to sell. I knocked on each fancy door and asked if they wanted any vegetables.

I wanted a different mothering practice—one that prioritized emotional healing and parenting without violence. As a child, I had been ashamed and frightened, unsure what was wrong with me as I hid my chaotic home life. As an only child, I operated as family mediator, hoping to deflect the violence. Accepting the truth about a childhood that revolved around both shame and perfectionism meant that I would try to avoid family history repeating itself and create a kind of loving, peaceful family.

My Father

I received constant criticism and blame from both of my parents. They have told me, even as an adult, that my feet are ugly because I put on a pair of pointe shoes once as a child. It is my fault. "I never thought you would have a weight problem because I never made you clean your plate." I must have done something wrong.

My father was visiting when my children were small and smacked the older child, a toddler, when I was not watching. My son was crying and said that he had been pushed to the ground. Another time, I watched as my father snatched the children's toy helicopter from the air, annoyed that it was bothering him while he was trying to read. Could I have been exposed to this much violence as a child, and nothing was done about it? How could no one have intervened? My mother, a teacher, a family friend?

A memory: My mother held his keys and asked him not to go, and he hit her. When I told my mother that my father could no longer come to the house because he had hit my child, she said, "I think he deserves another chance." I am expected to be a giver of chances. How many has she given him, this violent person, over the past forty years?

My mother said, "Your father does not think much of women, but he does think highly of his daughters." One time, looking toward the future, she said to me: "When you get married..." and my father interrupted: "Who would have her?"

My father on women: "She drives like a woman"; "That girl looks like a little Lolita"; "Why are you dressed like that? Do you want people to notice your behind?" Other messages too: "Your mother is stupid." "You are just like your mother" is the worst insult he can offer.

Why? Because she reads romance novels and works a service job? The messages were clear: Man is the judge, and woman serves and takes the abuse. More messages: My mother "worried" and cleaned the house, and my father worked to provide for us. It must be that mothers take care of the house and often, it seems, are embarrassed by it. No one can come to visit. Fathers have no need for that household labour, it seems—they work all day and come home and drink beer.

As an adolescent, my mother slapped me while she was trying to help me with my homework, after I had made the mistake of looking away, ignoring her. I put my hand to my cheek.

My father looked up from his paper he hid behind while my mother was talking and mouthed to me, "She never shuts up." There is no need to respect women: they are lesser beings. Look at her cleaning on her hands and knees, making grocery lists, filling the sink with soapy water like it is her job. A woman with children does not deserve your respect, he is saying, this is how women are treated, do not expect to be treated any better than this.

Feminism

What I learned in college: feminism means women should not be beaten by their husbands. They should not be bullied.

"The mother-child relationship is unlike any other," so many readings, academic and otherwise claimed. They talked about how our views about ourselves and the world are shaped by our mothers. And then when women become mothers themselves, they can find their lives changed by their children—being completely attuned to another being and needing to put another life ahead of your own. Surely, I am not actually capable, I think, and to me, feminism does not seem to consider women as mothers.

Other understandings: I missed out on having a mother. I have a longing for maternal love, but I will have to find this myself. I am missing a mother.

Maternal love is supposed to be unconditional. What is a person who calls herself mother but is not?

Feminism, which encourages both reflective and reflexive practice, allowed me to think this through: mothering as feminist practice. How should I connect family violence to my own perfectionism? How do I become the peaceful parent I desired? How do I become the person I've always wanted to be while my mother has never been the person she wanted to be?

A feminist understanding of domestic violence leads me to think how I parent and model behaviour really matters. Don't put people down. Don't judge yourself. Be your children's advocate. How do I make sure I don't criticize my body, so my daughter doesn't criticize hers? How do I make sure I show them that I take time for myself even though I have so much to do, for work and for them? How do I make sure I don't just work all the time and show them that they too must not work all the time? How do I make sure they know I have failings as a mother, so they don't have to parent perfectly? How will I make it clear to my children that girls and women are valuable? That care work is valuable? That domestic labour is not just the responsibility of women but of all of us?

Reprise

The mother laughs out loud in one moment and then moves to criticizing her daughter. She does this so much that everything the daughter hears is criticism.

Here's a story I've never told: a loud intersection, a crosswalk, being told to walk across the street slowly and carefully and only when the orange walk sign turns green. My mother's hand in mine. Is it true she was holding my hand? How often did we touch when I was a child? I cannot remember.

My husband asked me recently if my mother has ever said anything nice to me. I have trouble answering this question. What would she have said? To my children, I say, "I love you. I'm so proud of you. I love everything about you." Reminder: This is what my mothering looks like. I try to highlight the difference.

My memory projects an impossibility—that my mother and I are moving and laughing and talking together, enjoying each other, but of course that never happened. I must have been running behind her at that crosswalk. Where were we going? What would we talk about as adults? How frightened was she of life, of me, of doing anything wrong? We are both mothers, but we cannot speak of it. We leave a legacy with our children. I am full of pain, of sorrow, and of great longing for a mother's love.

I hold my daughter when she is small and hold her hand in mine. Now that she is almost eight, I hold her hand when we cross the street. Is this what I did as a child?

To this day, my mother seems to be unable to accomplish much in a day, overwhelmed, perhaps, with guilt and self-doubt. A day filled with television schedules, meals, and shopping trips. How does she feel about the jobs she was unable to keep? She demonstrates her nervousness and is unable to make plans without saying, "Well, I don't know if that will work out." What does she think of me? Here is my tall and beautiful daughter, who is a writer, a professor, a wife, and mother, with friends and social engagements. Does she see me as I am? Even a little? I tell her, "We are renting a cabin in the mountains, near a lake, with friends next summer." I see her disappointed face; I am not inviting her. I have left the family. I have created my own.

I am sometimes equally nervous about not accomplishing much. Whose fault is this? This is the complicated anger of a mother towards her daughter and from a daughter towards her mother (Rich 244) that leads me to blame myself and her when I feel like a failure. Which one of us has failed? We have exchanged knowledge about each other, about childrearing, about other things, knowledge that is subversive and preverbal (Rich 220), perhaps, as we sit in silence or prepare a meal together. Is this my reflective narrative (Wong 135)? I wish it were more understanding and able to rescue both of us.

Children

I still wake up in the middle of the night, afraid of my parents. Sometimes I wonder if this is the fear and worry that my mother experiences. Will I become my mother? What can I do to prevent this?

There is so much risk in the world. So much loss and sorrow. So many of us who haven't had mothers are trying to be good mothers ourselves. How do we do it right? Things I am afraid of—a COVID-19 test that went too far up her nose, a dental appointment she didn't like, a strep test swab down her throat, and here I am crying. I cannot protect her.

When my daughter was born, her feet were huge. None of the baby booties or shoes fit, and I would kiss her foot as she nursed or slept on my postpartum belly. Now, her feet are long and slender, and she puts on my sandals and asks to wear them to school. She has glasses and a long ponytail, a few missing teeth, a silly giggle, and a big laugh.

I sometimes feel nurturing as a mother, a grown woman with wide, curved hips, and a rounded belly. My daughter pats this belly and asks if there's another baby in there. "No, it's just a belly," I say and laugh, wanting her to not be nervous about growing into a woman's body.

When my children were tiny, I started to realize that I was not going to be the kind of mother society seems to revere, nor was I the mother my younger self had once imagined. I imagined a motherhood in which I would love it and cherish every moment, and I'm afraid I've missed so many moments. At first, I was a busy graduate student panicked about finishing my dissertation and teaching well but noticed diminishing opportunities for a personal life. I wasn't sure how to connect with people who were mothers and didn't work outside of home and with colleagues who worked and weren't parents. There is a constant pull between what I wanted for myself and what I wanted for my children or, perhaps, what I think I am supposed to want for my children. Do I want to be a mother who is always present for her children and takes care of their every need? How do I assert my own needs? "Go outside and play," I have said to them. "I'm working." I say this especially as I try to work from home, to both care for them and for myself, and to ease the tension between the yearning to have the freedom to do what I want to and the desire to cherish my young children. Am I feeling rejected and lonely? Whenever I find the solitude I am craving, I start to wonder: Am I my mother? Do I give the children the attention they need?

Memory

The place of memory in mothering coincides with memories of places from our own childhoods. I do not want to repeat this.

My mother is an intelligent person. She went to college, but when I talk to her, I remember where she is from: the upper panhandle of West Virginia, a house on cinder blocks at the edge of a trailer park, close to the train tracks. I picture her as she always sat: with her finger above her upper lip, looking at the television, engaging more with life inside of it than with life outside of it.

She is often unkind. She judges everything, herself, me. Her words often stay with me. She has said, "I think you should study something where you can get a job" and "I don't think you're a size small anymore." My own judgment of her is the most offensive and she says, "I know you think we were bad parents."

A list of my mother's obsessions: cleaning the washer for mould, cleaning the drain in the sink, whispering, even about the right way to care for the recycling, the fear she has of tea leaves going down the drain. She has a fear of everything. I must be doing everything wrong. She spends time arguing with the children, turning their clothing around when they dress themselves and end up with a shirt on backward.

Whispering to my father about me: "I think she is moving away from us." I am supposed to remain close when there is no closeness.

When I was in Costa Rica after college, my father emailed me to say that he found her wringing her hands and talking to herself when he got home. A cry for help. I must be the only grownup; I am supposed to fix this.

A list of moments in which she released her anxiety on me: "We don't want you to go that far away" when I suggest applying to college a few hours from home. "You will probably get involved with drug traffickers and be kidnapped and killed" when I am leaving for the Peace Corps. Before my wedding: "I don't see how this is going to work. It's all a big mess."

In *Practicing Feminist Mothering*, Fiona Joy Green proposes that society may push mothers to conform to mainstream patriarchal notions of motherhood. As mothers, we can use the actual practice of mothering to challenge those norms—to create a changed world. We are critical of conventional motherhood, redefining what makes a good mother as well as practising autonomy, self-awareness, and social responsibility as parents. Read: Childrearing is not a neutral act. A feminist politics of mothering means that I should have self-compassion as well as compassion for my children. And compassion for my mother.

My mother criticized everything about herself. So many regrets: "We never should have moved here" and "I should have studied something different in school." She blamed my father: "He never wanted to move out of this town."

I learned to google this early on: "signs your mother may have a personality disorder," "how to deal with a narcissistic mother," and "this is what it's like growing up with a paranoid mother." I read scholarly articles on paranoid personality disorder and obsessive-compulsive personality disorder. What is the difference? Which one does she have? Can I diagnose her from these articles alone?

One internet article suggests: "Remember you do not hate your mother. You feel sorry for her." Really? Pity is the only allowable feeling? I am so full of rage, of disappointment. A mother and grown daughter at lunch, enjoying each other's company. This can be the saddest thing in the world to those of us who have never had that, even if your mother is very much alive. Is there no acknowledgment of the hatred we feel? The envy of other mother and daughter pairs, laughing and enjoying each other? How do we avoid putting our own daughters in this position?

Motherhood is glorious is many ways. I could imagine it, but I could never really picture it for what it is, the day-to-day caregiving. When I had my first baby to take care of, I remember feeling the happiness of having a baby who needs everything from you. He needed me, and I could soothe him. I could stop his crying with my body, nursing and changing and fixing everything. There is a real joy in meeting someone's needs, of taking care of them, of saying these things: "You're beautiful. I'm so proud of you. You're so helpful." Yes, there are many moments of frustration, of boredom, but mostly I am disappointed with the lack of time to do other things I would like to be doing. But is this really a problem? That my life is so full I can't do everything? My own mother, often full of anxiety and paranoia that limits her, may have never felt the joy of being so busy.

Whatever she was on her way to becoming before, a woman is somehow reborn as a mother with the birth of a child. Literature directed to new mothers insists we trust our natural impulses and instincts.

Children's picture books show a mother's steadfast love. Mothering comes naturally. Motherhood for each of us exists in a state of flux. We must become mothers for our time, apart from our own mothers, sometimes.

Conversation

I am having a conversation with my mother in which I have to assert myself. Is this a feminist conversation? I say I have to move away from the violence of my family and create my own.

"It's not really up to you," my mother replies, as if a threat, when I say we are not inviting her to move closer, now that my father has died. I am in my forties, and she is in her seventies, yet she is still in charge, threatening to never leave my life, and I am still terrified.

"She pulled out the big guns," my husband says, meaning the guilt she inspires with just a few words. She says, "We made sacrifices so you could have things," intending for me to understand that I owe her, something, I guess. My life? My husband points out that this is merely a description of parenting; all parents must sacrifice things for their children. She cannot say she has done anything other parents have not done, only that she was not able to parent. Somehow, I am to blame.

"You're not invited to move here," I have to say, calmly, keeping myself from crying. She is angry and defensive: "I'm going to need more information." I don't know what to say. What would the information look like? A picture of the past? A sudden understanding of what it's like to grow up with parents you are terrified of: "Maybe you have to put this in writing," she says. I must defend my position because she disagrees and cannot trust it. A bully is someone who wants to get their way. She needs me to say what is obvious—that I want to be left alone, in peace, with my family. I have no right to claim my feelings without justifying them.

I always have fantasies of no longer having to be in touch with them, my parents, yet I admit I am still longing for parenting and trying to rid myself of their constant criticism: my body, my weight, stories of what I have done wrong. These are stories I have heard multiple times: I blamed another child for something I had done or I snuck out of the house. None of this is true, but I have heard it so much that I think I must have done something terrible. The paranoia she has even extends to my husband: "He must be making fun of me," she says. He doesn't understand how hard it is to pack up your furniture, and she is angry. Here is a story I wrote, I said once, as a much younger adult, giving it to her. It had won an award. "I don't agree with this," she says, about a piece of fiction. More recently: Here is something I've done, here is coverage of it in the university magazine. An eyeroll, a scoff. The word "doctor" appears before my name on a museum pass I lend her once. She laughs. What is funny? That I have accomplished anything? That I am good enough? At mothering or at life?

What am I afraid of? Myself or my mother? Am I afraid of becoming my mother, which Adrienne Rich calls "matrophobia" (236)? Is it possible to adopt new rules and practices in mothering, such as empowering practices apart from one's own motherline (Wong 136)? Do I have pity for my mother or myself? I have only recently constructed my identity as a mother instead of a daughter, perhaps attempting to avoid feeling like a guilty daughter who never does enough to get her mother's attention. I have been longing for supportive and present parents, but I will not find them in my parents. I can't recall imagining myself as a mother when I was a child. Did I imagine myself with children when I grew up? I hear only the sounds of ridicule from my mother, who wasn't sure I could be a mother. Perhaps she was afraid I would struggle to love a child as she has.

Here I am, having much of the life I have always wanted. I am a writer, a teacher, a mother. I can't imagine feeling resentful towards my future adult children. I try to picture the parents I have known, all of us who find joy in our children's accomplishments, who want our children to be capable, autonomous beings. "Yes," they say, shaking their heads. "There is something wrong with parents like yours." We all feel joy when our children are amazing. "Yes, you can be better than they were." But how will I be good enough? Is there something I must do to prevent it from happening?

A picture in my office: two children, my hair perfectly combed. Is that a picture of an idealized soccer mom, or is it me?

My feminist practice is this: I will know what maternal love feels like. I will know it as a mother. And even though I will never know what this love feels like as a daughter, this will have to be enough.

Works Cited

Green, Fiona. *Practicing Feminist Mothering*. Arbeiter Ring, 2011.

Rich, Adrienne. *Of Woman Born: Motherhood as Experience and Institution*. Norton, 1976.

Walker, Alice. *In Search of Our Mothers' Gardens: Womanist Prose*. Harcourt, 1983.

Wong-Wylie, Gina. "Images and Echoes in Matroreform: A Cultural Feminist Perspective." *Journal of the Motherhood Initiative for Research and Community Involvement*, vol. 8, no. 1, 2006, pp. 135-46.

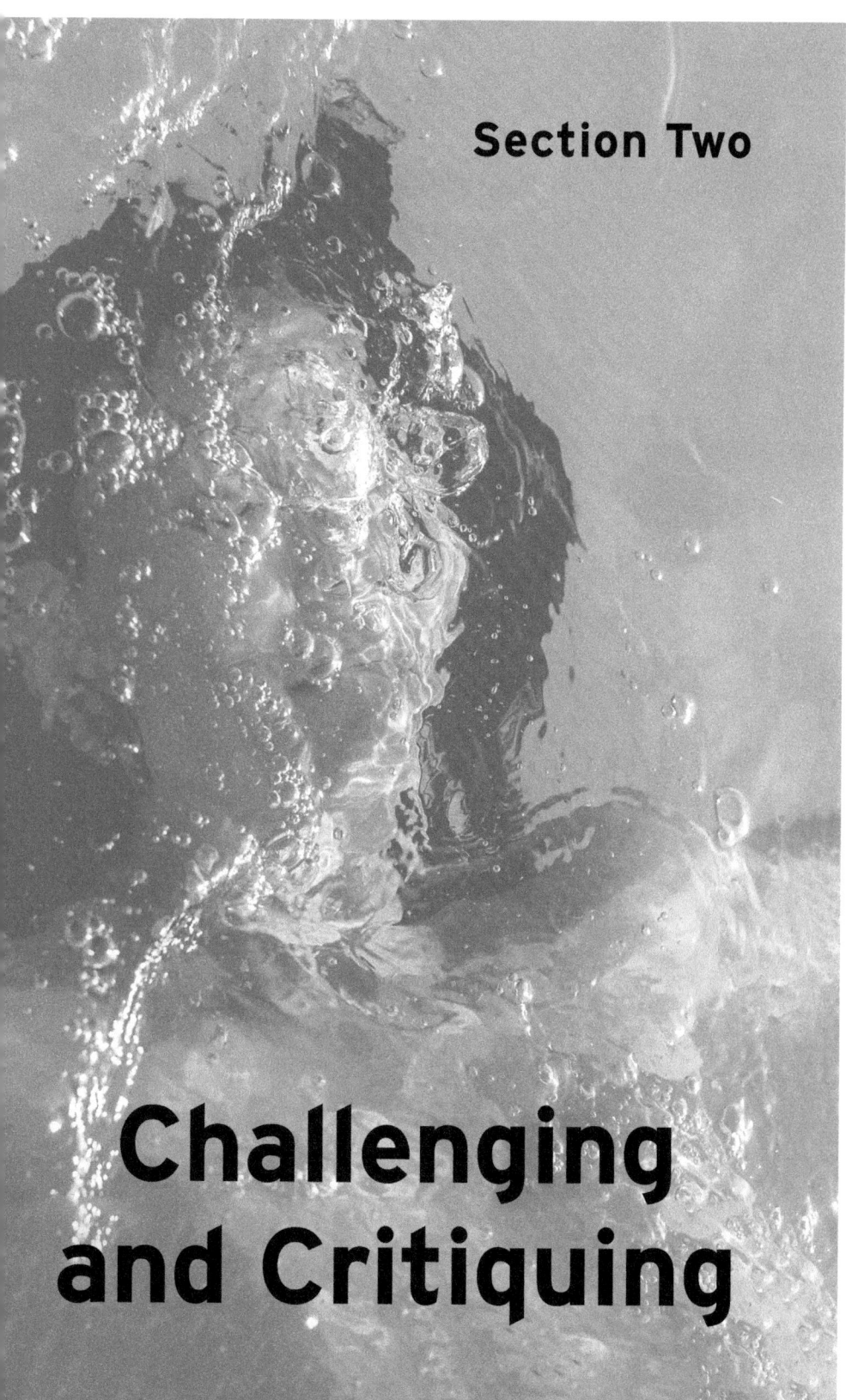

Section Two

Challenging and Critiquing

Chapter 8.

Coming into Motherhood: An Anishinaabeg Feminist View on Birth and Motherhood in Hospital Spaces

Renée E. Mazinegiizhigoo-kwe Bédard

Hospital Birth

Mothers come and go with babies in their arms.
I hear happy families out in the halls of this fort.
I try to sleep.
I try to rest.
I try to heal.
I try not to cry.
Every time the door swings wide, I cringe, retreat, and die a bit inside.
She comes again to judge and poke.
I hold back the tears and try not to let my voice crack.
I count down the minutes till I can leave this fort that does not want me here.
I feel like an outsider, a monster, the troll that has come out from under the bridge to find the villagers have pitchforks aimed at me.
Away with you! Away with you!
They snip and they snap at me.

The doctor with the scary eyes looms over me, pointing and judging.
They leave scars and scabs on my heart.
I wrap my baby up in my arms to protect us both.
We will survive.
We will retreat.
We will leave.
We will tell other women who follow behind.
Beware! Beware!

I wrote this poem as an expression of my memories and emotions that I carry deep in both my spirit and heart and that capture my experiences with medical colonialism. The poem, like this chapter, is rooted in Indigenous feminism, allowing me to confront medical colonialism and liberate me from the shackles of the pain. I release it!

As an Anishinaabeg[1] mother, feminism became a tool for me to decolonize my journey of coming into motherhood. My academic training and teaching in Indigenous feminism helped me shape and come to understand my own experiences of coming into motherhood in a hospital. The aim of this chapter is to explore how feminism provides the theoretical tools to enable me to decolonize my own experiences and thus heal from the traumas of medicial colonialism. I intend to discuss my Indigenous perspectives on feminism, which is rooted in the Anishinaabeg teachings of aazhawigamig (the space between two lodges). Next, I share my story of the birth of my daughters in hospital settings. Then, I explore the nature of medical colonialism in relation to Indigenous women and what it means for contemporary Indigenous women to come into motherhood in a colonized space, such as a hospital. This means looking to Dwayne Donald's theoretical model of Western institutions as symbols of the fort mentality and how this leads to the marginalization and, ultimately, the colonization of Indigenousness. Lastly, I explore what strategies Indigenous mothers can use to decolonize birthing spaces and create safe spaces for us as Indigenous women and mothers coming into motherhood.

From an Anishinaabeg worldview, coming into motherhood is a vulnerable time for all women, but in the hospital setting, Indigenous women face a host of dangers due to institutionalized racism, sexism, discrimination, and colonial-based negative constructions of female Indigeneity. In the hospital environment, as in other institutionalized settings, Indigenous women know that we are not safe. The joy of motherhood is often tainted by the fear of entering those buildings and the experiences we can endure within their walls from the staff and medical professionals who come with preconceived biases. Indigenous mothers across Canada face trauma in hospital settings every day, and some have the police and social services descend upon them to take their children away. They face pressure to make medical decisions that may not align with traditional customs or knowledge. They may suffer abuse: mental, psychological, emotional, and even, physical. As a mother, I have faced trauma, racism, and discrimination in medical institutions, and these experiences have shaped my path as an Indigenous feminist. Feminism has become a path forward to both heal and begin to articulate my experiences as an Anishinaabeg woman living under the mantle of colonization.

Feminism Is My Tool

For me, feminism offers a basketful of tools that I use when I need to knock down a few walls within the patriarchy or tear out the roots of colonialism across my miikana-bimaadizi (path of life). I pick up feminism like I pick up my garden tools when it is needed, and when it is not, I put them back in the shed. Feminism's methods serve me in particular ways and instances. I cannot fully immerse myself in its worldviews because I am not fully Euro-North American and cannot commit all of myself to it because its history and culture do not always align with my Indigeneity. My father, Joseph Bédard-*han*,[2] is French Canadian, but my mother, Shirley Ida Sheppard-*ban*, is Anishinaabeg (Ojibwe/ Nipissing/Omàmiwininiwak) and Kanien'kehá:ka (Mohawk), with English and French Canadian fur traders mixed in along the historical pathway. I was raised to see myself and to align with my Anishinaabeg mother's culture, traditional territory, and community of Dokis First Nation at Okikendawt Mnissing (Island of the Cauldrons or the Kettle Pots). My university degrees and publications all speak to Anishinaabeg maternal culture and philosophies. Yet as a woman who is a beadworker, I know that long ago the Anishinaabeg women of my culture adopted glass beads from fur traders to enhance their work in beading. They did not completely rely on them and continued their porcupine quillwork, so I know that it is good practice to pick up new tools if they do not compromise the integrity of my cultural traditions.

I see the value of feminism and understand that without feminism, I would not be able to vote as a woman in Canada. I would not be able to be out in the work force making as much as men, if not more, and I would have not been able to regain my Indian status and treaty rights, if not for the political space created by feminism for women of colour in Canada, which allowed First Nations[3] women to challenge the discriminatory gender inequalities of the Indian Act (1876). Through the door held open by feminists in Canada and the United States, First Nations women, particularly mothers, stepped into the political arena and took on the government to get amendments to the Indian Act to remove gender inequities. First Nations women brought about Bill C-31: Gender Equity in Indian Registration Act (1985), Bill C-3, Gender Equity in Indian Registration Act (2011), and Bill S-3, Act to Amend the Indian Act in Response to the Superior Court of Quebec Decision in Descheneaux c. Canada (2017). First Nations women activists—such as Mary Two-Axe, Yvonne Bédard, Jeannette Corbiere Lavell, Sandra Lovelace Nicholas, Sharon McIvor, Stéphane Descheneaux, Susan Yantha, and Tammy Yantha—picked up the feminist tools they needed to fight for and secure the reinstatement of their legal rights and benefits under the treaties, Indian Act, land, and resources. They did it not only for their own sense of self-determination but also for their families and descendants—those generations yet to come. These women are my role models for feminist activism within Indigenous contexts.

Each of these women has shown me that I can take up feminism as an Indigenous woman to deconstruct the patriarchal-colonial system that was designed to utilize gender discrimination as a method of denying rights to First Nations women and our descendants. Feminism can help us to purge our cultures and lives of the negative impact of patriarchal institutions. Indigenous feminism is activist in nature and voice, and Indigenous feminists seek to above all preserve, respect, and honour our traditional ways of knowing while using methods devised by feminists to dismantle Eurocentric-heteronormative-patriarchal systems that perpetuate the colonization of Indigenous women and those on the female gender spectrum as well as those who identify as LGBTTIQQ2SA+[4], two-spirited, or Indigiqueer. It is about restoring our inherent rights, restoring our power and traditions, as well as dismantling colonial systems that perpetuate the continued colonization, assimilation, and eradication of Indigenous peoples. Indigenous feminism is fluid because it sits between two lodges; two knowledge systems that require Indigenous women to stand between and navigate both Western and Indigenous ways of knowing, being, seeing, living, and relating. Shari M. Huhndorf and Cheryl Suzack write that Indigenous feminism "must aim to understand the changing situations, the commonalities, and the specificities of Indigenous women across time and place; it must seek ultimately to attain social justice not only along gender lines but also along those of race, class, and sexuality" (3).

For me, using feminism within Anishinaabeg contexts means embodying the concept of aazhawigamig, Anishinaabeg culture, and Western feminism (See Figure. 1).

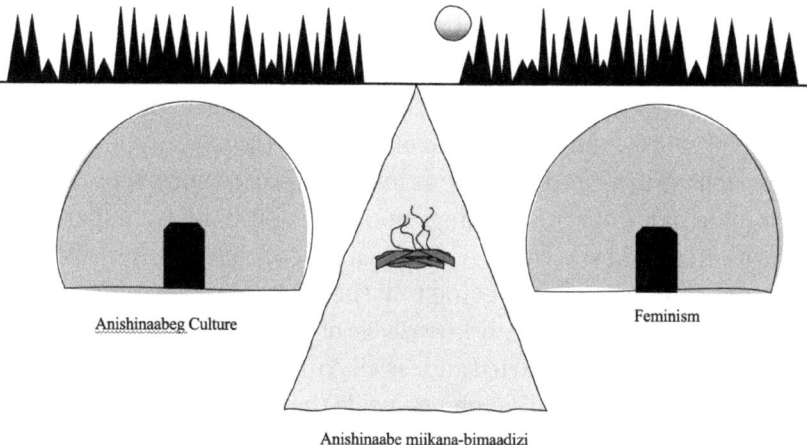

Figure. 1. Aazhawigamig Model

Between the two lodges is the sacred fire and the miikana-bimaadizi (path of life) that goes forward, and backwards, connecting past, present (i.e., the fire), and the future. The path is mino-miikana, which translates to "the good path of life." To walk that path in a good way requires Anishinaabe-mino-bimaadiziwin, which are the teachings and culture of how to live in a good way as Anishinaabeg. It requires Anishinaabeg to uphold the gchi-inaakonigewinan (Great laws; original laws; Sacred laws; Binding laws), which govern the lives and actions of everything in the universe. These laws were given to the Anishinaabeg at the time of human creation. The sacred fire in the middle of the two lodges represents the gchi-inaakonigewinan. That fire grounds me in my roles, duties, and responsibilities as an Anishinaabeg-Indigenous feminist while I move between the two lodges, and it acts as a safe space. So, when we choose to enter the aazhawigamig, sit down at the fire in between the lodges, and take part in using the tools of feminism for a time, we are never disconnected from our original lodge, but we can feel safe using those tools our feminist sisters share with us. When we are done, we put them down and return to our own lodge to attend to building, rebuilding, and renewing our traditions for the next generation. We do not have to compromise who we are to become what we want and dream to be—that is, decolonized.

As an Indigenous feminist, I look at my life as a space where decolonization is a life-time project where I tend to travel back and forth between the Anishinaabeg and feminist lodges. Currently, I am living in the phase of life described by Anishinaabeg peoples as the third mountain, or the parenting stage of life. I am in the western quadrant of the medicine wheel, and it is fall. The teachings of this side of the medicine wheel tell me to focus on my role as mother and decolonize those aspects of my life that impact or impinge upon any ability I have to parent or mother in a good way as an Anishinaabe-doodoom (mother). When I thought about what I was going to write about, I decided I wanted to share my experiences and my knowledge of what it is like to be a mother. So, I will share how it started and, as all Anishinaabeg do, begin with a story of the births of my daughters inside the hospital institution. Hospitals are colonial spaces and, thus, a perfect place for the tools of feminism to begin its work in the aazhawigamig. My story is about medical colonialism as lived by an Indigenous woman.

Dibaajimowinan

The hospital births of my two daughters were vastly different. Feminism taught me to see them for both their beauty and for the trauma they produced due to the hospital as a site of colonialism, discrimination, and racism towards Indigenous women and mothers.

Willow's Birth Story

My first daughter, Willow, made me a mother. With my first daughter's birth, I had intended to either have a natural birth at home or with my midwives at the Six Nations Birthing Centre: Tsi Non: we Ionnakeratstha Ona:grahsta (The Place They Will Be Born), which resides at the Six Nations of the Grand River territory. I had two First Nations midwives. One was Haudenosaunee and the other Anishinaabeg. They were supportive throughout the whole pregnancy. I received traditional teachings, herbal plant medicines that they had handpicked, and they brought a box of fresh food each month, filled with fruits and vegetables. I was instructed on how to care for myself: mind, emotions, body, and spirit. The whole holistic process of having traditional midwives felt right and made me feel like I was training to be a mother in a good way. Towards the end of my pregnancy my midwives informed me that my daughter was in the wrong position for birth and gave me homework to try to flip her. I tried all sorts of positions to move her into proper alignment, but nothing worked. My daughter would not budge. The midwives sent me for an ultrasound, and the results confirmed that my daughter was in a severe frank breech position, and their recommendation was to have a caesarean section. The midwives said it was my decision if I wanted to try for a natural birth, but they did not recommend it. I did not want to endanger my baby, and the looks on the midwives' faces told me to have the surgery. We found a doctor who would respect my cultural needs to collect the placenta and umbilical cord so that I could perform the burial ceremony of nitaawigiwin. The whole introduction to birth in mainstream medicine was starting out in a good way, and I felt confident.

The day of the caesarean section, I was extremely nervous. My doctor reassured me that it would be okay, and he informed the nurses that my husband would be collecting the placenta and umbilical cord. Then he introduced me to the resident doctor. She was Anishinaabeg from a community in Northern Ontario. I bonded with her quickly, and I felt like my people were with me in the room. The caesarian section birth was the best thing for my family. During postpartum care in the hospital, the nurses and doctors were nurturing and supportive. My midwife came and visited with me. She checked the baby and me, and then we chatted for an hour. I felt that the whole experience was healthy and honoured my wellbeing as a new mother.

In contrast, my second birth in the hospital was traumatic, and I received a full dose of what medical colonialism looks like for Indigenous women.

Juniper's Birth

Juniper's pregnancy flew by because I already had a child who needed me constantly, and I did not have time to sit there staring at a pregnant belly and marvelling at what was happening. The magic of the first pregnancy was not completely there. I now had a two-year-old yelling at me for goldfish and juice. My husband and I decided to go with an obstetrician with the second pregnancy due to the complications with the first. I was nervous and scared.

The obstetrician we went with was so supportive and laid back. She wanted us to try a vaginal birth. We agreed, wanting to give my body the chance to birth a child. I really wanted to be able to say that I welcomed one of my daughters through that eastern doorway of birth (i.e, vaginal birth) like my friends had talked so romantically about in their birth stories, but I also feared it. I feared complications and emergency surgeries. The women in my family have a history of serious complications in birth. I was a caesarean birth baby because my cord was wrapped around my neck. When my doctor went on vacation right before I was about to give birth, she reassured me that she would be back for my birth. My care was temporarily transferred to another doctor, and when we met with her, I expressed my fears to the new doctor about having a vaginal birth due to all the previous complications with my first baby. We discussed my options and together we decided that a caesarean would be best for my physical and mental health. I was happy with the meeting, and I set about waiting to be called by the hospital to come in for the surgery.

We arranged for someone to watch our daughter, and my husband and I went to give birth. At first, the birth experience was great and moved along Willow's birth. The doctor reassured me that my cultural needs would be protected and supported. My husband was able to collect my daughter's placenta and umbilical cord without any issues. One complication was that my daughter had inhaled amniotic fluid, so she was congested, which made sleeping on her back difficult. The first night was great. The first nurse I had was so wonderful and nurturing towards me. She helped me with breastfeeding and walking me to the washroom.

She even took the baby to the nurse's station to let me get a bit of rest. The next morning, the nurse told me she was going off shift, and I thanked her for all her help.

Now I was alone at the hospital because my husband had to care for our daughter, and we didn't have anyone that could come watch her for us. I was sore, achy, bleeding, and coming off heavy medications from surgery. It was difficult for me to get around. When the new nurse came in, she was different—cold and aloof. I introduced myself and told her that I had a daughter, so I knew what I was doing. Telling her that was a mistake. She didn't smile at me and was sharp with her words, but also her criticism. When I didn't do something right in her mind, she scolded me and stated, "Don't you already know how to do all this? Why don't you know how to do this? You should know how to do it if you are a mother! Is that how you treated your first baby?" She would constantly snap at me when I couldn't get out of bed fast enough to attend to my daughter who coughed due to chest congestion. I couldn't get out of bed fast because I had just had major surgery. All day I tolerated a perfect stranger's cutting words and berating me for not being perfect. Every time she left the room, I was in tears and felt helplessly alone. I counted down the minutes and hours until my husband came, or I could leave.

I understand that nurses can get tired doing shift work because I have nurses and a police officer in my own family who do shift work that is utterly exhausting. However, what was to follow was outright discrimination and racism. The nurses knew I was Indigenous. I remember lying in my hospital bed, and my feet had become really swollen. I was in pain from the tension of it. The scary nurse came in, and I asked her to look at my swollen feet. She said it happens sometimes from too much IV fluids and informed me she would consult with the doctor. Then she asked if I was in pain. I said yes. She then asked me another question that at the time I didn't think was a loaded question. She asked, "Do you want pain meds?" She specifically asked if I wanted morphine. I said, "Oh no! I just have some sore feet. Can you just make my feet stop swelling so they don't explode!" I laughed, trying to lighten the mood, but she didn't laugh at my joke and walked out of the room. From her reactions, I sensed she didn't like me. As I waited for her return, I took a nap while the baby slept. I was woken by a doctor poking my foot with a pen. He had removed the blanket on my legs and was jamming a pen at my foot. I was startled awake and groggy. He peppered me with questions about my feet and then asked me questions I will always remember. "I hear you want morphine for pain. Are you asking for more pain meds? Why are you asking for more pain meds?" He had a dark look on his face. I stammered no and that I didn't want pain meds and that I hadn't asked for pain meds. He informed me that the nurse who was standing in the doorway had said I was demanding pain meds and morphine. He explained to me that morphine was a powerful drug, and as he kept talking, I watched the face of the nurse. She was emotionless as she looked at me. It was not a friendly look. She had made him think I was begging for drugs. I looked at my daughter wearing a funny little purple knitted hat that had been donated for babies born at the hospital; some grandmother had probably knitted it. I became worried about where the direction of this conversation was going, which was really a confrontation at this point. The doctor's voice became louder and scarier. These people could take my child, or have her taken, based on how this situation unfolded. I was an academic in the field of Indigenous studies, and I knew what happened to some Indigenous women in hospitals. Our women can have a baby seized under the mildest of suspicions that we are a danger to the child. I have heard horror stories from both my friends and students about their experiences in the hospital.

My heart raced in that moment, and I realized what the nurse had done. She had the doctor thinking I had a problem with medications. By the tone of his questions, he was fishing around for information and making assumptions based on whatever the nurse had told him. My whole body went cold, and my spirit panicked. All I could think about was my baby. I fixed my eyes on her and took a deep breath. I focused on my breathing and her face. I knew I had to stay calm and not start crying, which is what I had wanted to do. I put on my big professor voice, my professional voice, and talked the doctor down. As I regained control of the situation and clearly showed that the nurse was lying, my husband came in with my eldest daughter. When the doctor saw this white man come into the room, his whole face and body changed. The doctor was no longer puffed up and big. His dark and serious expression was gone. He held out his hand in greeting and a smile plastered across his face. The doctor talked to my husband as if I wasn't in the room. There were smiles and laughter. The doctor asked if I wanted the IV out that was causing my feet to swell, and I quietly said yes. I was quiet because I wanted to hide and be small. In fact, I was holding back tears. Abuse makes you feel small. I felt tiny in the face of the threat of potentially having my baby taken from me for suspected drug use, the lies of the nurse, the patriarchal power play by the doctor, the erasure of my voice by the mere presence of my white non-Indigenous husband, and the medical staff talking to him and not me. No apologies were made to me for the misunderstandings, and no reassurances were made that the nurse would be talked to about her treatment of me. All I was left with was trauma and my story, but more importantly, I had my baby; I could heal from the rest of it.

I thanked the doctor politely, playing nice. I smiled and pretended I was not terrified. The nurse disappeared at some point, having lost the battle she had tried to create. Maybe she fled before she could be challenged or told she was in the wrong. To me, she will always represent a maji-manidoo (bad spirit). I am still traumatized by this incident and recognize that my experience with facing racialized medical trauma in a hospital environment is not an isolated incident.

As the news often demonstrates, Indigenous women have had children seized due to discrimination present within the institutions and culture of medicine. In Ontario, where I live, there was a system of birth alerts in place until October 15, 2020. The Ontario Association of Children's Aid Societies defines the birth or hospital alert practice as the following:

> A birth alert was the practice of child welfare agencies notifying a hospital and birth centres of safety concerns before a baby was born. Those concerns might be due to previous involvement with child welfare, drug use, issues surrounding mental health or other challenges that could impact their parenting. The practice could result in the baby being immediately taken away from its mother after being born.

These birth alerts disproportionately affected racialized parents (Lambert). In some cases, there are false allegations of drug and alcohol abuse in hospital settings (Favaro, Philip, and Jones). The practice of birth alerts was abused to target Indigenous mothers who faced already prejudice, discrimination, and outright racism from the medical community, including doctors, nurses, and other staff. The Ontario Association of Children's Aid Societies states the following:

Before the *National Inquiry into Missing and Murdered Indigenous Women and Girls,* we didn't really look at the practice critically. We never reflected on its long-term impact on the infant or their mother, or that the other components of the baby's safety, for example their emotional, spiritual, and intellectual safety, were compromised in those situations. We also didn't consider how the practice was inequitable, and led to overrepresentation of Indigenous, Black, and other marginalized communities in the child welfare system.

As of October 15, 2020, the practice of birth alerts is no longer conducted, but their legacy, as well as their mythos as part of Canadian history, will be long lasting in the minds of Canadians. The myth of the birth alerts only adds to the complex narratives of negative constructions already in place about Indigenous women in this country. These myths damage and endanger the social-cultural reputations of Indigenous mothers within Canada. Although the steps towards repealing the birth alerts is a positive movement towards reconciliation and decolonization of medical institutions, they will remain safe spaces for Indigenous mothers for a long time to come.

Medical Colonialism: Why Are Western Institutions Unsafe Spaces for Indigenous Women?

Healthcare was a popular policy tool of colonisers as a means of controlling and containing indigenous populations ... indigenous women were targeted by gender-specific measures aimed at their disenfranchisement in both their own and settler communities. The measures imposed by the Indian Act resulted in the direct removal of indigenous women's rights and the assimilation of indigenous culture and perceptions which increased indigenous women's vulnerability to abuse and mistreatment.

—"The Fatality of Bias" Global Policy Review

Dragging up the memories of the birth of my second daughter is always hard on me, and I spend days reliving these events—rationalizing, fretting, and mostly crying. To understand my trauma, move past it, and begin to heal from it, I have put on my feminist hat and collected some theoretical tools to begin to decolonize these events in a way that helped me and maybe will help others to see why this happens every day to other Indigenous women. Colonial institutions, such as the hospital and education system, have traumatized not only me but also all the women in my family on some level.

While writing this chapter, I was reminded of the work of scholar Dwayne Donald who talks about Canadian institutions representing sites of colonization. He uses the model of the fort to describe this colonial legacy we all live within—both Indigenous and non-Indigenous. Donald's work got me thinking of the parallels between the education system that he highlights and the healthcare system. All Canadian institutions carry with them the same DNA, collective memories, and traditions of the fort. As Simon Schama notes:

> It is clear that inherited landscape myths and memories share two common characteristics: their surprising endurance through the centuries and their power to shape *institutions* that we still live with. National identity ... would lose much of its ferocious enchantment without the mystique of a particular landscape tradition: its topography mapped, elaborated and enriched as homeland. (15; my emphasis)

Long before I entered the hospital, my ancestors faced the fort as a site to colonize Indigenousness into the Canadian mythos—to take it, manage it, transform it, and feed the new images back to us. Donald writes the following:

> The fort is a mythic symbol in Canada of high historical status that recapitulates the perceived civilizational frontier—a kind of cultural ditch—separating Aboriginal from Canadian. In Canada, the fort, as concept and organizing principle of Empire emanating from colonial processes, has taught, and continues to teach, a particular curricular and pedagogical message that reinforces these perceived divides. ("Forts" 93)

This mythic dynamic of the fort mentally permeates Canadian consciousness and is the foundation for every institutional or even public space within Canada: hospitals, schools, courthouses, jails, libraries, parks, malls, beaches, and so on. Every institution became a fort—that is, a space of Eurocentric colonization, patriarchy, heteronormativity, and Christianization.

Canadians resurrect and maintain the symbol of the fort within all its cities and cultural knowledge systems that work to generate Eurocentric intellectual traditions and culture. The pedagogy of the fort is used to teach and perpetuate the myth that Canadian institutions are places designed for citizens, who are non-Indigenous peoples in this narrative; here, Indigenous people are not a part of the myth of Canada. We are outsiders and alien to the myth of Canada. Donald states that there is a "metalanguage" at play here that rewrites the stories of the landscape and socially constructs a reality that "others" the Indigenous populations right to occupy the same lands and spaces as non-Indigenous peoples ("Forts" 98). He explains that the function of the forts and fortresses in Canada, both physically and metaphorically, is to gain sovereignty over an area or people. Terry Goldie provides significant insight on this:

> The white Canadian looks at the Indian. The Indian is Other and therefore alien. But the Indian is Indigenous and therefore cannot be alien. So the Canadian must be alien. But how can the Canadian be alien within Canada? There are only two possible answers. The white culture can attempt to incorporate the other, specifically through beaded moccasins and names like Mohawk Motors, or with much more sophistication, through the novels of Rudy Wiebe. Conversely, the white culture may reject the indigene: "This country really began with the arrival of the whites." (234)

These scholars and theorists paint a troubling picture of the impact of the myth of the fort on our collective sense of relationality as Indigenous and non-Indigenous peoples. Embedded in every institution—be it a hospital, school, university, or courthouse—the myth of the fort sets forth an "unquestioned authoritativeness" (Donald, "Forts" 101). Donald contends that the alienness of Indigenousness makes it unimaginable to the narrative of Canadianness because it cannot be reconciled with the vision of nation and nationality (Donald, "The Curricular Problem").

Another layer is that all women's privileges within the fort are fragile and never innate; they are bequeathed by men. The fort is therefore the domain of Eurocentric-Christian-white-male-heteronormative culture and power. Is there any reason why we, as Indigenous women, do not feel safe in a hospital? Why did I feel the need to shrink back from the doctor? And why did the nurse, who had been caught lying, flee? We both feared the male white doctor in the room. Why did the doctor's demeanour change with the entry of my white male husband holding a child? He recognized a fellow occupant of the fort—a family man with his own seat of power—and he knew he had an equal in his presence. Both men were certain of their power, whereas the women were left powerless and cast out. I was silenced, and the nurse fled the scene to protect her job, or she too would be exiled from the fort. Feminism allows me to see this clearly now, but for years, I did not want to confront this experience for what it represents for me and for other women: Indigenous and non-Indigenous alike.

Hospitals, like residential schools, are places where First Nations, Métis, and Inuit women fear for our lives and those of our children. Beginning in the early 1800s till 1996, the residential school system stole the culture, mental and psychological wellbeing, and the lives of thousands of Indigenous children. Boarding schools and day schools sought to colonize Indigenous peoples to absorb them into the Canadian populations as a means of eliminating Indian status in just a few generations and, consequently, obtain legal rights to First Nations land and resources. Duncan Campbell Scott, an architect of the residential school system, often referred to First Nations rights to land and resources as the "Indian Problem," which was to be done away with. He cared little for the poor conditions, abuse, or deaths of First Nations children inside these schools. All he saw was that these institutions were a means to an end goal—Canada claiming all First Nations territory to increase its wealth and sustain itself as a country. He stated:

> It is readily acknowledged that Indian children lose their natural resistance to illness by habituating so closely in the residential schools and that they die at a much higher rate than in their villages. But this does not justify a change in the policy of this Department which is geared towards a final solution of our Indian Problem. (qtd. in "The Legacy of Duncan Campbell Scott")

The residential school system was never a safe place for Indigenous females. Medical experimentations and sterilizations took place on

Indigenous bodies in residential schools, aligning educational institutions and medical institutions in a symbiotic scheme to violently reduce and eradicate the Indigenous population. Both Alberta (1928) and British Columbia (BC) (1933) passed Sexual Sterilization Acts. The BC Sexual Sterilization Act (1933 to 1979) gave "the B.C. Eugenics Board the right to make decisions to sterilize people living in government-run institutions without their consent and without their knowledge of what was happening." Moreover, "this treatment was approved as a means of controlling behaviour and ensuring the disability was not passed on to future generations" ("Eugenics," 2022).

Eugenics was prevalent in BC residential schools; students were forced or coerced into sterilization. The BC Sexual Sterilizations Act "allowed school principals in Residential Schools to carry out the sterilizations, and as their legal guardian could have any Indigenous child under their charge sterilized…. Sterilization procedures were carried out on whole groups of Indigenous children once they reached puberty" (Compton). However, residential schools were not the only space where Indigenous peoples were sterilized.

The 1928 legislation allowed for, and actively encouraged, the sterilization of those deemed undesirable (Kersten). The Sexual Sterilizations Act was drafted to protect the gene pool, which targeted the sterilization of persons with mental disabilities, intellectual disabilities (e.g., learning disabilities or any neurodevelopmental disorders, which used to be termed "mental retardation" during that time period), epilepsy, alcoholism, poverty, criminal behaviour, and social defects, such as prostitution or sexual disorders. Sterilization was deemed acceptable to prevent the transmission of traits to offspring deemed undesirable (Kersten). In Alberta, Métis and First Nations people "made up around 3 per cent of Alberta's population at the time, they made up 25 per cent of the number of individuals ordered to be forcibly sterilized under the act" (Compton). Ireland Compton notes the following: "Before the act was repealed, an astounding 2800 sterilization procedures were performed in the province of Alberta. Many individuals who were sterilized under the act were not told they were undergoing a sterilization procedure and remained unaware of their sterilization until many years later. These surgeries were often passed off as other surgeries and given without consent."

According to witnesses and victims interviewed by scholar Leonardo

Pegoraro, the government offered stipends to doctors willing to perform the surgery. One unnamed survivor who was sterilized at a BC medical clinic in 1952 recounted hearing that a sum of three hundred dollars would be given to doctors for each Indigenous woman sterilized, noting that "If you were seen to be a troublemaker, you got the operation" (Pegoraro 162). The woman was forcefully sterilized as punishment for refusing to marry a Christian Indigenous man; instead, she chose to marry a community chief. Others faced experimental sterilization methods (Pegoraro 162). During the 1950s, at the Nanaimo Indian Hospital, the doctors experimented with new methods of sterilization of First Nations patients. Joan Morris, of the Songhees people, was forced to drink a substance she believed was "radioactive iodine" (Pegoraro 162). Another witness shared the following: "Doctor Darby [a missionary doctor who sterilized non-Christian Indian women between 1928 and 1962 at the W.R. Large Memorial Hospital] told me in 1952 that Indian Affairs in Ottawa was paying him for every Indian he sterilized, especially if they weren't churchgoers. Hundreds of our women were sterilized by Doctor Darby, just for not going to church" (Pegoraro 162). It is unimaginable to think that doctors held a view that First Nations women mattered so little that they not only experimented on them but also took away their ability to have children.

Although it is easy to dismiss these cases as happening only in the past, they still continue today among Indigenous women throughout Canada. Karen Stote has demonstrated that thousands of Indigenous women have faced violence and abuse from Canadian governmental, medical, and educational institutions. Melika Popp said she was sterilized against her will in 2008 at the Royal University Hospital in Saskatoon ("Another Saskatoon Woman"). According to her interview with *CBC News*, Popp also had had prior experiences. At six-months pregnant, Popp went to the hospital with gestational diabetes, only to be asked by a nurse, "What birth control she'd been taking and why she hadn't used condoms" ("Another Saskatoon Woman"). At eight months, she returned to the hospital with a placental abruption and agreed to have a caesarian section, but she found herself pressured to sign consent forms for a tubal ligation and was told it was reversible. A tubal ligation is not medically reversible. Popp told *CBC News* that "As a mother I cannot tell you what this has done to my inner core ... having my reproductive organs crippled, robs my children of future siblings and my ability to pass on future aboriginal title and rights to land" (qtd. in "Another Saskatoon Woman").

Many contemporary First Nations Women face dangers upon entering medical institutions, and some even lose their lives to these forts of Western medicine. Joyce Echaquan, a thirty-seven-year-old Atikamekw woman from Manawan First Nation and mother of seven, died in her hospital bed. According to her husband, Carol Dubé, Echaquan suffered from heart-related problems and had a pacemaker. She went to the hospital for stomach pains. Echaquan was not fluent in French and had to have a translator, which seemed to frustrate the staff. They proceeded to only provide pain medication instead of treating her medical symptoms (Shingler, "Racism"). Echaquan reported to the nurses that she felt she was being given too much morphine from them (Shingler, "Investigations"). Using her phone, she recorded her interactions with the medical staff on Facebook Live. One nurse can be heard referring to her as stupid (Shingler, "Investigations"). Echaquan recorded herself calling for help only to be degraded and told that she had "made bad life choices." She was asked "what her children would say if they saw her in that state" (qtd. in Shingler, "Investigations"). Echaquan's neglect and poor treatment by staff led to her dying in the hospital. Stories like this, and many others, articulate the trauma resulting from entering Canadian medical institutions, which has led Indigenous women throughout Canada to fear for their lives within these spaces, which are supposed to save lives and do no harm.

Feminism's gift to me was the ability to see what happened to me with clear eyes and what all these stories represent for Indigenous women in Canada. The fort is a dangerous place if you are Indigenous and a woman. I think of all the women who do not survive the onslaught of the hospital as a fort of colonialism, and those who do, we are left violated, battered, and bruised—physically, emotionally, psychologically, and mentally.

Decolonizing the Hospital Space

If colonialism is indeed a shared condition, then decolonizing needs to be a shared endeavour.

—Dwayne Donald, "Forts" 102

Medical colonialism continues to this day for the thousands of Indigenous peoples who seek medical aid. It is hard to decolonize the hospital setting because it is a fort maintained by the residents of the fort, who are indoctrinated to protect it at all costs. The reality is that the nature of that fort will likely not change much unless the residents of the fort wish it so, but as Indigenous peoples, we can advocate for ourselves to be treated and recognized as human beings and also to have our rights under Canadian law upheld. We can learn from Black feminists, like Audre Lorde, to be wary of the house of our colonizer and be aware of our position in society:

> Those of us who stand outside the circle of this society's definition of acceptable women; those of us who have been forged in the crucibles of difference; those of us who are poor, who are lesbians, who are black, who are older, know that survival is not an academic skill. It is learning how to stand alone, unpopular and sometimes reviled, and how to make common cause with those others identified as outside the structures, in order to define and seek a world in which we can all flourish. (Lorde 99)

For Indigenous mothers, the fort mentality still seeks to dehumanize us, so we must perpetually remind those who maintain these metaphoric forts that we are human beings and that we are now also citizens of the fort. History, literature, media, politics, law, and economics have trained non-Indigenous people in Canada to see ourselves as less than human beings and as not deserving of respect. We must demand respect, protection, and safety from those working within the medical institutions.

Concluding Thoughts

Writing this chapter has been both liberating and difficult. I relived some dark times in my past, which are stories that I carry close to my heart and do not share with many. Right now, I do not tell my daughters the difficulties of their births, only the beauty. Every child should feel the beauty of their arrival into the world. I tell my daughters they were born of waves of water and brought to the safety of my arms by those doctors that caught them as they travelled through the eastern doorway from the Spirit World to this earthly realm.

Indigenous women were not the first to be colonized by Western medicine. For Indigenous women, feminists have shared with us their tools of decolonization. Be they words, stories, cultural resurgence, political action, or legal knowledge, many of us have readily embraced these tools to protect ourselves. Feminists supported us as we speak our truths, even if sometimes we tell them to let us speak alone and stand alone. They have shared space so that our cultural ways of knowing, being, and living can be included in the Western North American evolution of Feminist narratives. I could not have talked my way out of the dangers of the hospital environment following the birth of my second daughter without knowing the empowering lessons of my sisters in feminism. Miigwech, nimisenyag, thank you, my sisters.

Endnotes

1. Anishinaabeg are Indigenous peoples from the lands around Nayaano-wiishkbiwii-nibiimaang Gichigamiin (The Five Freshwater Seas: Great Lakes). Our traditional territory crosses the borders of Canada and the United States. We have lived on the lands of Turtle Island (the North American Continent) since time immemorial.

2. In Anishinaabemowin, *-ban* or *-ba* is a preterit suffix that is added to a noun stem to indicate a past state, absence, or loss. For example, *-ban* is added to a noun to indicate that the person is now deceased. To honour that they have passed to the Spirit Realm, I have chosen to write it as *-ban* at the end of their name. To not bother or draw the attention of the Spirit of the deceased who is busy with their existence in that Spirit realm, Anishinaabeg are told to alter or add to the name *-ban* or *-ba*. In this chapter, I have chosen not to attach it directly to the name of each deceased person repeatedly. Furthermore, I have chosen to italicize *-ban* to make it visually resonate as different and alter the name in the traditional manner.

3. First Nation(s) is a legal term found in the Canadian Constitution, Section 35 (2). It describes those Indigenous peoples who are not Métis or Inuit. First Nations also defines those who have been historically defined as "Indian" and continue to still be defined as "Indian" in either the Indian Act (1876) or within treaties. First Nation can also describe a band community as defined by the Indian Act. This territory was originally put aside in treaties and held by the

Crown (i.e., the Federal Government of Canada) for the exclusive use of First Nation groups.

4. LGBTTIQQ2SA+ means lesbian, gay, bisexual, transgender, transsexual, intersex, queer, questioning, two-spirited, and asexual.

Works Cited

"Another Saskatoon Woman Says She Was Sterilized against Her Will." *CBCNews*, 16 Dec. 2015, https://www.cbc.ca/news/canada/saskatoon/saskatoon-woman-says-she-was-sterilized-against-her-will-1.3366464. Accessed 1 Apr. 2023.

Compton, Ireland. "The Coerced Sterilization of Indigenous Women in Canada: A People's History of Canada Column." *The Link*, 2 Oct. 2018, https://thelinknewspaper.ca/article/the-coerced-sterilization-of-indigenous-women-in-canada. Accessed 1 Apr. 2023.

Donald, Dwayne. "Forts, Colonial Frontier Logics, and Aboriginal-Canadian Relations: Imagining Decolonizing Educational Philosophies in Canadian Contexts." *Decolonizing Philosophies of Education*, edited by Ali. A. Abdi, Sense Publishers, 2011, pp. 91-111.

Donald, Dwayne. "The Curricular Problem of Indigenousness: Colonial Frontier Logics, Teacher Resistances, and the Acknowledgement of Ethical Space." *Beyond Presentism: Re-imagining the Historical, Personal, and Social Places of Curriculum*, edited by J. Nahachewsky and I. Johnston. Rotterdam, Sense Publishers, 2009, pp. 23-41.

"Eugenics." *Canadian Institute for Inclusion and Citizenship*, The University of British Columbia, 2022, https://cic.arts.ubc.ca/the-eve-decision-1986/eugenics/#:~:text=%E2%80%9CThe%20Sexual%20Sterilization%20Act%2C%20which,knowledge%20of%20what%20was%20happening. Accessed 1 Apr. 2023.

Favaro, Avis, Elizabeth St. Philip, and Alexandra Mae Jones. "Indigenous Families Disproportionately Affected by 'Birth Alerts'; B.C. Lawsuit Seeks Damages." *CTVNews*. 31 Oct. 2021, https://www.ctvnews.ca/canada/indigenous-families-disproportionately-affected-by-birth-alerts-b-c-lawsuit-seeks-damages-1.5646384. Accessed 1 Apr. 2023.

Goldie, Terry. "The Representation of the Indigene." *The Post-Colonial Studies Reader*, edited by B. Ashcroft, G. Griffiths, and H. Tiffin,

Routledge, 1995, pp. 232-236.

Government of Canada. "Background on Indian Registration." *Crown-Indigenous Relations and Northern Affairs Canada, Collaborative Process on Indian Registration, Band Membership and First Nation Citizenship: Consultation Plan*, https://www.rcaanc-cirnac.gc.ca/eng/1540405608208/1568898474141#_Bill_C-31_. Accessed 1 Apr. 2023.

Government of Canada. "Differences between Self-Governing First Nations and Indian Act Bands." *Crown-Indigenous Relations and Northern Affairs Canada*, https://www.rcaanc-cirnac.gc.ca/eng/1100100028429/1616789617763. Accessed 1 Apr. 2023.

Huhndorf, Shari M., and Cheryl Suzack. "Indigenous Feminism: Theorizing the Issues." *Indigenous Women and Feminism: Politics, Activism, and Culture*, edited by Cheryl Suzack, Shari M. Huhndorf, Jeanne Perreault, and Jean Barman, UBC Press, 2010, pp. 1-20.

Kersten, L. "British Columbia Repeals the Sexual Sterilization Act." *Eugenics Archive of Canada*, 14 Sept. 2013, https://eugenicsarchive.ca/discover/timeline/5233c89f5c2ec50000000091. Accessed 1 Apr. 2023.

Lambert, Steve. "Video Sparks Outrage after Manitoba Officials Seize Newborn from Indigenous Mother in Hospital." *The Globe and Mail*, 11 Jan. 2019, https://www.theglobeandmail.com/canada/article-video-sparks-outrage-after-manitoba-officials-seize-newborn-from/. Accessed 1 Apr. 2023.

Little Bear, Leroy. "Jagged Worldviews Colliding." *Reclaiming Indigenous Voice and Vision*, edited by Marie Battiste, UBC Ppess, 2000. pp. 77-85.

Lorde, Audre. "The Master's Tools Will Never Dismantle the Master's House." *This Bridge Called My Back: Writings by Radical Women of Color*, edited by Cherríe Moraga and Gloria Anzaldú, Kitchen Table Press, 1983, pp. 98-101.

Pegoraro, Leonardo. "Second-Rate Victims: The Forced Sterilization of Indigenous Peoples in the USA and Canada." *Settler Colonial Studies*, vol. 5, no. 2, 2015, pp. 161-73.

Schama, Simon. *Landscape and Memory*. Knopf, 1995.

Shingler, Benjamin. "Investigations Launched after Atikamekw Woman Records Quebec Hospital Staff Uttering Slurs before Her Death."

CBC News, 29 Sept. 2020, https://www.cbc.ca/news/canada/montreal/quebec-atikamekw-joliette-1.5743449. Accessed 1 Apr. 2023.

Shingler, Benjamin. "Racism at Quebec Hospital Reported Long before Troubling Death of Atikamekw Woman Social Sharing." *CBC News*, 1 Oct. 2020, https://www.cbc.ca/news/canada/montreal/quebec-joliette-hospital-joyce-echaquan-1.5745150. Accessed 1 Apr. 2023.

Stote, Karen. "The Coercive Sterilization of Aboriginal Women in Canada." *American Indian Culture and Research Journal*, vol. 36, no. 3, 2012, pp. 117-50.

Stote, Karen. "The Myth of Reproductive Choice: A Call for Radical Change." *Without Apology: Writings on Abortion in Canada*, edited by Shannon Stettner, Athabasca University, 2016, pp. 227-88.

"The Fatality of Bias: The Legacy of Colonialism on Indigenous Women and the Canadian Healthcare System." *Global Policy Review, IWI: International Women's Initiative*, 19 Dec. 2020, https://www.theiwi.org/gpr-reports/indigenous-women-and-the-canadian-healthcare-system. Accessed 1 Apr. 2023.

"The Legacy of Duncan Campbell Scott: More than just a Canadian Poet." *First Nations Child and Family Caring Society of Canada*, July 2016, https://fncaringsociety.com/sites/default/files/duncan_campbell_scott_information_sheet_final.pdf. Accessed 1 Apr. 2023.

"The Practice of Birth Alerts in Ontario is Ceasing October 15th. What's Next for Child Welfare Agencies and Their Approach to Working with Expectant Mothers?" *Ontario Association of Children's Aid Societies*, 13 Oct. 2020, http://www.oacas.org/2020/10/the-practice-of-birth-alerts-in-ontario-is-ceasing-october-15th-whats-next-for-child-welfare-agencies-and-their-approach-to-working-with-expectant-mothers/. Accessed 1 Apr. 2023.

Chapter 9.

Meandering through the Intersections: Feminist Mothering as a Transnational Migrant Academic Mom

Lili Shi

My journey of feminist mothering is uniquely located around my intersecting identities. Among the many labels known in the English language, I am most comfortable with the following tags: immigrant, feminist academic, transnational subject, and woman with a mixed-race marriage and children. Writing this chapter about coming into being as a feminist mother is an exploratory journey reflecting on how I try to translate my transnational and intersectional feminist consciousness into my everyday mothering in different sociocultural and geopolitical contexts for my two biracial children. I write to share an autobiographical account of how I became a mother, the flashpoints of my interiority, my frustration, doubt, self-critique, and small victories. In doing so, I explore the meanings and habits of my feminist mothering, its complexity in transnational, cross-racial contexts, and the never-ending, pulverized nature of its labour.

How It Began: Becoming an Immigrant Academic Mom

To start, I should perhaps introduce how I have come to be. I was born in the early 1980s and raised in a mid-sized city in Southwest China's Yunnan Province in the 1980s and 1990s, when China had just opened up to the world and enforced its "one-child policy" (1980–2015) for urban families. I belonged to "China's unique urban generation of single daughters" (Wang, "A Special Interview"), who grew up with support and resources from family and society, which was unprecedented in Chinese history for girls. As my father often says: "I have raised you like a son and like a daughter as you are the only one."

I was pushed to study hard and turned out a better student than all my cousins. I went to college in the cosmopolitan Shanghai area of China, where I learned English and came to the United States for graduate education in the early 2000s. During those years, I was drawn to courses on feminism and came across many writers and professors who empowered and reshaped my consciousness. I became an interdisciplinary researcher and did my dissertation work (2010) on middle-class Chinese immigrant women's acculturation in the Washington D.C. area as a feminist critique of acculturation theories that privilege masculinist migrants' subjectivity and experiences.

While writing my dissertation, I got married to my husband, whom I met in graduate school, a white American who studied East Asia politics. I then graduated, became a migrant with a green card through my marriage, and after much searching and waiting, landed a job teaching and doing research on communication, race, and gender at a large public institution in New York City. That transition from an international student to an immigrant academic settling down in Brooklyn was transformative in many ways. I meticulously calculated and timed my first pregnancy to my teaching cycles and tenure clock and gave birth to my daughter almost exactly at mid-tenure point; I had my son, five years later, right before my sabbatical began as a tenured associate professor. We travelled back and forth from New York to Yunnan, China every year for two to three months until the pandemic struck, and we plan to maintain that transnational shuttling lifestyle as a family, if and when traveling is possible again.

In retrospect, I have miraculously programmed my body, career, immigration process, and my personal life to the heteronormative reproductive timeline for women, the neoliberal university's timeline for a genderless faculty's productivity and success, and the timeline of my family's expectations for their only daughter. "I can go to sleep every night because you did what you were supposed to do at every stage of your life," my mom used to say, confessing her long-lasting fear that I would never marry or have children, like many highly educated female friends of mine who also belong to the single-daughter generation in China. From my own perspective, I have internalized all those timelines and their respective expectations for a woman in both the traditional and neoliberal contexts out of my aspiration to achieve the American dream. Every step I took and choice I made was a deliberate act of extreme caution and planning—that I need to have it all to prove my success in my parents' known story of the American dream.

The Migrant Academic: Motherhood at the Neoliberalist University

In my own mind, and as part of my family history, striving for excellence and participating in public labour as women are core values. Giving up work to be a stay-at-home mom never crossed my mind. My mother and my many aunts—whose jobs ranged from factory technician (my mom) to village doctors, teachers, and a prominent railway engineer in Beijing—all grew up in Maoist China where "women held up half the sky"—a slogan of socialist China encouraging women to take social responsibilities and presence as men, and that women should work while raising a family. "It's going to be hard, especially for the first few years," my Dama (first aunt), the Beijing railway engineer told me. She continued: "You need your own income and your own social circle and not to depend on any husband. This is especially true for women like you and me, who left our hometowns and have an education." Dama is from a rural town in north China and graduated from China's best engineering school in 1964. She raised my cousin almost singlehandedly and maintained her railway design career while my engineer uncle travelled all year designing railways. Dama was my first feminist impression before reading anything feminist or knowing the word "feminism." My mom, who held a factory technician job through spousal hire (because of my dad's employment at that same factory) and retired in her forties, called Dama a "woman hero."

With a figure like my Dama, and other doctor and teacher aunties in the family, working while mothering was a normalized part of life for women growing up. When I read the "work-or-home" choice dilemma that dominates white feminist mothering discourses, I thought that it was so white feminism, so bourgeoisie, and so last century until my own coming into being as a feminist mom turned out to be a journey of everyday visceral experience of work-life struggles. Allow me to share the following vignette:

January 2014. 7:40am on a freezing morning. We have just moved to the suburban part of New York City where housing was cheaper, but driving was required. My car was frozen from the night before and was covered with thick snow. My husband left an hour earlier to catch the bus for an early meeting in his office in Manhattan. In the dark and in a hurry, he left without digging our car out of the snow. Both of our commutes to work were about one and half hours. But I had the car, so I dropped off our one-year-old baby at daycare daily. My department chair was going to do my teaching evaluation in my class that day—I must be there on time at nine. Walking out of the house with baby in arm—after at least two hours of changing, dressing, feeding, changing her again, and preparing myself—I was in shock to see the thick snow covering my car and the driveway. I could not leave the baby alone in the house while I shovelled, but I could not open the car door to put her in either. I strapped her in a baby rocking chair, put her by the car where I could keep an eye on her while shoveling, and covered her with all the blankets I could find in the house. I finally dug the car door open and started the car, only to realize my hybrid car would not heat up unless the engine was running. I put the baby in her car seat and relocated all the blankets with her. I kept shovelling. She started crying and screaming because of the cold and not being able to see me through the snow-covered windows. I dropped my shovel to the ground and sat in the snow. My family in China were having dinner at that hour, I thought. I had never really seen snow until I came to the US. Why was I here? Why did the world leave me? I cried with my daughter, in and outside the car, out of my loneliness, despair, tiredness, and the injustice that my husband and the rest of the world had just left us there. And yet somehow, in the end, I managed to shovel us out while crying, dropped her off, arrived at classroom on time, received an "excellent" rating for my teaching evaluation, and quietly walked back to my office with my own myth as the model minority faculty.

That was the day I realized how much I was hurting and hiding the fact that I was struggling. The women who worked in my family lived in an era of socialist China where housing and daycare were provided for free, and in proximity to their worksites, by their employers. The neoliberal university today, however, is a "childless and male space" that rewards "multitaskers with hyped schedules" (Shahjahan 491) who are expected to be "infinitely flexible, always on call, de-gendered, de-raced, declassed" and prioritize efficiency and productivity rather than relationships, creativity, and well-ness of the self. (Amsler and Motto 11). This hurtful work culture also affects my transnational life, as it follows me to my parents' house in China during our summers there. My parents were aging fast and could not handle childcare for extended periods of time. And without daycare or camps, and with my parents' adamant refusal to have hired nannies in their house, I worked inhumane hours in the summer to keep up with my writing during those years before my tenure review; I went to bed with my daughter (my son was not born yet) at 8:30 p.m., got up at 3 a.m., worked till 7:30 a.m., when she got up, and then carried out my other mothering and daughtering duties throughout the day.

Those countless sunrises at my childhood home became my feminist space where I spent time with myself and reflected on my being. Breathing the familiar crisp air and listening to the familiar birdsong reminded me of the girl, the only child, who studied so hard at that desk and how far she had travelled and worked to become the woman that I am, a professor half a world away. Those moments were of both empowerment and abjection, of joy and sadness, with both clarity and confusion about the future. It gives me great pride to think that I never gave up my work and myself after becoming a mother and that my young family, with my governance and work, was on its way towards a secure middle-class future. Yet my body and mind were always occupied with exhaustion, anxiety, a sense of guilt of not doing enough, constant self-doubt, and the never-ending repetition of all those feelings.

Those feelings are conditioned by capitalist neoliberalism. My effort of coping has been threefold. First, I finally realized, at least for me and my family, that work-life balance is a myth. I accepted that there will be no balance. The quest towards it is futile, as there is in fact only sacrifice. I discovered that quitting is sometimes radical self-love, an essential feminist lesson. As of this week, I withdrew myself from a competitive fellowship program after noticing its workload and competitiveness were harming my and my family's health, despite the prestige it could have added to my resume. Second, I worked endlessly to find allies to foster a feminist culture that brings structural changes in my immediate professional world. Together with colleagues who think like me, we elected a feminist department chair that listened and offered flexible schedules. I also became part of the administration after tenure and made every effort to invite candid conversations, offer mentoring, and make individual instructor's needs and vulnerabilities heard. Third, I sought refuge, strength, and wisdom from memorialized moments of quiet affirmations of my mother and grandmothers. My Popo (maternal grandma) was illiterate—she was the only one who did not mind my childhood whining and crying about homework and took me into her lap while I worked. I finished my first years of elementary school homework on her lap, feeling her patient warmth and her loving fingers in my hair while I learned the importance of learning, working, and carrying on. When discussing reincarnation after Popo's death (Popo was Buddhist), my mother mentioned once in the simplest words, which shall remain the most healing words in my heart, that she herself would like to reincarnate to a woman like me if there is another lifetime—her own daughter, who gets to see the world and make ideas and money of her own. Those memories of ancestral love gave me strength on my quest to find my own feminism and to become a feminist mom, with the belief that my daughter will find a path and live a life that is envious to me.

My Mixed Babies: Against the Gazes

Besides my battles against the neoliberalist capitalist work-life balance myth, another important aspect of my intersectional feminist mothering is to find identities and belonging as a biracial transnational family that prioritize not only gender equality but also racial justice. All four of us, as individuals and as a collective, need to develop a way of everyday talking, thinking, and behaving that leads us to a liberatory sense of self and selves as well as making a difference in the world. As my children grow, we encounter increasingly richer and more complex sociocultural situations, relations, geographies, and racial, gender, national, and class politics. The next section revisits some of our flashpoints.

My daughter was born with dark, long, curly hair, darker skin than both myself and my husband, big European-looking brown eyes, and a flat nose like my own. "She looks like a Mexican boy," a tactless friend jokingly commented when my daughter was two weeks old. Up until that moment, my daughter was raceless and genderless; she was simply my baby. It dawned on me that day that she had become public—that she had entered the eyes and perceptions of the world and started her own journey of socialization that is out of my control. She is bound to be racialized in various contexts by ranges of "floating signifiers" of race (Jhally and Hall 3). Her body will be read as text under public gazes across the global identity-scape—a chaotic space with dynamic borders of race, nation, gender, ethnicity, and language. That space is rich in quick-and-easy discursive identifications, such as "white" or "Asian," "good baby" or "tough cookie," "artsy" or "nerdy," "girly" or "boyish," as well as in its perception shortcuts about physical looks and geographical markings, often times captured by the ubiquity of Instagram or TikTok. And her experiences of racialization will be different from mine, with challenges and stakes unknown to me. My experiences will be irrelevant or dated. She will have to find herself—her Chineseness, her feminism, her clarity, and her sense of direction—not through me but by herself. And I, now with a mixed-raced baby by my side constantly, will experience a whole new stage of racialization. My premonition was right. While in the US, depending on where we were, she has been called "Uzbek," "from middle Asia," and "Thai"; she has also been mistaken for mixed-race toddlers at her daycare, for a sister to her Hispanic classmate, or for her Filipina American teacher's daughter. I was told at the beach by a white couple that they "would kill" for their kids to have her skin tone to save money on sun lotion. When my son was born five years later, he looked different, with fairer skin and a pointier nose. Our friends said the following: "He looks just like a little white dude"; "He's white passing", "He's the white version of you"; and "He's going to be your Keanu" (my friends know I love Keanu Reeves, whose paternal grandma is Chinese Hawaiian).

When with strangers, the moment I disclose that my children are biracial, I always get showered with comments like "Mixed babies are the cutest and smartest." In China, in public spaces and when with my family, they are adored and photographed nonstop. One day, a tactless auntie of mine, a former OB-GYN and a feminist hero of my childhood, said after staring and smiling at them for an entire meal: "It's a pity that the boy looks more American [she meant white] and more beautiful than the girl." I was mortified. She meant whiteness is more beautiful, and girls could take more advantage of that in life, more so than boys.

This example brings forth the paradoxical racial position that my family occupies in relation to whiteness. My children and I benefit from our whiteness adjacency—that they were seen as extra cute and that with their Gap Kids' animal-graphic clothes, "they have the shopping magazine kids' look that represent global urban cosmopolitanism" (my cousin's words). In the US, they will never be told to "go back to China," unlike many other children whose parents are both Asians. Yet embracing whiteness adjacency without calling out white supremacy is dangerous for my children, as it breeds self-hatred and alienation towards their Chineseness in the long run. The possibility of internalizing such notions as "whiteness features are more beautiful," announced by my unbashful aunt, would be catastrophic to my daughter's sense of self and the health of our relationship. Teaching my children "you are simply multicultural, both American and Chinese" is age appropriate for now. But developing an intersectional, a feminist, and a justice-oriented parenting that teaches, and critiques, white privilege, model minority myths, heteropatriarchy is always in the back of my mind.

One helpful strategy has been to use my autoethnographical notes, like the above, in my own teaching to connect my feminist mothering and feminist pedagogy. My mothering struggles about gender and race are points of theoretical inquiry and/or lived experiences that invite interpretations and critique. My classroom is part of an urban public university's community college campus in Brooklyn, where "mixedness" is the norm. Our discussions usually meander from theories of multicultural identity development to President Obama to Zendaya and then back to me and my children and the student body in the class. My perceptive students comment that "mixed race is smart and cute" is valorized and mythologized in popular media to ensure whiteness' survival in the capitalist economy of multiculturalism. That the "mixed-raced cuteness" is more often than not conditionally granted only when whiteness is part of that mix; and only when that mix inhabits middle-class or upper-class able and fit-looking bodies—that "working-class minority mix" (e.g. Black and Asian, Black and Hispanic, etc.) as acutely described by a student, is "basically our classroom" and "a large demographic group among working immigrants' NYC" that is not part of the mixed cuteness sensation.

Finding Chineseness and facing Asian hate in NYC

After having my privilege checked from such classroom conversations, I return to my home where I try hard to decentre whiteness and centre immigrant Chineseness. I was careful with our choices of food, films we watch, books we read. A couple of months ago, however, my daughter (eight years old) commented that my husband and I liked "cultural food and books," whereas she and her little brother preferred American food like burgers and fries and American stories like Disney ones and superhero movies. This episode of her expressing her perception of the generational cultural gap inside our family was quite revealing and shocking; she thought whiteness American culture is normative, a nonculture, contrasting with everything else. This was a transformation for my daughter, who used to believe that all planes and trains go to China, and the heroines of her stories were named "Guoguo" and "Chock," not "Daisy" and "Sarah." The pandemic has disrupted our family's yearly travel and transnational lifestyle and has caused our children's identity development to be sheltered in place. Building her sense of connection and belonging with local Chinese immigrant communities became a priority for us.

In a recent family tree project, she drew a tree of our faces and the Statue of Liberty and my hometown Fortune Pagoda in the background, signifying two cultures. I wanted to encourage her to look beyond the binary of our origin and settlement, beyond the nation-centred emblems and look for something local in the Chinese diaspora to represent us as immigrants and overseas Chinese. So I probed: "There is Chinese stuff here in New York that you visit all the time, too, right? You don't want to add something you see from Chinatown every week? That's your Chinese community here." She replied: "But we are not from Chinatown, mama. We only go food shopping there. It smells bad and is so crowded, and people don't speak English!"

I was speechless. I could not believe that was my own child speaking. I thought she and I shared the same feelings about Chinatown: the familiar sights, smells, and sounds. Even the chaos and crowdedness are so familiar, therapeutic, and energizing. Chinatown feels like home for a new immigrant like me. But she, on the contrary, was problematically conscious and protective of her middle-class Chineseness and language privilege. Angered, I lectured her about our immigrant roots, the hardships of immigrants' lives—mine included—about language and citizenship, about overcrowdedness and gentrification in Chinatown, and about the lack of environmental justice regarding having enough trash cans on the streets. She stared at me with a blank look and said: "Okay. But you know sometimes you talk too much, and I don't understand a thing." I forgot that she was eight years old and that I needed to give her time. "Just think, Gonggong and Popo [my parents] would like to rent and live there for a few months next year [it didn't happen due to the pandemic] because that's the only place they can get around by themselves in New York. Would you still say the same thing about Chinatown then?" She gasped, looking thoughtful.

After the incident, I reflected and realized that her feelings were in fact my failures of not making meaningful local connections between our family and local Chinese immigrant communities—communities that both host my belonging as diaspora and nurture my values as a feminist. There are so many different versions of diasporic Chineseness in New York City that complicate our journey of identification. As a global nomad who relocated constantly in the past two decades, my closest circle of friends has always been women of colour feminist academics, who are now scattered all around the world. Many of them stayed childless and could not relate with my mothering experiences. I talk to and do research with Chinatown mothers regularly, but none of them married interracially, nor do I live close enough to participate in their social events. I have only one Chinese colleague mom friend at my entire college. But her kids are college age, and our parenting struggles are different. From the extensive social experiences that I've had through my daughter's school and extracurricular activities, I also do not identify with, and frankly detest and flee from, the "crazy rich Asians" moms who clear out luxury stores buying their toddlers designer clothes. I also friended and then unfriended a few middle-class Chinese immigrant moms at my daughter's school after hearing their anti-Black and transphobia chats during the Black Lives Matter movement around the country. I then connected with a few professional immigrant Chinese moms in my area, only to get triggered and scared away by their anxiety-laden "Tiger Mom" (Chua) culture of overscheduling and ardent Ivy-League obsessions. It is hard for me to find a local Chinese mom community where I belong, no wonder my daughter's sense of Chineseness is limited to the abstractions of her memories of visiting China and my family.

Lacking a core local mom community where I can find my diasporic and intellectual belonging results in a lack of socialization, which produces coping wisdom for challenging situations. Allow me to share a vignette of such:

December 2018. Bryant Park's Christmas market. My daughter and I were wandering around the market with hot cocoa in our hands. She was attracted to a crystal Christmas ornament shop where sparkly animal crystals were displayed with beautiful Christmas décor. I was worried that my daughter's excited small hands would break the ornaments easily or she could spill her cocoa all over the decorations. "Only look. No Touch, okay?" I said it first in Mandarin and then in English. The shopkeeper, a white woman in her sixties with an Eastern European accent, looked at me and my daughter with a sarcastic, unfriendly look. "You Oriental people only look, and touch, and never buy, right?" she asked. Shocked, I responded: "It's not nice to use that term." She was aggravated, and my daughter was confused. She stood up from her chair and challenged me aggressively: "What? What term? You are not Oriental people? What are you? Chinese? Korean?" I paused a second to gather my thoughts, wanting to make it a textbook moment for my daughter to learn how to fiercely denounce racism in public. But I could not find any words, and instead I grabbed my daughter's hand and fled. On the subway ride back home, I tried to tell her what is colonialism and why the word "Oriental" should not be used. She was completely confused. "Who are colonial powers? Who told stories that we were not ordinary and mysterious? Why?" I kept preaching my college lectures at her, and she kept getting lost. I felt like I always overdid it. And I was so disappointed in myself for not giving a more powerful response at that moment, which demonstrated feminist fierceness and pride. I wish I had a group of Chinese or Asian moms with younger kids who think and feel like me so we could discuss. I had none then. I had to do this alone with my husband. We revisited the topic several times at home; each time I experienced mild trauma, which my husband understood but could not relate to.

About a year later, my daughter one day aptly pointed out that world maps in English and in Chinese "have a different East"—that a country likes to centre itself on a map. It felt like a small parenting victory. I was of course overjoyed but also sad that I alone had to bear the weight of teaching antiracism, to pay the emotional cost, to take on this invisible labour and that I didn't have anyone else to relate to.

Then the pandemic hit. News stories of rising Asian hate crimes around the city and the country circulated in the air along with ubiquitous soundbites of President Trump's anti-China speeches. I then had social media groups of Asian feminist moms that were my go to for life challenges. With the groups' collective wisdom, I sheltered my daughter from hearing about the tragedies of Asian men and women being hit, pushed off subway platforms, stabbed, and set on fire around our city. "We need to practise Asian pride and joy for our children," my feminist Asian American mom friends said, so did my husband. But after we decorated our front yard with red lanterns for the Lunar New Year 2020, we found dog poop in the yard. I lost sleep worrying about everything and did not feel well, not to mention the additional mothering work, postpartum issues, and lack of sleep quarantined with my then eighteen-month-old son.

It was then I learned that my second-grade daughter was on her way to become her own active agent of feminism. I realized that feminist mothering is not and should not be unidirectional—that I should let go of my own burden of trying to figure everything out for her all the time, as if she were just a passive recipient (which my constant college lectures suggested). Feminist mothering could be an interactive journey of me learning from our children, granting them the space and trust to let them practise their own wisdom and power, and subsequently drawing wisdom to empower myself. Here a vignette of my daughter's response to racism she experienced at school:

March 2020. One week before the shutdown, my daughter's teacher called me on the phone. A classmate had mocked her during lunch, saying: "Stinky cheese, you are Chinese!" The teacher told me my daughter had cried and reported the classmate to the lunch monitor. The teacher apologized to me again and again, assuring me that the school took the issue seriously and had already summoned the classmate's parents for a talk.

I was furious, tense, and worried sick all day. I picked my daughter up early from school and was surprised to find her in a great mood. When I asked her what had happened and how she was feeling, she gave me a long-winded account of the full event in a matter-of-fact happy tone, with details of lunch-table seating arrangements, everyone's reactions, the lunch monitor's response, teacher's responses, the classmate's apology, etc.

"And you are fine now? You're not sad anymore?" I asked her.

"Yeah! I was sad and angry at first, and I'm glad that everyone was on my side when I spoke up for myself! But you know, mama, J [the classmate who made the comment] was also the one who told me happy China Day when I did my presentation on Lunar New Year last month. I think he was interested in our culture and wanted my attention, or maybe he's jealous that I'm Chinese and can speak Chinese. Like you said, a person learns to say those things from hearing others talk. I'm glad I stopped that."

She always talks beyond her years, but I was proud she separated the individual from the discourse and gave her analysis.

"It sounds like you know what to do if it happens again," I said.

"Oh. I'm just going to walk away next time. That stuff cost me all my recess time."

That day, I learned from my daughter to speak up against racism and to not overextend my time and emotional labour. I learned from her that we should take on social justice work but not to be overburdened by it at the expense of our self-preservation. I also learned that feminist mothering includes putting down my own sense of authority, intellectual superiority, and letting her generate her own knowledge and power.

A Feminist Migrant Mom Must Relearn Her Mother Tongue

In this next section, I reflect on another important aspect of my mothering—the linguistic struggles in my intercultural feminist mothering endeavours.

As an immigrant mom, I always aspired for my children to be completely bilingual. But as a working professional with a non-Chinese speaking husband at home, our children's immersive Mandarin experience was limited to their trips to China. (My son only went once.) Not getting enough exposure and practice, my daughter can speak little but understands it all when I speak. In my understanding, her Chineseness and intelligence are not dependent on her Chinese language proficiency. Yet my extended family in China disagree. As her mother, a feminist mom who is known to speak well, I often find myself tongue-tied and speechless, unable to voice my feminist values for my children and myself. Here is another vignette:

February 2019, Lunar New Year. Twenty-four extended family members from my father's side gathered at my parents' house to celebrate the New Year. While playing together, my cousin's nine-year-old son asked my then six-year-old daughter a series of questions about her Lego sets she was sharing. My daughter stared at him uneasily, not understanding the technical terms he was using about Legos and could not respond. After a couple of questions, the boy asked the room: "Is she dumb or something?! She's quiet, like an idiot." My aunt, who is the grandma of the nine-year-old, indirectly affirmed the sentiment instead of disciplining her grandson for being rude and said to me: "You need to really work on her Chinese. We know a kid who was diagnosed with child depression due to language deficiency. He moved to our town not knowing the local dialect and couldn't fit in."

I was completely furious but completely speechless. Same silent rage happened to me often when these relatives commented on my children's shapes of noses and eyes. My Western-educated feminist consciousness called on me to speak up and to legitimize my daughter's humanness and Chineseness. Yet I felt paralyzed most of the time, especially when those comments or treatment came from elders or the young, which they usually did. Growing up as a girl in a collective society following middle-class Confucian familial codes, where seniority and social hierarchy mattered a great deal, I was taught to always respect elders, to care for the young, to always avoid conflicts, and to save face for others in public spaces.

The notion of speaking up is also loaded with a Western ideology of individualism and a certain assumed discursive infrastructure already in place—that one is always-already an autonomous being with a right to speak and that one's speaking is legible to the ears that hear. To speak up for my daughter would not only risk my effort to sustain my diasporic ties with my family in China but also jeopardize my parents' social relations in my hometown. I also worried that even if I spoke, I would not likely be heard correctly, that it may lead to my aunties' further misinterpretation that I no longer love them, and that I'm American now and better than them. They already told me that I laugh like an American and that I smell like a foreigner. To simply speak up is not empowering but damaging in my own emotional construct as a returning migrant whose belonging and Chineseness were put to question due to my daughter's lack of Chinese fluency. It will not lead to my liberation or empowerment, only a deeper cultural divide in a torn self with an even more precarious sense of home.

I also had to reconsider my Yunnanese in the sense that patriarchal expressions and jokes slipped through my tongue if I did not pay attention. Yunnanese is the heartbeat of my soul, but it is also a language loaded with problematic gender stereotypes and the toxicity of some aspects of my parents' parenting that caused me trauma. For example, when my daughter was four years old, she was trying on hairclips one day, and I said "哎哟，没看出啦你还挺爱臭美" ("Okay, I didn't know you are so narcissistically into stinky beauty!") This is typically said in a shaming tone in my hometown culture. Or I once told my toddler son: "小男子汉有什么好哭的?!" ("What would even be worth your crying, little man?!") I would never have said those things if I had been speaking in English to them. Shocked at my own words at moments like those, I immediately switched to English: "I'm so sorry, baby. Mama is sorry. I shouldn't have said that." English is the language of my work and reason, of my learned feminist consciousness from American colleges, and of the psychologists-written baby talk from *Daniel Tiger's Neighborhood* I learned in my thirties. I had to constantly translate, pause, rethink, and make up new ways to transport my English feminist consciousness over to my Chinese mothering self.

Making My Children Aware of Global Inequality

Making global inequalities legible to my children has always been an important task for my feminist mothering because seeing and experiencing some of those inequalities during my own transnational and intercultural journey were reasons why I became a feminist in the first place. To make visible the incredible first-world privilege we carry, I tried to share with my daughter stories of my own upbringing with little material wealth and that of our current Chinese relatives, especially those who live in rural areas who struggle on a scale unimaginable for Western middle-class families due to economic challenges, physical disabilities, or lack of medical support and education. Those stories sometimes, but not always, registered with her. We have travelled to the villages, and to my surprise, she said "It's more fun than Disney World." Our distant aunties chaperoned us to feed the free roaming chickens and cattle on the road, showing us pigs living with people in the back of their house, and letting us watch a donkey give birth. The whole village came to see her, the American guest, with their best treats. "She's treated like a princess here," I told my husband. "I hope she grows up understanding her privilege and is not going to be blinded by them," I said.

A turning point happened when she was seven during our visit with my parents in China. One day when watching local news, she was drawn to a story featuring a twelve-year-old girl from the rural area near my parents' town taking care of her paralyzed father singlehandedly since she was ten. As a solution to her tiny body's inability to carry the weight of the father, the girl engineered a simple and effective pulley system at home to help her father get in and out of bed to use the bathroom. This pulley attracted villagers and reporters. According to the news, this girl never went to school. Her mother left when she was a toddler. Her older brother went to school under the support of a distant uncle, and she stayed home and cared for the sick father. The family relied on neighbors' charity and a small government stipend to live. And to support the family, the girl farmed vegetables outside the house and picked bricks at local construction site for money. My daughter was quite taken aback by the story. Her face changed from an expression of curiosity to confusion and then to sadness, with big tears coming out from her eyes. I was not sure which part of it had particularly triggered her sensitivity. "What made you sad?" I asked her. "That her house looked like that." She thought hard and said, "The wall was made of dirt. They don't have any furniture or toys. And her dad looks dead." Before I could say anything, she asked: "Is she a kid or a grownup? Are you sure she's a kid? Maybe she's a grownup but just short?" I confirmed that girl was twelve according to the news. In the following weeks, my daughter kept bringing up the story. She would suddenly pause in the middle of playing with her dolls and ask if the girl in the news really had to help her paralyzed dad to go potty and to wipe and wash him. (She watched me changing her baby brother's diaper daily and rightfully could not imagine a girl doing that to her grown father.) She also asked how much money she could make by picking bricks and how much food it could buy. I was honest in all my responses. The more we talked, the more important questions she started to ask. Why was she the one staying at home doing hard work while the brother who is supposed to be older and stronger went to school? How can people around her not see that the work she does was not right for her—that a girl her age should not help a grown man use the bathroom? And how come the story was only known because of the pulley she made? What if there are girls who just suffered and worked in similar situations without making pulleys?

I did not have answers to all those good questions, but I was happy she asked them. Those questions directly centred issues of gender inequality in education, about the ableist social structure, and media biases in making gendered care labour invisible (e.g., whereas the pulley was sensationalized, the awkward and hard labour of washing her dad's naked body was not mentioned.) It was feminist of her to ask and care about those questions. There is a budding feminist consciousness in her. I also sensed that the story was an important moment where my daughter learned a different kind of global feminism from this Chinese news story, a feminism different from the girl power stories that she is familiar with in her American life—stories from *She Persisted* series of books with women historical figures making a difference, or girl adventure and warrior stories like those of Hermione Granger and Moana. This story was also a girl's persistence story (as it was framed in the reporting), but it is nowhere near the self-actualization stories that are popular in the West. The girl was almost nameless, and her suffering was normalized and glorified. To be a feminist, one needs to not merely be inspired by the young heroine but to develop a much more critical engagement with her story that involves questioning, investigating, contextualizing, and critiquing the culture and the circumstances that legitimize her suffering.

From then on, I noticed that both my daughter and I have become more conscious in noticing issues of gender and labour on the streets, both in the US and China. My daughter developed an interest to collect stories from her own life about children working on site with their moms, from our Didi (the Chinese version of Uber) woman driver who worked all day with her three-year-old son in her front seat, to the Guatemalan cleaning lady employed by our New York neighbour, who works with her young daughter at her side as a helper and translator. Hopefully, these early experiences of noticing and inquiring, of unpacking complexity, and of building connections will help my daughter and eventually my son (whose current triumph is getting potty trained) develop a global consciousness of gender equality as well as of the different paths, not stages, that different feminisms take.

Final Thoughts

By highlighting some flashpoints of mothering my transnational biracial family, I explore the messiness of my intersectional feminist mothering that prioritizes gender and racial justice as well as global awareness. When I was first pregnant with my daughter, I had a rough draft of a feminist mothering design in my mind, as if it were a school project that included a thesis and strategies which would carry out my feminist ideals I learned from books (e.g., gender neutral clothing and naming choices). I quickly learned to abandon that design during my postpartum struggles of depression, exhaustion, and loneliness, realizing that mothering, especially feminist mothering, is an exploratory journey and that every woman may have her own version.

In this chapter, I have shown how I orient my thinking and practice towards intersectional feminism, in which concerns about race, class, nation, ability, and colonialism are equally prioritized with that of gender and sexuality. I am a feminist mother holding a unique social position; my intersections as an immigrant and transnational Chinese academic mom have brought me distinctive challenges as well as unique resources, privileges, and opportunities. I delineate my feminist mothering journey by reflecting on my own personal transnational history, histories of women in my family, my journey struggling with neoliberal university's work-life culture, as well as my long process of negotiating identity and finding belonging for my biracial children in the pandemic culture of Asian hate. I also explore issues of translating feminism into the discursive infrastructures of different languages and my effort to raise my daughter's awareness of global disparity in gender equality. One important lesson of my journey is that feminist mothering works best when I am mothering with my children and not to my children. My feminist mothering works best when it is invitational, dynamic, and not unidirectional. As a feminist mother, I am always on the journey of becoming.

Works Cited

Amsler, Sarah, and Sara Motta. "The Marketized University and the Politics of Motherhood. *Gender and Education*, vol. 31, no. 1, 2017, pp. 1-18.

Chua, Amy. *Battle Hymn of the Tiger Mother*. Penguin Press, 2011.

Jhally, Sut, and Stuart Hall. *Race: The Floating Signifier.* Media Education Foundation, 1996.

Lorde, Audre. *Sister Outsider: Essays and Speeches.* Crossing Press, 1984

Lorde, Audre. *I Am Your Sister: Collected and Unpublished Writings.* Oxford University Press, 2009.

Shahjahan, Riyad. "Being 'Lazy' and Slowing Down: Toward Decolonising Time, Our Body and Pedagogy." *Educational Philosophy and Theory,* vol. 47, no. 5, 2015, pp. 488-501.

Wang, Zheng. "A Special Interview with Prof. Zheng Wang on International Women's Day." *University of Michigan News,* 6 Mar. 2017, https://news.umich.edu/zh-hans/%E5%9B%BD%E9%99%85%E4%B8%89%E5%85%AB%E5%A6%87%E5%A5%B3%E8%8A%82%E7%8E%8B%E6%94%BF%E6%95%99%E6%8E%88%E4%B8%93%E8%AE%BF/ Accessed 1 Apr. 2023.

Chapter 10.

Coming Home to Myself: On Single Black Motherhood

Kahaema Byer

Other mothers, unlike their White counterparts had to try and make a home in the midst of a racist world that had already sealed our fate, an unequal world waiting to tell us we were inferior, not smart enough, unworthy of love. Against this backdrop where blackness was not loved, our mothers had the task of making a home.
—hooks, *Salvation: Black People and Love* 35

"They will have dark, buttery skin like mine!"
"But of course!" He was surprised that I didn't retort.
"And they will have almond eyes like mine." I added.
"No, they will have irresistible eyes like mine...Whatever, fine. Your eyes are fine!"
"Thank you!" I grinned.

Playfully envisioning what our offspring might look like, my daughter's father and I mixed in our internalized racism, colonial histories, and our longings for freedom to be confidently Black. We were drawn to each other because we found a home place of belonging in each other. As returning Black Caribbean nationals who spent time in predominantly white ivory towers, we had a shared identity and language. We were immigrants who reached for big dreams with limited financial resources and who struggled as a result. Together, racism, finances, and our immigrant status made our journeys uniquely challenging.

My daughter's father and I both knew the hardship of racism that intersected with class. He achieved his dream while suffering loss and enduring the dynamics of being a Black man at an elite university. As a woman, gender-based violence struck my world, and I abandoned my dreams for safety. Becoming mommy to a little girl was both the best and scariest thing to happen to me. Her dad's illness of thought that manifested in forms of violence and control led to us parting during the first trimester. I faced pregnancy alone.

This chapter begins with a personal narrative of my pregnancy, birthing, and postpartum experience, which crucially set the stage for understanding my social location as a Black single mother navigating a landscape dominated by racialized patriarchy, and ultimately my feminist homecoming. Through lived experience, I focus on themes of violence against mothers by women, the socialization and policing of mothers into silence and passiveness, and the potential of single mothers to destabilize patriarchy. The various stories throughout this section illustrate the ways in which patriarchy disrupts the fabric that binds women together in community.

Next, I introduce the intersectional themes of race and mothering by way of social media, which served as an important catalyst in integrating my mothering with Black feminism. Using my experiences as a backdrop, I highlight how the momosphere—online communities of mothers is based predominantly in the privatized, white patriarchal institution of motherhood with little room for intersectionality. In the final section entitled, I describe my own matricentric feminist praxis as a single Black mother in relation to whiteness.

Understanding the Single Mother Location through the Lens of Maternal Health

I was already performing motherhood as I adhered methodically to what Jane Ussher describes as "rigorous body management" (286) during pregnancy, a marker of the so-called good mother. My weekly routine included running several miles and swimming in the ocean or a pool. Then, out of the blue, complications began, and I was cycling in and out of hospital, and exercise took a backseat among my priorities.

Violence against Women (and Mothers) by Women (and Mothers) in Maternal Health

The abuse in the public health system was endless. Nurses (women) yelled and swore at me, scolded me for asking questions, shoved me, touched parts of my body without warning or permission, and more. Maternity patients shared a floor, separated by open sections, each with about twelve beds. In general, the assumption was that all patients who were opting to deliver at the public hospital were poor, uneducated, and pregnant (again) due to bad choices. This was particularly so if unaccompanied by a male partner. Although a majority of providers in maternal care are women, they fiercely uphold the patriarchy as though it were their own, resulting in diverse forms of violence against other women. This behaviour is especially reserved for women who are viewed as vulnerable in imperialist, white supremacist, capitalist, patriarchal society (hooks, "Writing beyond Race"). Like an initiation into what lay ahead, patriarchal motherhood formed the backdrop of obstetrics.

Although feminism was not a prominent part of my consciousness at the time, it grew increasingly important to me that I assert myself. I was becoming a mother to a Black child and passiveness would no longer suffice. I had noticed how otherwise verbally expressive and seemingly confident Black women became helpless and deferential in the presence of medical experts. I overheard the conversations in which women angrily protested decisions about their care and how they were mistreated and misunderstood. Yet rarely would they express to providers how they felt. They were afraid.

The scenarios that follow give some insight into the culture of violence in maternal health. I was admitted to the hospital for complications again at around six months. I had just returned from doing additional tests that night and my pillow was gone. The other ten or so patients watched as I struggled to lie down on an already uncomfortable hospital bed. I complained and looked around for support, but their eyes were averted. "Where's my pillow?" "Who took my pillow?" I asked. I had learned by this time that I had to speak up for myself and conceal weakness. After an unsuccessful search, I attempted to ask a few nurses about the pillow, each of whom walked past me without saying a word. Switching strategy, I announced my plan to go to the nurses' station to make a request. One patient warned, "You sure you want to do that?" The rest, otherwise chatty, watched in silence.

I persisted for some time in calling out to the nurses who were engaged in casual conversation. Based on the exchange of glances between them, I assumed they had heard and had chosen to ignore me. Eventually a nurse responded: "You think this is the Hilton!? Honey, if you have no pillow, that's your problem!" She subsequently turned to the group and commented briefly. They collectively laughed and continued their chatting where they had left off.

I returned to my bed, and about an hour later, another nurse brought a pillow, but it came with consequences. First, a bit of verbal abuse. She then proceeded to check my vital signs, shoving and squeezing me as she did so. Providers had mastered the use of routine procedures to assert power. Their behaviour reveals how they assert domination over mothers in their most vulnerable state. Intersectional identities, such as those occupied by single (Black) mothers, exacerbate patriarchal violence towards this group.

It was not just the nurses or some doctors. From where I sat in the waiting room earlier in my pregnancy, I observed the phlebotomist working. Patient after patient, she drew blood without consistently changing her gloves. It was finally my turn. She was writing in her book and rarely made eye contact when giving instructions. "Sit there, and pull up your shirt," she instructed. I waited, hoping she would remove her gloves from the last patient, but she did not. I had been practising a humble tone in my head. As she reached for the vials, I said gingerly, "Just a little reminder to please change your gloves." She grew angry and a lecture followed about her importance at the hospital. However, she did change her gloves, which was good enough.

These experiences are common in obstetrics at local public hospitals. Perhaps providers acted this way because they feared their authority being threatened in a resource-strained environment with the socioeconomically vulnerable. Whatever their motivation, their behaviour worked to create a culture of silence as women entered motherhood. Paulo Freire shows how the oppressed become "sub-oppressors," as they identify the oppressor as their "model of humanity" (45). This vulnerable time in a mother's journey is an opportunity for the power of women to be subverted by other women through the mores of patriarchal motherhood.

The Stripping of Agency: Socialization and Policing of Mothers into Passiveness and Silence

In her reflection on obstetric violence, Nicole Hill describes how her interactions with the hospital staff led to her feeling that her "agency was increasingly unwelcome" (241). In my case, exercising agency was followed by punishment. I thought about what could explain their behaviour. What could be so difficult for these women? Were their actions a result of burnout? Were they a consequence of how they themselves were treated as women and mothers? Did they have such horrible experiences that they resented me for my entitlement? Or was it "the cruelty and harshness that Black women reserve for one another [which] is a piece of the legacy of hate with which we were inoculated" (Lorde, 159). Perhaps it was all of these.

The violence continued through the birthing process until my daughter finally arrived. I had a hunch that something was wrong, but as usual, no one listened. For the healthcare providers, it was as if becoming a mother had stripped me of my sensibilities, including my training in child development and paediatric health. What did I know? The prevailing perception appears to be that mothers are emotionally charged caregivers who are unable to make logical decisions about our own bodies and the wellbeing of our children. Such perceptions warrant interrogation through a matricentric feminist lens. Andrea O'Reilly writes that the patriarchal ideology of motherhood "requires the repression or denial of the mother's own selfhood" (177). A part of that selfhood is the mother's agency.

The day after giving birth, my daughter and I were discharged. By that first night, we both had high fevers and had to go to another hospital, where we would spend the subsequent two weeks.

"First time mom? Oh, that's why you're so worried!" The doctors' eyes would widen with condescending excitement during their rounds or consults. Although we were admitted, they still did not believe anything was wrong. I insisted on routine tests. My baby screamed constantly, and sure enough, hospital personnel insisted it was my fault: inadequate feeding, inexperience, etc. During their rounds, the doctors giggled at my perceived ignorance and anxiety when I described my daughter's pain. "Children cry, scream, kick, and arch. That's normal!" they would say.

My daughter protested. Attempts to insert an IV into her arm or foot took approximately six doctors. She was born just days before and yet, the doctors held her down as though she were an uncontrollable adult. I could not shake the triggering thoughts of how Black men and boys are treated with excessive force. Although we were in a different hospital from where I had delivered, the violence continued.

I was scolded and critiqued constantly, at least so it seemed. "You don't know what you're doing!" they would say. The nurses seemed to take greater liberties because I was usually alone and dared to ask for appropriate tests to be done and be kept informed of the results, and so on. In response to my attempts at agency, they withheld food from me, turned off the lights abruptly, refused to provide water for me to warm my milk, and more. What would happen if the tables of power turned? I wondered. In my state of powerlessness, the thought of having power over them was appealing. Perhaps it was this sort of cycle that maintained this violence.

In patriarchal motherhood, women as mothers are ideally devoted, selfless, "sweet" beings who relinquish their autonomy (Douglas and Michaels). According to O' Reilly, a theory of feminist mothering "begins with the recognition that a mother must live her life and practice mothering from a position of agency, authority, authenticity, and autonomy" (178). It is a mothering that is founded on respect for the whole woman—not a disjointed, compartmentalized self.

The Power of Single Mothers to Destabilize the Patriarchy

In this section, I reference my personal experience to primarily highlight the experience of single mothers within patriarchal motherhood and the power of single mothers to destabilize the patriarchy.

I have advocated for others for most of my adult life, but I was really struggling at this point and felt I needed help. I wanted to ask questions and advocate for us. I found myself wishing that I had a male partner to passively show up. Within patriarchy, a man need not be informed, invested, or engaged. Ignorant and distant, he will still access his unearned privilege of basic respect. In contrast to my earlier stance, I began to grow silent except in exceptional circumstances.

From all the standing and walking, my stitches unsurprisingly came undone. Although there was a women's hospital adjacent to where we were, they could not care for my wound due to policy. I would stay up all night, then leave my breastfeeding baby in the care of nurses I did not trust to go to the next hospital, which was twenty minutes away by car without traffic. How would they respond to her irritability (pain) in my absence? Would they leave her to cry? Friends could not disrupt their mornings to assist, so I took a taxi to the next hospital and waited in line. I tried sharing my story, to explain that I needed to get back to my baby. "We all have to get back to our babies," someone said. It was true. Everyone who was there had recently delivered. I tried explaining my situation to the nurses, but they replied "You're not special. You need to wait your turn." That could be anywhere from half an hour to four hours. I cried a lot.

Alas, the tests confirmed that my daughter was in significant, unrelenting pain due to a primary diagnosis and a comorbid condition that would be diagnosed post-discharge. We were finally discharged with medication, but she still suffered a great deal. I paced the living room throughout the night for months. I then discovered that the television distracted her, so I broke the rules and let her watch while I held her in a position that minimized her discomfort. I was riddled with guilt every time I broke another expert rule in a desperate attempt to cope. The gaping absence of an intersectional framework for these rules keeps some mothers out of the "good parenting" club by discrediting their efforts and reinforcing a sense of disempowerment. Feminist mothers interrogate expert rules and recognize how they can work in tandem with the oppressive construct of good mothering if diversity is not considered. For and by whom were the rules written? Generally, the rules neglect to integrate the nuances of the social context that impact many single women of colour who are mothers. A critical intersectional approach would have significant implications for research in family and child development and for researchers themselves who need to confront the bias that informs their work.

Associates from my personal and professional life wanted to see the baby, which allowed me the occasional break. I would hurriedly shower, run to the grocery, and cut up ingredients for the slow cooker. Half-jokingly, I would barter "Sure, come see the baby but bring food." Some verbalized their irritation about my request. One woman brought leftover food from the day before. It had a pungent smell, and I had to discard it, but she did get a chance to play with the baby. In the face of a pattern of exclusion by white mothers and white maternal health providers, it was two white women who regularly checked in and came by to lend a hand. They did not know each other but I later realized that they were both about twenty-five years my senior, had experiences of single mothering, and were deeply committed to feminist values. "How can I help?" each would ask. I felt supported. They understood the context of mothering. In patriarchal motherhood, isolation increases, and mothers are expected to do it all alone. In feminist mothering, there is support and community.

We finally found a specialist who required weekly visits but would leave us for hours past our appointment time and attend to us for no more than ten minutes. During those longer waits, I paced the waiting room and cried quietly. I was worried that my daughter never stopped crying. She was sleep deprived, and that could not be good. Again, I imagined how different my experience would be if a man were present. I would not be left waiting indefinitely. I feared expressing my dissatisfaction because it might have implications later on, so I would enter the office, angry as ever, and force a smile. The specialist would ask a few questions, undress my daughter like it was a race, touch her belly, and then send us on our way with another bill and an expensive task. I could barely afford the diet he prescribed, let alone visit the dietitian. Eventually, he discontinued my dietary restrictions and prescribed milk, which lasted three days at a cost of a whopping $250TTD ($64 CAD) a can. Additionally, it could not be sourced locally, and whenever my supply finished, I had to drive well over an hour to the distributor that imported it. At the time, I thought that I had no choice. I later learned that providers will often have financial arrangements with companies, which informs local treatment recommendations.

Luckily, I had a good counselling job, but I wondered how other single mothers would afford this. Soon, the benefits of my job ran out. Two months into maternity leave, I received a phone call. Because I had delivered earlier than my estimated due date, I was apparently in breach of contract and was asked to return the income received. My maternity leave was rescinded. My eyes welled up as I spoke face to face with the human resources personnel who initiated the process. "The same thing happened to me with my last baby," she replied. She had not suffered income loss due to the terms of her position. I had no other source of income. Patriarchal motherhood began with a bang.

I was hoping for a break, but daycare was merely an extension of the violence that was located in the healthcare system. I distinctly recall completing a long admission process, which included an interview. What could be under review for a baby who was just a few months old? I got dressed up and attended the interview with a white male associate who had a powerful and well-known family name. I told him that I needed to "borrow his privilege." We were accepted, but his presence did not lead to any more benefits. Frustrated by my daughter's health challenges, a new round of abuse began—this time in my absence and perpetrated in the daycare facility. When attempts to rectify the issue did not work, I removed her at significant financial expense.

Once again, being a single mother, I was subject to aggression. I felt shame for using strategies that were based in a privilege that other single mothers did not have. I feared being perceived as aggressive, and I felt ashamed that as someone who worked with trauma, I was struggling to speak up. Talia Esnard describes the "pathologization of matrifocality that imposes functional, heteronormative, Eurocentric notions of the family" (239) in the Caribbean. Superimposed on (or emerging from) a colonial, racist history, it is no wonder that as a Black single mother, I was not respected.

Although single motherhood in some ways seems far from a male centredness, single mothers arguably do the closest dance with patriarchy. Through our daily interactions as women and mothers, we are reminded that without a man's presence, we are entitled to no respect. Curious about the impacts of Black single motherhood across class, I asked a friend who is also a Black single mother and a managing partner in corporate America whether racism affected her parenting. She confirmed it did and described it as "extremely difficult" and "very frustrating." Mothers are oppressed under patriarchy as both women and mothers (O'Reilly). As women unpartnered by its key actors, single mothers face another layer of that oppression that creates unique barriers and harms. Lack of time and resources result in single mothers spending way more energy in the mom space, like it or not. Yet, the same time-starvation prevents single mothers from ever competing for the good mother position as constructed by intensive mothering. It seems like a lose-lose battle, resulting in a profound sense of inadequacy that is reinforced by patriarchal narratives about single mothers. However, single mothers are simultaneously powerful and pose significant threats to the patriarchy. As hooks writes, "The quality of care of Black single mothers makes this group worthy guides of anyone examining the impact of a love ethic in Black life" ("Salvation" 118).

Yet the contribution of single mothers is silenced, and this group is rewritten with specific negative stereotypes: "When Black single mothers raise children who become healthy, self-loving, productive citizens, no one calls attention to the strategies they have used to create a positive family life that stands as a complement or alternative to the patriarchal model" (hooks, "Salvation" 119). Additionally, single mothers are strategically positioned to construct "feminist motherlines" (Green)—that is, to convey enduring counternarratives across generations that contrast with the patriarchal institution of motherhood. As these counternarratives thicken through representation of multiple, intersectional storylines, they move from the fringes and provide new ways of mothering that are grounded in feminist discourse. Why make such effort to discredit and silence the contributions of single mothers? It must be because this group has remarkable power to destabilize the patriarchy.

An intersectional matricentric feminist discourse calls for moving single mothers from the margins to the centre. It goes without saying that single mothers face unique oppressions as a function of social location. However, the single mother experience can also be thought of as an unadulterated version of the experience of all mothers. Her story is that of all mothers when the superficial benefits of other mothers' relationships with men are removed. Single mothers can advance feminist movement and scholarship against patriarchal motherhood but doing so demands that all mothers see themselves as connected to this group; it calls for collective resistance to the dehumanizing and disempowering patriarchal narratives about this group.

My healthcare ordeals provided much needed context for the terrain ahead. I understood my social location as a single mother as another layer of my identity within an imperialist, white supremacist capitalist, patriarchal context. As a result, I began to craft my mothering practice strategically to facilitate my empowerment.

Shaping Matricentric Feminist Praxis through Race Relations in Online Mothering Communities

I turn to the momosphere to illustrate some dynamics of race and motherhood, which ultimately became the catalyst for my feminist homecoming.

I started to feel like I was getting the hang of this motherhood thing. I had found a routine that worked and managed to integrate my then core parenting values while taking care of myself. As I listened to the frustrations of married mothers who appeared to have extensive support systems, it dawned on me that as a single mother, I was doing quite well. In a search for community and an opportunity to share or perhaps gain legitimacy, I decided to start a platform on social media. Focusing on Black mothers, I sought to promote maternal self-care as a precursor to child wellbeing. I did not explicitly use terms like "racism" and "sexism"; rather, I theorized that these sources of stress affected the wellbeing and parenting of mothers.

In her article "Enacting Motherhood Online," Charity Gibson suggests that "women of colour are reticent to conform to White motherhood mandates" (4). While my experience online was that Black women indeed have communities that centre comparative aspects of motherhood, what I was doing did not align, and Black mothers were not interested. Predominantly Black spaces for mothers (that I found at the time) were complex—empowering in some ways and steeped in patriarchy and neoliberalism in others. I was doing what I had learned in my training in psychology and human development, and that was akin specifically to white motherhood. Racial bias and the colonial underpinnings of psychology and human development should be noted. Before I knew it, I was quickly absorbed by a community of white mothers with similar interests.

Initially oblivious, I thought it was a good fit. I got into discussions about gentle parenting and attachment. I affirmed the approaches of other mothers, and they did mine. There were mompreneurs, mom coaches, mom wellbeing experts, sleep experts, attachment specialists, and more. The albeit contrived community was a better match for me than the harsh parenting and shaming that is predominant here in the Caribbean. bell hooks devotes an entire section of her book *Salvation: Black People and Love* to the effects of shaming and humiliating Black children. Even before my daughter was born, I had disavowed that.

It had never occurred to me that I had been absorbed into the new momism: an online patriarchal motherhood that had no space for my Black identity. It was not long before I realized that the group subscribed to excessive rules and had unrealistic expectations of themselves, which paradoxically worked to exacerbate their stress. Then, as white women sometimes do in their interactions with Black women on and offline, intellectual property theft began. Claiming intellectual property online is tricky. Soon after I had shared my thoughts in print, they would appear on the platforms of my online mom friends—without crediting me. I was new and trying to gain traction online. They had larger platforms, which meant my material easily became theirs and earned them their desired gains. I debated what to do. Should I assert myself and run the risk of alienating these women with whom I had grown fond and with whom I had developed relationships including outside of social media? Or should I stay silent, withholding my authenticity and continuing with the status quo? Back in North American academia, I had learned that staying silent is best. Speaking up as a Black woman had dire consequences.

Patricia Hill Collins and bell hooks describe the impact of controlling images on Black women. University-educated Black women often have the sense that we have two options at the university: be aggressive or be silent. I did not want to teach my daughter that to avoid the former, she had to accept the latter. I thought of what mothering meant to me and what it meant to raise a little Black girl. I was certain it did not mean teaching her to silence herself.

Fearing the consequences, I decided to speak up. I centred my identity as a Black woman and addressed how racial inequity was at play in these online dynamics. Because of the relationships we had constructed, I added qualifiers like "loving" my readers and not wanting "to offend" but needing to "speak my truth." Gibson writes that "it is necessary to recognize a racial component at work regarding the ideology of the new momism as the idea of a good mother, who dedicates her life solely to motherhood is a predominantly white mandated expectation" (2) This racial component intensified once it was made explicit. I had been in Zoom and other meetings with some of these women, yet in lieu of merely moving away from me, they used creative means to express their aggression. It was so striking that I wondered if it was organized. Initially, I was confused, but then I realized that mothers of the new momism—which is based in white femininity and patriarchy and to which I had inadvertently subscribed—do not do social or racial justice. Rhetoric like raising kind, thoughtful, or self-aware children had its limits. I was expected to assimilate and, possibly, be grateful for their feigned acceptance. I learned then that good mothers seeking to raise kind children did not mean teaching them to be antiracist, socially conscious, or even self-aware.

I started to make connections between the anxiety underlying maternal ambivalence (and other painstakingly concealed contradictions of the new momism) and racism. It occurred to me that the denial of their own humanity, which resulted from efforts to conceal the unsanctioned realities of an imperfect motherhood, would inevitably be projected onto me as a Black woman who dared to recognize and respect her own. In response, these fellow mothers grew enraged, and effort was made to shame and injure me. Validated by their own racist beliefs, their got a chance to air their internalized anger at me. This motherhood community was based on white supremacy. Self-care, yes, but for white mothers and perhaps those confining to their standards. I no longer belonged. What was I expecting? I never belonged.

Locally, I had felt excluded. Patriarchy continued to rear its head and open its insatiable mouth. Heterocisgender men continued to engage with me as though nothing had changed—inviting me out to late night parties with full knowledge of my pregnancy and then recent birth. My relationship with a few friends with young children was strained by my glaring nonwifehood status. Once the husband topic came up, conversations would abruptly end or become coded as if to say it was off limits, even if they initiated it. Sometimes they were direct: "You're not married so you can't understand." But most of the time, they were not. I am uncertain whether they felt badly for beginning to complain about their darlings to a single mother or whether it was guilt based on the assumption that they had something I desired: a husband. It became exhausting. The other mothers I knew subscribed to shaming and harsh parenting. I did not want that either.

So, I fell in with this group that represented the good or the hegemonic mother, who does what she should according to patriarchy's rules. A hum of guilt tortures me in hindsight. Where did I lose myself? I desired community, but I was largely oblivious to my self-betrayal. Losing a community, though contrived, was hard. Despite my delusions, I felt grief. I also was harmed by their passive aggressiveness. Regardless, I am grateful that their sophistication did not extend so far as to maintain my delusions of belonging.

In the past, I had gotten feedback by psychologists that I was "too radical" to become one myself. Over time, I had learned to hang my

Black feminist head in shame. In some sense, motherhood and rejection by white femininity helped me to find my voice and reunite with this core part of myself. My passion for racial justice reawakened with the intensity that I had had years before. In an article on mommy blogs and representations of motherhood, Kate Orton-Johnson writes that "The digital terrain of motherhood can both liberate and constrain" (2). One thing led to another, and before I had such language as "matricentric feminism" (O'Reilly), I started calling myself a "mother-activist" and asserting that mothers had a key role in the landscape of social justice. I made a pivotal shift.

Maternal Acts of Power

At once, I reconciled with Black feminism and activism and felt whole again. Oblivious to the academic literature, I proposed that motherhood is a social justice mandate, and I began facilitating online dialogues with white women about raising antiracist children. I began my journey towards empowered motherwork (O'Reilly).

Access to Black Bodies and Visibility

The issues of touch and consent as they relate to children's bodies are intricately linked to patriarchal narratives about mothers. When touch in turn intersects with race, the terrain also involves access to Black bodies. The following scenarios (not reported chronologically) focus on the latter, and touch continues to be relevant throughout my motherwork regardless of race.

Two women (one white and the other white passing), the property owner and her friend, showed up unannounced at my new home, where we recently moved. Uninvited, they walked inside while I was still on my couch, gave me unsolicited parenting advice, and commented on how I should decorate. Under the guise of bringing a document, they overdid their stay. On numerous occasions, I articulated that it was time for them to leave and each time, they did not respond.

They departed on their own time, as if to assert that I don't get to end the conversation or request that they leave. My daughter, who was obviously frustrated, had tried multiple strategies to end the visit and regain visibility, since they had not engaged her. She wore her diaper alone but was eager to escort them out. They stopped just outside the patio when one of them commented on my daughter's "cute belly." As she extended her arm to touch my daughter's belly, I leapt out and said, "No, no, no, we have a rule. Ask before touching please." "But she doesn't speak!" the woman contested. "If she wants you to touch her, she will let you know." I politely stated.

They seemed stunned. I was young, a renter, Black, and a single mother. By all counts, I was supposed to be relatively powerless. My thought process was simple: I would not be so presumptuous as to touch your child, so do not touch mine. I am a mother who expects basic respect, and being a Black woman does not disqualify me from that. My daughter indeed replied that she did not want to be touched. The women said goodbye and quietly walked away, probably pondering what had just happened.

I was starting to gain a sense of "empowered mothering" (O' Reilly). For some mothers, setting boundaries over touch is a given. As a Black woman, I am hyperaware that boundary setting is itself a site of empowerment, and, thus, I view it as a political endeavour within my mothering praxis. Setting boundaries represents the capacity to assert myself despite what my social location dictates in relation to white people. As a Black mother, setting boundaries is to exercise the agency to restrict access to a Black body—in this case, my daughter's. My interactions with white women took on patterns similar to the incident described above.

At another encounter in a parking lot with another chatty white woman, my daughter tried an array of distractions after waiting for a long time (over half an hour), including running towards a moving car. Each time, the woman continued chatting as though my daughter's safety or needs did not matter. My daughter was invisible. I would walk away or run to attend to her, and as I attempted to end the unreasonably long monologue, the woman would casually resume. Despite my own social consciousness, I seemed to be in an uncritical autopilot of deference, and I remained engaged far too long.

On one particular occasion, my daughter decided to throw stones at a white woman who also made her wait for a long time and who continued to talk in response to my attempts to end the conversation. My daughter had never done anything like that before. I contemplated. Should I correct her for this behaviour? If I do not, onlookers will perceive me as the dreaded bad mother. The expectation that a toddler would quietly wait for up to an hour was unreasonable. Was this a function of colonialism? A lack of respect for children? Or was it racism? Would she engage in this behaviour with a white mother and child? I further reflected. I want my daughter to know that she is visible and is entitled to take up just as much space as anyone else, but am I setting her up for rejection, aggression, or a sense of entitlement? hooks discusses the many ways that shaming and silencing of Black children take place, including by Black mothers, as we negotiate our own space in white-supremacist societies. Perhaps a certain level of child centredness is necessary to counter the silencing and invisibility of Black children.

For years, Mr. Hart was the only white man in the neighbourhood to speak to us. Still, I had to say something quickly as I noticed him getting closer to my daughter. "Please do not pick her up without asking permission." I yelled as I observed his body language. Shirtless, he leaned over to pick her up while simultaneously asking, "Can I pick you up?" I hurried to get within arm's reach of my child. "Please wait until she says it's okay to pick her up. She will let you know." Stopping, and obviously irritated, he stared briefly at my daughter and without a word, walked back inside his house. I worried both about how she was processing his sudden shift and about the consequences of my assertiveness. Fortunately, Mr. Hart was not so cunning as to find ways to make me a scapegoat in the community. Touch comes up often and at times is a challenge in public and private spaces. My stance is uncommon and perhaps even offputting to others in the moment, but everyone has had to ask her permission at least once. As long as I can help it, she will not be touched without consent—certainly not by a white man.

On another occasion, Mr. Hart called from his living room and asked me to wait a second. He hurriedly walked outside to meet us during our morning walk and then he leaned towards me and stated, "You have the body of a model." Stunned, I replied, "Okay, not sure how to respond to that!" "You should be proud! That's a great thing!" he responded. With a strained smile, I attempted to call my daughter away, but she was just learning to pedal her bicycle. With that, he leaned in close to her, and said, "Hey you want a beer?" "First, even if you're joking, she's a toddler," I said politely, confused that this was coming from him and aware that he and his family owned the neighbourhood. Continuing to push boundaries, he asked, "Maybe mommy wants a beer?" "No, I don't, thank you. And it's morning time!" I said and calmly walked away, paralyzed by the potential repercussions of responding otherwise.

We encountered Mr. Hart often because his home was adjacent to the area where my daughter preferred to play. Mr. Hart was a friendly man who had a gentle, humble, and honest disposition about him. On that day, he took the liberty to violate boundary after boundary with a single Black mother who had respectfully greeted him and his wife for years. White male privilege and internalized racism in the Caribbean combined manifests a confidence among White men that even their sexual advances will not be rejected by nonwhite women.

Mothering is a community effort, but in the absence of a healthy community that protects and respects all children, mothers are expected to be friendly with strangers seeking to approach our children. Persons take all kinds of liberties in these interactions, whereas mothers are expected to abandon boundaries and politely engage. Untimely comments get a pass as does touch. There is a sense that anyone is entitled to access. When mothers veer off script, offense or aggression ensues. Here in Trinidad and Tobago, children are physically and sexually assaulted as part of daily life, often without consequence. Could it be that the same entitlement to touch is what fuels our society's violence towards children?

Recently, a Black man whom I did not know but who was an associate of my friend was being introduced to me and my daughter for the first time. He immediately attempted to pick my daughter up. She jumped back, and I stopped him. He grew angry and verbally aggressive. My friend, a Black woman, was both embarrassed and grateful. She had not previously thought of access to a child's body and was grateful for my perspective. I later asked my friend if the man would do the same with a white person. Her response: "Absolutely not!" This incident underscores the importance of an intersectional analysis in mothering praxis. Although there are shared experiences, they affect mothers differently based on identity.

These maternal acts of power are a work in progress. Over the course of writing, I have critiqued my own values of patriarchal motherhood, including my preoccupations with intensive motherhood and expert theories, which have been particularly draining in the time-starved environment of single motherhood.

Forging Identity in Motherwork

I am keenly aware of my Blackness, my womanhood, and how these intersect with my day-to-day motherwork. Giving up does not run in the women of my family's bloodline. My grandmother passed the year I was born. I recently learned that she worked in a time when women did not work, especially Black women. Saving money from secretarial work at the United States naval base in the Caribbean, she even started a school. Although I do not subscribe to superwoman delusions of total resilience, neither do I abandon concepts of diligence and persistence. When it comes to legacy building and creating new narratives across generations in the face of adversity, a certain Harriet Tubman-like focus is necessary. I am unapologetic about it. My daughter will know that whether you go slow or you go fast, should you desire, you keep going. This is what mothering means to me.

According to hooks, "Most Black folks first experience racist wounding in our own homes when our worth is judged at birth by the color of our skin or by the texture of our hair" ("Salvation" 56). I am intentional about cultivating pride in her dark, beautiful skin. Through these everyday choices, I hope to instill values that will support her as she navigates necessary encounters with the violence of this world. She will be better at it than me and will teach the next generation.

Raising Black children in a racist world is complex. In *Salvation*, hooks also reflects that "Mama's wise parenting could not protect us from the world outside the home, which constantly reminded us that black was not the color to be" (35). Audre Lorde once suggested that Black mothers have two options: kill their children or send them into the white labyrinth. I am not romanticizing my ability to facilitate my daughter's empowerment as a Black person, but I am surely going to try.

It took me a long time to be proud of the middle spaces that I occupy. Here in the Caribbean, I speak of racism, which is largely misunderstood. I have both experienced and held space for Black rage as a function of racism in North America, and I am painfully aware that the fight is a global one.

As a member of the Black Caribbean diaspora, rarely do I see my story. Racism is alive and well and, dare I say, thriving unchallenged in my predominantly African Black (and Indian) country. Trinidad (of Trinidad and Tobago), like the Dominican Republic, struggles with colorism, internalized, subtle interpersonal and structural racism, which is deeply intertwined with class and is also so entrenched that we rarely speak of it. Like a dirty secret, many Caribbean writers will go so far as to minimize or discredit it. Although Collins has laid the foundation to explore Black feminism in a transnational context, the literature has been slow, if not stagnant, to build. However, there are Black mothers worldwide who are fighting the scourge of racism and demonstrating maternal acts of power (O'Reilly). They are in Trinidad and Tobago, Barbados, Haiti, the Dominican Republic, Cuba, Jamaica, Germany, Brazil, Colombia, South Africa, Denmark—all around the world. When I browse online to find communities of women who are resisting white supremacy outside of North America, I usually find small coalitions, some of which disband within a few years. My hope is that our voices and our stories will collectively be amplified to reduce the isolation and bolster our collective strength.

I am a transnational Black feminist scholar and activist with Indigenous ancestry. Becoming a mother brought me home to myself.

Works Cited

Collins, Patricia Hill. *Black Feminist Thought: Knowledge, Consciousness, and the Politics of Empowerment*. Routledge, 2002.

Douglas, Susan, and Michaels, Merideth. *The Mommy Myth: The Idealization of Motherhood and How It Has Undermined All Women*. Free Press, 2004.

Esnard, Talia. "Towards Matricentric Feminism in the Caribbean: Inroads and Opportunities." *Journal of the Motherhood Initiative for Research and Community Involvement*, vol. 10, no. 1-2, 2019, pp. 257-272.

Freire, Paulo. *Pedagogy of the Oppressed*. Continuum, 2005.

Gibson, Charity L. "Enacting Motherhood Online: How Facebook and Mommy Blogs Reinforce White Ideologies of the New Momism." *Feminist Encounters: A Journal of Critical Studies in Culture and Politics*, vol. 3, no. 1-2, 2019, pp. 1-11.

Green, Fiona Joy. "Practicing Matricentric Feminist Mothering." *Journal of the Motherhood Initiative for Research and Community Involvement*, vol. 10, no. 1-2, 2019, pp. 83-99.

Hill, Nicole. "Understanding Obstetric Violence as Violence against

Mothers through the Lens of Matricentric Feminism." *Journal of the Motherhood Initiative for Research and Community Involvement*, vol. 10, no. 1-2, 2019, pp. 233-243.

hooks, bell. *Salvation: Black People and Love*. Harper Perennial, 2001.

hooks, bell. *Writing beyond Race: Living Theory and Practice*. Routledge, 2013.

Lorde, Audre. *Sister Outsider: Essays and Speeches*. Crossing Press, 2007.

O'Reilly, Andrea. *Matricentric Feminism: Theory, Activism, Practice*. Demeter Press, 2021.

Orton-Johnson, Kate. "Mummy Blogs and Representations of Motherhood: 'Bad Mummies' and Their Readers." *Social Media+ Society*, vol. 3, no. 2, 2017, pp. 1-10.

Ussher, Jane M. *Managing the Monstrous Feminine: Regulating the Reproductive Body*. Routledge, 2006.

Chapter 11.

Reflections from a Settler and an Immigrant Mother of Colour: How Motherhood Helped Me Develop My Feminist Politics over the Last Decade

Shruti Raji-Kalyanaraman

Introduction

This chapter explores my journey of realizing my feminist positionality, politics, and their development throughout the last decade. I spatially and temporally reflect on my current social location by critiquing normative motherhood dictates as discussed by Andrea O'Reilly in her book *Matricentric Feminism,* which recognizes mothers and motherwork as a separate social category of inquiry. I specifically argue that any realization of gender disempowerment, for me as a feminist, is incomplete without acknowledging my privileges as a caste privileged and middle-class settler from India. I aim to share through my personal experiences that any understanding of feminism that is lived or theorized must address one's privileges, complicities, and disempowerment. To explain further, I reflect on three distinct experiences that caused me to turn to feminism and examine my social privileges and highlight my gender disempowerment. First, anchoring my research in Haunani-Kay Trask's term "settler of colour" and immigrant hegemony, I reflect on why do I not call myself a settler mother of colour. I aim to contextualize my racialization as an immigrant woman and mother within the broader concepts of colonialism, slavery, and dispossession (Alook; Coulthard; Diverlus et al.; L.B. Simpson, *As We Have Always Done*; L.B. Simpson, *Noopiming*; Wynter). These concepts include historical experiences of mothering intersecting with class, race, ethnicity, religion, gender, ability, and sexuality variables that would deem these experiences unique and multiple. Second, I explore how a master's of philosophy degree in women's studies helped me embrace my caste privilege. On the path to realizing my feminism as a mother, I recognized that my mothering and my motherhood experiences are affected by a combination of my privileges and disadvantages. The intersectional (Nash; Crenshaw) identities arising out of my race, class, and ethnicity also include the social variable of caste, which often gets buried under my dominant identity as a racialized immigrant mother of colour in the land that is now called Canada. In the section below, I highlight my caste privilege by unravelling and detailing my caste privileged, Indian brahmin identity. I draw upon the scholarship of caste-oppressed scholars to explain my caste advantage across transnational borders. Third, I address how turning to feminism helped me make sense of the loss of my first child in India. Within this section, I look at how feminist politics helped me articulate the patriarchal gaze of a society that body shamed me for the loss of my child. Before I proceed, I want to clarify that mothering in my household and in my community is not an individual's labour. Through thought and actions, mothering is constantly influenced by the family, neighbourhood, and community. I am grateful for this reality. Hence, this chapter is not about my interpersonal dynamics with different mothering relations in my life (mother, mother-in-law, brother, father, husband and so on) but how through realizing feminism, I am able to unpack the way in which these relations as actors get co-opted into the vicious system of patriarchy.

Realizing Feminism as an Immigrant Mother through Indigenous-Immigrant Relations

An excerpt from my journal entry July 1, 2021:

It is Canada Day today. In the Canadian benevolent multicultural narrative (Lawrence and Dua), I am called a "newcomer immigrant" and a "woman of colour" (Bannerji), who is privileged to live and work in a place of my choosing. I am a very passable, unnoticeable mother of colour in the broader nation building project of over 150 years. I was in the comfort of my home office, when I first learned about the uncovering of 215 graves of Indigenous children at the Kamloops Indian Residential School, British Columbia. As a mother who has lost a child, I was triggered even as an immigrant parent with a marginal spatial or temporal connection to the Indigenous communities that have existed on this land for thousands of years (Lawrence and Dua). As a maternal activist and through my affiliation with the Aurora Black Community and Association, situated in Aurora, Ontario, I reached out to my community to initiate a vigil. A group of parents, many of them mothers, and community leaders came together to honour the lives of these innocent, young victims of genocide. Kim Wheatley, Ojibwe Anishinaabe Grandmother from Shawanaga First Nations (Wheatley, Kim–CRESTWOOD), led this vigil of over a hundred people with her healing medicines and prayers. All this happened within seventy-two hours of me reaching out to the Aurora Black Community and Association Facebook group. The Indigenous Grandmother emphatically helped us contextualize our settler, immigrant complicity with a simple direction of centring Indigenous knowledges and communities in this prayer. By the end of this month, over a thousand, mostly unmarked, graves were identified in Saskatchewan and Cranbrook, British Columbia. Our community realized we could not help each other grieve. Why? Because we understood that the colonial violence directed to Indigenous communities (Coulthard; Byrd; L. B. Simpson, *As We Have Always Done*) has been historically destructive. This destruction is far more powerful than our community's everyday politics to help protect Black expression and other racialized families in our community.

This entry helped me understand the importance of continuous support and commitment to knowing the history of Indigenous dispossession and genocide in Canada. Responsible understanding of Indigenous-immigrant relations has been an important journey for me to realize my feminism, especially as an immigrant mother. Part of this process is to understand that I, as a settler, am complicit in the nation building project of Canada. The following quote by Haunani Kay-Trask, in the context of Hawaii, directly corresponds to my immigrant complicity and subsequent community initiatives as a maternal activist:

Finally, it must be recalled that history does not begin with the present nor does its terrible legacy disappear with the arrival of a new consciousness. Non-Natives need to examine and re-examine their many and continuing benefits from Hawaiian dispossession. Those benefits do not end when non-Natives begin supporting Hawaiians, just as our dispossession as Natives does not end when we become active nationalists. Equations of Native exploitation and of settler benefit continue. For non-Natives, the question that needs to be answered every day is simply the one posed in the old union song, "which side are you on?" (22)

The first step in contextualizing non-exploitative Indigenous-immigrant relations for me is to not call myself "a settler mother of colour." This heightens my racialization and undermines my complicity as a settler. If I position myself as a settler first and then as a mother of colour, it would centre my experiences as a racialized mother without taking away my complicity as a "preferred" immigrant who immigrated through the popular Canadian Federal Skilled Worker program—an initiative by the government that aims to better serve immigrant settlers who wish to be integrated as working professionals in the colonial fabric of Canada (Corntassel et al.; Lawrence and Dua; Tuck and Yang). State policies and practices that address my immigrant racialization as a mother must not further dispossess and invisibilize Indigenous ways of mothering and their mothering communities.

Finding Feminism to Acknowledge My Caste Privilege: Being a Brahmin Learner in an Indian University

South Asian scholars have discussed caste privilege in certain universities across Turtle Island (Patel et al.; Corntassel et al.). It has been decades since caste reservations and representations were authorized by government bodies in various Indian universities, government positions. This authorization is supposed to include involving caste-oppressed communities in decision-making roles in governing bodies to help them access learning opportunities in higher education institutions for socio-economic mobility. This state-led affirmative action initiative aims to counter centuries of caste oppression (Gidla 67; Umar, "The Identity of Language" 190). However, caste discrimination is still evident in these government spaces, especially in universities ("Remembering Rohith Vemulah"; Tamalpakula). As Sujatha Gidla—a Dalit-identifying (caste-oppressed community) author residing on Turtle Island and belonging to a family in India that understands caste oppression and reforms intimately—explains below, caste oppression in practice is still existent. My brahmin caste privilege is explained by Gidla (8-9) in an emphatic manner below:

> In Indian villages and towns, everyone knows everyone else. Each caste has its own special role and its own place to live. The brahmins (who perform priestly functions), the potters, the blacksmiths, the carpenters, the washer people, and so on—they each have their own separate place to live within the village. The untouchables (hereby, referred to as Dalit community), whose special role—whose hereditary duty—is to labor in the fields of others or to do other work that Hindu society considers filthy, are not allowed to live in the village at all. They must live outside the boundaries of the village proper. They are not allowed to enter temples. Not allowed to come near sources of drinking water used by other castes. Not allowed to eat sitting next to a caste Hindu or to use the same utensils. There are thousands of other such restrictions and indignities that vary from place to place. Every day in an Indian newspaper you can read of an untouchable beaten or killed for wearing sandals, for riding a bicycle.... If you are educated like me, if you don't seem like a typical untouchable, then you have a choice. You can tell the

truth and be ostracized, ridiculed, harassed—even driven to suicide, as happens regularly in universities. (8-9)

As Gidla explains, caste-based restrictions and indignities continue to exist for Dalit communities, including in universities. Any understanding of gender and feminism for a brahmin learner, like me, is incomplete without understanding the problems other learners from marginalized castes, sexualities and genders face. In 2016, I was a master's student studying women's studies at the Tata Institute of Social Sciences, Hyderabad. My supervisor—hereafter, referred to as Dr. SH —was negligent and disrespectful of my time, labour, and research goals during the entirety of my dissertation and fieldwork timeline. I would not get consistent and timely feedback or guidance regarding my work. My emails often went unanswered. Funding was limited to two years, and my supervisor was indifferent to my economic instability. Fortunately, I advocated for a change in supervisor, and my request was granted. While I lost a year, my subsequent supervisor—Dr. Nilanjana Ray and program chair Dr. U. Vindhya—set me up for success by intervening at the right time. I must acknowledge, however, my success was also connected with my brahmin privilege. Although policies are in place to support the inclusion and mobility of caste-oppressed communities, in practice, the Indian education system supports caste-privileged learners. Me being a brahmin meant that I received more support in my conflict with my supervisor than other-caste disadvantaged students facing their own problems.

Whereas I was able to resolve my issues by advocating for a change in my supervisor and complete my degree, not many other students, especially those that are caste oppressed, can expect much advocacy on their behalf. In the same city, during the same semester, I heard the tragic news of another university student, Rohith Vemula, who died by suicide. Vemula belonged to the Dalit community and was pursuing a PhD in sociology (Leonard; Mondal). He was one of the five student leaders of Dr. Ambedkar's Student Association at the University of Hyderabad who were struggling against a social boycott by the university officials and spaces: "[These] Dalit PhD scholars from the University of Hyderabad were mandated to be punished by the administration; they were not allowed to gather in groups, were denied access to the library and common places in groups, and, more importantly, were locked out of their hostel rooms" (Leonard 520). Vemula's advocacy and fight against his social boycott by caste-privileged university officials and systems was criminalized (520). To protest being locked out, the student leaders created temporary shacks in the ostracized university space, their own Dalit living space (Leonard and Mondal). Two weeks after creating this space, Vemula committed suicide, which created an uproar in caste-oppressed and other caste-aware student communities. Many aspects of Rohith's life, including his educational dreams and his caste status, were questioned by the university and state officials.

The maternal activism done by Radhika Vemula, Rohith's mother, on the part of her son has been important to me as a mother trying to understand feminism. Vemula travels across the country and meets various student bodies and associations to mobilize them to work against caste discrimination in university spaces (Mondal; Teja). Alternative yet powerful Indian YouTube channels, like "Dalit Camera," have highlighted this activism (Paul and Dowling). Also important is this maternal activist's call for coalition building among Dalits, Adivasis, and Bahujans (other caste-oppressed groups) Muslims, and women to fight caste and religious discrimination (Paul and Dowling 1246). However, Radhika Vemula's activism and her process of seeking justice for her son's suicide have been equally undervalued by dominant caste social groups and officials, and there is hardly any academic scholarship on her activism. From character assassination, to being disrespected in meetings with government officials, and to having to prove her son's caste, Radhika Vemula has undergone tremendous physical and mental suffering (Mondal). From this mother, I learnt that my acts of feminism and solidarity can never be fulfilled unless I address casteism and patriarchy together (Tamalpakula), which is the double burden that Dalit mothers, children, and women endure.

I lost my first born to premature birth in 2013. He lived eighteen days. I was twenty-six and devastated. But reading about the maternal activism of mothers like Radhika Vemula as well as about the scores of Black, Indigenous, and other racialized, marginalized mothers who have lost their children to caste, racial, and religious violence has helped me contextualise my loss and trauma (Alook; Barker; Diverlus et al.; Simpson, *As We Have Always Done*; Umar, "The 'Other' Muslim"). Even in the loss of my child I had been privileged, because my child did not have to experience the violence that the children of the mothers mentioned above did. I carry this privilege in every space where my maternal activism takes me.

From Losing a Child to Understanding Body Shaming and Patriarchy

My entry to finding feminism was subconsciously informed by the loss of my child. It was 2013 when I lost my child. At the time, as a business graduate, I was working as a qualitative consumer researcher where my audience was mostly women. I was exposed to plural understanding of women's issues, which led me to pursue a master's program in women's studies. What connected me with feminism was this question: Just like intersectionality (Crenshaw; Nash) questions universal nature in feminism, could mothering experiences be plural? (O'Reilly, *Mothers*). I thought that I was no longer a mother when I lost my first born to premature birth. However, my disempowering mothering experiences never left me. I continued to experience marginalization, as the loss of my child was seen as a failure of my fat body. Additionally, in a typical brahmin patriarchal family, the onus is primarily on the women's family to take care of childbirth and the last trimester of pregnancy.

As in many Indian families, we had relatives who helped us to the best of their abilities. I am thankful for this help, but it must be noted that they were not socially obligated to support me. Right from the time we were trying to save the child, to even after his passing, many comments were made to my parents about their not doing enough, about me being fat, and about my body not being the ideal type to carry a pregnancy. The doctors stated I had pre-eclampsia (a sudden onset of high blood pressure), which affected my bodily functions and eventually led to a premature caesarean section. My baby was removed from my womb at about thirty-one weeks. He fought to live for eighteen days, all of his six-hundred-odd grams, but he could not make it. It was a difficult period for my family. My mother lost her mother the week my son was born and rushed back from another city after hearing about my hospitalization. A doctor on duty who was supervising my floor, a woman herself, very insensitively remarked in front of my husband and mother-in-law that I must lose weight.

It is important to note here that the medical professional made this passing remark about the need for me, the patient, to lose weight without knowing my history. I could not make sense of this passing diagnosis, as I had lost weight before the pregnancy, even though my child was unplanned. As evident in my medical reports, they could not find a reason for the loss of my child and sudden termination of the pregnancy.

But "I am fat and that is why I have pregnancy issues" became a conversation within my husband's family. My mother-in-law, who was otherwise very helpful during my second pregnancy and even helps now with childcare that immensely helps my PhD goals, repeated the same to me when I was eight-months pregnant with my second child. It must be noted that according to her, her comments were coming from a place of concern, which is often how body shaming gets masked as advice and counselling by brahmin elders. I do not blame her because even though Western education may mean more modern thinking, many elders in a patriarchal society, like mine, can feel privileged enough to pass demeaning comments about daughters-in-law and their families.

It was only after my second pregnancy in Canada that I found out from my doctor that placental inefficiency has no possible solution or cure, and there was no evidence to prove that it was related to my body weight. I ensured that my mother-in-law heard this observation from the doctor to change her perspective. My doctor and other healthcare practitioners worked extensively with me over a period of eight months and never once targeted my body weight for any potential pregnancy-related complications. My daughter thrived, even as a premature baby. As Donna Haraway writes, "Social constructionists make clear that official ideologies about objectivity and scientific method are particularly bad guides to how scientific knowledge is actually made" (576). This statement is relevant for my pregnancy and for other mothering experiences. Pregnancy, mothering, and mother-work can never be a result of one individual alone (Aggarwal and Das Gupta; Cortes; O'Reilly, *Maternal Theory*; Rich); it is heavily influenced by factors, such as the environment, family situation, race, class, ethnicity, caste, and religion, to name a few. Through patriarchy and gender subjugation, an unnatural onus is placed on certain bodies, which are then seen as responsible for reproducing the next generation.

These bodies are expected to be cisgendered, heterosexual women—like me, my mother, my mother-in-law—and their only role must be of cultural carriers, cultural enforcers, or gatekeepers. They must be able to reproduce and rear individuals that adhere to dominant caste and cultural ideas and perpetuate dominant gender, sexual, and religious ideologies. These ideologies in my family are often dictated by caste and patriarchy. Going back to the main argument of this chapter, an important step in understanding feminism, for me, was to make peace with this question: Why some women in the family I married into did not acknowledge or support me after the loss of my child but instead perpetrated my gender disempowerment by body shaming me?

Here is my understanding and analysis. Caste-privileged hindu women who end up donning mothering roles and becoming mothers-in-law, sisters-in-law, and other actors with more agency can choose to question their role as cultural carriers or gatekeepers. They must, however, acknowledge the caste privileges that give them power in relationships, for example—a relationship between a mother-in-law and a daughter-in-law, disempowers and isolates them when the power dynamics are reversed—in a situation or a relationship where they do not hold the same power.

As I write and edit this chapter, I am constantly thinking of how my mother-in-law is a widow, having lost her husband recently, which makes her vulnerable in patriarchal brahmin spaces, especially during her visits to my house here in Turtle Island, which is not a space she can own. I am constantly thinking of how I must check my privilege and build a symbiotic relationship that helps us both exist in peace and helps me grow as an individual. I can see her trying, too—by holding herself from commenting on other people's bodies before me, and by helping me with childcare while I navigate my PhD program. In addition, I am fortunate to be friends with women in my husband's family who identify as daughters-in-law and sisters-in-law. They provide me a safe space to discuss my experiences of alienation and disempowerment as a daughter-in-law. Many of our experiences are shared, which helps me realize I am not alone. It helps me make meaning of the term "the personal is political" (Hanisch). These shared experiences have led to a sense of consciousness raising, in that our oppressive situations are not our fault (Hanisch 2). As a woman, when I fill many shoes—as a mother, a sister, a sister-in-law, and maybe in the future a mother-in-law—I must realize the benefits of feminist friendships with other women in the family.

Conclusion: Towards a Nonexploitative, Mutually Beneficial Feminist Politics and Positionality

My experiences of gender disempowerment, caste privilege, and complicity as a settler have brought me closer to envision how I want my feminist politics in mothering to be. I want a non-exploitative, mutually beneficial relationship in my mothering experiences, my maternal activist networks, and my research collaborations. These goals help me question the norms dictated by patriarchy, casteism, and colonialism, which have affected my everyday experiences as a mother. I introduce here what O'Reilly has termed "the ten dictates of normative mother-hood":

> Essentialization, privatization, individualization, naturalization, normalization, idealization, biologicalization, expertization, intensification, and depoliticalization. Essentialization positions maternity as the basis of female identity, whereas privatization locates motherwork solely in the reproductive realm of the home. Similarly, individualization causes such mothering to be the work and responsibility of one person, and naturalization assumes that maternity is natural to women—that is, all women naturally know how to mother—and that the work of mothering is driven by instinct rather than intelligence and developed by habit rather than skill. In turn, normalization limits and restricts maternal identity and practice to one specific mode: the nuclear family wherein, the mother is a wife to a husband, and she assumes the role of the nurturer, and the husband assumes that of the provider. The expertization and intensification of mother-hood—particularly as they are conveyed in what Sharon Hays has termed "intensive mothering" and what Susan Douglas and Meredith Michaels call "the new momism"—cause child-rearing to be all consuming and expert driven. Idealization sets unattainable expectations of and for mothers, and depoliti-calization characterizes child-rearing solely as a private and non-political undertaking, with no social or political import. Finally, biologicalization, in its emphasis on blood ties, positions the cis-gender birthmother as the "real" and authentic mother. Norma-tive motherhood is only available to mothers who can enact and fulfil these ten dictates: mothers who cannot, or will not, do so because they are young, queer, single, racialized, trans, or non-binary are defined and positioned as de facto bad mothers. (O'Reilly, *Matricentric Feminism* 10-11)

As a mother to a three-year-old, I often find my feminist beliefs and practices in contrast to what normative motherhood dictates. O'Reilly's work helps me contextualise my brahmin, caste privileged, immigrant, hindu mothering. When I juxtapose these dictates to my particular social location, it helps me reiterate the need for a separate category of feminism to theorize mothering, motherhood, and motherwork beyond gender (O'Reilly). I am particularly disadvantaged by the essentialization, privatization, individualization, idealization, and naturalization dictates of normative motherhood. In my experience of child loss, essentialization and idealization of motherhood reduced my identity as a person to a mother who could not see a pregnancy to term because of a so-called fat body. Privatization, individualization, and naturalization simultaneously expect me to be a mother who must engage in not only paid work but also unpaid carework. This situation was exacerbated during the pandemic, when everyone in my family was overworked.

Many times, I have experienced scrutiny from my in-laws when they visit me in Canada to help with childcare. It must be noted again that I have the privilege of community support few immigrant mothers have. During the pandemic, my overworked family concluded (often aloud) that my PhD work and mothering cannot go together. When I struggle with writer's block or understanding concepts and need to put in a few extra hours, my husband who works round the clock as an information technology worker, points out that I do not work part time, as I claim, and these extra hours mean time away from our daughter. I did, however, get better support from my husband and other family members when my research was supported by federal and provincial scholarships and by internal university awards, which have ensured some income and marginal economic stability. This funding has helped me advocate for my education and further my economic independence.

My mothering experiences are far more privileged as a settler and as a caste-privileged individual. Our household has two incomes, and we can pay our monthly mortgage. I have a community of loving grandparents, uncles, and aunts across borders and within Canada who helps me with childcare, a privilege few first-generation immigrant mothers have. It was only possible for me to write this chapter because my mother and father helped care for my daughter. My mothering is political in my community work (Tungohan) with the Aurora Black Community Association as well as when I document my experiences of resistance. My feminist politics are situated within these mothering experiences of privileges and precarities. I turn to Haraway's call to action: "I would like a doctrine of embodied objectivity that accommodates paradoxical and critical feminist science projects: Feminist objectivity means quite simply situated knowledges" (598).

I want my politics to highlight situated knowledges that belong to a particular land, as argued by various Black, Indigenous, and other racialized scholars (Byrd; Coulthard; Collins; Da Costa and Da Costa; hooks; A. Simpson). Allyship must exist with Black motherhood collectives that fight against anti-Black racism, with Indigenous mothers who have been relentlessly pursuing justice for missing and murdered Indigenous girls, women, two-spirit people, and with many other racialized activist mothers who fight discrimination in their communities.

My mothering experiences will be affected by these situated knowledges, and to make meaning out of them will be a complex process. I will be required to juxtapose, read, and analyze complex concepts of intersectionality, caste politics and settler colonialism simultaneously with my mothering experiences. Mothering experiences are as equally complex and plural as feminist politics. It is important to not look at these plural concepts separately but to look at them in opposition as well as collaboration with one another.

Acknowledgments

I thank my colleagues Jasleen Arora and Zahra Nader for helping me with their feedback on my chapter. Generous peers like these teach me that research is always a collaborative exercise. My research has had the privilege of receiving funding from the Social Sciences and Humanities Research Council 2022-2024, the Ontario Graduate Scholarship 2021-2022, and the Nirvan Bhavan Fellowship 2021 (York Centre for Asian Research).

Works Cited

Aggarwal, Pramila, and Tania Das Gupta. "Grandmothering at Work: Conversations with Sikh Punjabi Grandmothers in Toronto." *South Asian Diaspora*, vol. 5, no. 1, Mar. 2013, pp. 77-90.

Alook, Angele. "Indigenous Families: Migration, Resistance, and Resilience." *Continuity and Innovation: Canadian Families in the New Millennium*, edited by Amber Gazso and Karen M Kobayashi, Nelson

Education Limited, 2018, pp. 99-112.

Bannerji, Himani. "The Paradox of Diversity: The Construction of a Multicultural Canada and 'Women of Color.'" *Women's Studies International Forum*, vol. 23, no. 5, 2000, pp. 537-60.

Barker, Joanne, editor. *Critically Sovereign: Indigenous Gender, Sexuality, and Feminist Studies*. Duke University Press, 2017.

Byrd, Jodi A. *The Transit of Empire: Indigenous Critiques of Colonialism*. University of Minnesota Press, 2011.

Collins, Patricia Hill. *Black Feminist Thought: Knowledge, Consciousness and the Politics of Empowerment*. 2nd ed. Routledge, 1999.

Corntassel, Jeff, et al. "Unsettling Settler Colonialism: The Discourse and Politics of Settlers, and Solidarity with Indigenous Nations." *Decolonization: Indigeneity, Education & Society*, vol. 3, no. 2, Sept. 2014, pp. 1-32.

Cortes, Krista L. "AfroBoriqua Mothering: Teaching/Learning Blackness in a Bay Area AfroPuerto Rican Community of Practice." *Journal of Ethnic and Cultural Studies*, vol. 7, no. 2, July 2020, *DOI.org (Crossref)*, https://doi.org/10.29333/ejecs/351.

Coulthard, Glen Sean, and Taiaiake Alfred. *Red Skin, White Masks: Rejecting the Colonial Politics of Recognition*. University of Minnesota Press, 2014.

Crenshaw, Kimberlé. "Demarginalizing the Intersection of Race and Sex: A Black Feminist Critique of Antidiscrimination Doctrine, Feminist Theory and Antiracist Politics." *University of Chicago Legal Forum*, vol. 1, no. 8, 1989, pp. 139-67.

Da Costa, Dia, and Alexandre E. Da Costa. "Introduction: Cultural Production under Multiple Colonialisms." *Cultural Studies (London, England)*, vol. 33, no. 3, 2019, pp. 343-69.

Diverlus, Rodney, et al., editors. *Until We Are Free: Reflections on Black Lives Matter in Canada*. University of Regina Press, 2020.

Gidla, Sujatha. *Ants among Elephants: An Untouchable Family and the Making of Modern India*. Farrar, Straus and Giroux, 2017.

Hanisch, Carol. "The Personal Is Political." *Notes from the Second Year: Women's Liberation*, edited by Shulamith Firestone and Anne Koedt, 1971, p. 5.

hooks, bell. *Ain't I a Woman: Black Women and Feminism*. 2nd ed. Routledge, Taylor & Francis Group, 2015.

Lawrence, Bonita, and Enakshi Dua. "Decolonizing Antiracism." *Social Justice*, vol. 32, no. 4, 2005, pp. 120-43.

Leonard, Dickens. "Rohith-Movement, Conversion, and Renaming." *Critical Times*, vol. 3, no. 3, Dec. 2020, pp. 519-27. *DOI.org (Crossref)*, https://doi.org/10.1215/26410478-8662408.

Mondal, Sudipto. "A Year on, Rohith Vemula's Death Still Caught in Caste Web." *Hindustan Times*, 17 Jan. 2017, https://www.hindustantimes.com/india-news/a-year-on-rohith-vemula-s-death-still-caught-in-caste-web/story-Et7w946WDSWIhz5SqXAVaI.html. Accessed 2 Apr. 2023.

Nash, Jennifer C. "Re-Thinking Intersectionality." *Feminist Review*, vol. 89, no. 1, June 2008, pp. 1-15.

O'Reilly, Andrea, editor. *Maternal Theory: Essential Readings*. Demeter Press, 2007.

O'Reilly, Andrea, editor. *Mothers, Mothering and Motherhood across Cultural Differences: A Reader*. Demeter Press, 2014.

O'Reilly, Andrea. *Matricentric Feminism: Theory, Activism, and Practice*. Demeter Press, 2016.

Patel, Shaista, et al. *Complicities, Connections, & Struggles: Critical Transnational Feminist Analysis of Settler Colonialism*. no. 4, 2015, p. 15.

Paul, Subin, and David O. Dowling. "Digital Archiving as Social Protest." *Digital Journalism*, vol. 6, no. 9, Oct. 2018, pp. 1239-54.

"Remembering Rohith Vemula: On His Sixth Death Anniversary, a Look at the PhD Student's Demise and Its Aftermath." https://www.firstpost.com/india/remembering-rohith-vemula-a-look-back-at-what-happened-six-years-ago-10292711.html. Accessed 2 Apr. 2023.

Rich, Adrienne. *Of Woman Born: Motherhood as Experience and Institution*. Norton, 1995.

Simpson, Audra. *Mohawk Interruptus: Political Life across the Borders of Settler States*. Duke University Press, 2014.

Simpson, Leanne Betasamosake. *As We Have Always Done: Indigenous Freedom through Radical Resistance*. University of Minnesota Press, 2017.

Simpson, Leanne Betasamosake. *Noopiming: The Cure for White Ladies.* Anansi, 2020.

Tamalpakula, Sowjanya. "'Annihilation of Caste' and 'Annihilation of Patriarchy' Must Go Hand-in-Hand." *The News Minute*, 7 Dec. 2020, https://www.thenewsminute.com/article/annihilation-caste-and-annihilation-patriarchy-must-go-hand-hand-139165. Accessed 2 Apr. 2023.

Teja, Charan. "Not a Single Day Goes by without Remembering Him: Rohith Vemula's Mother Radhika." *The News Minute*, 17 Jan. 2021, https://www.thenewsminute.com/article/not-single-day-goes-without-remembering-him-rohith-vemula-s-mother-radhika-141642. Accessed 2 Apr. 2023.

Tuck, Eve, and K. Wayne Yang. "Decolonization Is Not a Metaphor." *Decolonization: Indigeneity, Education & Society*, vol. 1, no. 1, 2012, pp. 1-40.

Tungohan, Ethel. "Reconceptualizing Motherhood, Reconceptualizing Resistance: Migrant Domestic Workers, Transnational Hyper-Maternalism and Activism." *International Feminist Journal of Politics*, vol. 15, no. 1, Mar. 2013, pp. 39-57.

Umar, Sanober. "The Identity of Language and the Language of Erasure." *CASTE / A Global Journal on Social Exclusion*, vol. 1, no. 1, Feb. 2020, pp. 175-99.

Umar, Sanober. "The 'Other' Muslim: Spatial-Temporal Cartographies of the Gendered Muslim World." *Religion and Gender*, vol. 11, no. 1, June 2021, pp. 113-20.

Wynter, Sylvia. "Unsettling the Coloniality of Being/Power/Truth/Freedom: Towards the Human, After Man, Its Overrepresentation—An Argument." *CR: The New Centennial Review*, vol. 3, no. 3, 2003, pp. 257-337.

Chapter 12.

I Am Never Sleeping with You Again: Reflections on Mothering, Community Building, and Unstable Allyship

Zaje A.T. Harrell

Introduction

Modern motherhood, in the Western context, is a role that is largely centred within the individual nuclear family. This limits the imagination of reach beyond the family unit. However, throughout human history, mothering has been a communal experience. Women in ancient and modern societies have bonded and shared the responsibilities and tasks associated with caretaking. Children are raised in multigenerational families and extended-family social networks (Omolade 74). These bonds, rooted in community, are often harder to establish among mothers living away from their family of origin. In these instances, one must make a community. This chapter explores the implications of building bridges and allyship through my early motherhood experiences as someone in a chosen mothering community. The community focused on sharing breastfeeding knowledge and prioritizing attachment-related nurturing practices. Although I felt that these practices were feminist, there were dimensions of racial and gender oppression in the group. The respect I had for the knowledge and instincts of these women when facing sleepless nights with a newborn or a child on a nursing strike did not hold in the face of the more reactionary beliefs held by some and a culture of silence around issues of social justice. Because this chapter is written over a decade after my initial parenting years, I have come to understand my experience in such a community and the fragility of the allyship I shared within the group through a Black feminist lens.

First, I use my breastfeeding relationship, which was initially fraught, as a point of departure for finding community with other mothers. I then explore motherhood as a radicalizing force and relate that to themes of womanhood emergent in nineteenth-century feminist theory and political groundings. This background establishes that feminist politics share some overlap with what I term here "maternal politics" but that there are also reactionary threads in the latter that should be problematized. Finally, I explore the impact of the relationships that I built in community during my earliest mothering days as I emerge as a more fully formed feminist mother.

Foundations

I grew up during the Black political and cultural movements of the 1970s and 1980s. As a child, I was nurtured by my biological mother as well as a community of "othermothers" (Collins 380). This community nurturing and caregiving evolved to respond to a sociocultural ethos that inoculated Black children against racism while providing a strong cultural foundation (Collins 372). This had practical implications for maternal practices. Babywearing, cooking healthy meals from scratch, making homemade clothes, and using alternative healing modalities were considered liberatory in that they represented separation from oppressive institutions and economies. Furthermore, resistance against systems that negatively affected the wellbeing of Black children were central to parenting. For example, the lack of inclusion of Black perspectives in mainstream entertainment and school curricula required that Black parents develop supplemental content and creative outlets (Burke 40).

Upon reflection, I can point to areas of privilege that enabled the women in my community to mother in this manner. They were largely partnered, employed, and educated. However, privileges, such as being college educated or married, were not the primary catalyst for their parenting approach. These women's ideas of cultural pride, uplift, and solidarity were central to their view of family. For example, activist Tarana Burke, founder of the #MeToo movement, speaks about similar types of cultural education in her memoir *Unbound*: "My mom, heavily influenced by my grandaddy, was engaged in the Black liberation struggles of the 70s and put me in Afrocentric daycare, where I was learning Swahili and African dance at just three" (39). Whereas Burke grew up in a working-class neighbourhood, and I was raised in a middle-class one, our experiences resonated. I also took African dance for several years and Swahili lessons in an effort to immerse myself in culturally relevant activities. This was also a political project aimed at raising children to resist the anti-Blackness of the dominant culture. My earliest world was affirming; this was in contrast to the larger world, which was hostile to Blackness. My intersectional perspective grew from this foundation. Even within a nurturing community, I observed that Black women struggled to find avenues to reach their full potential because of patriarchal systems within their communities and outside as well. These were my earliest Black feminist musings.

The Gateway

> So, you nurse and you keep nursing wherever and whenever the mood strikes, but there's a catch. As it turns out, public breastfeeding is the gateway drug to attachment parenting.
> —Susanna Schrobsdorff, "Confessions"

I became a mother in 2009. At the time, my husband and I were living in a majority white Midwestern town. As is the case for many young professionals who have had to relocate for educational and career opportunities, we were left to navigate building a supportive community for our young Black family without the benefits of our families of origins being in proximity.

My firstborn arrived at half-past six on a Friday evening, after eighteen hours of labour. As had been my plan, she was delivered without pain medication. For as long as I could remember, I had heard Black women critique the experience of maternity care in the hospital setting.

My instinct was to avoid the hospital for as long as possible. I arrived at hour twelve of my labour. I pushed for nearly three hours to overcome her posterior position—"sunny side up." Then, in one final push, all eight pounds and five ounces of my firstborn child slid onto the hospital bed. I was delirious and marvelled at the strength and brokenness of my body. The euphoria that had been described in my natural childbirth learnings overwhelmed me. It was dizzying. It was also dizzying because my body was exhausted. During those post birth moments, I briefly fainted twice.

As a researcher, I was versed in racial differences in infant mortality and maternal health outcomes. I was aware that racism was implicated in these poorer birth outcomes for moms and babies. I knew that being a person with a postgraduate degree would not protect me (Jackson et al. 91). I knew that the concerns of Black patients were often ignored (Bridges; Tello). In those moments, in the hospital, I knew that this could quickly turn into a fight for my life.

Even though I had been in the hospital for hours, for the first time, I fully noticed the whiteness of my surroundings. There were no Black doctors or nurses on my team. Now I was weak and drained, with a new life to consider. My husband advocated for me; he began to ask pointed questions about which tests were being ordered. The team, which had been generally kind, became more attentive and slightly deferential. One of the labour and delivery nurses told me that I would stay in that room until I could walk.

The baby had been taken by a team to monitor her vitals. My husband went with them, leaving me alone with the nurse. She turned to me and asked, "Do you want me to do your hair?" I had forgotten that I was a person who others could see. I had no idea how wrecked I must have looked. At that moment though, I did not care if the white delivery nurse was experienced in the intricacies of Black hair care. I was grateful. She parted my hair and brushed it into two ponytails. I could tell that my hair had been matted and tangled by sweat. I needed a shower and a nap. Upon returning to the room, the baby bassinet was wheeled close to my bed. I picked up our newborn and began to nurse, feeling the strength of her latch. I called my daughter by her name and sang her a lullaby.

Two days later, before our discharge, we were visited by the hospital paediatrician. The doctor, a middle-aged white woman, came in to evaluate our daughter before release. She headed for the baby who was in the bassinet and barely looked at me. "Is this your first child?" she asked. I still had the ponytails that the nurse had styled, and I realized I could have looked younger than my years. "Or do you have several?" Several? Something about the way that word slipped out of her mouth made me uncomfortable. "She is my first." I replied.

Our daughter had lost greater than 10 per cent of her birthweight. She was still a good-sized newborn. Nursing was going well, and she had passed her meconium the night before. Thus, I was surprised when the doctor recommended formula. As a part of my natural childbirth classes, I had been attending a breastfeeding peer support meeting. There I had been warned about the hard sell for formula in the hospitals, especially targeting women of color. I also knew from other Black mothers that they had not met their nursing goals after having discouraging experiences in the hospital. The literature supports these disparities, with Black and Indigenous women having lower overall rates of breastfeeding initiation in the hospital (Chiang et al. 770). I argued that the baby was nursing well and that I was committed to breastfeeding. She was terse as she heard that our plan was to consult a paediatrician of our choosing. We declined the formula.

By this time, my mother had flown into town. As a veteran nursing mother, she was certain that she could help me get the baby established at the breast. She could see that I was stressed about having to make sure that the baby gained weight quickly before we had the next visit with the doctor. My mother also implored me to call one of the organizers of the peer support group, just to ease my mind.

I did call one of the group organizers, Katie. She was a soft-spoken mother of two girls, one of whom was a nursing toddler and the other a homeschooled seven-year-old. Katie talked to me for a long while. She reassured me that the baby would be fine and gave me practical steps. She stressed skin-to-skin contact and nursing as frequently as the baby would take the breast to establish my supply. Within a few days, a second paediatric examination gave my daughter a clean bill of health. She gained back her birth weight plus a few ounces for good measure.

After that first parenting win, I saw it as my duty to make informed and supported decisions. I was also experiencing the health and bonding benefits of nursing and connecting these to other nonmainstream practices, such as cosleeping. The fact that I had already been attending the support group meetings and had developed a rapport with a few organizers made it seem like a natural place to return, baby in arms. I returned to the group when my newborn was about six weeks old, and I would attend those monthly meetings for the next four years.

The World We Made

Becoming a mother radicalized me. I entered motherhood as a feminist, and that worldview has only been strengthened through my parenting experiences. It became obvious to me that our social systems were largely ill equipped to adequately support mothers, babies, and families. Mainstream parenting advice seemed to only prioritize expedience and consumption. The focus was on finding the right products to buy or experts to consult rather than on the work of nurturing. I also found the United States' lack of government support for families to be abhorrent. The fact that there was no federally supported paid parental leave and that breastfeeding was not yet fully normalized was infuriating. My maternal support community was riddled with assumptions of whiteness; threads of feminism and antifeminism intertwined. I began to ponder the implications of being an active member in a community such as this: Was my connection to these women and groups contributing to oppression and anti-feminist praxis?

Early parenting both expanded and contracted my world. The intensity of adjusting to first-time motherhood and then having a second daughter thirty-one months later left me with little time outside of work and childcare. The peer support groups with other mothers became a lifeline and social outlet. My breastfeeding support group met in a progressive, Midwestern college town. We convened in a cohousing community's common space. Some of the women, like me, came from a bit of a distance. I had consciously chosen this particular group because I thought that the meetings in the more conservative county where my husband and I lived would not be welcoming to women of colour.

Our discussions were practical in terms of meeting the demands of motherhood and philosophical in musings about empathy as central to (our) parenting practice. This meant responding to a baby's cries rather than forcing them to cry it out. This also included breastfeeding frequently and keeping the baby close. The women in the group often wore their babies in wraps or semistructured carriers. These practices were a part of several gentle and holistic approaches to baby care, including attachment parenting (Sears and Sears) and natural parenting (Feder).

The attachment-parenting philosophy focused on maximizing the nurturing time between caregiver and baby. This was facilitated initially through the nursing relationship, skin-to-skin contact, and sleeping close to the baby to respond to their needs. William Sears was commonly referenced by group members. His expertise was considered credible, as he was a paediatrician and his wife a nurse. They had raised eight biological and adopted children. William Sears and Martha Sears conceded that there was value in fathers being supportive in the nurturing role but focused on the mother as the primary caregiver (147). This was a comfortable delineation for more conservative women in the group.

Other group members seemed to focus more on scientific arguments related to research explaining the origins of attachments. They referred to the natural and holistic needs that met those of the whole child. Natural parenting was another common descriptor used to characterize parenting that rejected mainstream interventions. This approach argued that because the medical field was preoccupied with treatment instead of prevention, parents should be critical consumers of these interventions. Natural parenting also noted that "many age-old traditions" have been used successfully for generations (Feder 14). Natural parenting was often also more neutral with respect to questions of gender.

Natural- and attachment-parenting advocate, actress, scientist, and now *Jeopardy* host, Mayim Bialik, articulated her view that walked a line between evidence and instinct in her own book focused on attachment parenting:

> By understanding basic theories of attachment and infant development, by surrounding ourselves with a community (and a culture) that seeks to support healthy and natural choices that make intuitive sense, and by trusting that everything a baby needs is communicated honestly and simply, without malice or manipulation, we can truly be the parents that nature intended us to be. (5)

During our group meetings, attendees were encouraged to focus on what they found useful in the discussions. Yet even though we kept our focus on breastfeeding and family life, there were glimpses of other beliefs and political leanings of some of the other attendees. For example, some of the women did not seem to have any attachment to a professional identity and had quit their jobs as soon as they became mothers. There was some veiled judgment towards working mothers. The assumption of the financial privilege of being able to afford such a lifestyle was rarely fully acknowledged. There was no full interrogation of how limitations on material resources and stress may impact parenting behaviours, such as the ability for a mother to sustain a breastfeeding relationship.

As often the only Black person in the room, I was troubled by the norms that required we stay away from topics that were relevant to our identities beyond motherhood. By not discussing our contexts more fully, we were limiting our ability to build an authentically honest community in the group. The assumptions of white middle-class heteronormativity silenced those of us who did not fit neatly into those categories. Over time, I became more interested in helping to organize the group to address these issues of inclusion.

Because of my professional work as a professor and presenter on issues of diversity and community building, I was asked to facilitate workshops on these topics. I led two workshops over the course of four years with the statewide gathering of this peer support group. In these sessions, participants were able to explore how race, culture, gender, and class affected mothering practices and their interactions with others. The intention was to take these learnings back to community building in our own local groups. These were well received by many attendees who seemed poised to take on some issues of inclusion more directly. Others seemed less on board. After one of my presentations, a woman raised her hand during the question-and-answer portion to say that there had never been racism in her neighbourhood growing up, even though some of her neighbours were German, Irish, and Italian. She seemed to have missed the points I was making about inclusion and oppression, and some of the other attendees were clearly annoyed. I found myself caught in some of the classic tensions that emerge between Black and white women when engaging in community work.

The Nature of True Womanhood

> Enslaved black women had no control over their own children. Their sons and daughters could be sold away from them without their consent or brutally disciplined without their protection. So, when a Black woman proclaims public ownership of her children she helps rewrite that ugly history.
> —Melissa Lacewell Harris-Perry, qtd. in Cooper 50

The tensions I felt as a Black woman in majority white peer support spaces can be understood through an integrated analysis of feminist theory. Feminist theory provides frameworks for understanding women's lived experiences and material conditions as related to their public and private lives. Theoretical frameworks inform the understanding of history and feminist political actions. Thus, integrating theory illuminates mothering as an intersectional political practice. The following section explores feminist theories that inform the trajectory of my early mothering experiences.

The nineteenth-century cult of true womanhood still permeates the understanding of womanhood and motherhood today. The assertion of true womanhood is that women are by nature more attached to the domestic sphere and that this focus on family and home making was a social good (Giddings 47). However, as political goals of education and suffrage began to shape nineteenth-century feminist endeavours, the concept of true womanhood perhaps offered a more resonant notion than more aristocratic ideas of womanhood. Nancy Cott points out that this was a way to address diversity of "ascriptive character, achieved status, and opinion" (6). Thus, opening the door for inclusion of more than just upper-class women in the struggles for gender equality. In sum, Cott argues that all women could aspire towards true womanhood, whereas only some women could aspire towards public-facing achievement. This argument, however, did not fully address the context of race in an evolving feminist context.

Black feminist historian Paula Giddings argues that the role of Black women in the domestic sphere was more complex. This view of white domesticity does not foreground the experience of Black women who are essential to the building of this private sphere for white women (Giddings 47). For example, the ideal of womanhood does not account for enslaved Black women who engaged in domestic labour. It also does not address the desire of Black women to care for their own families rather than to perform physical and emotional labour for the white slave-owning class (Cooper). To this end, the conception of motherhood idealized by the cult of true womanhood foundationally privileges upper middle-class whiteness as the standard for entry. When the intersections of race, class, and politics are applied to the domestic focus of the early feminist movement, particularly in the racial caste system of the United States, women of colour, and working-class women are largely excluded.

Black feminist theorists have asserted distinct epistemological positions independent of Western idealizations of womanhood. These assertions are made to resist the hierarchy, individualism, and materialism that are prevalent in Western philosophy, including feminist theories. As argued by Patricia Hill Collins, the epistemological standpoint of Black women is informed by contact between Afrocentric and feminist analysis. Collins does not accept the binary of public and private spheres in the lived experiences of families of colour. Rather she asserts that for racially marginalized women "motherwork" is both work within the household and public engagement and community building (Collins 373). Motherwork is nurturing and resistance.

When I apply this lens to my early mothering support groups, I was community building in spaces focused on breastfeeding and other nurturing practices as motherwork. However, we were in community with one another as mothers and women, where the hierarchies of race, class, sexual identity, and ableism are ever present—a space where white women do not acknowledge the privilege of their positionality is not liberatory. The assumptions of racist hierarchies are being reinforced in the silence.

The role of nature and instinct also required further interrogation. In a sociological analysis of narratives of women who practised natural mothering, Chris Bobel found that the roles of nature and instinct are central (149). In this analysis, she characterizes "natural mothers," her informants, by their rejection of mainstream parenting practices in favour of focusing on the bond between mother and child. This is a labour-intensive parenting style, which relies upon a mother making sacrifices to meet the needs of children without the resources that are considered typical in modern parenting. For example, the use of bottles, disposable diapers, and daycare would be criticized and interrogated within the framework of natural mothers. Bobel describes her informants as believing in a maternal knowledge that is instinctual: "The natural mothers believe that they have wrested control away from institutions and experts and others who claim to "know best" and returned it to the site of the individual family. The natural mothers exalt nature as a force to be trusted and respected, and this realization sometimes shocks them" (26).

The "shock" that natural mothers experience is characterized by an understanding of systems that are accepted by the mainstream as worthy of rejection and detrimental to the development of children and families. It is this critique of social structures that allows room for both liberal and conservative women to find themselves among natural mothers. Bobel argues that natural mothering, as a cultural phenomenon, has both progressive and regressive elements. My own experience, to a large degree, resonated with that of many of Bobel's informants. My instincts led me to reject many mainstream practices. Because my trajectory was that of a second-generation natural mother, I was simultaneously resisting social norms for parenting and conforming to my cultural socialization.

This language of "control" and "institutions" merits further consideration. It underscores that natural mothering is both personal and political. I did not want to see a world that limited women's ability to reach their full potential. Instead, it is arguable that the revelations of natural mothering allow for the imagining of a world that is more materially supportive of motherhood and normalizes nurturing as a public good. This does not require a repressive return to the domestic sphere for women but instead could be the foundation for a more equal society that recognizes parenting is relevant and requires accommodation and investment.

Maternal Politics and Feminist Politics

There are many historical threads and antecedents that illuminate why mainstream American mothering exposes certain sociopolitical fault lines and hierarchies while obscuring others. In my work in mothering communities, the political distinctions between groups of women organized around nurturing practices and a feminist project became more evident. This is the distinction between what I identify here as "maternal politics" and "feminist politics."

Maternal politics are the dimensions of practice and power related to the role of the mother. They can be represented as having conservative and progressive elements. For example, maternal politics can focus on essentializing the role of woman as mother to reinforce patriarchal structures and undermine women's participation in public life. This is a thread that is evident throughout Western women's history (Cott 49). However, maternal politics can also be radically progressive in advocating the use of societies' material and political resources to materially support mothers. For example, the debates of paid family leave are progressive in the argument that there is a societal investment in making sure that there is opportunity for caregivers to take time with their infants.

Maternal politics can also critique how mothering is particularly labour intensive for women. Hannah Rosen's article "The Case Against Breastfeeding" asserts that the trend for upper middle-class women to breastfeed proforma was not a universal good. "Let's say a baby feeds seven times a day and then a couple more times at night. That's nine times for about a half hour each, which adds up to more than half of a working day, every day, for at least six months. This is why when people say that breast-feeding is 'free,' I want to hit them with a two-by-four. It's only free if a woman's time is worth nothing" (Rosen).

As more educated parents in Western societies have spent more time with their children over the past forty years (Dotti and Treas 2), a disconnect has developed between the need for efficiency and the practices of nurturing among educated middle-class parents that require increasing amounts of time and labour. Although maternal politics can be reactionary, they are not necessarily reactionary.

In contrast, feminist politics are necessarily oppositional to oppressive hierarchies and highlight the limiting impact of patriarchal systems on women's lived experiences. Feminist politics centre women's lived experiences but do not privilege motherhood as essential to that lived experience. Feminist politics also focus on modifying social structures that limit the ability for women to fully participate in society.

As a Black woman and a feminist, I have a baseline skepticism of institutions and practices that reinforce the status quo. For example, the reliance on external domestic labour to support a career and lifestyle begged several questions for me about the exploitation of other women for my own benefit. I knew that my daycare workers were not paid equivalent to their societal value. As my own relationship to breastfeeding evolved, I became more suspicious of the infant-feeding industrial complex. I educated myself about the way that the infant-feeding industry had engaged in targeted marketing, which would affect the breastfeeding rates among Black women for generations to come (Freeman 65). I found some community groups that addressed these disparities more directly, and I began to apply my professional skillset in collaboration with them. Here, I felt like I was engaging in the necessary work of serving Black families.

As my understanding of a maternal politics that fit my feminist politics grew, my support group looked different to me. The space required obfuscation of the differences between mothers. This was an act of erasure because individuals from marginalized groups would be welcome only if they did not disrupt the power hierarchies. The groups gave me the support I needed for mothering practices, but the assumptions of time, peaceful home lives, middle-class resources, and heterosexuality were right underneath the surface. This was an unstable foundation on which to build anything lasting.

Strange Bedfellows

We were resting across a tall queen-sized bed. My friend Tracy was in the middle of a major home renovation. She and her husband took over their teen daughter's bedroom while the master suite is being remodelled. We were in the girl's room listening out for the children but also catching up with each other. I had completed a long day at a feminist conference in Utah, where I had presented on inclusive pedagogy. I travelled by plane with my two daughters. My eldest was then almost three years old, and the youngest was sixteen months. Tracy offered to help me with the children while I was at the conference. This meant that I did not have to enlist a family caregiver to come to support us. Instead, Tracy met me at the hotel and took my children back to her house. This allowed me the opportunity to focus fully on my work.

As we talked that evening, I felt for a moment that maybe I had found some equilibrium—a way to have it all. The only way the fleeting moment of balance emerged was because I had other women. I was not isolated. Tracy and I were not of the same race or background. Before motherhood, she had been a teacher. She was also a wife and a devout

Mormon mother of four. Our paths had crossed when our husbands had worked together, and we found a friendship.

Motherhood can provide an opportunity for women to deepen connections across backgrounds. I have older children now, but I still am in contact with some of the women from those days in the breastfeeding support group. However, I now have come to a stronger belief that the time I spent with the group was largely a journey into antifeminist maternal politics. I resent the fact that I spent time on my diversity work that was a political project ill-suited for the audience. I resent that the solitude and loneliness of modern life delivered me to places where my whole self, and by extension that of my children, could not be affirmed. However, I do not regret the experiences of those early days of motherhood. Watching the way that this group was ineffective in achieving inclusion was a valuable lesson for me about the tentacles of antifeminist forces. I saw up close how white supremacy is practised in female-led spaces that are depoliticized. I saw how the vision of true womanhood seems genteel and narrow but is really a pillar holding up larger systemic inequities. These lessons and the women who remain in my life make it worth it. I will always have the kindness of those afternoons, when we gathered in our common cause and were simply there for one another.

Coda

This chapter tells the story of my earliest time as mother. In telling this story, I must acknowledge the background of the political climate in the United States. All of my children were born under the presidency of Barack Obama. They were born at a time when a Black family, like ours, was in the White House. It is tempting for the Obama years to become in memory, a halcyon time, representing a period of a promise for inclusion and progress, compared to the jolt of the years that would follow. However, the undercurrent of right-wing antidemocratic forces was barely contained during Obama's tenure.

By the time Donald Trump was elected to the US presidency in November of 2016, I had finished pregnancy, birth, and breastfeeding. My youngest was almost three at the time of Trump's accession to power, and my concerns became more focused on what it meant to raise Black children under creeping autocracy in a country that was becoming more racially polarized. According to the Pew Research Center, 47 per cent of white women voted for Trump compared to 45 per cent who voted for Senator Hillary Clinton (11). The same reports found that 98 per cent of Black women voted for Senator Clinton. Perhaps these findings tell us that Black women prefer qualified candidates and democracy more than their white female fellow citizens. This speaks to a race and gender divide in politics, which is a divide in beliefs about power and resources. Moreover, it speaks to a denial of gender solidarity as a thread among white female voters.

Living through the rise of Trumpism as a Black American woman caused me to reevaluate coalition building as a potential strategy for maternal politics. For example, the common cause that can sometimes be found between conservative and progressive women in policy questions, such as paid family leave, can be evidence of alignment. However, the conservative movement in the United States is a well-funded movement that includes many factions, not limited to fiscal conservatives, religious fundamentalists, and reactionary populists (Posner). All of the factions in some ways are invested in the validation of hierarchies that are central to white supremacy and systemic racism. When white women reinforce this worldview with their vote, they lend legitimacy to a heinous project. Therefore, even when we may share a common short-term goal, I do not think that it is sensible or safe to align with groups that support reactionary politics in any form.

*Pseudonyms have been used to preserve anonymity.

Dedication

To the mothers who nurtured me, then and now.

Works Cited

Bialik, Mayim. *Beyond the Sling: A Real Life Guide to Raising Confident Loving Children the Attachment Parenting Way*. Gallery Books, 2012.

Bobel, Chris. *The Paradox of Natural Mothering*. Temple University Press, 2002.

Bridges, Khaira M. "Implicit Bias and Racial Disparities in Health Care." *Human Rights Magazine*, vol. 43, no 4, Aug. 2018. American Bar Association. https://www.americanbar.org/groups/crsj/publications/human_rights_magazine_home/the-state-of-healthcare-in-the-united-states/racial-disparities-in-health-care/ Accessed 8 Apr. 2023.

Burke, Tarana. *Unbound*. Flatiron Books, 2021.

Chiang, Katelyn V. "Racial and Ethnic Disparities in Breastfeeding Initiation—United States 2019." *Morbidity and Mortality Weekly Report*, vol. 70, no. 21, pp. 769-74.

Collins, Patricia Hill. "Shifting the Center: Race, Class, and Feminist Theorizing about Motherhood." *Representations of Motherhood*, edited by Donna Bassin, Yale University Press, 1994, pp. 371-89.

Cooper, Brittney. "Ain't I a Lady: Race, Women, Michelle Obama and the Ever-Expanding Democratic Imagination." *Melus*, vol. 35, no. 4, 2010, pp. 39-57.

Cott, Nancy F. *The Grounding of Modern Feminism*. Yale University Press, 1987.

Dotti, Giulia M., and Treas, Judith. "Educational Gradients in Parents' Childcare Times across Countries 1965-2012." *Journal of Marriage and Family*, vol. 78, no. 4, 2016, doi: http://dx.doi.org/10.1111/jomf.12305

Feder, Laura. *Natural Baby and Childcare*. Hatherleigh, 2006.

Freeman, Andrea. *Skimmed: Breastfeeding, Race, and Injustice*. Stanford University Press, 2020.

Giddings, Paula J. *When and Where I Enter: The Impact of Black Women on Race and Sex in America*. Bantam Books, 1984.

Omolade, Barbara. *The Rising Song of African American Women*. Routledge, 1994.

Jackson, Fleda, et al. "Examining the Burdens of Gendered Racism: Implications for Pregnancy Outcomes Among College-Educated African American Women". *Maternal and Child Health*, vol 5, no 2, 2001, pp. 91-107. Accessed 3 Apr. 2023.

Pew Research Center. "For Most Trump Voters 'Very Warm' Feelings for Him Persisted." *Pew*, 9 Aug. 2018, https://www.pewresearch.org/politics/2018/08/09/for-most-trump-voters-very-warm-feelings-for-him-endured/#:~:text=In%20November%202016%2C%2087%25%20of,more%20negative%20views%20of%20Trump. Accessed 3 Apr. 2023.

Posner, Sarah. *Unholy: Why White Evangelicals Worship at the Altar of Donald Trump.* Random House, 2020.

Rosen, Hannah. "The Case Against Breastfeeding." *The Atlantic*, 2009 Apr. 1. https://www.theatlantic.com/magazine/archive/2009/04/the-case-against-breast-feeding/307311/. Accessed. 3 Apr. 2023.

Schrobsdorff, Susanna. "Confessions of an Accidental Attachment Parent." *Time Magazine,* 10 Mar. 2012, ideas.time.com/2012/05/10/confessions-of-an-accidental-attachment-parent/. Accessed 3 Apr. 2023.

Sears, William, and Martha Sears. *The Attachment Parenting Book.* Hachette Book Group. 2001.

Tello, Monique. "Racism and Discrimination in Health Care: Providers and Patients." *Harvard Health Blog,* 16 Jan 2017, www.health.harvard.edu/blog/racism-discrimination-health-care-providers-patients-2017011611015. Accessed 3 Apr. 2023.

Chapter 13.

The "Wildness of Motherhood": Transforming Maternal Rage and Transgressing Patriarchal Motherhood to Realize Maternal Empowerment: A Reading of Rachel Yoder's *Nightbitch*

Andrea O'Reilly

In an interview on her novel *Nightbitch*, Rachel Yoder emphasizes the difference between the experience of mothering and the status of motherhood. She elaborates: "Motherhood feels very different than mothering. Motherhood is a status that locks you into gendered scripts and limits you in so many societal arenas" (qtd. in Fox and Valez). Mothering, in contrast, is "wonderful ... and makes the mother in the novel a stronger and braver person" (qtd. in Fox and Valez). Compellingly, Yoder's words recall the important distinction between motherhood and mothering that Adrienne Rich develops in her classic work *Of Woman Born: Motherhood as Experience and Institution*. Rich writes: "I try to distinguish between two meanings of motherhood, one superimposed on the other: the *potential relationship* of any woman to her powers of reproduction and to children; and the *institution*, which aims at ensuring that that potential—and all women—shall remain under male control" (lxi). Rich emphasizes that her work "is not an attack on the family or on mothering, *except as defined and restricted under patriarchy*" (14). For Rich, motherhood refers to the patriarchal institution that is male defined and controlled and oppressive to women, whereas mothering refers to women's own experiences that are female defined and centred and potentially empowering. In *Of Woman Born*, Rich explores how maternal power has been stolen and withheld from women through the institution of motherhood. However, there is little discussion on how the potentiality of mothering may be realized other than Rich's brief reference to a holiday when her husband was absent, and she and her sons lived as "outlaws from the institution of motherhood" (195).

Through a reading of Yoder's novel *Nightbitch*, this chapter considers how maternal power may be reclaimed and how the potentiality of empowered mothering may be realized. More specifically, the chapter explores how the mother in *Nightbitch*, through claiming and harnessing maternal rage, moves from motherhood to mothering to achieve maternal empowerment and become Rich's outlaw from the institution of motherhood. The chapter will first introduce a theoretical model of maternal empowerment developed from Australian scholar Megan Rogers's concept of empowered maternalism, and my own concept of empowered mothering. Next, the chapter will discuss maternal rage as necessary for the development of a theory of maternal empowerment. The final section will explore how Yoder's novel *Nightbitch* positions maternal rage as a transformative power that prompts insight and propels resistance and how the mother, in harnessing and directing this rage, achieves empowered maternalism and empowered mothering to realize maternal empowerment. Indeed, as Yoder emphasizes, it is the wildness of motherhood that "is the mother's wisdom." She continues: "It's the energy that can no longer be contained or looked away from and is trying to wake her up" (qtd. in Dominque Sisley).

Maternal Empowerment

In *Of Woman Born*, Rich proposes that "We do not think of the power stolen from us and the power withheld from us, in the name of the institution of motherhood" (275). The aim of empowered mothering is to reclaim that power for mothers and to imagine and implement a mode of mothering that mitigates the many ways that patriarchal motherhood, both discursively and materially, regulates and restrains mothers and their mothering. However, empowered mothering, or what may be termed "mothering against motherhood," has yet to be fully defined, documented, or dramatized in feminist scholarship on motherhood. Rather, empowered mothering is understood for what it is not—namely patriarchal motherhood. Indeed, as Fiona Green notes, what is still missing from discussions on motherhood is "Rich's monumental contention that, even when restrained by patriarchy, motherhood can be a site of empowerment and political activism" ("Feminist Mothers" 31). Rich uses the word "courageous" to define a nonpatriarchal practice of mothering, whereas Baba Copper calls such a practice "radical mothering." Susan Douglas and Meredith Michaels use the word "rebellious" to describe outlaw mothering, and "hip" is Ariel Gore's term for transgressive mothering. In my work, I use the term "empowered mothering" to signify maternal practices that resist and refuse patriarchal motherhood to create a mode of mothering that is empowering to women.

Interest in, and concern for, the empowerment of mothers—both in the home and in the larger society—has been a central concern of feminist research and activism worldwide over the last thirty-plus years. Feminist scholars contend that motherhood, as it is currently perceived and practised in patriarchal societies, is disempowering if not oppressive for a multitude of reasons—for example, the societal devaluation of motherwork, the endless tasks of privatized mothering, the current incompatibility of waged work and motherwork, and the impossible standards of idealized motherhood. Empowered mothering is essential for maternal wellbeing, as it enables women to mother comfortably, competently, and confidently. More specifically, empowered mothering enables mothers to balance motherhood more effectively with paid employment; in fact, findings from my study on academic mothers suggest that empowered mothering is more a determinant of employment success than family friendly policies in the workplace (O'Reilly, "I Should"). Feminist scholars likewise emphasize that empowered mothers are more effective mothers for children, that such mothers are healthier women and more productive workers, and that empowered mothering is beneficial for families and society at large.

Overall, empowered mothering allows mothers to effect real and lasting change in their lives, in the lives of their children, and in the larger society. However, even as feminist researchers concur that empowered mothering is better for mothers and their children, discussions continue on how empowered mothering, as both practice and politic, may be achieved and sustained (Green, "Developing a Feminist Motherline"; O'Reilly, *Matricentric Feminism*). In other words, how do mothers individually and collectively refuse and resist the ideology and institution of patriarchal motherhood? What makes this possible? Although researchers agree that "the process of resistance entails making different choices about how one wants to practice mothering" (Horwitz, "Mothers' Resistance" 58), the larger question remains: What is needed at both the individual and cultural level to empower women to engage in this process of resistance?

Over the last two decades, I have sought to define and develop a theory of empowered mothering. I begin with Wanda Thomas Bernard and Candace Bernard's definition of empowerment, which refers to "naming, analyzing, and challenging oppression" and "occurs through the development of critical consciousness," with concern for "gaining control, exercising choices, and engaging in collective social action" (46). Most pointedly, the overarching aim of empowered mothering, I argue, is to confer on mothers the agency, authority, authenticity, autonomy, and advocacy-activism that are denied to them through the institution of patriarchal motherhood. "Maternal agency," as Lynn O'Brien Hallstein explains in her encyclopedia entry on the topic, "draws on the idea of agency—the ability to influence one's life, to have a power to control one's life—and explores how women have agency via mothering" (698). A theory of maternal agency focuses on, O'Brien Hallstein continues, "mothering practices that facilitate women's authority and power and is revealed in mothers' efforts to challenge and act against aspects of institutionalized motherhood that constrain and limit women's lives and power as mothers" (698). "Authenticity," as explained in Elizabeth Butterfield's encyclopedia entry, "is an ethical term that denotes being true to oneself, as in making decisions that are consistent with one's own beliefs and values [whereas] inauthenticity is generally understood to be an abdication of one's own authority and a loss of integrity" (700). In the context of empowered mothering, maternal authenticity draws on Ruddick's concept of the "conscientious mother" (70) and my model of the "authentic feminist mother" (O'Reilly, *Matricentric Feminism*) and refers to "independence of mind and the courage to stand up to dominant values" and to "being truthful about motherhood and remaining true to oneself in motherhood" (Butterfield 701; See also O'Reilly, *Matricentric Feminism*). Similarly, maternal authority and maternal autonomy refer to confidence and conviction in oneself, holding power in the household, and the ability to define and determine one's life and practices of mothering, which mean the refusal to, in Ruddick's words, "relinquish or repudiate one's own perceptions and values" (112). Finally, the topic of maternal advocacy-activism foregrounds the political and social dimensions of motherwork, whether such is expressed in antisexist childrearing or maternal activism. Overall, empowered mothering functions as a counternarrative to challenge patriarchal motherhood and change the many ways that it, both materially and discursively, oppresses mothers and their mothering.

In my recent writing on empowered mothering (O'Reilly, "Matrifocality"), I use Australian maternal scholar Rogers's concept of empowered maternalism and integrate it with my theory of empowered mothering to create a theoretical model of and for maternal empowerment. According to Rogers, for a woman to embody and enact an empowered maternalism, she must "assimilate elements of her private and public life so that they are integrated and so that both halves are as important and respected as the other" (142). Empowered maternalism also requires, as Rogers explains, "a transference of allegiance from a heterosexual relationship to one of intimacy between women" (142). With an empowered maternalism, a woman integrates and values all dimensions of her identity, and she creates and expresses this identity in and through intimacy between women. Empowered mothering, as noted above, bestows on agency, authority, autonomy, authenticity, and advocacy-activism to women, whereas empowered maternalism enacts self-integration and identification with women. Together, they form maternal empowerment to counter, as Rogers explains, "not only patriarchal motherhood but also patriarchal notions of how women occupy private and public spheres in general" (168).

From Mother to Nightbitch: The Transformation of Maternal Rage to Transgress Patriarchal Motherhood and Realize Maternal Empowerment

The novel *Nightbitch* tells the story of a mother who leaves her career as an artist to become a full-time stay-at-home mother. However, with her husband travelling five days a week for work, the mother finds herself alone and isolated in motherhood, and in her rage and desolation, she becomes convinced that she is turning into a dog. As Yoder explains, "The story of a mom turning into a dog [was] a vehicle for me to unleash all these thoughts and feelings I had in motherhood ... to work out this whole problem of ambition and maternal love and marriage and how to take all of that and make it work" (qtd. in Fox and Valez). The novel explores how the mother learns to assert, harness, and direct her rage as a transformative power to create and claim an empowered selfhood.

Maternal Rage: "Once We Understand This Anger, It Can Become Useful"

I argue that the mother's transformation into a dog and the subsequent shift in her identity from mother to Nightbitch signify and enact the character's maternal rage that makes possible a movement from motherhood to mothering and the achievement of maternal empowerment. As the mother reflects in the novel, "One day the mother was a mother, but then, one night, she was quite suddenly something else ... a nightbitch" (6, 9). The mother further reveals: "She knew the horrible truth, Nightbitch has always been there, not even that far below the surface ... no one could have predicated such an arrival, for years she had been the very picture of a mother; self-sacrificing and domestic, un-gripey, un-grumpy, refreshed even after unrefreshing nights of nonsleep" (9). In an interview, Yoder explains that she "considers the novel a sort of coming-of-age story ... [of] how we come into our womanhood, into our motherhoods in a way that is empowering rather than in a way that feels like we're abandoning ourselves" (qtd. in Audie Cornish). I suggest that the mother comes into this empowered maternal identity precisely by reclaiming her suppressed Nightbitch self and that the released rage of Nightbitch is what propels the character's movement from motherhood to mothering to achieve maternal empowerment. Indeed, as Adrienne

Westenfeld argues, "It's only through her surreal transformation into 'Nightbitch' that she experiences liberation from the pressure cooker of motherhood." In an interview, Yoder questions: "How do women move from self-denial into power? This is *Nightbitch's* central question" (qtd. in J.A. Tyler).

For the mother in *Nightbitch,* it is her claim and expression of maternal rage that moves her from self-denial to power, and in this, the novel foregrounds the centrality and necessity of maternal rage to transgress and transform patriarchal motherhood and realize maternal empowerment. Speaking of her own experiences of mothering, Yoder comments:

> I really wanted to explore what I was going through in early motherhood, this sort of rage at where I found myself, this rage at the structures of society that I felt had led me to this point. I was angry because this had not been my vision of motherhood.... I thought it was going to be this endeavour my husband and I did equally. It was going be modern, I was going to be able to feel fulfilled in my career and in my art and also have a child.... I expected more. And I think the biggest feeling was that I felt tricked—that somehow the stories that I had been told were false. (qtd. in Cornish)

Interestingly, the necessity of maternal anger has largely been absent in maternal theory on maternal empowerment with the notable exception of Rich's writing in *Of Woman Born*. In the preface to the third edition of *Of Woman Born,* Eula Biss writes: "Rich's embrace of rage is liberating.... What she gives us, as mothers, is a model for understanding our own rage... Once we understand this anger it can become useful" (xix). In her book, Rich references the goddess Demeter to signify every mother's longing for power and the efficacy of her anger. In patriarchal culture, where there are so few examples of empowered mothering, in both life and literature, Demeter's triumphant resistance serves as model for the possibility—and power—of maternal empowerment. Indeed, as Rich writes, "Female anger threatens the institution of motherhood" (30); "If we want to destroy the institution," Biss asserts, "we cannot deny ourselves this anger" (xx).

This is why the novel *Nightbitch* is so crucial for current theorizing on maternal empowerment. It demonstrates how, as in the title of this collection, mothers may find and realize feminism precisely through maternal rage. The mother's rage in the novel is what enables her to see the oppressions of patriarchal motherhood and then empowers her to challenge and change them. Yoder elaborates, "Anger can be and has been for me so transformative, to unleash it instead of letting it snarl and fight inside you" (qtd. in Fox). Rage prompts insight and propels resistance. In the first sections of the book, when the mother is called "Mother" and before she transforms into Nightbitch, there are numerous examples of how her rage delivers insight. The morning her husband calls her a Nightbitch, the mother questions:

> Nightbitch... Was is it her [own] fault that she had bought into the popular societal myth that if a young woman merely secured a top-notch education she could free herself from the historical construction of motherhood, that if she had a *career* she could easily *return to work* after having a baby and sidestep the drudgery of previous generations, even though *having a baby* did not, in any way represent a *departure from work* to which one might one day *return*. (29)

Rather, the mother thinks: "[Motherhood] actually, instead marked an *immersion in work, an unimaginable weight of work, a multiplication of work* exponential in its scope, staggering, both physically and psychically" (29). When she is at the grocery store getting groceries she did not want but got anyway, the mother reflects: "Society, adulthood, marriage, motherhood, all these things, were somehow masterfully designed to put a woman in her place and keep her there.... And once she was stripped of all she had been, her career, her ambition ... an anti-feminist conspiracy seemed not only plausible but nearly inevitable" (49). The mother continues: "How could you *not* be pissed after having a baby?" (50). As the mother is leaving the store, she meets a colleague from the community art gallery where she worked before having her son. When her colleague asks her how she is doing, the mother thinks: "I am now a person I never imagined I would be.... I would like to be content, but instead I am stuck inside a prison of my own creation.... I feel as though societal norms, gendered expectations, and the infuriating bluntness of biology have forced me to become this person.... I am angry all the time" (53). One Saturday morning when her husband is home after his weekly five days away for work, the mother must end her longed-for uninterrupted shower because the father is unable to comfort their crying son. The mother tells her husband, "one moment" while thinking: "Take care of your child, she wanted to scream. Just take care of it! What was so hard about it?" (56). And later when her husband complains that she forgot to buy milk, the mother thinks: "Couldn't he see how much I struggled? ... If he could not offer his actual hands-on help, at the very least he could offer his gratitude.... Instead when she tried to bring up the division of labor, the invisible labor of her life, the psychic load, he would offer something like *I suppose the money I make means nothing*, but that wasn't what she was saying" (57). In each of these instances, the mother's rage yields clarity, allowing her to see and understand how patriarchal motherhood—in its gendering and devaluing of carework and rendering of the mother as the one responsible for this labour—robs the mother of her power and results in the loss of her selfhood.

However, as this rage provides insight, it also propels resistance; as the mother's understanding is awakened so too is her power. This awakening to her power is enacted and symbolized through the mother's transformation into a dog. With each moment of clarity, there is an accompanying physical marker of this transformation. The novel opens with the mother discovering a growth of black hair at the base of her neck. Immediately following her understanding of the gender inequities of her marriage, she discovers a lump which she believes to be a tail (28, 31). Then, after acknowledging her anger at the grocery store, "the locus of [women's] oppression" (51), she is ravenous for red meat and purchases ten pounds of it as she thinks: "Vegetables were very civilized. Dogs wouldn't buy vegetables" (52). Later at the grocery store, as she reflects upon the "enormity of patriarchal society loom[ing] behind every box of farm-themed crackers, in the crackle of her every pretzel bag," she notices her "heightened near-animal sense of smell" (52) and realizes that she "was alive in a new way" (51). And when her husband arrives home after another week away for work and complains that the house is a mess—explaining that "it *stressed him out*, and couldn't he just have a calm re-entry" (54)—the mother discovers that the "hair was already back in full force and then some" (55) and that there were new nipples on her torso (56).

Initially, as the transformation evolves, the mother is resistant to the wildness and power it awakens and is resolved to "calm down, not be so angry, be grateful and happy" (62). When three dogs appear at her front door, the mother's heart "thudded with horrible terror, a horrible delight" (59). While normally she would recoil at such a show of affection by dogs, the mother instead finds their bodies lovely and allows herself to be led by the dogs "with the air of a waking dream" (61). She then scolds the dogs and chases them away. However, immediately after she does this, she "tilted her head back and howled from the cavern in her chest where everything was, the crushing anger, joy, loneliness, all came out of her in one giant sound" (62). Later when she tries to explain to her husband about the dogs, she realizes that he "didn't understand anything, not her sadness or her anger, not why the dogs had been so oddly disturbing" (64). She could not explain to him how she "felt called by the retriever, how it had spoken to her, how it had been so alluring, so comforting, as if it understood all her inner most urges and struggles" (64). When the dogs visit her again, this time in a pack of twenty, she realizes: "They had come for her, as she had both feared and hoped they would. They wanted her to join them, to take her, but she wouldn't go, she would not" (72)—that is, until she realizes that she is not afraid and allows the dogs to nip at her and tear off her clothing. As they do, she feels her hair "growing into a monstrous spectacle" as one thought comes to her: "You are an animal" (74). The next morning, as she wonders what happened the previous night, she "understood [that] she should be scared, but she simply wasn't. *A fresh power animated her body*, and she loved her body, loved being a body, and loved the boy, another body she had made" (75; my emphasis). And later she thinks, "I am becoming a better mother because I am becoming a better dog" (83).

The first section of the novel concludes with the mother's complete transformation into a dog sprinting from the house, and the second section opens with the mother transformed into Nightbitch: "She was Nightbitch, and she was fucking amazing. It seemed she had been waiting for this for a very, very long time.... [She was] overwhelmed by her strength and awash in her own violence" (90). Nightbitch kills a rabbit, realizing that was "what she needed all along ... to sink her sharp teeth into something living and bloody" (91). After killing the rabbit, Nightbitch feels "strong and alive ... and was awake in a way she had not been since her child was born, maybe even before" (92). As she enters her home the morning after becoming Nightbitch, she feels "as Eve must have that first morning out of the garden ... to understand yourself anew ... to know the truth" (93). Remembering this night later in the novel, the mother reflects: "While all the usual worries and insecurities ... the marital resentments, feminist rage were back, [they were] somehow transformed" (102). The mother "felt she could abide them as long as she had Nightbitch" (102). Yoder explains: "There's an embodied truth that I was trying to get at through the transformation of the mother.... After refusing what her body is trying to tell her, once Nightbitch embraces it, she comes into this deeper understanding of who she is and how she can actually transform in an internal and meaningful way" (qtd. in Westenfeld). However, Yoder emphasizes that Nightbitch's "anger has become unwieldy ... she must find a way to wield her rage that's not destructive but, rather, creative" (qtd. in Tyler), and it "demands that she make a choice: destroy her feelings or transform" (qtd. in Fox). Speaking of her own experiences of mothering Yoder comments: "I was very scared of my anger in early motherhood. I didn't know how to relate with it. I was afraid of it getting out of control" (qtd. in Tyler). She continues: "I felt like a feral monster. My anger felt like a terrifying creature inside me, whipping and snapping and screaming to be let out, to exert a physical force" (qtd. in Fox). In the second section of the novel, there are several instances of Nightbitch's out-of-control anger, including a dinner when she, envious of her working mother friends' successes, felt "a tidal-wave of rage and hopelessness," and then "monsters" from the restaurant, as she "snarls and barks" at her friends, overturns cups, and steals a meat patty from a patron's plate. (147). The second section of the novel concludes with Nightbitch, in "her silent rage," brutally killing the family cat, whereas the third opens with Nightbitch realizing "that she could not go on like this, with the unhappiness and this now uncontrollable rage" and that "she needed to change" (169). Initially, Nightbitch believes that if she "maintained a placid disposition of motherly care" (170), she could contain the "pure yearnings and rage" (168). However, and as Yoder explains:

> The question [to be asked] is what happens when we turn toward that sort of wild, perhaps rageful, feral part of ourselves and move into relationship with it.... rather than suppressing it and pretending it's not there and sort of pushing it to the back. What happens when we explore that part of ourselves that in motherhood can really flourish? This really wild creative, powerful self. (qtd. in Cornish)

The novel explores how Nightbitch moves into relationship with this anger so that it becomes, in Biss's words above, "liberating and useful." I suggest that it is precisely in and through maternal empowerment as enacted in empowered mothering and empowered maternalism that Nightbitch's rage becomes liberating and useful and allows her to be that wild, creative, and powerful self. There is, as Yoder emphasizes, "a wildness that this character learns to embrace" (qtd. in Cornish) and comes to harness to achieve maternal empowerment.

Empowered Maternalism and Empowered Mothering Allegiance between Women: "How Desperately I Needed a Community, a Pack"

Yoder argues that "Nightbitch's rage becomes a part of her self-care once she figures out how to wield it. Her rage becomes a source of great power and propels her into asking for what she needs" (qtd. in Westenfeld). Once claimed and used constructively, Nightbitch's maternal rage gives rise to maternal empowerment, as it is enacted in empowered maternalism and empowered mothering. As explained above, empowered maternalism requires "a transference of allegiance from a heterosexual relationship to one of intimacy between women" and the "assimilation of the mother's private and public life so that they are integrated and so that both halves are as important and respected as the other" (Rogers 142). Within an empowered maternalism, a woman integrates and values all dimensions of her identity, and she creates and expresses this identity in and through female allegiance. In *Nightbitch*, this empowering allegiance of women is enacted through the mother's affinity with the magical women of Wanda White's book *A Field Guide to Magical Women* and through the friendships she builds with other mothers. This female allegiance then makes self-integration possible and gives rise to empowered mothering.

The mother is transformed by the empowered maternalism of the magical women she encounters in Wanda White's book. Yoder explains that *A Field Guide to Magical Women* is in the novel to "showcase how we share wisdom and communicate knowledge through the generations." She "wanted to place Nightbitch within this lineage" (qtd. in Westenfeld). The magical women of this book model and mentor the transformative power the mother seeks to acquire as she harnesses her rage for maternal empowerment. Significantly, the mother reads the book "as if the book itself was her most cherished friend. As if its pages knew her heart" (65). As the mother is searching for an identity and life in which she can be both self and mother, the foreword to White's book asks: "To what identities do women turn when those available to them fail? How do women expand their identities to encompass all parts of their beings?" (40).

The book includes the Bird Women of Peru—who sprouted feathers and beaks in their sixties but only if they had never married or had children, and once these women learned to fly, they never returned (41)—and the mothers from Bangladesh, who appeared sometimes as a playful mongoose (112). However, it is the WereMothers from Siberia that the mother is most drawn to—a dozen of them, both human and animal, raising their children together and who were the most "gentlest of creatures though with their large canine teeth were terrifying" (176). Reading the description of the WereMothers, the mother reflects: "There was truly something so enticing and exhilarating at the thought of rejecting all established society for something remote and magical, for a community suited particularly and only to the community's needs" (179). The mother then wonders: "Was being free to do what you needed and be who you wanted—truly free—not *monstrous*? If so, it was not a wrong kind of monstrous, but a beautiful one" (179). In the creation of their matrifocal community, the WereMothers enact the female allegiance of empowered maternalism to become Rich's outlaws from the institution of motherhood. And importantly, the mother as she transforms her rage to power understands that this maternal freedom is not, as patriarchy defines it, monstrous but beautiful. At the conclusion of the novel, when the mother learns that Wanda White is not an esteemed author and is instead only a persona on an online profile at a defunct school, she realizes that "Wanda White is not a person. Wanda White is a place at which a person finally arrives" (231). And this place is the empowered maternalism of both female allegiance and self-integration.

Significantly, it is after the mother reads about the WereMothers in White's book that she decides to join the Book Mommies at the herb party to achieve this freeing and magical maternal community in her own life. However, at the start of the novel, the mother confides that "she did not enjoy the company of moms and felt to begin a friendship merely because of shared motherhood was repugnant" and so she "actively resisted making friends in a mom context" (35). She thinks that while she is a mother "she wasn't that kind of mother, the sort that built her entire life and being around her child" (35). Every time the mother encounters the group of mothers, whom she disparagingly calls the "Book Mommies," at the park or the library, she is "nauseated" by them and "their wretched contentment" (67). The mother is consistently rude to these mothers and rebukes their overtures of friendship. In an interview, Yoder explains that the "mother's disdain for other mothers reveals an internalized misogyny [as] she dismisses connections with other moms because she is trying to distance herself from the idea of motherhood, that it is not of much value and that moms aren't interesting" (qtd. in Cornish). However, Yoder continues: "[She] really wanted a way for this mother to overcome that. How she can kind of start looking at the moms as her pack as opposed to women who aren't cool enough for her to hang out with" (qtd. in Cornish). Yoder further elaborates: "It became really clear to me in motherhood, how desperately I needed a community, and I needed a pack.... And so that old sort of way of communally raising children really started resonating with me when I was feeling isolated and at home. I desperately wanted to connect with other moms but, I couldn't quite do it and didn't know how" (qtd. in Sarah Aswell).

When Nighbitch, following her transformation into a dog, joins the Book Mommies in the library in the second section of the book, she comes to this same realization on the necessity of community: "A horrible loneliness ballooned in her chest.... She must, must, forge a real human bond, or she might actually go insane" (105). Significantly, in the third section of the novel, as the mother is harnessing and directing her anger in and for maternal empowerment, she joins the Book Mommies one night, and when they ask her about her current art project, she explains that it is about "feminine power finally wielded" (184). And later when she meets Jen, one of the mothers, Nightbitch realizes that she "needed other women, other mothers, and even if these weren't the right ones, they were a start" (191) and that through them she achieved "an equilibrium, a return to her self, or at least to a transformed self that owned her dreams and desires, but wielded her power with even determination" (191). Inspired by her newfound allegiance with the mothers—"a brilliant magnanimity and feeling of goodwill to all women" (212)—and empowered by the magical women's enactment of it in

White's book, the mother transforms her rage into power and moves towards self-integration, the second dimension of empowered maternalism.

Self-Integration: "Art Is Essential, as Essential as Mothering"

Yoder emphasizes that it is "important to hold tight to the most essential parts of yourself in parenthood, even if it's hard [as] it will make you more sane in the long run" (qtd. in Kelly Luce). She elaborates: "One of the lessons of *Nightbitch* is that despite all the beautiful biological mandates of your body, you still must attend to your dreams. You still must attend to the part of you that makes you you.... For me parenthood was this negotiation of giving part of myself away, while at the same time holding fast to the piece that I most needed, which was my creativity and my writing" (qtd. in Sisley). Once a fulfilled and successful artist, the mother now censors and denies her own desires, ambitions, and dreams as the patriarchal institution of motherhood dictates and demands: "Now there was nothing. Not a single creative impulse inside her, no matter how much she searched. Her son now was her only project. She had done the ultimate job of creation, and now she had nothing left. To keep him alive—that was the only artistic gesture she could muster" (23). Later in the novel, when the mother tries to compile a list of the ten things she wanted to do before she dies, she realizes that she could not even think of one: "Did she really have no desires anymore? No deep passions? Where had the vitriolic emotions and sweeping gestures of her twenties disappeared to?" (177) And in a letter to Wanda White, the mother writes: "There is no room for art within my house with my child. It is as if all my dreams have been reset. The walls are blank, and with them I am blank too" (82). However, as the mother harnesses her rage to power, she returns to her art and achieves the self-integration of empowered maternalism—"the assimilation of the mother's private and public life so that they are integrated and so that both halves are as important and respected as the other" (Rogers 142). The mother turns the guest room in their home into an art studio and explains to her son: "Never go in there.... This is where Mommy works, and her work is very important and not for little boys or doggies" (202). The mother also begins to sleep in the guest room when her husband is home and explains its importance to her family: "I need alone time. Time ... to myself" (206). In claiming this space and time for her art, the mother finally enacts what she shared earlier in her letter to Wanda White: "Art is essential, as essential as mothering" (82). On weekend nights, the mother roams the neighbourhood as rehearsals for her artistic project, "ruling and presiding over it as its monster, its mistress" (207). The mother realizes that she now "trusted the strength of her body, and the depth of her rage, the rage now tempered by her vision, her singular direction deep into mystery and into creation itself" (207). The mother's rage, harnessed and directed through vision, empowers the mother to return to her art and delivers a transformed self in which both halves of the mother's identity as artist and mother are fully integrated and lived.

The empowered maternalism the mother acquires—self-integration, alongside the female allegiance discussed above—is enacted in the mother's formidable and confounding artistic performance that concludes the novel. The audience at her enigmatic and powerful performance, both the Book Mommies and the working mothers included, "were stupefied by the spectacle, so perplexed by what they were seeing, unable to separate reality from artistry" (235). They witness "goddess-like apparitions that conjured in the viewers the most profound feelings of unity" (237), and those members of the audience who did not flee at the end of the performance witness the mother holding her son and "emanating a beauty they had not seen before" (238). The most devout fans of the widely successful performance don pins asking "WHERE DO YOU GO AT NIGHT?" with the image of a ferocious dog, and sales for Wanda White's out-of-print book skyrocket (237). When asked about the meaning of the performance at the conclusion of the novel, the mother explains: "It is meant to underscore the brutality and power and darkness of motherhood, for modern motherhood has been neutered and sanitized.... Womanhood and motherhood are perhaps the most potent forces in human society, which of course men have been hasty to quash, for they are right to fear these forces" (237). In acknowledging and expressing her rightful rage and transforming it into power, the performance enacts the female allegiance and self-integration of empowered maternalism to make possible empowered mothering.

Empowered Mothering: "To Demand Things—All Sorts of Things"

Empowered mothering is also necessary for, and central to, maternal empowerment. The mother in the novel, as Yoder explains, must "find her voice and say this is what I need, to make demands" (qtd. in Westenfeld). However, as Yoder continues, "the mother "is not able to have that conversation [the negotiation of roles] for a long time until something finally opens up for her and she is able to start talking about it with her husband and come out of this rageful silence" (qtd. in Cornish). I suggest that it is precisely the mother's anger transformed into power that enables her to finally have this conversation and make these demands. In their marriage, the mother assumes all the work and responsibility in caring for their son. Even when her husband is home on the weekends, she is responsible for "the night nights" because her husband, as the mother explains, *"had to wrap up some work emails,"* even though he had had all week to do it (55). But as the mother asks: "Shouldn't he undertake night-nights happily, gratefully, in honor of the many nights—the years—when she had been in charge of the task? (129). The mother realizes that although "She wanted to exit it would really be inconvenient for her husband, for *the entire family,* as he put it, so she stayed" (55).

Indeed, as Rich emphasizes, patriarchal motherhood demands "selflessness rather than self-realization, relation to others rather than the creation of self" (42). However, as the novel concludes and the mother is waiting for her husband's return, "the old night-night rage ballooned inside her, but instead of erupting ... she grew calm, clear" (204). When the husband arrives home, she hands him their son and says, "I'm done. You're doing night-nights every weekend night from now on" (205); to which he replies, "Sure. Seems fair" (205). The mother realizes that she only had to ask but then became irate, thinking: "If it was this easy for him to do things, then why had he not been doing them from the start?" (204). She then wonders why "she had not claimed the power and authority that were hers" (204). As an empowered mother, the mother now asserts her authority—"to demand things—all sorts of things" (205). She embraces her transformed self as "a wild, complicated woman with strange yearnings" (219). She is stubborn and angry—soft and sweet (219). Transforming her anger into power, the mother can now be both mother and Nightbitch; and in being both self and mother, she is empowered in motherhood. Yoder elaborates: "What seems to me like it would be of most benefit to families and communities is the embrace of a vibrant, dynamic, and full-bodied womanhood that Nightbitch ultimately claims. Kids are much better parented by whole human beings who are fulfilled and happy, who have these dynamic facets of themselves, rather than by women who are denying vital parts of themselves" (qtd. in Westenfeld). Compellingly, Yoder's words here evoke a central and crucial insight of maternal theory—namely, that empowered mothers are more effective mothers, and empowered mothering is better for children. Therefore, and contrary to patriarchal wisdom, empowered mothering asserts that what a child needs most in the world, as Janna Malamud Smith argues, "is a free and happy mother" (167). Smith elaborates:

> [W]hat a child needs most is a free mother, one who feels that she is in fact living her life, and has adequate food, sleep, wages, education, safety, opportunity, institutional support, health care, child care, and loving relationships. "Adequate" means enough to allow her to participate in the world—and in mothering.... A child needs a mother who has resources to enable her to make real choices, but also to create a feeling of adequate control—a state of mind that encourages a sense of agency, thus a good basis of maternal well-being, and a good foundation on which to stand while raising a child. Surely, child care prospers in this soil as well as, if not better than in any other. (240)

The mother in *Nightbitch* becomes this free mother valued by Smith, which is essential for the wellbeing of children through the transformation of her anger into power from which she creates and enacts empowered mothering.

Conclusion: "Motherhood Itself Is Power"

Yoder argues, "Motherhood itself is power. Women understand this power in their bodies, especially during childbirth" (qtd. in Tyler). She continues: "I had a baby that I had grown in my body, I pushed it out of a small hole. Do you see how powerful this is?" (qtd. in Sara Petersen). And she further elaborates: "Honestly, how are men not terrified of us?"

(qtd. in Sara Petersen). However, and as Wanda White writes in her book, "Perhaps most peculiar, most magical women are not aware of their powers" (85). What the novel *Nightbitch* shows us is how mothers may recognize, claim, and realize, in the mother's words, "the transformative power of anger" (143) to achieve maternal empowerment as it is enacted in both empowered maternalism and empowered mothering. The power of the *Nightbitch*, in Yoder's words, "comes in its rebellion, in saying the things we are normally not supposed to say or express, or even think" (qtd. in Petersen). And this rebellion, transforming the power of maternal rage to transgress patriarchal motherhood and realize maternal empowerment, is indeed "a radical act of feminism" (Yoder qtd. in Westenfeld).

Works Cited

Aswell. Sarah. "'Nightbitch' Author Rachel Yoder Talks Motherhood, Art, And Getting Personal." *Scary Mommy*, 25 Aug. 2021, https://www.scarymommy.com/rachel-yoder-interview-nightbitch. Accessed 3 Apr. 2023.

Bernard, Wanda Thomas, and Candace Bernard. "Passing the Torch: A Mother and Daughter Reflect on Their Experiences across Generations." *Canadian Women's Studies Journal/cahier de la femme*, vol. 18, no. 2-3, summer-fall 1998, pp. 46-50.

Biss, Eula. "Of Institution Born." In *Of Woman Born: Motherhood as Experience and Institution* by Adrienne Rich. W.W Norton & Company, 2021, pp. ix-xx.

Butterfield, Elizabeth. "Maternal Authenticity." *Encyclopedia of Motherhood*, edited by Andrea O'Reilly, Sage Press, 2010, pp. 700-01.

Copper, Baba. "The Radical Potential in Lesbian Mothering of Daughters." *Politics of the Heart: A Lesbian Parenting Anthology*, edited by Sandra Pollack and Jeanne Vaughn, Irebrand Books, 1987, pp. 186-93.

Cornish, Audie. "The Rage and Wonder Of A Motherhood Unleashed (Literally)." *NPR*, 26 Jul. 2021, https://www.npr.org/2021/07/26/1020866511/the-rage-and-wonder-of-a-mother-unleashed-literally. Accessed 3 Apr. 2023.

Douglas, Susan J., and Meredith Michaels. *The Mommy Myth: The*

Idealization of Motherhood and How It Has Undermined Women. Free Press, 2004.

Fox, Pamela, and Elizabeth Valez. "Read Our Interview with 'Nightbitch'' Author Rachel Yoder." *Reading Motherhood*, 28 Oct. 2021, https://www.readingmotherhood.com/post/interview-rachel-yoder. Accessed 3 Apr. 2023.

Gore, Ariel, and Bee Lavender, editors. *Breeder: Real Life Stories from the New Generation of Mothers.* Seal Press, 2001.

Green, Fiona J. "Developing a Feminist Motherline: Reflections on a Decade of Feminist Parenting." *Journal of the Association for Research on Mothering*, vol. 8, no. 1-2, 2006, pp. 7-20.

Green, Fiona, J. "Feminist Mothers: Successfully Negotiating the Tensions Between Motherhood and Mothering." *Mother Outlaws: Theories and Practices of Empowered Mothering*, edited by Andrea O'Reilly, Women's Press, 2004, pp. 31-42.

Horwitz, Erika. *Mothers' Resistance to the Western Dominant Discourse on Mothering.* 2003. Simon Fraser University, PhD dissertation.

Luce, Kelly. "In 'Nightbitch,' Motherhood Turns You Feral." *Electric Lit*, 30 Sep. 2021, https://electricliterature.com/nightbitch-rachel-yoder-novel-book/. Accessed 3 Apr. 2023.

O'Brien Hallstein, D. Lynn. "Maternal Agency." *Encyclopedia of Motherhood*, edited by Andrea O'Reilly, Sage Press, 2010, pp. 697-699.

O'Reilly, Andrea. "'I Should Have Married Another Man; I Couldn't Do What I Do Without Him': Heterosexual Intimate Relationships and Their Impact on Mothers' Success in Academe." *Academic Motherhood in a Post Second Wave Context: Challenges, Strategies, Possibilities*, edited by Andrea O'Reilly and D. Lynn Hallstein O'Brien, Demeter Press, 2012, pp. 197-213.

O'Reilly, Andrea. *Matricentric Feminism: Theory, Activism, Practice.* 2nd ed. Demeter Press, 2021.

O'Reilly, Andrea. "Matrifocality, Maternal Empowerment, and Maternal Healing: Conceiving Empowered Young Motherhood in Miriam Toews' Summer of My Amazing Luck." *Feminist Perspectives on Young Mothers and Young Mothering*, edited by Joanne Minaker, Deborah Byrd and Andrea O'Reilly. Demeter Press, 2019, pp. 207-26.

Rich, Adrienne. *Of Woman Born: Motherhood as Experience and Institution.* W.W. Norton & Co., 1986.

Rogers. Megan. "Resolving the Madwoman: Unlocking the Narrative Attic by Writing the Maternal Journey." 2014. University of Melbourne, PhD dissertation.

Ruddick, Sara. *Maternal Thinking: Toward a Politics of Peace.* Beacon Press, 1989.

Sisley, Dominique. "Nightbitch Author Rachel Yoder: 'Motherhood Is Feral, Dirty and Intense.'" *Another Mag*, 28 Jul. 2021, https://www.anothermag.com/design-living/13475/rachel-yoder-motherhood-is-feral-dirty-and-intense. Accessed 3 Apr. 2023.

Smith, Janna Malamud. *A Potent Spell: Mother Love and the Power of Fear.* Houghton Mifflin Company, 2003.

Tyler, J. A. "Ferocious and Violent: The Millions Interviews Rachel Yoder." *The Millions*, 22 Jul. 2021, https://www.scribd.com/article/516901502/Ferocious-And-Violent-The-Millions-Interviews-Rachel-Yoder. Accessed 3 Apr. 2023.

Westenfeld, Adrienne. "In 'Nightbitch,' A Mother Reclaims Her Power ... By Becoming a Dog." *Esquire*, 20 Jul. 2021, https://www.esquire.com/entertainment/books/a37051500/nightbitch-rachel-yoder-interview/. Accessed 3 Apr. 2023.

Yoder, Rachel. *Nightbitch.* Alfred A. Knopf, 2021.

Section Three

Connecting and Conversing

Chapter 14.

Becoming a (Better) Feminist: Autoethnographic Lessons I Learned about Feminism by Becoming a Mother

Molly Wiant Cummins

Dear Bear and Monkey,

Before either of you were born, I stumbled across the idea of creating email addresses for you to which I could periodically send emails, then giving you the passwords at some later point in life. The inbox would serve as a repository of memories and ideas, which I could share with you when they were salient and on which you could later reflect. The emails are as much for you as they are for me; they offer me a chance to model honesty about my experiences of mothering. I write about precious memories I have shared with you, important milestones you have crossed, my feelings about the state of the world, and the difficulties of parenting. I hope as you read through the emails, you are overwhelmed with the sheer love I have for you, you see the memories that mattered so much to me (even if you can't remember them), and you find moments of truth—moments where I felt defeated, overwhelmed, or overjoyed as a mom. I wanted you to see it's a messy, complex life we share, and I wanted you to see it all.

All my love,
Mom

Introduction

Lola Olufemi opens the introduction of *Feminism, Interrupted: Disrupting Power* by claiming, "Feminism is a political project about what *could* be" (1). The expanse of this claim, the potentiality inside it, became clearer to me when I had children. Although certainly not true for everyone, having children made me a better feminist. It sounds trite to claim that birthing babies was similarly about birthing myself, yet I have come to understand my own feminism more deeply by birthing and raising two children assigned female at birth.

In this chapter, I use autoethnography in the form of letters (emails) to my daughters to explore how becoming a mother helped me become a better feminist. Autoethnography allows me to examine my personal experience to better understand cultural experiences of motherhood (Ellis, Adams, and Bochner). I argue that birthing and raising girls has created a unique space for me to reflect, grow, and be reflexive about my feminism. In the emails, I explore ideas about trusting and loving my body, intersectionality as a privileged mother, and learning to advocate for myself and my children. I do not claim a universal experience, but I aim to model a legacy my daughters can build on to create a more humane and socially just world.

Situating Feminism and Motherhood

Writing for *The Guardian*, Eliane Glaser argues, "Motherhood is feminism's unfinished business." Even after more than one hundred years of feminism, mothers are still overworked, underpaid, and "perpetually guilty." Glaser says that despite feminist gains, expectations of mothers have increased. What Glaser identifies but leaves unnamed is intensive motherhood (Hays), which is also called patriarchal motherhood (O'Reilly, *Matricentric Feminism*). Intensive motherhood is the normative discourse conferring good mother status to those who fit the ideal —namely, white, middle-class, cisgender, heterosexual, married, and able-bodied women (Wiant Cummins and Brannon). Specifically, intensive mothers should devote all their time, energy, empathy, and money to raising their children (Hays). Unfortunately, trying to live up to this unrealistic ideal leaves mothers exhausted, weary, and often isolated (O'Reilly, *Matricentric Feminism*). In the world Glaser describes, mothers are left putting on public good mother performances for audiences also well versed in the normative discourse, which once again relegates mothers' questions, concerns, and even boredom to the private sphere, where it is often experienced alone and in shame. Glaser argues that families deserve better: "Realism is a political act: it builds solidarity and better conditions." I write this chapter in response to Glaser's call, writing from the real emotions of motherhood rather than upholding an intensive motherhood ideal.

Writing about motherhood, for me, is underscored by feminism. In a virtual talk given for the University of Texas at Arlington, Lola Olufemi posited: "How we come to politics, I think, is as important as what we do with it." Although I identified as a feminist before my children were born, I came to a new understanding of my own feminist politics because of becoming a mother. Part of how I come to feminism now is through my identity as a mother. Olufemi elaborated in her talk: "How we arrive and what's crucial when we think about how we arrive is understanding that our task is to denaturalize a world premised on misery, alienation, and dispossession. And this has to become, I think, our political imperative, no matter how we arrive at feminist politics." In a world premised on pain and misery, part of my feminist duty is to work against that pain and oppression. As trying as motherhood can be, counteracting the pain in the world, even through motherhood, is part of my "political imperative," especially when trying to write against the isolation and individualization of intensive motherhood (O'Reilly, *Matricentric Feminism*). As Andrea O'Reilly ("Introduction") contends, "Feminist mothering functions as a counterpractice that seeks to challenge and change the many ways that patriarchal motherhood is oppressive to women" (10). Feminist mothering must focus on all women (e.g., all races and classes, including transwomen and nonbiological mothers) as part of a political imperative to counteract and alleviate the suffering and oppression of the world. I write about my own feminist growth through autoethnography, which I detail in the next section.

Autoethnography

Autoethnography is "an approach to research and writing that seeks to describe and systematically analyze (graphy) personal experience (auto) in order to understand cultural experience (ethno)" (Ellis, Adams, and

Bochner 273). Focusing on their relationships with others and with culture, autoethnographers write about their lived experiences to help readers make connections to their (the autoethnographers') stories. Patty Sotirin posits that autoethnography invites readers to "participate in the creative act of authoring a meaningful life" (5). I use autoethnography because this method reveals the "fractures, sutures, and seams of self interacting with others in the context of researching lived experience" (Spry, "Performing Autoethnography" 712). This approach grants me a way to humanize research to show that the writer, reader, and implicated others matter (Adams, Ellis, and Holman Jones 8).

Moreover, autoethnography is a useful framework for feminist writing and research. As a method of inquiry (Richardson), autoethnography works with a feminist perspective to extend "the relationship between experience and culture," moving the "locus of inquiry from identifying *how* private/individual and public/cultural domains intersect to asking *why* they intersect in specific ways" (Foster 57). For Elissa Foster, telling (women's) stories from a feminist perspective is about conflating private and public spheres to muddle systemic structures that reify (women's) subjugation. In fact, autoethnography is a popular approach by feminists exploring gender and social media (Lauricella), race (Ghabra; Griffin), as well as a host of other topics, including addiction of a family member (Stern) and chronic illness (Edley and Battaglia).

I use autoethnography in this chapter as an approach to explore growth of my feminist self through stories I share with/about myself and my children. Autoethnography allows me to write the particulars of my/our life situation, even from a privileged position (e.g., white and cisgender), and create points of entry for the reader to dis/identify with the story. Through glimpses of a life, readers are invited into the story to find places where they can make meaning alongside us, where they do not find entry, and even where they might be challenged by our stories. Specifically, through three emails, I use autoethnography to address both the reader and my children, explore my feminist growth, and expose the places I still need to grow.

Email One: Body Love

Dear Bear,

I hate that you're going to learn as you get older that you should be suspect of your body. I'm doing what I can to help you love your body now, and it's so refreshing to see you get excited about what your body can do. (Right now, it's cartwheels!) I hope you always keep that love and amazement of your capabilities. I, however, learned that lesson all too well. Growing up, I was often suspect of my body. It never quite did the things I thought it should be able to do, never fit in the moulds just right. It always seemed too chubby to me, and it didn't help that a family member had said as much.

When I was pregnant with you, I decided I wanted to track our progress. Every week, I'd ask Dad to take our picture so I could look back on how much growth we really had. I documented it, trying to map the ever-shifting changes we experienced, including pictures a few days after you were born of my still-swollen belly looking much more deflated. Although I will probably always have issues with all the bits of my body that aren't what I want them to be (hey, I'm still a work-in-progress), those pictures mean so much to me now. When I look back on them, I remember parts of the experience, like what it felt like to turn over in bed. I joked that a three-point turn in bed became a twenty-nine-point-turn by the end. I remember what it felt like when you'd have your nightly "Peanut dance parties," rolling and flipping to let me know that even though I was ready for bed, you were not.

Those pictures remind me of the amazing things my body was able to do, even when it wasn't always pleasant—to grow, nourish, and birth you. I experienced labour as a connection to generations of women who have borne the pain and changes of the world to make it a better place. You, Bear, have taught me it's time to listen to my gut and trust that my body speaks for a reason. You have taught me that "our bodies are never silent or invisible to the interactions that we are involved in" (Kannen 189). Instead, we learn through our bodies. Our bodies have been interacting since long before you were born. You teach me through how you view your body, how you interact with it, and how you interact with mine. It is knowledge we have "gained by paying close somatic attention to how and what our body feels when interacting with others in contexts" (Spry, *Body, Paper, Stage* 64).

I remember the first day it happened—that those audiencing our shared growing felt compelled to offer their feedback on my/our growing shape. At twenty-two weeks and a few days pregnant, I stopped in at our local sweet shop to see what they had to offer. As you know, an indulgent treat for myself is not out of the ordinary, so I thought nothing of my body shape as I walked into the store. I ordered one chocolate chip cookie, and when the woman behind the counter asked if I'd like anything else, I said, "You'd better make it two." She smiled, wrapped up my two chocolate chip cookies, and walked them to the person at the cash register. The woman who'd helped me chuckled and said, "Well, you are eating for two." My understanding of this phrase was that she was helping me justify my ordering two cookies, instead of just one. I understood this comment from her to be a mutual, if vague, understanding that I was pregnant, and two cookies would be okay to eat. I responded merely with, "Yeah," before I left the store a bit dazed. I didn't need her permission to order, let alone eat, the cookies. She had no idea if both or either of those cookies was for me, yet she still felt the need to help me justify eating them.

What might she have said if I wasn't pregnant in that moment? Would I have been allowed to have the cookies, or would I have been shamed because of my order? And why couldn't I come up with a better response? When I remember this exchange, I am sad that I couldn't love my body enough to be happy about cookies—to have explained to the person selling them that it didn't matter how many people I was eating for, I was going to enjoy those cookies. I hope you, too, choose what you want when you want because you are nurturing your body, not because someone gives you permission, however well intentioned.

Recently, you and I were watching a show when a person came on screen wearing a skin-tight silver dress with cutouts in the midriff. You said, "Mom, that dress would look so pretty on you." Without thinking, I replied, "That dress wouldn't work well on my body." You told me it would. You were adamant. As I reflected on that moment later, I wish I would have reacted differently. I wish I could have explained to you that your comment was flattering and that I appreciated you thinking I would look nice in the dress. Instead, I'm afraid that what I communicated was another reason to shame or hide the body—my body doesn't look like the person's body on screen; therefore, I shouldn't wear that dress. I am so hopeful that this moment, which now sits with me, was but a passing comment to you. I hope it brushes past you and doesn't become one chip of millions in the armour of your self-esteem. Yet I know the cultural conditioning I bring to our relationship. No matter how aware of these fleeting moments I am, I will assuredly miss other teachable moments or contribute to the cultural discourses you're inundated with.

In the years since you were born, I have worked to better understand what my body can do and how to nourish and respect my body to optimize my health and wellbeing. I hope to now model for you ways to take care of myself, not for weight loss or some impossible standard of thinness (like fitting in a tight, silver dress), but to show you that the food you eat becomes the fuel you can use and that some fuel is better for your body than others. That doesn't mean, of course, that we can't still get ice cream; sometimes loving your body is allowing yourself to indulge in treats you enjoy. I hope that I model for you movement—both for your physical and mental health—and that we can do that movement together. Mostly, I hope I teach you to respect the body you have, to learn to love it so it can help you live a long, healthy life. May I always learn from you and may you forever keep your appreciation of your body.

Love,
Mom

Email Two: Learning about Privilege

Dear Bear and Monkey,

As you no doubt know, the world can be a scary and hard place. When I was pregnant with Bear, I remember talking with a professor friend about the fear of bringing a child into a world that is so unfair, so prejudiced. Her response has stayed with me. She said, "We need good people to raise good people." Although that may seem boastful now, it is my hope that you two will be good people who help change the world. I hope you stand up to bullies and make the world, or at least your corner of it, brighter with your kindness, generosity, and radical love. You know these are values we have for you and try to model in our family. We've talked about differences and the importance of loving people who look and/or are different from us just like we love our own family. We have been to marches as a family, and we try to make it clear to you not only what we believe but why we believe it. We want you to be able to make your own decisions, even if we hope you'll embrace kindness, empathy, and love.

Here we are, in the middle of a pandemic that is both terrifying and boring. But our hearts were broken when we heard about George Floyd's murder. Bear asked us why we were upset. It became a lesson I wish we could shield you from, but one I didn't learn explicitly as a child, so we wanted you to have the truth. You can't make the world a better place until you can understand why it isn't the best place already. I was encouraged to see you enraged, Bear, to see you upset that the world could be cruel. This became a critical moment for us to help frame the world for you—to show you that racism affects all of us (McGhee) and that it's up to us to be antiracists in the world. We explained to you what Black Lives Matter is and its importance in affecting change. I was heartened when Bear began saying it, too, proclaiming in a video assignment for her remote Kindergarten class "because Black lives matter!" We were disappointed when her teacher responded, "Yes, all lives do matter." I couldn't help but see the language change as purposeful, so we talked through why "all lives matter" was not sufficient to address the racial problems facing Black lives now.

I am grateful to you for holding me accountable. Your presence requires me to contend with privilege; I have extra incentive to confront it if I want your world to be a better place than mine. I think about taking an evening walk with Bear one holiday season. In front of one house was a blow-up decoration of gingerbread people where one of the people had fallen. Bear said, "Oh, no! One of them fell over!" I responded, "Yup. The girl has fallen down." Without missing a beat, Bear said, "No, Mom. They. We don't know if it's a girl or a boy." I stopped, tipped up her chin, and told her I loved her. I was astounded. I came to an understanding of whiteness, gender, and privilege far later in life than I care to admit, and in this small interaction, I am hoping we (your parents) are correcting that course for you, providing the chance to grow up with an understanding of how privileged and lucky you are. I'm determined not to let any of us off the hook (Johnson). I do not want to raise children who contribute to the problem. Rather, your presence requires me to reflexively face hard truths about myself, my life, and the ways I affect the world so that I may teach you how to do the same. Because of you, I have learned to be a better feminist, focused on intersectional politics and on creating a better world than the one I feared bringing you into. May your strong wills be a force for good, mercy, and justice always. Don't grow up too fast.

Love,
Mom

Email Three: Modelling Advocacy

Dear Bear and Monkey,

I grew up a Midwestern kid. To me, that meant a certain level of politeness was at my core—that it was part of my nature to be polite to others. It's a value I hold dear, and I believe it has served me well. Yet the older I get, the more I realize how that value has also meant I've given time to people out of politeness or a sense of duty rather than a genuine level of respect. But I want more for you. As I've told you before, it matters to me that you are good, kind, and caring people. I want you to be respectful and thoughtful, but I'm not sure I want you to be polite. Certainly, decorum is called for in social situations, but I don't want you to waste your time being polite when it's not what you want to do (but still, be kind).

I think about our trip to the store the other day. After I got you both in the cart, we headed in to track down the items on our list. A salesperson approached us. I made brief eye contact but tried to focus on talking to you, hoping to passively indicate to said salesperson my complete noninterest in whatever they were selling. Unfortunately, the salesperson ignored that message and asked us how we were doing. These are the moments where I feel like an observer of the situation. My communication training kicks in, and I want to point out to the salesperson that I see the rhetorical strategies they're deploying and that I am not easily swayed because I'm too busy judging their choice of strategies. Yet I stood there and listened as the salesperson told me how we could get a free estimate on our roof, windows, or siding. We didn't need (nor want) any of those things, so I deployed my next passive Midwestern politeness tool: the clipped voice. As the salesperson spoke about the benefits of their program, I tried to indicate with my short answers that I wasn't interested. In the end, I walked away with a sheet of paper for a tentative appointment for someone to come look at our windows, which I didn't want.

I pushed the cart ahead a few aisles and turned the corner. Angry at myself, I looked at you two and said, "You never owe anyone your time, not even Mommy, do you understand me?" You both looked a bit taken aback—and really, how could you not? I was more or less yelling at you but not mad at you. I explained to you some of what I've written, that I've grown up giving people time, and that I don't want you to be people pleasers who feel you owe others your time. You get to decide who is important enough for you to give attention to, and I hope that person has earned your respect. I was almost shaking I was so upset. I called Dad and told him about the exchange and that we'd have to cancel the appointment. Ultimately, I called and cancelled and explained it was because I didn't want it. This felt like a turning point for me.

Without knowing it, you girls taught me, too, in that moment. I realized that my passive Midwestern roots, which I know have failed me, were being witnessed. This moment wasn't affecting only me, regardless of how mundane and trivial it might have felt. For me, it was a monumental lesson in advocacy. I had the power, now, in the moment, to change course. If I wanted different—better—for you two, then I needed to model better. I hope that lesson sank in. I hope that is what I'm seeing when we stopped for a break on our holiday trip, and as I am carrying Monkey into the gas station, I thank the person (who appeared to be a man) holding open the door. I realized that Bear had walked up, turned her back to hold open the door, and promptly told the person, "I've got it." Once inside the store, I told Bear that she could say thank you when someone holds the door. She responded, "I know, Mom, but I wanted to hold it." May I never take these small moments for granted, watching you assertively declare and achieve what it is you want and know you can do. I hope the situation in the store continues to be a turning point—that you see me better advocating for myself, and especially, advocating for you. May you never question whose side I'm on.

I love you dearly,
Mom

Lessons Learned

My children have taught me so much; my experience of motherhood has helped me become a better feminist. I learned more about loving my body and appreciating what it can do through pregnancy, early motherhood, and watching my children grow and learn about their bodies than I could have learned otherwise. For me, I needed the stark contrast of a life before and a life after to understand that love for my body was more than something I should do; it was something I already did. There are certainly other ways I might have learned this lesson, but the literal act of birthing children helped me understand that part of my feminism had to come with loving my body. In a culture premised on an impossibly narrow standard of beauty, my feminist politics had to include learning to love bodies, my own being first. Moreover, raising two children assigned female at birth means I have to model how to love my/other bodies. I do not want to perpetuate stereotypes and damaging narratives about how their bodies should look. I want to teach them how to love and nurture the bodies they have.

One of the hardest and most rewarding lessons becoming a mother has taught me about feminism is how much I still do not understand about privilege and intersectionality. Although I try to learn, grow, and be reflexive, the honesty of children is a powerful reminder of the growing I have left to do. My children have opened my eyes to so much about the world around me with simple questions. Their desire to better understand the world means I must as well. Choosing books and shows that feature representation of people who look and live differently from us is but a fraction of my responsibility to raising the next generation of feminists who can resist the patriarchy while also recognizing their privilege to do so. Whether that is learning to assert themselves and their desires or understanding how their lives have been privileged in ways their friends' lives may not have been, advocacy, intersectionality, and radical love are part of the feminist legacy I hope to model for and ultimately leave my children.

Conclusion

In an essay exploring the aims and meanings of feminist mothering, Andrea O'Reilly explains that feminist mothering of girls "is not about choosing blue over pink, or trucks over dolls but about *living*, to use the title of Marilyn Waring's work, *as if women counted*" ("'That Is What'" 200). This is my desire and goal in raising children assigned female at birth—to show them through the way I live that they count and that we all count. In this chapter, I used autoethnographic emails I have sent my daughters to detail some of the ways becoming their mother has helped me become a better intersectional feminist. Using autoethnography allows me to mine my personal history to connect my story to larger cultural narratives, such as intensive motherhood, which individuates mothers from working collectively towards feminist action that would benefit all parents and families. Sharing these emails, both for my children and for the readers of this chapter, is in answer to Glaser's call that realism—sharing what is real about a life lived—is a political act capable of building solidarity and a better world, a world that Olufemi claims is feminism's political project of potentiality. May the small moments of realism I share here and continue to share with my daughters be building blocks towards a better, more inclusive, more joyful, loving, and just world.

Works Cited

Adams, Tony E., Carolyn Ellis, and Stacy Holman Jones. "Autoethnography." *The International Encyclopedia of Communication Research Methods*, edited by Jörg Matthes, 2017, https://doi.org/10.1002/9781118901731.iecrm0011. Accessed 3 Apr. 2023.

Edley, Paige P., and Judy E. Battaglia. "Dying of Dismissal: An Autoethnographic Journey of Chronic Illness, Feminist Agency, and Health Advocacy." *Women and Language*, vol. 39, no. 1, 2016, pp. 33-48.

Ellis, Carolyn, Tony E. Adams, and Arthur P. Bochner. "Autoethnography: An Overview." *Historical Social Research*, vol. 36, no. 4, 2011, pp. 273-90.

Foster, Elissa. "Desiring Dialectical Discourse: A Feminist Ponders the Transition to Motherhood." *Women's Studies in Communication*, vol. 28, no. 1, 2005, pp. 57-83.

Ghabra, Haneen Shafeeq. "Disrupting Privileged and Oppressed Spaces: Reflecting Ethically on My Arabness through Feminist Autoethnography." *Kaleidoscope: A Graduate Journal of Qualitative Communication Research*, vol. 14, 2015, pp. 1-15.

Glaser, Eliane. "Parent Trap: Why the Cult of the Perfect Mother Has to End." *The Guardian*, 18 May 2021, https://www.theguardian.com/lifeandstyle/2021/may/18/parent-trap-why-the-cult-of-the-perfect-mother-has-to-end. Acccessed 4 Apr. 2023.

Griffin, Rachel Alicia. "I AM an Angry Black Woman: Black Feminist Autoethnography, Voice, and Resistance." *Women's Studies in Communication*, vol. 35, no. 2, 2012, pp. 138-57.

Hays, Sharon. *The Cultural Contradictions of Motherhood*. Yale University Press, 1996.

Johnson, Allan G. *Privilege, Power, and Difference*. 2nd ed. McGraw-Hill, 2006.

Kannen, Victoria. "Pregnant, Privileged, and PhDing: Exploring Embodiments in Qualitative Research." *Journal of Gender Studies*, vol. 22, no. 2, 2013, pp. 178-91.

Lauricella, Sharon. "Bam! Pow! Vanish? A Feminist Autoethnography of Gender Performance and Covert Influences on Twitter." *Women and Language*, vol. 41, no. 2, 2018, pp. 62-78.

Olufemi, Lola. *Feminism, Interrupted: Disrupting Power*. Pluto Press, 2020.

Olufemi, Lola. "Redefining the F Word: A Talk with Lola Olufemi." Women's History Month, 24 Mar. 2021, University of Texas at Arlington, Arlington. Lecture.

O'Reilly, Andrea. "Introduction." *Feminist Mothering*, edited by Andrea O'Reilly, University of New York Press, 2008, pp. 1-22.

O'Reilly, Andrea. *Matricentric Feminism: Theory, Activism, and Practice*. Demeter Press, 2016.

O'Reilly, Andrea. "'That Is What Feminism Is—The Acting and Living and Not Just the Told': Modeling and Mentoring Feminism." *Feminist Mothering*, edited by Andrea O'Reilly, State University of New York Press, 2008, pp. 191-202.

McGhee, Heather. *The Sum of Us: What Racism Costs Everyone and How We Can Prosper Together*. One World, 2021.

Richardson, Laurel. "Writing: A Method of Inquiry." *Handbook of Qualitative Research*, edited by Norman K. Denzin and Yvonna S. Lincoln, Sage, 2000, pp. 923-48.

Sotirin, Patty. "Autoethnographic Mother-Writing: Advocating Radical Specificity." *Journal of Research Practice*, vol. 6, no. 1, 2010, Article M9, www.researchgate.net/publication/49611627_Autoethnographic_Mother-Writing_Advocating_Radical_Specificity. Accessed 4 Apr. 2023.

Spry, Tami. *Body, Paper, Stage: Writing and Performing Autoethnography.* Left Coast, 2011.

Spry, Tami. "Performing Autoethnography: An Embodied Methodological Praxis." *Qualitative Inquiry*, vol. 7, 2001, pp. 706-32.

Stern, Danielle M. "Engaging Autoethnography: Feminist Voice and Narrative Intervention." *Women and Language*, vol. 38, no. 1, 2015, pp. 83-102.

Wiant Cummins, Molly, and Grace Ellen Brannon. "The Balancing Act is Magnified: U.S. Mothers' Struggles amidst a Pandemic." *Mothers, Mothering, and COVID-19: Dispatches from a Pandemic*, edited by Andrea O'Reilly and Fiona Joy Green. Demeter Press, 2021, pp. 211-20.

Chapter 15.

Recognizing Their Feminist Selves through the Journey of Mothering: Reflections of Urban Indian Mothers

Ketoki Mazumdar, Sneha Parekh Gupta, and Isha Sen

Introduction

Indian feminist Jasodhara Bagchi asserts: "Motherhood without the mother's selfhood is not complete" (20). This chapter explores how a cohort of urban Indian mothers with children below the age of ten years are recognizing their feminist selves and challenging traditional mothering practices in the urban twenty-first century. For years, women have endeavoured to make meaning of one of the most critical roles they are required to assume in our societies—that of being a mother. There are gendered social structures which are prescriptive and meant to be followed and performed within familial roles to maintain social order. However, as noted by Leela Dube, "It is within these limits that women question their situation, express resentment, use manipulative strategies, utilize their skills, turn deprivation and self-denial into sources of power, and attempt to carve out a living space" (113). Mainstream media is suffused with traditional mothering practices, whereas there is a lack of matricentric feminist research in academe within the Indian context.

This situation led the authors to engage in in-depth interviews with a cohort of Indian heterosexual mothers of children below the age of ten years to unpack their lived experiences of mothering in today's age in an urban landscape. The authors interviewed seven mothers living in large cities in India. All the respondents have at least one child (50 per cent of the mothers have one child and 50 per cent have two children), ranging in age from new-born to ten years. The mothers (aged between thirty-two and forty) who were interviewed all belonged to the upper middle class or the middle class and had the cultural capital of being educated with a minimum of a bachelor's degree and were either homemakers (n=three) or professionals (n=five). Young children are more dependent on their mothers for daily functioning, which increases the amount of time and effort mothers put in to raise them. This dynamic creates a space in which mothers feel conflicted between providing the best nurturing environment for their children while trying to maintain a similar environment for themselves. Through this process of conflict and evolution, emerges a feminist mother (Gordon 149). As the authors delved deeper into the lived experiences of the participants, through the process of thematic analysis, three themes were identified from their narrations: recognizing one's feminism and gaining agency; feminism for the future; and gender-neutral parenting. These themes, along with the voices of the respondents, are unpacked under the lens of feminist and sociocultural perspectives and discussed in the following chapter.

The association between motherhood and womanhood, alongside the magnification of maternal work in Indian society, puts a lot of responsibility on the mother. Although parenting has become a more collaborative process, the buck still stops with the mother. Mothers are often left with no option but to accept all the responsibilities they are given. Thus, it is important to listen to mothers to achieve a more egalitarian society. Matricentric feminism positions mothering as a site of empowerment, where mothers have a voice to challenge patriarchal motherhood. In "It Saved My Life," Andrea O'Reilly discusses the importance of a mother-centred position:

> In affirming the importance of mothers' voices, this mother-centered standpoint leads to the development of critical consciousness by linking personal experiences with wider structures of power and inequity. Through this, women are able to name, analyze and challenge patriarchal motherhood by gaining control, exercising choices, and in engaging in collective social action (197).

In the current study, interviews were transcribed verbatim and were thematically analyzed. The respondents were assigned pseudonyms in order to protect their identity and anonymity. The authors would like to state that this is not meant to be a representative sample of Indian mothers or even of mothers who identify as feminists. Their narratives are, moreover, not representative of all middle- and/or upper-middle-class women, even though their interviews were located within a generally defined construct of middle-class India. The mothers' narratives have been used to portray the newer wave of feminist mothering that a certain cohort of mothers are employing and reflecting upon to navigate mothering within a sociocultural context that is deeply heteropatriarchal in nature.

The Mothering Discourse

"Mother" is one of the oldest words in the history of humankind. Mothering as a phenomenon has been noted to be a complex and deeply personal experience, largely guided by the affective and cognitive processes of maternal thinking discourse (Ruddick 349-351), which is constructed from "reflection, judgement, and emotion" about their maternal roles (Ruddick 77). Motherhood refers to the patriarchal institution of motherhood, which is deeply oppressive in nature towards women, whereas mothering refers to "the *potential relationship* of any woman to her powers of reproduction and to children; and the *institution*, which aims at ensuring that that potential—and all women—shall remain under male control" (Rich 13). Andrea O'Reilly notes the following: "The term motherhood refers to the patriarchal institution of motherhood that is male-defined and controlled and is deeply oppressive to women, while the word mothering refers to women's experiences of mothering that are female-defined and centred and potentially empowering to women" (*Feminist Mothering* 3). The term "mothering" is viewed as lived experience and is used to denote a woman who cares psychologically and physically for the child, which also includes feeding, washing, and other daily activities, whereas the other family members, especially the father, are largely not engaged.

Sara Ruddick argues that the work of mothering is akin to the real act of caring practices that a mother engages in while raising a child. These acts can undergo a change guided by the mother's feminist consciousness, nurturing, and caring experiences. Ruddick highlights the transformations that mothering practices can bring when they are informed by feminist consciousness, as it "shifts the balance away from illusion and passivity toward active responsibility and engagement," thus affirming "its own criteria of acceptability" (222). Moreover, when mothers have a conscious feminist lens guiding them, they find ways to resist the values of the existing dominant heteropatriarchal culture. This also gives them a chance to appreciate, and make informed decisions regarding, how many of those dominant values and tropes to actively challenge and, thus, not blindly follow them (238).

The Indian Mothering Experience

In Indian culture, motherhood is tied to a woman's a priori dharma, which is associated with morality and righteousness. Mainstream literature is peppered with maternal tropes that represent the ultimate purpose of a woman. "Every woman is a mother in embryo. That is her supreme function in life. That is her social mission," said Lala Lajpat Rai, a leader of India's independence movement, at the beginning of the twentieth century (qtd. in Kishwar 105). Swami Vivekananda, an acclaimed nineteenth-century philosopher and saint, described an ideal woman in India as "the mother ... marvellous, unselfish, all-suffering" (2473). Even though these instances are from the past, they still represent the larger sociocultural discourses happening today. The contemporary Indian mother is considered to be devoted to her family. She takes care of her children, often at the cost of her own needs and life ambitions, thus becoming another product of the traditional heteropatriarchal construct of motherhood (Sarkar 2; Dutta 132; Sharma 2). As Amrita Nandy argues: "Among all gendered roles, motherhood is a rich realm to understand what we have come to know and refer to as the 'Self.' Self-sacrifice, self-abnegation or simply selflessness are assumed, expected and extolled as inherently feminine and specifically maternal traits" (2). The sacrifices a mother makes to meet the demands of her roles are often made invisible or taken for granted; her own desires are also thwarted.

Sashi Deshpande argues that these unrealistic demands thrust upon Indian mothers are done in an effort to associate their maternal roles with self-sacrifice: "Actually, as far as women are concerned, the mother myth, an immensely powerful one, is a huge burden.... We have made it almost impossible for us to get past the image of the ever-forgiving, the always-sacrificing mother" (97). This idea is not only limited to India. Western feminists, too, have argued that the predominant image of the "ever-bountiful, ever-giving, self-sacrificing mother" is "a socially supported myth designed to keep women in their place" (Bassin et al. 3). This thinking is suffused with tropes wherein a mother births sons to carry forwards the family lineage, and daughters are expected to follow in the mother's obedient footsteps and take the onus of carework on their shoulders. Indian culture has over centuries glorified and worshipped the sacrificing nature of mothers who are devoted to their family and home: "An Indian woman's individual identity is subsumed under her identity as a mother, even more so than being a wife. In Indian cultures, motherhood is exalted as nearly divine and is positioned to everything human and mundane" (Dasgupta and Dasgupta 133). India is possibly one of a few countries where goddesses are worshipped, as per the Hindu religion; women are called "ghar ki Lakshmi," or 'goddess of the house,' and their status is put on a pedestal. Yet this glorification involves the subjugation of their agency, compromising their empowerment (Hegde 26; Krishnaraj 5). This dynamic limits a woman from engaging in activities that are not devoted to the household; if they do, they are not revered like those who focus on their energies on the household.

Dube notes how girls growing up in the patrilineal structure of Indian society become socialized into acquiring a particular identity through several rituals and ceremonies, language, and other practices (88). The identity of a daughter is often that of a temporary one in traditional heteropatriarchal societies, where the young girls are moulded to leave their house and prepare for their future role of wife, daughter-in-law, and mother. One may also observe a stark difference between a woman's and man's work starting in early childhood, which is reflected in the tasks and roles assigned to them. Girl children are continuously and consciously trained to get ready for their future roles as wives and mothers—roles they would perform in another family, the family they get married to (Dube 102). The traditional heteronormative, patrilineal family, thus, becomes the heart of patriarchal social systems and the epicentre of gender inequality practices, quelling women both within the family and outside as well. Women therefore end up internalizing these practices as prescriptive norms, which prevent their feminist selves from developing or being expressed. This internalization applies to the context of Indian mothers, for whom it has become a normalized practice to put themselves last or perhaps not even consider their own needs. Indian mothers find themselves juggling their household responsibilities, extensive mothering duties, the phenomenon of intensive mothering, and the expectations of being a wife and daughter-in-law, often at the cost of their own wellbeing (Grewal, Bottorho, and Hilton). Alternatively, feminist mothering practices are considered to be a seat of empowered mothering:

> Empowered mothers do not always put their children's needs before their own nor do they only look to motherhood to define and realize their identity. Rather, their selfhood is fulfilled and expressed in various ways: work, activism, friendships, relationships, hobbies and motherhood. These mothers insist upon their own authority as mothers and refuse the relinquishment of their power as mandated in the patriarchal institution of motherhood (O'Reilly, *Rocking the Cradle* 47).

In the following sections, this chapter will portray the lived experiences of urban Indian mothers' engagement in feminist mothering practices and processes.

Feminist Mothering

With the advent of modernization, under the influence of globalization and neoliberalism, a larger number of Indian women are becoming professionals (Kadale, Pandey, and Raje 1; Manimekalai, Sivakumar, and Geetha 168) and have chosen to continue to work after having children (Bhaumik and Sahu 2905; Dey and Das 68). This situation has led to women making huge strides in their education and professional careers, which have given rise to the concept of "supermom"—a mother who effortlessly balances both their personal and professional lives while keeping invisible the actual lived experiences of being a mother. Alongside taking these strides, mothers have also, in their own ways, started to challenge and resist the idealized institution of motherhood; they have highlighted the need to make their mothering experiences more visible and recognized. Acts defying traditional sociocultural constructs of motherhood can be found in everyday instances, such as recognizing the need to change the family system so that mothers can better express their agency through mothering now and in the future.

Motherhood studies provides a matricentric perspective to allow narratives of resistance wherein mothers share their lived experiences and express themselves through various forms of writing, artwork, poetry, and blogs—as a way of confronting the homogeneous cavernous patriarchal illustrations and single dominant stories of stereotypical motherhood that subjugate mothers. O'Reilly states the following in her book *Mothers, Mothering and Motherhood*

> I understand feminist mothering to refer to an oppositional discourse of motherhood, one that is constructed as a negation of patriarchal motherhood, seeking to interrupt the master narrative of patriarchal motherhood, and to imagine and implement a view of mothering that is empowering to women. Feminist mothering may refer to any practice of mothering that seeks to challenge and change various aspects of patriarchal motherhood that cause mothering to be limiting or oppressive to women. (187)

When using the term "feminist mothering," we also refer to the practice of gender-neutral parenting, where children are brought up as human beings and not pigeonholed into rigid and socially constructed gender roles, which are often hierarchical in nature. Thus, according to O'Reilly, feminist mothering is a process to "create a mode of mothering that is empowering in and for mothers" (*Mothers, Mothering and Motherhood* 187) and a "practice that seeks to grant mothers agency, authority, authenticity, autonomy, and advocacy/activism denied to them in patriarchal motherhood" (O'Reilly, *Mothers, Mothering, and Motherhood* 189). Matricentric feminism takes on a mother-centred perspective, in which motherhood is understood to be "socially and historically constructed, and positions mothering more as a practice than an identity" (O'Reilly, "Matricentric Feminism" 57). No wonder then that mothers as individuals have been seeking an identity beyond the halo of motherhood (Krishnaraj 5) in an attempt to navigate traditional heteropatriarchal social systems as well as to break single dominant stories in an attempt to narrate preferred stories for themselves. Tuula Gordon summarizes her idea of a feminist mother as:

The way in which they challenge and criticize myths of motherhood; the way in which they consider it their right to work (in the labour force); the antisexist way in which they bring up their children; the way in which they expect fathers of their children to participate in joint everyday lives; and the way in which many of them are politically active (149).

Findings

The following quotes by mothers interviewed in the study potently exemplify the reasons why it is so critical that their lived experiences be shared. Mothers are burdened with much invisible labour. For example, Aanya[1] expressed: "If I tell my husband, I had to do this twenty times today, he would say, 'So what if you had to do it, you're a mother, you should be doing it.' I think that he's ignoring the extra effort that I put in, and if it was left to him, then probably my child would be just watching television, have unkempt hair, and things like that." As highlighted by the interviewee, even with the time and effort that mothers put into their mothering practices, there lies a vacuum in how their efforts are perceived. Three respondents discussed the sheer lack of understanding from the husband's side. For example, Sabrina[2] shared: "There is also that ignorance from my husband's side where at times he thinks that it [parenting work] is anyways expected of me to do, so it is not something that needs to be acknowledged." Mothers are often left unacknowledged and unappreciated. And when they do express themselves and their needs, they are often disregarded and left without a voice. Whereas the role of the mother is diminished as the primary caregiver, her presence is spotlighted if the child is perceived to be behaving incorrectly. This sentiment is lucidly highlighted by Ira[3]: "Whatever bad happens, it's like your mom has not taught you this; your mom has not taught you that, it always circles back to the mom." Socially unacceptable behaviours or traits of children are solely attributed to the mother, disregarding the other influences the child has, including family members and societal interactions, thus adhering to the notion of "glorification without empowerment" (Krishnaraj 5). This applies to the Indian context, as expressed through A.S. Altekar's words when he states that the zenith of the "mother" is higher in India than anywhere else (100). In

India, motherhood is glorified tremendously while simultaneously existing in parallel with the domination of mothers as well as women in general (Dey and Das 66). This dichotomy prevails across intersections of class, caste, or location. Gender inequalities that are prevalent in patriarchal society are often hidden by this overt and explicit glorification of mothers.

The following section will discuss the emergent themes along with narratives of mothers to elucidate the findings.

Recognizing Feminism and Gaining Agency

Feminism believes that women are individuals first and that their roles as mothers are one of the multiple roles they embody. By empowering a woman's right to choose to become a mother or not, feminism acts as a reminder for mothers that they have lives outside their roles of a mother. While being a feminist and a mother, women are often bound by stereotypes and struggles peppered with situations that induce guilt, especially as they traverse the heteropatriarchal sociocultural landscape. When mothers start to challenge and seek answers for these set-in-stone cultural norms about how mothers ought to be, how they ought to present themselves, and how they raise their children, feminism helps in unravelling and challenging these prescribed norms about mothering. To understand what feminism is, one often needs to unpack what feminism is not, which the mothers in this study did. For example, they reported that they had identified what was not aligned with their feminist and mothering ideologies and made efforts to change them. One example of this kind of challenge included that of their identities being limited to that of a mother by their family members. As Reena[4] explained:

> It's about what others think I should do. For example, on a Sunday, when I have my parents around, and I want to do something for myself, people constantly keep asking me to spend time with my baby. There are so many people at home. It doesn't mean that the mother has to be completely attached with the baby the whole day for the baby to feel good. I found this a little difficult because I get only one day off. I also need some time for myself.

These thoughts resonated with our understanding of matricentric feminism, in which mothering is seen more as a practice than an identity (O'Reilly, *Matricentric Feminism* 16). Instead of conforming to the traditional expectations of mothering while adhering to patriarchal sociocultural norms, the mothers in this study reported that they asserted themselves by establishing boundaries, engaging in other activities, and embodying roles they wished to have, along with mothering. Ira elaborated: "You first need to understand whether whatever you have thought is logical and practical. If you feel it is required and others are not permitting, you will have to explain to them what is reasonable and what is not." Traditionally, Indian mothers have spent their days—and are therefore expected to—being engaged in caregiving chores focussed on family and children, often at the expense of having time for themselves. The respondents in the study challenged this notion by putting in place boundaries and asserting aspects of their identities outside of being a mother while simultaneously not compromising their mothering duties. In order to navigate the traditional heteropatriarchal social systems, mothers have been seeing an identity beyond that of motherhood (Krishnaraj 5).

With men being the breadwinners in traditional heteropatriarchal Indian families, women typically have not had financial autonomy, and this has been an acceptable part of their daily familial lives. Over the years, with more women gaining higher academic qualifications and being engaged in paid labour, their financial dependency on male partners has reduced, allowing them more autonomy in making financial decisions. The study's cohort of mothers expressed their need to be engaged professionally in paid labour. Rupa[5] shared. "When I want something, and he [husband] decides it isn't the right time yet, I think I would be in a better place if I were financially independent. I should have been working." Ira had the same thoughts and further explained her desire for getting into paid employment: "Maybe teaching or any work, which is a little away from the house and gives me time for myself and also supports me financially." As highlighted by the interviewee, being professionally engaged not only transformed them into being financially independent but also allowed them to have an identity for themselves beyond the four walls of their household. Sabrina also added: "I think any woman should be a little stubborn and determined to work. It could be anything, a job that could make you happy. I mean financial independence is also necessary. Otherwise, you're always dependent on everyone, both financially and emotionally." Whereas Sabrina spoke about financial and emotional independence, Rupa spoke about inspiring future generations, like her daughter. She explained: "Whatever I do will set the example for my daughter. If I tell her to study, I have to give her a realistic picture of what lies in the future if you study. If she sees that I am a chartered accountant and a stay-at-home mother, but I do nothing with numbers and only clean, she would question me as to why would I study so much if this is what I have to do in the future." Although mothers in the study wanted to be professionally engaged for personal reasons, it was also to set an example for their children.

Mothers in the study experienced both gender bias and inequality in the way they were raised. This was powerfully demonstrated by Aanya: "My dad really pushed me to be ambitious, like, study harder, and he pushed me to do different things. He never made me feel like there's something I can't do because I am a girl.... But at the same time, when we were growing up, my dad would say that I have to serve the food, not my brother. I would have to clean up once we finish eating, not my brother." This disparity in parenting practices based on gender was a part of the study cohort's upbringing. It is these gaps or differential parenting coupled with unequal treatment that allowed their feminist identities to develop. Reflecting back, they could identify what they would have liked to be different in the way they were raised and decided to further implement it in their parenting towards their children. Srabani Maitra discusses in her work that "agency needs to be understood in its full complexities and ambiguities rather than blindly equating it with outright collective defiance or resistance" (48). Thus, these expressions of agency by the respondents may not be perceived as extremely powerful by both their families and society at large because they are not as overtly expressed towards the oppression that mothers might experience; nevertheless, they hold significance for the mothers engaged in such practices.

Feminism for the Future

Rupa, a mother of a daughter and a son shared her thoughts on how she wished for her children to grow up:

> In the kitchen, what is to be cooked and what should be cleaned? I don't think he's [husband] capable of doing that. And I want to change that. I want Karan [son] to be somebody who's capable of

doing that, and I want Alia [daughter] to grow up to be somebody who does not have this thing in her head that my husband is not capable of doing kitchen related and/or domestic chores. You know, I want her to feel that we are the same, and if I am capable, my husband should also be capable, too. I want to raise them both equally.

By engaging in feminist practices as such, these mothers question preexisting gendered prescriptions and prejudices regarding how boys and girls must be raised, which, in turn, changes how mothers view themselves—both as mothers and as women. Applying a feminist lens to mothering can create certain conflicts by showing that mothering is loaded with social stereotypes and plagued with feelings of guilt. Mothers no longer wish to be constrained within the socially imposed boundaries of what a mother's role has been typically defined to be. Thus, feminism challenges multiple stereotypes and gender biases about childrearing, women, and mothers. A world with egalitarian gender-neutral values can only be achieved when all sexes and genders are trained and raised to perform all types of chores and develop a variety of caregiving, parenting, household, and professional skills.

As O'Reilly argues, "A feminist mother, in other words, is a woman whose mothering, in theory and practice, is shaped and influenced by feminism" (*Mothers* 191). These ideas resonated in the narratives of the mothers in this study. Reflecting on her experiences, Ivy[6] shared the following: "I have experienced situations where the household has to be run by females only, and I don't want my daughter to go through this. I want her to understand that the responsibility of home is on everyone, be it male or female." This participant provides insight into how vital it is to break gender stereotypes.

Gender roles and norms are not innate to human beings; rather, they are a product of socialization. These biases can be changed not just from female perspectives and experiences but also from those of males. Boys can be taught to not adhere to masculine tropes and express themselves freely and be accepting of traits traditionally seen as feminine (such as crying or cooking). In traditional Indian households, there is a clear distinction between men's work and women's work. As observed by Dube, girls, from early childhood, are trained for future roles as wives and mothers, which is reflected in the tasks assigned to them (102), whereas boys are encouraged to avoid household chores and instead focus on their future careers. The mothers were aware that such values are not solely imparted by parents; societal influences also play a large role. Children learn from their surroundings—from their friends, schools, relatives, to count a few. This was reflected in Reena's words: "In her [daughter] school, the teacher was showing a story with photos of the mother wearing a saree and cooking and the father going to the office. However, in our home, both mother and father go to the office. I don't think my daughter relates to the story, and I don't want her to." Reena was aware of the external influences on her child's upbringing. Even with more women involved in professional paid labour, deep-rooted gender stereotypes and gender-role biases are still prevalent within families and societal norms. As understood through feminist literature, women are seen as individuals before anything else. They have multiple roles, one of which may be that of mother. Although a woman may choose motherhood or not, it is important to note that they all have a life outside of their mothering journeys. O'Reilly in her book *Mothers, Mothering and Motherhood* states as follows:

> Mothers resist patriarchal motherhood simply to make the experience of mothering more rewarding for themselves and their children. In so far as this aim challenges the patriarchal mandate of maternal selflessness, sacrifice and martyrdom, these mothers are resistant in their insistence upon more time for themselves and support from others.... In contrast, feminist mothers resist because they recognize that gender inequity, in particular male privilege and power, is produced, maintained and perpetuated (i.e. though sexist childrearing) in patriarchal motherhood.... Thus, while in practice the two seem similar—i.e. demanding more involvement from fathers, insisting upon a life outside of motherhood—only with feminist mothering does this involve a larger awareness of, and challenge to, the gender (among other) inequities of patriarchal culture. (*Mothers* 192)

Gender-Neutral Parenting

Pioneering author and feminist Adrienne Rich notes the following: "Perhaps for a long-time men will need a kind of compensatory education in the things about which their education as males has left them illiterate" (216). For the mothers in this study, through an egalitarian upbringing of children within the home, they aimed to counter and navigate deeply entrenched heteropatriarchal discourses. For example, Kyra[7] shared how she ensured gender neutrality through her parenting:

> We consciously don't use words like "pretty." We consciously use words like "smart," "strong," "brave." To even acknowledge her [daughter], we say, "That was a very smart thing to say," or, you know, "Today you're looking nice." These are consciously chosen words, not saying, "Today you are looking very pretty." I think what we say typically is "This is really suiting you well."

The respondents realized the importance of using gender-neutral words and made conscious efforts to do the same. This kind of feminist learning used by the mothers in their home is a way for them to offset the patriarchal socialization within which children and families have traditionally grown up. Reena shared a small success of her mothering efforts: "Today we had a haircut, and my daughter asked, 'Do I look like a boy?' and I said, 'Oh, you don't. You're wearing a dress." "Even boys can wear dresses," she said. And I felt so good about that because, I feel somewhere I'm succeeding in imparting gender neutrality. I feel the right thing to do is to be gender neutral about things." Rupa shared something similar about her daughter: "She loves the Lion King, and her best friend is a boy. They used to play the Lion King, and she would be Simba, and he used to be Nala. I love the way she has been able to be gender fluid about characters she loves and impersonates." The mothers in the study shared the joy of small successes in instilling gender-neutral values in their children. In heteropatriarchal societies, such as India, mothers are expected to be the primary caretakers and therefore impart norms to their children. While they may sometimes be gender neutral, the norms often veer towards being gender specific. For instance, mothers should teach girls to be good, domesticated future wives and mothers and teach them such skills as sewing and cooking. In contrast, boys are taught to be assertive, daring, and fearless. These forms of prescriptive gender stereotyping typically begin and are reinforced during the early years of a child's life by their mother.

Feminist mothering purposefully steers away from a gender-biased form of upbringing and moves towards a more progressive and egalitarian approach. The narratives in the study showed that mothers work to ensure a gender-neutral approach in their daily activities, including (but not limited to) choices regarding colours, games, sports, clothes, words, and stories as well as behavioural expectations and engagement in household chores. As Chimamanda Ngozi Adichie emphasizes "[For] a fairer world ... a world of happier men and happier women who are truer to themselves ... this is how to start: we must raise our daughters differently. We must also raise our sons differently" (25). We must shift the existing gender-biased discourses

Concluding Thoughts

In her edited collection, *Motherhood in India*, Maithreyi Krishnaraj states the following:

> It is not the fact of mothering that makes women vulnerable, but their social construction, the implications for women owing from the meaning attached to the idea of motherhood, and the terms and conditions under which it is allowed to express itself. Being a mother is a fulfilling experience. However, in reality, it becomes a burden to be borne by women, because they do not get adequate support from society. (7)

Although India has made noticeable progress over the past few decades, it is still considered a traditionally heteropatriarchal society in which women's roles are centred around the home, often under the hegemony and surveillance of the male members of the family. After becoming a mother, a woman gains some semblance of agency through her role as a mother within the traditional family system. What does it mean to recognize one's feminist self through the journey of motherhood/mothering in twenty-first-century urban India, especially when feminists are increasingly being considered a difficult group of people? Mothers practising matricentric feminism in the current sociocultural space are navigating the demands of mothering to engage in breaking the chain of traditional mothering practices and laying the foundation for an egalitarian future for themselves and their children. Amber E. Kinser notes: "The terrain of motherhood ... is still difficult ground for most women to navigate.... Despite feminist effort and accomplishment, women still are largely thought of first in terms of maternal capacity"

(161). The primary reason for this is the still prevalent link between motherhood and lesser social status, which is being thrust upon mothers. Home can be a good starting point for mothers to initiate conversations and practices around more egalitarian gender-neutral parenting, raising conscientious individuals, and finding one's agency towards recognizing their feminist selves while being mothers. There has been a growing number of feminist maternal scholars who, in their pursuit of maternal agency and empowerment, have identified active resistance as a response to dominant ideologies (Green; Horowitz; Lopez; Miller; O'Reilly). Maternal agency is described as "mothering practices that facilitate women's authority and power and is revealed in mothers' efforts to challenge and act against aspects of institutionalized motherhood that constrain and limit women's lives and powers as mothers" (O'Reilly, "It Saved My Life" 189).

Due to India's cultural diversity, its class and caste differences, as well as its rural-urban divides, there is a certain amount of variation in how mothering is experienced and represented. Throughout this chapter, we have endeavoured to represent the voices of mothers located within the sociocultural contexts of Urban India, and we hope these voices are encouraging steps for mothers across the country to embody the empowering matricentric feminist approaches towards rewriting and redefining the rules of mothering for themselves. The mothers reflected on how they realized the need to change existing patterns within the family and larger society. This bolstered connections with their feminist identities and encouraged the development of their agency—both as mothers and as women. This is also a process whereby mothers are finding their own agency and raising strong, independent, egalitarian, and resilient children as part of larger and deeply personal feminist mothering practices. At the same time, they are also crafting their own stories instead of following the dominant single story of how to be a mother (Green).

Endnotes

1. Aanya is a thirty-four-year-old homemaker with a background in investment banking. She lives in a nuclear family with her husband and six-year-old daughter.
2. Sabrina is a thirty-two-year-old chartered accountant, working part

time. She lives in a joint family with her husband, mother-in-law, and her nine-months-old infant.

3. Ira is a thirty-three-year-old stay-at-home mother with a master's degree in accounting and finance. She lives with her husband, parents-in-law, and two six-year-old children.

4. Reena is a thirty-year-old assistant professor at a national university, holding a doctorate degree in human resources. She lives with her extended family, consisting of her four-year-old son, husband, parents, in-laws, and a pet dog.

5. Rupa is a thirty-three-year-old homemaker with a background in chartered accountancy. She lives with her husband, parents-in-law, brother-in-law, sister-in-law, and two children, aged six and three.

6. Ivy is a forty-year-old woman with a postgraduate degree. She lives with her husband and two children, aged nine and six years, in a nuclear family.

7. Kyra is a thirty-seven-year-old MBA graduate, currently working in the television industry. She currently lives in a nuclear family with her husband and four-year-old daughter.

Works Cited

Adichie, Chimamanda Ngozi. *We Should All Be Feminists*. Fourth Estate, 2014.

Altekar, A.S. *The Position of Women in Hindu Civilization: From Prehistoric Times to the Present Day*. Motilal Banarsidass Publishers, 1959.

Bhagchi, Jasodhara. "Foreword: Motherhood Revisited." *Janani: Mothers, Daughters, Motherhood*, edited by Rinki Bhattacharya, Sage Publications, 2006, pp. 11-21.

Bhaumik, Sanjukta, and Sahu, Sudhansubala. "My Motherhood, My Way: A Sociological Study of Contemporary Employed Mothers in Kolkata." *Journal of International Women's Studies*, vol. 22, no. 6, 2021, pp. 66-75, https://vc.bridgew.edu/jiws/vol22/iss6/8. Accessed 4 Apr. 2023.

Bassin, Donna, Margaret Honey, and Meryle Mahrer Kaplan, eds. *Representations of Motherhood*. Yale University Press, 1994.

DasGupta, Sayantani and Shamita Dasgupta. "Motherhood Jeopardized:

Reproductive Technologies in Indian Communities." *Global Motherhood*, edited by W. Chavkin and J. Maher, Routledge, 2010.

Deshpande, Shashi. *Writing from the Margin and Other Essays.* Penguin, 2003.

Dey, Arpita, and Das, Dipendu. "Motherhood in India: Myths, Theories, and Literature." *Research Journal of English Language and Literature*, vol. 8, no. 3, 2020, pp. 65-67.

Dube, Leela. *Anthropological Explorations in Gender: Intersecting Fields.* Sage, 2001.

Dutta, Sangeeta. "Relinquishing the Halo: Portrayal of Mother in Indian Writing in English." *Economic and Political Weekly*, vol. 25, no. 42/43, 1990, pp. WS84-94. J.

Gupta, Nandini. "Deconstructing the Hailing of 'Mother India.'" *Journal of International Women's Studies*, vol. 22, no. 9, 2021, pp, 128 -141.

Gordon, T. *Feminist Mothers.* New York University Press, 1994.

Green, Fiona J. *Practicing Feminist Mothering.* Arbeiter Ring Pub., 2011.

Grewal, Sukhdev, Joan L. Bottor, and Ann B. Hilton. "The Influence of Family on Immigrant South Asian Women's Health." *Journey of Family Nursing*, vol. 11, no. 3, 2005, pp. 242-63.

Hegde, Radha, S. "Sons and M(others): Framing the Maternal Body and the Politics of Reproduction in a South Indian Context." *Women's Studies in Communication*, vol. 22, no. 1, 1999, pp. 25-44.

Horwitz, E. *Through the Maze of Motherhood: Empowered Mothers Speak.* Demeter Press, 2011.

Kadale, Prajakta G., Aastha N. Pandey, and Swati S. Raje. "Challenges of Working Mothers: Balancing Motherhood and Profession." *International Journal of Community Medicine and Public Health*, vol. 5, no. 7, 2018, pp. 2905-10.

Kinser, Amber E. *Motherhood and Feminism*: Seal Press, 2010.

Kishwar, Madhu. "The Daughters of Aryavrata." *Women in Colonial India: Essays on Survival, Work, and the State,* edited by J. Krishnamurthy, Oxford University Press, 1999.

Krishnaraj, Maitryei. *Motherhood in India: Glorification Without Empowerment?* Routledge, 2009.

Lopez, L. K. "The Radical Act of 'Mommy Blogging': Redefining

Motherhood through the Blogosphere." *New Media & Society*, vol. 11, no. 5, 2009, pp. 729-47.

Maitra, Srabani. *Redefining 'Enterprising Selves': Exploring the "Negotiation" of South Asian Immigrant Women Working as Home-Based Enclave Entrepreneurs.* 2011. Ontario Institute for Studies in Education, Unpublished dissertation.

Manimekalai, K., I. Sivakumar, and S. Geetha. "Working Mothers and Parenting: Health Status in India." *IJAR*, vol. 5, no. 9, 2019, pp. 168-73.

Miller, T. *Making Sense of Motherhood: A Narrative Approach.* Cambridge University Press, 2005.

Nandy, Amrita. "Shadow of Motherhood: Writing the Outlier Self." *UCLA: Center for the Study of Women*, 2014, https://escholarship.org/uc/item/38x7122z. Accessed 4 Apr. 2023.

O'Reilly, Andrea, editor. *Feminist Mothering.* State University of New York Press, 2008.

O'Reilly, Andrea. "Matricentric Feminism" *The Routledge Companion to Motherhood*, edited by Andrea O'Reilly, 2019, pp. 51-60.

O'Reilly, Andrea. *Matricentric Feminism: Theory, Activism and Practice.* Demeter Press, 2016.

O'Reilly, Andrea, editor. *Mothers, Mothering and Motherhood Across Cultural Differences: A Reader.* Demeter Press, 2014.

O'Reilly, Andrea. "'It Saved My Life:' The National Association of Mother Centres, Matricentric Pedagogy, and Maternal Empowerment." *Journal of the Motherhood Initiative*, vol. 4, no. 1, 2013, pp. 185-209.

O'Reilly, A. *Rocking the Cradle: Thoughts on Feminism, Motherhood, and the Possibility of Empowered Mothering.* Demeter Press, 2006.

Rich, Adrienne. *Of Woman Born: Motherhood as Experience and Institution.* Virago, 1986.

Ruddick, Sara. "Maternal Thinking." *Mothering: Essays in Feminist Theory*, edited by J. Trebilcot, Rowman & Allanhead, 1984, pp. 213-30.

Ruddick, Sara. *Maternal Thinking: Towards a Politics of Peace.* Beacon Press, 1989.

Sarkar, Sucharita. "'Working for/from Home': An Interdisciplinary Understanding of Mothers in India." *Rupkatha Journal on Interdisciplinary Studies in Humanities*, vol. 12, no. 5, 2020, https://dx.doi.org/10.21659/rupkatha.v12n5.riocls26n6. Accessed 4 Apr. 2023.

Sharma, Prasun. "An Analytical Review of Cross-Cultural Child-Rearing and Care Practices: A Special Reference to India." *Central European Journal of Educational Research*, vol. 2, no. 3, 2020, pp. 7-18.

Vivekananda, Swami. *Complete Works*. Advaita Ashram, Mayavati. 11th ed. 1999.

Chapter 16.

A Conversation: A Mother and Daughter Discuss Feminism

Tara Carpenter Estrada and Emily Rae Robertson

The text for this chapter is excerpted from a conversation on September 3, 2021, between Tara Carpenter Estrada and her then sixteen-year-old daughter, Emily Rae Robertson. Included with the text are artworks created by Tara that illustrate typical family interactions.

Background

Tara married Emily's father, Ty Robertson, in 2003. Emily was born two years later, and Tara became a stay-at-home mom. After a rocky marriage, Tara and Ty divorced in 2010. While pursuing a MFA and subsequently working as a professor, Tara raised Emily as a single mother with the support of nannies and daycare. When Emily was twelve years old (in 2017), Tara married Nick Estrada. Their daughter, Evie, was born in 2020. For most of Tara and Nick's marriage, Nick has worked part time so that he can be the main caregiver for the family.

Figure 1. Tara Carpenter Estrada, *Emily and Tara*, Digital painting, 2022.

Tara: What does feminism mean to you?

Emily: I guess it's a movement that says women should have equal opportunities as men and to be viewed as equals to men.

Tara: What would you say has shaped your view of feminism?

Emily: I would say mostly you.

Tara: I see.

Emily: And feminist picture books.

Tara: Interesting. What is a favourite feminist picture book?

Emily: *Princess Smartypants* is one. It's about a princess who doesn't want to get married, but her parents tell her she has to, so she tells the princes that they have to do all of these challenges in order to marry her. Only one guy is able to do all of them, but her kiss turns him into a toad, and she lives happily ever after on her own.

Tara: I feel like that book could give a misleading view of feminism though. Feminism doesn't mean you're antimarriage or antimen.

Emily: I mean, that's an extreme version, I guess. But in a lot of princess stories the girls are just plot devices, and the guys are the ones that actually do stuff. In this book, she's in charge of herself, and she doesn't need a man.

Tara: She can make her own choices.

Emily: Yeah.

Tara: When we recently re-read that book to Evie, I realized that the suitor she turns into a toad could actually be a good match for her because he can keep up with her. He can deal with all the stuff that she throws at him, you know?

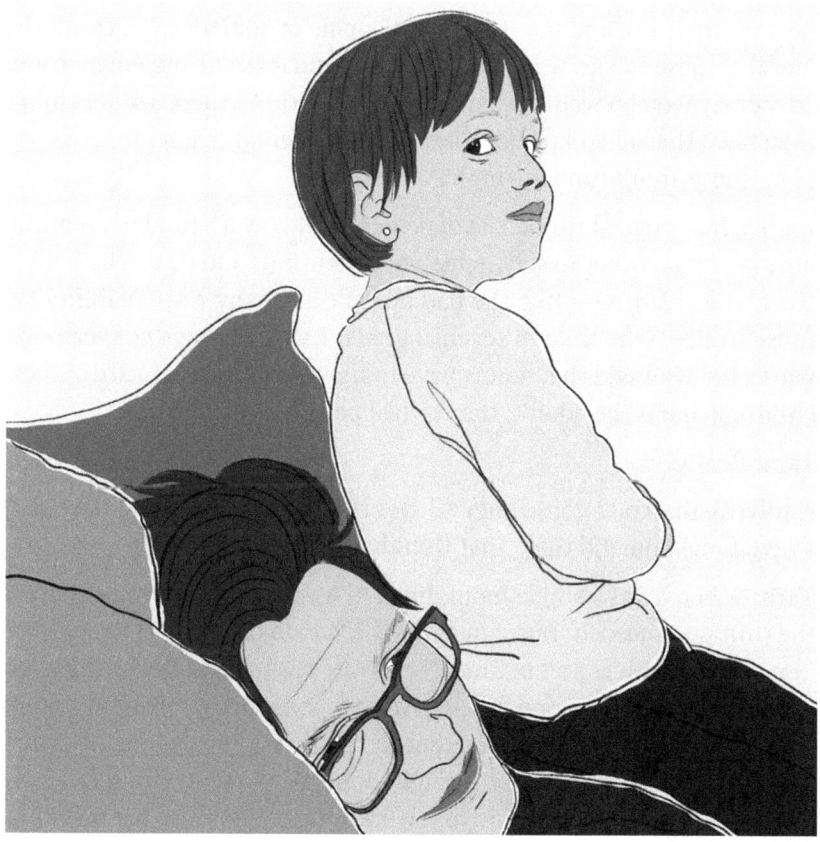

Figure 2. Tara Carpenter Estrada, *A Good Place to Sit (Nick and Evie)*, Digital painting, 2022.

Emily: I kind of thought that, too. But I like that it flips the script on princess stories. You don't have a princess that's in need of rescue or marriage that gets saved by some dude.

Tara: Do you think that people look at feminism like it's portrayed in *Princess Smartypants* and think that feminism goes too far?

Emily: I think people sometimes think feminism says that women should be better than men or women should have power over men. One time, I was talking with my friend, and he said, "I don't support feminism or masculinism. I believe that both sexes should be equal." And I was like, "Oh, but that's what feminism is."

Tara: Growing up, I heard feminists referred to as "bra burners" or "feminazis." And we'd hear stories about "crazy women" who would take off their bra and put it up on a flagpole or something. I think the moral of these stories was that a bra is so fundamental and normal, and only crazy women would rebel against that. I think there's other things (like bras) that a lot of people view as fundamental that feminism says, "No, those aren't fundamental."

Emily: That's true. I think a lot of people would say it's fundamental and normal for a mother to stay home with their kids and do all the housework and cleaning—like the dad doesn't have any responsibility for those things. One time in seventh grade, I was having a conversation with a kid who said that moms have to stay home and take care of their children, and if they don't, they're bad people.

Tara: Really?

Emily: Yeah. And I got so angry. I was thinking—I wouldn't have survived if my mom did that. That wouldn't have been possible for us.

Tara: When I was a single mom, I had to work so that we could pay for the things we needed. But somebody still had to take care of you, right? You had babysitters and nannies. Someone has to be there for the kids, whether that's the dad or mom or daycare or extended family. But I think in our society, it's just assumed that the mom is going to do it. What do you think about our home setup right now? With me working full time (sometimes from home) and Nick working part-time so that one of us can be home with Evie?

A CONVERSATION: A MOTHER AND DAUGHTER DISCUSS FEMINISM

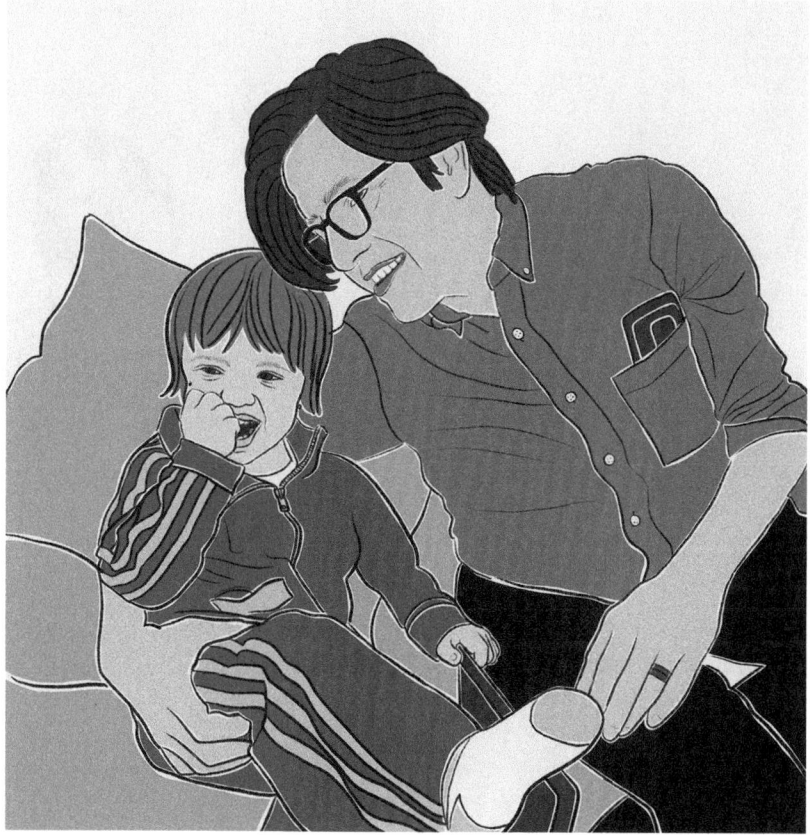

Figure 3. Tara Carpenter Estrada, *Nick and Evie*, Digital painting, 2022.

Emily: I think it's good. I think it works. It's made me realize the sacrifice that it takes to raise kids. Nick doesn't have his ideal job and he can't because he can't work a full-time job and still take care of Evie. I think that's interesting, and I've realized there has to be sacrifice sometimes.

Tara: Nick and I really wanted one of us to be home—to trade off if we could. I don't know how our choices might have been different if I hadn't already had a full-time job when Nick and I got together. Nick made a conscious choice when we got married to work part time so he could be home for you in the afternoons. When you were little, I was a full-time mom for your first three years. Then you were in preschool and aftercare while I went to graduate school, and since then, I've been working.

Figure 4. Tara Carpenter Estrada, *Sisters Getting Ready*, Digital painting, 2022.

Emily: I don't know, honestly, if I could stand being a full-time stay-at-home parent. That sounds just really draining.

Tara: There are a lot of things that are draining but important enough to do, though.

Emily: Yeah. But when I spend three hours with Evie, I already feel done. You know what I mean? It seems really hard. But at the same time, because I want to be a graphic novelist and I'll be at home anyways, it might make sense for me to be home with my children. I hope I'm with a partner who is willing to negotiate responsibilities and who is willing to support me in what I decide to do.

Tara: You want to be able to make choices for yourself, too. It's hard because, like you said, having kids means sacrifices. It's a question of whose dreams get put aside for a while. I was listening to the *Hidden Brain* podcast recently, and the guest, Anthony Burrow, said that having a baby adds at least thirty hours of work to your week. The question is who takes on those thirty hours? Everybody has hopes and dreams, and you don't want to be the coparent whose hopes and dreams are not validated or pursued because of the children. There's got to be give and take.

When I was married to your dad, we had very traditional roles—he went to work, and I stayed home with you. Do you think your ideas about feminism would have been different if things had gone differently with me and your dad? If we had stayed together and had kept up those traditional roles?

Emily: Maybe I would have had more of the mentality of that's just what moms do.

Tara: Looking back, I didn't think a lot about feminism or roles until I was already married. I married young—barely twenty. Feminism wasn't something that I had been exposed to (except negatively) or considered. But when things fell apart between your dad and me, I realized that the gendered role I'd taken wasn't working for me. Then, being a single mom, I started to get curious about feminism and started reconsidering what I wanted out of life. I realized that the stories that I had absorbed in childhood (in fairy tales, pop culture, and my conservative religious upbringing) were all from the perspective of men, with women playing minor roles. That's when I started buying you feminist versions of fairy tales like *Princess Smartypants* and *The Paper Bag Princess*. I wanted you to see strong women making choices for themselves. I wanted you to feel like you could be the protagonist in your own story—that you had choices for what that story would look like.

Emily: I think that's been really helpful in my life. I think if things hadn't been different, I would just be in the mentality that I should graduate, go to college, then get married and have a family.

Tara: Like it's all figured out. Like it's all a package or something.

Emily: Yeah. But it's not a package deal. Now I just have an open mindset about that. I still want to get married and have a family, but I know I don't have to do it right away, and I can choose what my family gets to look like.

Figure 5. Tara Carpenter Estrada, *Trio*, Digital painting, 2022.

Tara: Right. But you've also talked about feeling afraid of commitment?

Emily: Yeah. Definitely. Because of my open mindset, I guess I also know that things can go wrong, and that scares me.

Tara: I see. I don't think I'd ever considered that things could go wrong. I think a lot of people go into their adulthood thinking that everything's fine with the way our society works. Everything's okay, and everything will magically work out for everybody. You don't realize that there are societal challenges and roadblocks that make it harder (for women and others) to do what they want to do.

Emily: Yeah. And sometimes the role society gives you is not the role that's best for you. Like what if you married someone who was super good with kids? And maybe you're just not good with kids. In that case, it makes more sense for the partner to care for the children. Or what about our situation, where you already had a good full-time job when you married Nick? Should you have given it up to be at home?

A CONVERSATION: A MOTHER AND DAUGHTER DISCUSS FEMINISM

Tara: I guess when I was younger, I didn't know that parental roles were something that had to be figured out or that they even could be figured out. I think it's so much better to have a partner that's willing to work things out, but it's also a little hard. There are more things up in the air and questions to negotiate, and it's not easy. But at least it's on the table, you know? I think there's also this magical belief that taking care of children should come naturally to women. You become a mom, and you'll just be able to do it. And caretaking is devalued because of that—because it's just something that mothers do.

Emily: I mean like physically, yes, women can breastfeed. But that's the only advantage we have.

Tara: Oh, my gosh, breastfeeding! I mean, you watched me trying to breastfeed Evie. That was so hard! Especially when Evie went on a nursing strike at eight weeks and stopped eating. I felt like my body was supposed to be able to do this thing for her, but I couldn't make it work. There's this idea that all parenting, even breastfeeding, will come naturally to women. But then on the other hand, there's this expectation of intensive mothering, or the idea that mothers have to do everything perfectly for their kids. You're supposed to make beautiful little bento boxes full of organic food for lunches, and your children are supposed to look perfect all the time. Your life is supposed to be represented perfectly on your Instagram feed.

Emily: Yes! Your house should always be clean. You have to find time to do makeup in the morning. You have to go on a jog at four a.m. before your kids get up.

Tara: You have to get up so early because you're supposed to do all of these things. You're supposed to stay skinny, and you're supposed to have everything looking perfect. You should have a carefully curated, beautiful, amazing life, but it's also supposed to be easy and come naturally to you. Do you think by the time Evie is old enough to have kids, society will have gotten over this nonsense? Or do you think we'll still be in the same spot?

Emily: Yeah. I definitely think things will have changed. Twenty to thirty years ago, the expectations were different. I mean, things haven't changed that much, but they've changed. So, I hope that things will be even better in another twenty to thirty years. For example, the way the media shows women in the last twenty years has changed. It's funny the differences between how me and my dad see feminism in the media. We watched *Spider-Man 2* with Toby Maguire, and I was like, "This movie is ridiculous!" I mean, Mary Jane is not a real person. The scenes with her are super cheesy, like her running in her wedding gown. And she's like, "Go get 'em tiger," at the end when Spider-Man goes off to save the day. It's just so cheesy and weird. I was laughing while we watched it because it was so absurd. My dad said, "But it's so good! Don't you love Doc Ock and all the fighting?" And I'm like, "I guess so." But in literally every fight scene, there's a screaming woman that's going insane. And I think, "What is up with that?" The movie's not treating women as actual people. I think oftentimes in movies women are there to further the plot, and so their decisions just don't make sense. And it was just interesting to see how my dad didn't really even think about those things.

Tara: So from a feminist perspective, a good female character is just one that's an actual character who has her own reasons for doing things?

Emily: Yeah, definitely.

Tara: What about female characters in books for teens and adults? I know we're both fans of Ursula Le Guin's *Earthsea Cycle*. The first book [*A Wizard of Earthsea*] is from the perspective of a guy who only really interacts with men. And then by the end of the series, Le Guin is writing the stories of women and girls [*The Tombs of Atuan; Tehanu; Tales from Earthsea*] with a feminist perspective.

Emily: Well, I don't like *A Wizard of Earthsea* much because it's a coming-of-age story about a male wizard, and that feels cliché. I mean it's good. I just don't like it as much as the other ones. I wonder if the author had to start her series with something that publishers would be more likely to pick up. The later books are more feminist and creative in their story structures, so they might have been riskier to sell. *A Wizard of Earthsea* establishes the whole universe but using a more stereotypical character. In that series, I especially like *Tehanu*. It's a less dramatic story in some ways. The main character, Tenar, used to be famous, and she had done big important adventures in the past. But in this story, she just lives on a farm. She's a normal lady. She just goes about her life. I love how it describes when they're walking, and her adopted daughter Tehanu stops to take a rock out of her shoe. The story talks about mundane moments and makes them valuable. And I think that's really cool.

Tara: There's a lot of little mundane moments in parenting. I think my hope as a woman is to be able to have a full spectrum of opportunities. I want it to be possible for women to make real changes in the world and do big things like Tenar did when she was younger. I also want it to be okay and valuable to do small things. I want a bigger range of possibilities. I want the work that women do to be equally valued and considered legitimate—whether they choose to work in the home (which is still work), or outside the home, or some combination of both.

Figure 6. Tara Carpenter Estrada, *Energetic*, Digital painting, 2022.

Emily: Both are equally important. I mean you can make big changes in the world all you want, but there still needs to be someone to do those mundane things.

Tara: This semester has been interesting for me as I've worked from home a couple of days a week and then worked on campus the other days. One day, I go to a meeting that affects my whole college, and I have a say there. And then the next day, I'm at home just trying to keep Evie busy.

Emily: Evie's the boss there ….

Tara: I'm giving her a bath and cleaning her food off the floor.

Emily: Or changing her diapers.

Tara: Yeah, exactly.

Emily: Making weird noises, trying to make her laugh, to entertain her.

Tara: I think that's something that gets missed when you don't take care of children. We can be much sillier around her than I think we can be around other people.

Emily: There's no expectation of normalcy from her.

Tara: Yeah. No expectations, no shame. You can say and do weird things.

Emily: Yeah. And she likes it.

Tara: I feel like being around little kids allows you a more full expression of yourself as a human being.

Emily: Yeah. I definitely know what you mean. Also, you feel obligated to be a better person to set a good example for them.

Tara: If we're trying to set an example for Evie of being good feminists, what does that look like for you?

Emily: I think it looks like teaching her that she can be anything she wants to be through how we talk about women and feminism. If we talk about her future as not a set course, then she can see that it isn't. She doesn't have to be a stay-at-home mom or have a full-time job. She can make choices for what is best for her. I hope that we're already setting a good example, with your and Nick's relationship. I hope, most of all, that we can help the world through our influence on her—to be kinder and more accepting of all women, no matter what they choose to do.

Tara: Amen.

Works Cited

Cole, Babette. *Princess Smartypants*. Puffin Books, 1997.

Le Guin, Ursula K. *The Books of Earthsea: The Complete Illustrated Edition*. Saga Press, 2018.

Munsch, Robert. *The Paper Bag Princess*. 1980. Annick Press, 2018.

Raimi, Sam, director. *Spider-Man 2*. Sony Pictures, 2004.

"You 2.0 Cultivating Your Purpose." *Hidden Brain*, 2021, https://hiddenbrain.org/podcast/cultivating-your-purpose/. Accessed 5 Apr. 2023.

Chapter 17.

Motherhood, Art, and a Revolution

Jillayna Adamson

Introduction

Motherhood is hard. This is a statement that seems mostly accepted. But for decades, it has been predominantly quietly hard, and the understanding of this difficulty has been minimally explored. This quiet struggle is not unlike many of the experiences of girls and women themselves across history. From patriarchal regimes, girls have learned to exude a certain silence about their experiences— their bodies, their thoughts, and their feelings and desires. They have been led into the belief system of a certain privacy and discretion. No one needs to know this. No one needs to hear the things that are not pretty or polite. We all know the story of oppressed women. But what about motherhood? The motherhood experience has historically remained tight lipped—from the transition to becoming a mother, to daily struggles of mothering, to feelings of inadequacy, guilt, and a lost sense of self. To mother has historically been seen as a virtuous and selfless role, with little room for grievance or criticism (Tubbs). We know that women have traditionally become mothers by expectation and judged specifically by nuances surrounding childbirthing and childrearing (Lerner). From the residue of this patriarchal expectation, to yearn for more or seek more than being "just" a mother becomes a radical act. We have come far enough societally to relinquish the radicalism of the not-just-a-mother identity and to embrace how all-encompassing and variant it is to be a mother; the internal struggles of motherhood deserve a voice. As a psychotherapist and mother myself, I set out to explore the experiences of mothers. I began trailing the difficulties mothers grapple with within their roles and their connections to patriarchal backgrounds, eventually highlighting the changes that the motherhood identity specifically brings into women's experiences of feminism. I have ultimately come to observe that many women do not identify gaps in feminism until they become mothers. Motherhood serves as a reckoning in feminist awakening, yet it remains a largely unexplored component of identity development. For my investigation, I invited in-depth discussions with mother-creators about the evolution of their mothering experiences and their individual development. I came to explore artistry itself as an example of feminist means of continued identity expression throughout motherhood and noted the vital ways in which mother-creators are propelling this movement. I assess recurring themes in the narratives of the women I talk to, including the following: experiences of stereotypes and assumptions, underprepared motherhood, putting one's self on hold, emotional struggles with guilt and worry, choices between careers and motherhood, and the varied ways women have gone about integrating the mother self and individual self. Through these personal interviews with filmmakers, writers, photographers, and other creators, I observe the necessity of the expressive self and the ways in which this has highlighted feminist understandings. I see this as an unveiling of an overarching radical new understanding of motherhood—the bold necessity of being seen and understood as women and mothers.

Women in academia and mainstream media are bringing the realities of motherhood into the world in courageous ways, and creators are spurring the growth of this content. In *The Guardian*, Amy Westervelt notes that beginning around 2018, motherhood experiences seen in the media hit a notable boom; multiple books, essays, and think pieces began to come out including memoirs and feminist explorations. Magazines, which previously would scarcely take mother-related pieces, were suddenly seeking out more of these stories that were spilling motherhood's harder truths. Westervelt highlights what maternal-feminist scholars know—that motherhood has been a taboo area of women's studies and feminism; she notes that the topic "comes up in fewer than three percent of papers, journal articles or textbooks on modern gender theory." She describes the topic as a "bogeyman for feminists," inciting multiple views on what feminism truly means in conjunction with the motherhood role. Motherhood, she notes, has remained a kind of "time machine, shooting women instantly back to 1950." Although scholars have noted this theme, it is also one expressed by women as they enter motherhood. In other words, many women do not realize the ways mothers continue to be oppressed and disempowered until they are in the middle of it. Somehow, this lack of awareness surrounding mothers' experiences is still happening.

Today, a social shift has begun that explores mothering experiences from honest, in-depth perspectives. We see mothering realities expressed through emboldened television shows, books, writing, and movies, which address the less glamorous aspects of motherhood. We see leaking breasts, postpartum depression, isolation, boredom, vaginal tears, and identity crises. Examples of these works include the shows and films *Workin' Moms*, *The Letdown*, and *Tully*, as well as the motherhood novels and memoirs *And Now We Have Everything* (O'Connell), *Nightbitch* (Yoder), and *I'm Supposed to Protect You from All This* (Spiegelman). In these works, we are shown the loneliness and guilt, anxiety, and physical exhaustion that mothers experience. As a result, a fuller picture of motherhood is emerging. In *The Mommy Myth*, Susan J. Douglas and Meredith W. Michaels highlight the "chasm between the ridiculous, honey-hued ideals of perfect motherhood in the mass media and the reality of mothers' everyday lives" (2). The honesty presented in these new narratives daringly bridges this gap, critiquing the view of the perfect, noncomplaining mother. To abandon this long-held idealistic imagery is a radical stance and allows for a new depiction of motherhood.

This seeing is a vital step in the evolution of what Andrea O'Reilly has coined "matricentric feminism"—a necessary and specific branch of feminism that needs more recognition and support ("Feminism for Mothers"). O'Reilly explores motherhood as its own category of feminism that focuses on the needs and concerns of mothers. She notes that "motherhood matters and is central and integral to understanding mother women's oppression in patriarchy and their resistance to it" ("Motherhood Hall of Fame Keynote"). Such a position allows for motherhood to have its own branch of study, which is integral to liberating oppressive expectations for mothers. Matricentric feminism helps mothers critique patriarchal modes of motherhood and to express their needs as women and mothers. This chapter highlights the experiences of a collection of creator-mothers in coming to know themselves and to understand the mothering role and its complex relationship with feminism. I begin this exploration by dissecting the more common reckonings that mothers experience as key points in this feminist awakening.

Process

I met, both virtually and in person, with thirty-three mothers from around the globe. All of these women are western women of varying racial and socioeconomic backgrounds—from South Africa, Australia, Canada, US, Europe, and expats living in various countries. They each identify as a creator of some type—of which there are no stipulations. Of these thirty-three women, seventeen identify as either gay, bisexual, or pansexual. Twelve women identify as white or European, eight women identify as Black or person of colour, eight identify as Hispanic, and five identify as First Nations or Indigenous. Two women identify as having a physical disability. Eight women note that they fall into the upper-class bracket, whereas the majority identify as middle class. Eight women consider themselves lower middle class or working class. Because the interviewees are all Western women, this chapter is limited to general cultural iterations of modern Western experiences. Additionally, for length purposes, specific personal cultural iterations, including religion and racial or ethnic identity, are not further assessed, limiting the impacts of said backgrounds on worldviews and mothering experiences. Notably, none of these women struggle with basic needs of food, shelter, and safety, which is also vital in assessing one's ability to explore their needs beyond survival.

I spoke with actresses, writers, filmmakers, photographers, dancers, musicians, painters, and alternative-identifying creators. With some, we spoke for about ninety minutes, with others the conversations continued over days and months. They kindly let me into their lives and minds; they took me though their struggles as well as their states of empowerment and change. I decided to keep all these women anonymous for simplicity. Some requested it and expressed some anxiety about opening up about what they felt to be a sensitive issue; others were happy to express their thoughts and have their name on it. To encourage authenticity, openness and allot for privacy, I title all women simply by their identifying craft. I compile and discuss a number of narrative experiences and explore qualitative connections therein.

This exploration assumes a general awareness of the history of feminism in Western culture, with the MeToo movement representing a fourth wave of feminism that has focused on rape culture (Negar). I thus suggest that the work and influences of mother-creators are growing, which has allowed for motherhood experiences to be seen, studied, and understood.

Artistry as Medium

I became curious about the experience of creators and artists because of the pushback in the arts being seen as necessity. I began to see motherhood more boldly expressed in mainstream art and media—from photography to writing and cinema. And I began to wonder how the feelers and expressors—the people for whom art is paramount to who they are and how they live—experienced and embraced motherhood and identity. Some argue that creation is a hobby or an expressive side. For mothers specifically, if something is not generating significant income or is seen as a creative outlet (Hayasaki), it will be sacrificed to the demands of mothering (Meeussen and Van Laar). In my work, I have observed that mothers frequently put their own needs, wants, and elements of self-care on the backburner. I note two ways mother-creators are bringing motherhood issues to the forefront: For some, motherhood is the direct topic of their work, whereas others discuss the difficulties of their processes and decisions as mothers and creators.

Because I decided to focus on creators, there are limitations to this study. These findings do not represent the experience of every modern Western woman. Instead, what I hope to do is explore a variety of narrative experiences in feminist reckonings and explore motherhood through another lens, which can also fall victim to being overlooked—that is, artistry and creators.

Understanding the Interconnection of Feminism and Motherhood

Being a mother does not dictate facets of a woman's identity like it previously has—or at least, this is what women are working towards. Mothers seek change so that the role can be feasible and possible at a time when expectations remain outdated. For motherhood to not be the sole purpose of a woman and centrefold of her existence is radical. What might it mean if a woman is a mother and also wants to work out of the home, create art, change the world, study, and research? Would that mean she loves her role as a mother less? Or loves her children less? We know this is not so. Yet through my research, I found that many women find it difficult to accept this. We are not prepared for it. We do not have social systems in place to allow for it, and it is not what we have seen. What we have seen primarily are false ideals of the perfect mother and intensive mothering (Meeussen and Van Laar). At the same time, we are hearing that things have changed for women. Thus, women become mothers and can be surprised to find that society seems largely uncomfortable with their desires that fall outside of mothering. Women may become mothers only to realize that the enormous expectations of motherhood are unrealistic and that the need for feminist efforts and attention specific to motherhood remains.

Understanding the Interconnection of Artistry and Motherhood

When becoming mothers, our primary focus often shifts to our babies and children (and this has both a biological and social component) (Hoekzema et al.). At the same time, there is the expected cultural shift of the self and the social ideas of what one's new focus should be. Unless women work to tune back into their sense of individual identity, it can be hard to do. From my conversations with mothers, a majority struggle with continuing to care for themselves. Others struggle to understand their changing selves, establish a balance, or deal with enormous levels of guilt about even having other desires. Other women note being unable to shift their focus, even in small increments. From the basics of self-care to embracing one's own desires or interests, it is clear that many women grapple with balancing the components of their identities once they become mothers.

Artistry is a unique lens for approaching motherhood because frequently the remaining parts of our selves become seemingly unimportant in the urgency of motherhood. Mothers note that it can be hard to allow themselves the space to refocus on their selves and to see themselves as changed—to embrace this. Expressive and creative acts are even more difficult to reembrace and much easier to ignore than the basics of self-care.

Through my work as a psychotherapist and conducting narrative assessments with various mothers, I see that barriers to the individual self and creative self become numerous once one becomes a mother. Many mothers express surprisingly falling into long-held stereotypes about the motherhood role; others feel they no longer know themselves once they become mothers. Mothers routinely disclose putting themselves on hold, struggling with guilt and letting go of aspects of caretaking, as well as feeling pressure about making career decisions. Many of these themes are seen in various research studies of mothers' experiences, especially focussing on burnout and struggles with anger, anxiety, and depression (Meeussen and Van Laar; Hochschild; McLeish and Redshaw; Parker; Ross and Van Willigen). Ultimately, what I heard most steadily through these narrative explorations is the enormous emotional impacts of the motherhood experience—the guilt and worry as well as the self-questioning and expectations. The immense period of growth that comes with motherhood has been sorely neglected in being seen, explored, and validated in a sociocultural context.

The expressions of mothering experiences we are seeing have highlighted the need of mothers to be finally seen. For some, this includes presenting the more graphic realities of motherhood, such as depictions of postpartum depression in the film *Tully*, or the painful realities of breastfeeding or career balancing, such as those presented in *Workin' Moms*. In the 2021 novel *Nightbitch*, author Rachel Yoder seeks to make sense of the identity loss she felt in motherhood, as she explores the "overwhelming rage, loneliness and love she felt in the early days of motherhood" (Walsh) through the quirky story of a mother that turns into a feral dog at night. As a dog, the main character is able to escape her domestic duties, "shed the modern mold of motherhood" (Walsh) and explore herself as an artist and being. As noted by reviewer Brienne Walsh, the piece serves as some "comic relief" for mothers who might feel trapped in prescribed roles. Walsh notes the allegory of Yoder's "reminder that perfection is not only unattainable, but also corrosive" in the motherhood experience. Yoder herself notes the following: "In my own experience, so much of the performance of motherhood felt hollow or inauthentic to the sort of mom I wanted to be" (Yoder qtd. In Walsh). Yoder's expression is an artistic bursting of sorts—a narrative push to the comical extremes of confines prescribed by mothering. It is boundary pushing and graphic, which goes against the grain of standard mothering tales. The shock of the bloodthirsty feral dog-mother character is a scream for mothering ideals to be seen and reevaluated in a radical way.

Exploring the Reckoning as Feminist Awakening: The Surprising, Quiet Difficulty of Motherhood and Identity

In my professional career, and as a mother myself, I have learned that women's intricate struggles with identity in motherhood are increasingly common and that some are only more recently feeling the freedom to express this difficulty. Around 10 per cent of mothers that I surveyed online (requiring no identifying information) noted that they do not feel it is okay to be open about their struggles. Mothers feel that seeking careers or following their own interests once they become mothers becomes not only more difficult but also results in intense feelings of guilt and self-doubt (Hochschild). Interestingly, I repeatedly hear mothers say that they were unprepared for these feelings, which is telling. How is it that after years of feminist development in the West, women are still becoming mothers and realizing they had no idea about the reality of the experience?

Anna Malaika Tubbs notes how damaging expectations of selflessness can be for mothers: "The more you agree to being secondary, to put everyone's needs ahead of your own, to let your child shine while you sit in the background, the more you are congratulated." The disappearing individual identity of the mother is a standard historical narrative we continue to accept.

It is important to note that mothers are not appreciating motherhood any less. The mothers I spoke with are quick to point this out. They are not loving being a mother less or loving their kids less. Instead, they are simply noticing and demanding necessary change. Mothers are bravely allowing themselves to be known as humans with struggles. They are shedding the unwaveringly strong persona of the mother who is only allowed to be a mother. This radical social shift is a push towards recognizing empowered motherhood as its own branch of study.

Struggle with the Self: Identity Development through Motherhood

As a clinician, I have had patients say to me, "I don't know who I am now that I'm a mother. I feel like that's all that I am, and I feel guilty for that not feeling like enough." They want to know how they can keep being an individual with passions when motherhood consumes so much of their identity. They question if it is even possible. We love our kids so much that we may have to remind ourselves to think of ourselves. And with the weight of patriarchal frameworks, we have to remind ourselves that other aspects of ourselves still have worth. Societally, we continue to see a simplistic understanding of what it means to be a mom; it's not uncommon for stories of mothers to only follow their mothering role. But what does it mean to be individuals once we become mothers? How do we allow for this in the greater world? The following intimate narratives explore these questions.

The Narratives: How Have We Seen Mothers?
On the Stereotypes and Assumptions of the Role

I meet with a painter in her seventies through video chat, and she takes me through a colourful exploration of her girlhood: "We were taught to be discreet when we were menstruating, to be sure our bra straps were not visible, and that childbirth is just something women do so we needn't droll on about the stitches to our rectum." She continues, pondering about her own mother: "All along our mothers were also being told things that they didn't question, right? And I suppose felt not right in complaining." I ask her about what she thinks some of these things might have been: "In my own mom's day, it was to never express any dissatisfaction with [your role as a mother and wife].She never learned to drive, never worked. She had five kids, a meal on the table every night. I don't ever remember thinking twice about [all the weight on her]. If she did, I never knew. And she must have, right?" She further discusses her feminist art, which she describes as more "graphic" than some feel comfortable with, since expressing discomfort is a way of squashing decades of silence. As this painter expressed to me, it is time for these discomforts to be visible and heard. They have been politely covered long enough.

At the same time, I also hear the cultural iterations and heroic assumptions of motherhood among the mothers I spoke with. An actress tells me she frequently gets asked, and sometimes shamed, about how she manages to work and parent. She notes the following: "Men have never had to balance it all. It has never been their job. So we are watching women do this. We are amazed, and maybe we want answers. But what we are relaying instead is gender-biased question: 'Can you really be a good mother and do this?'" She continues to tell me that after the birth of her last child, well-meaning interviewers expressed sympathy to her male partner about the difficulties of having a new baby at home. She struggles with the sexism that women experience, but she also realizes that people see women as incredibly dynamic, versatile, and capable—"superhero like." As she explains: "They go to men and they say, damn! What a switch up for you. They go to women and say, yeah, I am assuming you got this."

Women have been doing this forever. We have taken on the mental load of children and home and work while also pushing to be seen, to be equal, and to be respected. But now, we are talking about it. And we have centuries to talk about. We have lifetimes of so much that has been kept quiet under the narrative of simple and easy. The seams of this narrative are starting to split. As the actress wonders: "What if I can't actually do all this expected super mom stuff? Or why am I expected to, to the point of depletion?" We enter into motherhood, and we realize we have been grotesquely underprepared. From girlhood, we have been told that so much of our existence is easy or shameful, and no one has to know a thing. Now, women are pulling back the curtains. "I can't lie," the actress tells me. "I had all the assumptions, too. That as women we just got this. I couldn't have possibly wrapped my head around all of the ways the [role of] mom feels impossible." Matricentric feminism allows for new narratives of motherhood to be heard, breaking decades of silence. It brings the potential to eradicate the harmful narratives that propel the fantasy of the perfect mother.

Some mothers have feared that exploring feminist aspects of themselves could potentially signal to a lack of love for being a mother. As a writer explains to me: "Thinking of myself under the bracket of a feminist project feels scary. Not because I'm not a feminist but [because] I know that some people equate feminists with somehow being against mothering or less of a mother." She ponders about the guilt she felt for thinking that being only a mom was not enough for her: "I spent hours wondering exactly where 'mother' should go in my biography and what that said about me. And then I wondered what that said about me."

Underprepared: On the Surprise of Motherhood Experiences

Many women tell me that they always wanted to be mothers or that they never considered otherwise. Although motherhood is a socially assumed and positively reinforced norm, they note that the stories and images they have taken in of it leave them completely underprepared. "I just had no idea," one artist relays. "Women have been doing this forever, and I went right into it all without much question." She tells me about her loneliness and the anxiety she felt unable to turn off: "I felt so overwhelmed by how much I loved my daughter that sometimes I just couldn't function. I'd just cry. I'd be near a meltdown if she had a cough." She describes her days as mostly alone in silence, minus the crying or babbling of her baby, and anxiety about embarking on outings with her child.

Photographer Tabitha Soren brings her mothering experiences into her art and has mounted cameras in her home. In a photo series, she shares the surprising images she captures and writes the following about the work: "*Motherload* is about what mothers don't show: the emotions and psychological states that we've all been socialized to bury. It's not so much about my personal existence as it is about the blurred existence, all that time spent keeping something alive." The photographs are blurred and show time lapse; they have an ethereal quality that she likens to expressing her own "not feeling like a whole person" (Soren). A writer tells me something similar: "I did not feel like I was even really there—for years." This sense of being lost is a theme shrouded in guilt and self-questioning. Is this right? Is there something wrong with me? How is it all this hard? How did I lose myself?

Ourselves on Hold: Finding a Sense of Self Later in Motherhood

A filmmaker I speak to tells me how she put her entire artistic passion and career on hold for the better part of fifteen years as she raised her children. Mothering was what she did, day in and day out. She notes that she did not really consider what she wanted as an individual; motherhood was all consuming. But she just accepted that this was how motherhood was supposed to be.

Reemerging into the art world more recently was not without its struggles for the filmmaker; it was a years-long endeavour. She experienced self-doubt and waning support of those around her. Her sentiments are mirrored frequently by other mothers. Personal interests become seen as some kind of extracurricular activity, not worth our time and energy. Artistry is a particular component of this because it so frequently can be seen as unnecessary.

When this filmmaker worked to make her way back into the art world, she felt lost and behind. She questioned if time away from her kids was really okay and if her work was really that important. She struggled to take herself seriously as an artist and wondered if her working was even justifiable.

When I ask the filmmaker about her turning point, she tells me that she does believe "artistry is a thing that chooses you." She continues, "It's not about a job; it's about a way of being in the world and understanding the world. It felt like living a lie as 'just a mom.'" It was not until her kids became more independent that she allowed herself to invest in this career path. She notes that being able to find herself as an artist was pertinent for not only her sense of self but also her mental health.

We also discuss the ways in which she often feels undervalued as a mother—another theme I often hear. Mothers are seen as doing little to nothing, and artistry falls into this same trap of devaluing. As the filmmaker explains: "Isn't it interesting that both artists and mothers are so likely to not be valued? That mother and artist are these two areas that are so similarly minimized?" People have been doing this for centuries. Yet imagine if the mothers stopped mothering or if artists and creators stopped creating?

The Cave: Guilt, Worry, and Emotional Struggle in Letting Go

The mothers I talk to frequently feel torn and confused; they experience deep guilt. In focusing solely on making decisions about the wellbeing of their children, they note feeling more emptiness, anger, or disconnect.

And in making decisions that allot for more self-care, they may experience guilt and apprehension. Both ends of the spectrum are difficult, and neither feels right. This tug feels undefinable. Women remain disempowered in this unknowing—a feeling of being never enough. We have not known how to make sense of the dissonance of our mother self and our individual self. And, so, we feel pulled into multiple worlds and not quite proficient in any.

Mothers have to reexplore themselves as people because so much changes in motherhood. Many of these experiences remain quiet and need space to be better understood. I talk with a writer who tells me that her male partner does not truly understand women's issues: "He supports me and my work, but he doesn't get it. He sees it as overhyped. He'll say women are equal and can do anything men can do, so what is the big deal? And you know, I don't think I did either until I became a mother."

While her partner tends to more of the parenting now than he previously did, she emphasizes that their roles have intentionally changed with effort. The decision proved pivotal to their continued partnership: "It was a lot of teaching. A lot of educating and reminding and explaining [to him]. If I was to go out into the world, I couldn't continue to have the weight of the all-knowing mom on me. It didn't turn off for me; there was so much I still did and do. I think women, mothers that is, don't quite know how to stop carrying." We have carried so long that it can be hard to feel confident in letting go of all of the complex things we have held and known so intimately.

The writer tells me that she stopped writing almost completely for close to fifteen years. She felt so drained from motherhood and caring for a house, her children, and her husband that no other aspect of herself could come to life. When her kids were older, she felt safer and began to let her husband take on some of the tasks. She explores how rational her decision to stay home had been. He had made more money, and she was needed in specific ways for years. For her to go into work made little sense. She felt unsure of being able to hand it all over and how that would feel for her. She notes that guilt primarily drove her decisions: "I have always loved my children more than anything, but I don't know that I can totally articulate what really kept me in a cave of not leaving and being my own person all those years." It took her years to feel empowered enough to advocate for herself—to not be the only all-knowing parent.

The pressure for a woman to pour her entire self into her children as her primary role is highlighted across research. The practice is known as intensive mothering, which often increases guilt, burnout, and gatekeeping tendencies. This pressure to be perfect and to do no wrong is paramount; it affects the ability of mothers to feel able to step away from their duties even a little bit for their self-care or their careers (Meeussen and Van Laar). Thus, the artist's sentiments are not unusual. All the mothers in this study speak about the difficulty in reducing their mothering responsibilities and embracing themselves outside the role. "The cave," as she had called it.

Choices

Mothers frequently bring up the weight and anxiety of making career and mothering choices. I speak to an actress who explains to me that she feared having children with her career path. She explains the ways it can be "career suicide" but also the potential impact of the job on her children: "I realized I have to be completely prepared to be seen by my kids if I do this. My stuff is out there. It's not all the greatest of things either!" She laughs as she describes the awkward photos of her on the internet, paparazzi harassment, and roles she has taken that may not have been her best. She says:

> Is some kid on the playground going to humiliate my kid because of me? I don't know! But being known—in any way—by more than just your inner circle invites for that, doesn't it? I decided that I needed to make sure I really believed in what I did and myself and my artistry. That I was okay with owning past mistakes and seeing it as part of the process—and teaching that to my kids. That that is okay. I look like a total idiot here, or I did some embarrassing pictures here.

She pauses a long moment before saying: "I decided it was worth it.... I believe in the artistry. I guess I believe that passing this along has some kind of worth." She laughs again and asks me if she was right in this decision or if "she's nuts." "When things happen or come up, though, anything related to these choices," she says a moment later, "It's all guilt. Not good enough. Somehow messing them up. Did I put myself first? Is what I choose to do even fair to my kid? Can I actually do both? What is wrong with me to want this?" Male coworkers, she notes, do not seem to grapple with these issues in this way.

The actress, and other artists agree, on having similar feelings: Am I less grateful to my experience of motherhood by wanting or needing other things? That people question a woman's identity so intimately reinforces feelings of inadequacy. They feel that they can never be good enough.

A dancer I meet with tells me she thought the integration would be easier—that becoming a mom would not mean she would give up dancing. But this was not the case: "I think I thought things had become more modern than they have." She explains that she truly thought this would be simple and doable. "I'll just have daycare!" she exclaims. She looks dejected when she tells me it really just was not possible to keep dancing, despite the efforts of her and her partner to allow for it. She envisioned that she would be able to get back to it after giving birth. But the months became years, and there was "always something" that kept it a lesser priority.

Integrated Identities: Art and Mothering as Survival, as Coping, and as an Integrated Identity

To mother and to create, as symbiotic healing, is another theme I hear about. I speak with a writer and filmmaker who identifies foremost as a mother. Her art has been a means of expression and survival—particularly through some of the more challenging parts of the parenting experience. Having a premature and medically fragile child brought incredible stress and hardship. Writing and creating were how she was able to work through it—to process her experiences and express herself. She notes that she found herself questioning her own drive towards her craft during these difficult times. She wondered "How can I be working on this?" and questioned if she might be crazy for even wanting to continue her work. Others questioned her too.

Her drive and creativity are a vital part of her identity, which she knows is important for her children to see, and are also instrumental to her own wellness. Although people may have questioned her dedication to artistry while also dedicating endless days and nights in caring for her child, this was her way through. What I see in this filmmaker is someone who is a passionately dedicated mother and one who is allowing her children to see her also as a human and an artist with the awareness that these are vital elements of her person. And this is radical. It is radical to allow our children to see us as so intimately human and not just as mothers. As noted by the actress who chose to embrace her visibility, it is radical to allow for our own flaws and passions to be made visible to our children.

Some of the filmmaker's projects convey her mothering journey, as well as the trying experiences of other mothers, with uncompromising authenticity. She notes that the voice her work has given to other mothers has inspired her to continue working. Heart-spilling fan-mail has helped her see the importance of her art when others were critical. She stays dedicated to sharing her truth with the world through her art and sees the importance in her truth becoming defined "beautifully," she notes, by motherhood itself.

A photographer tells me that her art is what saved her connection to her children and her ability to embrace motherhood. After battling severe postpartum anxiety and depression and questioning her decision to become a mother, her ability to photograph her way through it became her way through it: "I do think putting so much into photographing [her son and herself] is what allowed me to see and experience [motherhood] differently—maybe more ... beautifully than I was actually feeling it at the time." She continues: "My art is no longer what it was—at all. It won't change the world the way in which I may have once dreamed, which sometimes I feel sad about. It's more for and about [my kids] now, but it at least keeps it in my veins." We dissect her feelings about her art and what it means to "change the world." Although she has reshaped her expectations for herself, we discuss how influencing her children to value her work as an artist, woman, and mother is meaningful and may just be changing the course of feminism for mothers more than she thinks.

Another creator I speak with explains her feeling of luck and gratitude at having had numerous supporters to be able to work full time as an artist. She is one of the only women I talk to that tells me she could balance her creator self and mother self with support from her mother and husband. She notes, though, that what she sees is primarily people unable to separate and have an individual self—that is, mothers who grapple heavily with guilt and have little time away from their responsibilities as a mother. "It's okay to exist without carrying mother guilt around with me if I'm not tending to my children around the clock," she tells me. She realizes that a number of mothers feel unable to live this way and notes that others are frequently surprised at how she is able to separate her different responsibilities. She as well as other mothers have told me about the number of friends they have lost because their sole focus stays on their children, and they stop engaging with others outside of mothering.

A Radical Move: Seeking More Is So Radical, We Wonder If It Is Valid To Do So

Mothers describe to me how learning to prioritize yourself is a learning curve. In fact, self-care and creation are different for a mother. As photographer Tabitha Soren states: "I can't tell you how many times I've checked an artist's biography to see, Oh God, she's so great, but does she have children? Like, are we in the same race? Because it's like running with weights on" (Soren). A painter I have been speaking with sends me an email late one night, noting she has a baby on her boob and a toddler that continues to tiptoe down the hall. "It is hard to be more, to do more ... to not fall into some of the [social and cultural] traps within motherhood that take away our options. We can be making space for this now. Right?" She notes at the bottom of the email that in the morning, she will reevaluate whether her thinking makes any sense. "Mom brain," she says, laughing later as we speak, and this is another frequent term I hear—as if they are asking whether they can even think with all of their responsibilities. Motherhood does change our brains, but is the science behind the narrative reinforcing that the other components of us could become less than? It becomes clear that women are questioning this, whether consciously or not.

A musician tells me that she sometimes wonders if she is just "crazy," if it is impossible to attempt to have it all and pursue life outside of mothering. She questions aloud if it's selfish, laughs, and puts her head in her hands, saying: "No! God! No, it's necessary. And yet sometimes I really have to convince myself of that all over again." A photographer expresses this same phenomenon to me:

> You know how when your kids are little, and every day is the same long boring drawn out exhausting thing. Feeding, cleaning,

changing, crying—it's all you do. And you actually feel like you are doing nothing. You feel worthless and useless and like your days are accomplishing and coming to nothing. It messes with your mind. Trying to make personal choices as a mom kind of does that too. "Do I really need to shower? Is taking a class really necessary? Is going on this shoot really what I need to be doing?" And then it hits you: How sad is that. That's the whole system, isn't it?

It is a recurrent self-doubt I hear. Mothers feel crazy or unreasonable when society has made motherhood appear so simple and seamless. When they feel that it is not, they worry something is wrong with them; they assume they are not as good or are doing something wrong. In that self-questioning, I see mothers struggle to find the space for themselves, their art, and their creativity.

What Are These Narratives Telling Us?

As I spoke with all of these incredible women and took in their experiences and feelings, I was overwhelmed by the weight of all the considerations that so many mothers have had to make. Moreover, I am saddened when I think of all of this weight—centuries of it—mothers have had to quietly carry. Sometimes, they have had no choice or say at all. And now, they are trying to navigate how to have a choice, with some wondering if it is even possible or valid. Becoming a mother is a stark reckoning. Motherhood, it seems, is a force that brings an awareness of feminist needs and the realities of oppression to many.

We know that to mother is an understated role. For centuries, motherhood has been undervalued and its challenges underestimated, including the physical and emotional challenges as well as the many sacrifices a mother makes. Mothers love their kids, but some mothers have not felt there is any space beyond mothering. An aerial artist tells me: "[To pursue your passion] is liberating, and it is huge to allow it to be different now. It takes the risk of all that crap judgment [from others]—that we don't love our kids, [or] we aren't devoted." The judgment and the idea of being forced to choose are expressed as exhausting by many of the women. They feel it archaic that there have not been more accommodations for mothers. Mothers assume motherhood will be different because up until more recently, motherhood narratives have not truthfully explored the experience. Narratives of motherhood that convey both the positives and negatives of mothering have not been the norm. We have felt this dissonance continued in cycles of silence, shame, and a lack of social change. To honestly tell our stories is to finally feel the freedom to connect and be seen.

Conclusion

Motherhood is beautiful and powerful and yet remains astoundingly undervalued and unseen. Society is still creating space to understand the depth of the mothering experience for women and the ways in which mothers remain disempowered. We still lack many necessary accommodations to support mothers. Through the radical honesty of the women cited in this text, we have a glimpse into the ways that the reality for mother-creators is not flowery, seamless, or simple. Mothers deserve all the warmth and praise and Mother's Day poems, but the sacrifice and difficulty mothering entails must also be recognized. Mothers must be empowered not only to mother well but also to be individual women. Right now, this continues to be challenging and for some impossible. The demand for a new understanding of mothering is a radical push. From scholars hoping to widen the understanding of feminism, to artists putting mothering truths out into the world, and creators just trying to make it as creators and mothers, the shift is evident. It is being heard and seen, and many hope that this awareness signals a rebirth of mother narratives. Mothers are putting their stories out there boldly and intimately. Mothers are ready.

This chapter has barely skimmed the surface of the depths of mothering experiences. Instead, I see this chapter as a brief glimpse into a few experiences. In most of these experiences, these mother-creators grappled with their sense of self. Within this grappling, they questioned their worth and the value of their roles. Many made difficult decisions; some gave up their art or careers for a time, and some did forever. For some, motherhood changed their art, or their art helped them through mothering. All of them experienced the reckonings of the gaping holes in the transparency of the motherhood experience.

For each of the women I talked with, there was a sense of surprise at the difficulties, the hurdles, and the silences of motherhood. They had been presented a pretty picture of what motherhood would be, which did not match their actual experiences of mothering. That motherhood is not what many women expect and that mothers find themselves unprepared for the enormity of the mothering experience further highlights the need for matricentric feminism. Moreover, the beautiful honesty conveyed by the mothers in this study signals a readiness for a revolution in necessary social change.

Other Notes and Considerations

For the purpose of the chapter, I decided to focus on artists and creators. Artists are certainly not the sole holders of these experiences. Mothers everywhere have numerous hurdles to overcome in being able to express, live, and explore their own identities.

Due to length constraints, and to avoid repetition, not all interviewed women are directly referred to, but their stories and experiences are highlighted through the themes in this chapter. Even though these mothers' experiences are not specifically mentioned, their stories are by no means less valued or appreciated. I am deeply grateful to all of the lives I have had the privilege of being let into and allowed to explore.

Works Cited

Douglas, S. J., and M. W. Michaels. *The Mommy Myth: The Idealization of Motherhood and How It Has Undermined All Women*. Free Press, 2004.

Hayasaki, Ericka. "How Motherhood Affects Creativity." *The Atlantic*, Sept. 2017, https://www.theatlantic.com/science/archive/2017/09/how-motherhood-affects-creativity/539418/. Accessed 7 Apr. 2023.

Hochschild, Arlie. *The Second Shift: Working Families and the Revolution at Home*. Penguin, 2012.

Hoekzema, E., et al. "Pregnancy Leads to Long-Lasting Changes in Human Brain Structure." *Nature Neuroscience*, vol. 20, 2017, pp. 287-96.

Lerner, Gerda. "Placing Women in History: Definitions and Challenges." *Feminist Studies*, vol. 3, no. 1-2, 1975, pp. 5-14.

McLeish, J., and M. Redshaw. "Mothers' Accounts of the Impact on Emotional Wellbeing of Organised Peer Support in Pregnancy and

Early Parenthood: A Qualitative study." *BMC Pregnancy Childbirth*, vol. 17, no. 28, 2017, https://bmcpregnancychildbirth.biomedcentral.com/articles/10.1186/s12884-017-1220-0. Accessed 7 Apr. 2023.

Meeussen, Loes, and Colette Van Laar. "Feeling Pressure to Be a Perfect Mother Relates to Parental Burnout and Career Ambitions." *Frontiers in Psychology*, vol. 9, Nov. 2018., https://www.frontiersin.org/articles/10.3389/fpsyg.2018.02113/full. Accessed 7 Apr. 2023.

O'Reilly, Andrea. "Matricentric Feminism: A Feminism for Mothers". *Journal of the Motherhood Initiative for Research and Community Involvement*, vol. 10, no. 1-2, Dec. 2019, https://jarm.journals.yorku.ca/index.php/jarm/article/view/40551. Accessed 7 Apr. 2023.

O'Reilly, Andrea. "Motherhood Hall of Fame Keynote." *Museum of Motherhood*, 2014, Keynote Address, https://mommuseum.org/aint-i-a-feminist-matricentric-feminism-feminist-mamas-and-why-mothers-need-a-feminist-movementtheory-of-their-own/. Accessed 7 Apr. 2023.

Parker, Kim. "Women More Than Men Adjust Their Careers for Family Life." *Pew Research Center*, Oct. 2015, https://www.pewresearch.org/fact-tank/2015/10/01/women-more-than-men-adjust-their-careers-for-family-life/. Accessed 7 Apr. 2023.

Ross, Catherine E., and Marieke Van Willigen. "Gender, Parenthood, and Anger." *Journal of Marriage and Family*, vol. 58, no. 3, 1996, pp. 572-84.

Soren, Tabitha. "The Blurred Existence of Motherhood" *The Atlantic*, June 2021, www.theatlantic.com/magazine/archive/2021/06/tabitha-soren-motherload/618718/. Accessed 7 Apr. 2023.

Tubbs, Anna Malaika. "The Problem with Celebrating the Selflessness of Mothers." *Time*, May 2021, www.time.com/6045818/supporting-mothers-after-baby-is-born/. Accessed 7 Apr. 2023.

Walsh, Brienne. "In this Surreal Novel about Motherhood, a Mom Slowly Turns into a Bloodthirsty Dog" *Cable News Network*, 18 July 2021, www.cnn.com/style/article/nightbitch-rachel-yoder-culture-queue/index.html. Accessed 7 Apr. 2023.

Westervelt, Amy. "Is Motherhood the Unfinished Work of Feminism?" *The Guardian*, 26 May. 2018, www.theguardian.com/commentisfree/2018/may/26/is-motherhood-the-unfinished-work-of-feminism. Accessed 7 Apr. 2023.

Chapter 18.

Between Mothers: Dialogically Exploring the Mother-Scholar Relationship

Rachel E. Stough and Elizabeth A. Bennett

We approach writing about motherhood and feminisms while taking seriously our lived realities as feminist mother-scholars who enjoy a rich mentoring relationship. One author, Elizabeth, is an early-career professor and the other, Rachel, is halfway through a doctoral degree in the same field and program. Importantly, Elizabeth serves as Rachel's primary academic mentor and dissertation chair, and over the course of our nearly two-year mentoring relationship, we have written a great deal together: namely, scholarship about our mothering intertwined with scholarship about our mentoring relationship, which we both experience as radically and intentionally relational, nonhierarchical, and—in its eschewing of power—subversive within the patriarchal constraints of academe.

For us, the process of becoming and being mothers has been shaped by our feminisms, which, along with the tone of our feminist mentoring relationship, are likewise shaped by our motherhood. Importantly, our professional identities as mother-scholars and psychotherapists are shaped by this dialogic interplay between motherhood and feminism. In this chapter, we attempt to convey the unique timbre of our professional—and deeply personal—mentoring relationship in the language of a matricentric feminism. Our manuscript is written in a poetic letter form, in which we write to each other about our experiences of entering and deepening our relationship as feminist mother-scholars. Shared explorations of some central themes serve to connect the letter poems, including recognition of the other's maternity, disclosure(s) of motherhood, radical nonhierarchy of matricentric feminism, and encouraging a reclamation of the primacy of motherhood—without sacrificing intellectual identities. To connect the dialogue of our letter poems and to more richly explore the themes we introduce, we consider the ways in which motherhood has enriched, deepened, and transmuted our feminisms. In particular, we explore motherhood as a relational and hierarchical equalizer and as presenting a call to an even more vulnerable feminism. Perhaps provocatively, we consider what we have experienced as the subversive nature of mother-scholar mentoring mother-scholar while reciprocally cultivating a mother community. First, we begin with a brief exploration of the mentoring literature to ground the reader in the contrasting nature of our mentoring relationship before we transition to our matricentric feminist approach.

"Traditional" Mentoring: A Brief History and Contextualization

The term "mentor" stems from Homer's epic poem *The Odyssey*. In this classic work of Greek mythology, the hero, Odysseus, leaves his son Telemachus in the care of an older man named Mentor. Mentor guides Telemachus on both a journey to find his father and a journey to find self-knowledge and authenticity (Merriam). Since 1750, the term "mentor" has been used to describe a person with similar characteristics and relational function to Mentor. Like the relationship between Mentor and Telemachus, ideal mentorship is intentional, involving elements of support and protection. It is a relationship oriented towards fostering growth between one adult who carries wisdom and experience valuable to another less experienced adult (Anderson and Shannon).

Much of the contemporary conceptualization of mentorship has its roots in the work of psychologist Daniel J. Levinson. In his text exploring the seasons of adulthood and the role of more-experienced adults in facilitating adult stage growth, Levinson writes that "The mentor relationship is one of the most complex ... and developmentally important.... Mentoring is defined not in terms of formal roles but in terms of the character of the relationship and the function it serves" (97-98). Levinson and other adult development thinkers have conceptualized mentorship as a relationship between an older male who functions as an older brother to the protégé. This concept of a mentorship relationship involves an eight- to fifteen-year age gap and is time limited. Although contemporary mentoring relationships may not be limited by these constraints, mentorship still often carries a paternalistic and/or patriarchal tenor. Sharan Merriam describes the mentorship relationship as "a powerful emotional interaction between an older and younger person, a relationship in which the older member is trusted, loving, and experienced in the guidance of the younger" (162). This implies a hierarchical relationship in which a mentor is defined by their rank, seniority, and/or status. Given this hierarchy, it can be assumed that a mentorship relationship offers unidirectional nurturing and support from the older, more experienced mentor to the younger, novice protégé (Anderson and Shannon). Although some view mentorship as "an intense form of love" (Merriam 162), this love is constrained by time and norms of professionalism.

In the academic setting, "the faculty member seeks advancement for the student in order to enhance the field and the student's role in it" (Merriam 167). Many academic programs involve formal mentorship programs, in which the academic mentor is a role model who offers informational support and opens doors for the student protégé, in addition to the advisory structure more strictly focused on ensuring that students meet requirements for graduation. Despite the intimacy of these activities, a mentorship relationship can range from one of deep personal connection to one that is completely emotionally detached and strictly professional (Anderson and Shannon). Indeed, there remains disagreement regarding the exact definition and bounds of mentorship (Jacobi). In the academic setting, particularly in psychology graduate studies, students identify mentor relationships—characterized by mutual trust and self-disclosure on the part of the mentor—as essential for impactful mentorship (Wilson and Johnson). This expectation blurs the lines between personal and professional, implying a bidirectional vulnerability and somewhat subversive dismantling of the built-in hierarchy of academia: We can imagine a version of Mentor and Telemachus in which Mentor acknowledges the ways in which Telemachus reciprocally transforms him as well.

A Movement towards Feminism in Mentoring

The primacy of spontaneous, genuine, mutually vulnerable, and mutually beneficial mentoring relationships, as well as the importance of addressing power in mentorship, reflects essential feminist principles that seem to directly challenge the hierarchy and paternalism inherent in more formalized or traditional mentorship. Jennifer Wolgemuth and Clifford Harbour beautifully describe the ways in which graduate school privileges "a particularly *masculine* way of learning and producing knowledge" (our emphasis; 182). Feminine ways of doing scholarship—à la the letter poems we introduce in this chapter—embrace "emotions, vulnerability, and dependence on interpersonal relationships," in such a way that invites collaboration and mutual support (Wolgemuth and Harbour 183). A feminist comentorship promotes the mutual vulnerability and trust that, as previously discussed, makes a mentorship meaningful, genuine, and enduring in its impact (see also McGuire and Reger). This approach to mentorship has a particular attunement to power—a recognition and subversion of the inherent power differential as the mentor intentionally invites the graduate student to teach them.

A feminist approach to mentorship is not without complication. There is an inherently paradoxical nature to the kind of feminist mentorship we enjoy in our relationship. Although it challenges aspects of traditional mentorship that reinforce inequality, feminist mentors must also still prepare the protégé for success in academic or professional settings by working from their position of authority and power. Thus, there is a dilemma between hierarchy and closeness, professional and personal. Perhaps most important in balancing this paradox is the intentionality of exposing oppressive power structures, reflecting critically, and mobilizing student/protégé power. This is a feminist orientation towards care for a less experienced other in which difference (in age, experience, etc.) coexists nonhierarchically (Adams-Hutcheson and Johnston). Self-definition, the gateway to empowerment, is the goal of feminist mentorship. A feminist mentorship validates the student's own ways of knowing and is "replete with mutuality, respect, and collaboration; emphasized connection, challenge, honest communication, political analysis and self-awareness, and a valued difference" (Prouty Lyness and Helmeke 174-75). This dynamic allows students to develop the skill of reflexivity and the capacity to be vulnerable in a way that is generative. A feminist approach to mentoring also recognizes that whereas in traditional mentoring it is assumed that the mentor has greater relevant knowledge than the protégé, in reality, it is likely that there are domains in knowledge where that differential is flipped (Bozeman and Feeny). This implies that mentor and protégé can learn reciprocally from one another across different domains of knowledge, effectively breaking down the hierarchical nature of traditional mentoring.

Matricentric Feminism and Feminist Mentorship

Where the voices of women and other marginalized groups tend to be silenced in the dominant, patriarchal structures of academia, the voices of mothers tend to be silenced or rejected from dominant feminist discourse. Thus, the role of a matricentric feminism in feminist mentorship has yet to be considered. Andrea O'Reilly offers a nuanced perspective on motherhood and feminism—offering matricentric feminism as a means of emphasizing the ways in which mothers uniquely experience oppression in light of patriarchal expectations of motherhood as an institution. In *Matricentric Feminism*, O'Reilly calls for a nurturing mothering community, which tends to be lacking in the present zeitgeist, given the present cultural expectation of isolated and intensive mothering (i.e., without the support of a reliable community). In twenty-first-century Western society, it is rare and challenging to be a mother in professional and academic spaces, particularly given the expectation of a masculine way of succeeding in these spaces. (One need only consider the absence of maternity leave and support for mothering responsibilities within the academy to see how it is, at best, difficult to do mothering and scholarship.) Therefore, it is particularly radical to reclaim the tradition of the nurturing mothering community in such spaces, leaning into collaboration and connectedness where independence and emotional detachment are praised. A matricentric feminist scholarship is a radically feminine scholarship that challenges the unidirectionality of traditional mentorship and invites intimate trust. Though specific to motherhood, a matricentric feminist mentorship offers a theorical lens through which to view mentorship and what it offers both to mentor and protégé. It challenges the need to rationalize, standardize, operationalize, and reproduce mentoring relationships by underscoring the electricity that exists in spontaneity and genuine connection. Matricentric feminism humanizes both the protégé and the mentor in a distinctly and importantly feminine way that offers a gateway into conceptualizing effectiveness in mentorship as radically opposed to the structures in place in professional and academic settings—challenging professionalism and appropriateness standards with the humanity of what it means to see one's experience reflected in another's.

Relational Context and Authors' Positionality

Grounded in the above context, what follows reflects the relationship between two mothers: one a third-year clinical psychology doctoral candidate and the other an early career licensed clinical psychologist and assistant professor of psychology in the same academic program. One of us, Rachel, is a biracial Afro Cuban, and ethnically Jewish, cisgender woman and mother of one toddler. The other, Elizabeth, is a white, cisgender woman and mother of two young children. Both of us recognize the primacy of our identities as mothers while deeply valuing our identities as scholars, clinicians, and creators. We developed a connection when Elizabeth, just a few months postpartum from birthing her second baby, began teaching in the clinical psychology program just as Rachel returned from her extended maternity leave as an early-in-training doctoral student. Upon discovering that we were both mothers and shared many research and clinical interests—namely, centring the experience of motherhood as a primary site of scholarly activity and generativity—we began a mentoring relationship as advisor and advisee. (Our program uses the language of advisor/advisee rather than mentor/protégé.) Our closeness in age (we are about two and a half years apart, and in one of the few aspects of our mentorship that feels traditional, Elizabeth is older) has enabled a kind of generational resonance that has made connection feel extra easy. Though we occupy different ethnic positionalities, the moments of salience in our differences have largely served to enrich our getting to know each other.

We have committed to scholarly activities together—all focused in some way on our mothering, the nature of our mentoring relationships, or both. We have met with regularity for the advisor to inspire and guide the advisee to fulfill the requirements of her academic program and find professional grounding, whereas the advisee's desire for vulnerable, nonhierarchical connection has encouraged and inspired the advisor to more vulnerably lean into the kind of mentoring that feels most authentic and rewarding. Over time, sparked by many raw conversations about the experience of womanhood, motherhood, and mother-scholarship, we recognized a resonance that was deeply personal—an intimacy, a safety, a friendship. Acknowledging the ways in which a masculinized, patriarchal academic culture discourages the kind of intimacy that we share (often leaving one labelled as having unprofessional and poor boundaries), we explore the importance of the multifaceted and subversive nature of our relationship in the form of letter poems. We do not identify the author of each individual letter poem to keep the reader's focus on the radically relational and nonhierarchical nature of our relationship; our hope is that the reader experiences the kind of dynamic closeness and genuine care that we have leaned into cultivating together rather than focusing on whose ideas or words belong to whom. True to the above-described feminist theoretical values, the meaning here is in our vulnerable "yes" to prioritizing connection over individualized career gains as so-called professionalism, as is often the model in academe. Importantly, we hope to illustrate the ways in which our feminisms and feminist identities have been nourished and shaped by our shared maternity. We have selected letter poems as our means of exploring these phenomena due to our shared love of poetry coupled with its central role in qualitative and autoethnographic feminist scholarship. Poetry has been richly employed across a variety of academic contexts to evocatively explore lived experience, particularly within a feminism context (e.g., Faulkner) and is considered especially appropriate when examining a less-well-studied area, such as the nature and fruitfulness of matricentric feminist mentoring. We are unaware of the letter-poem medium being used in the way we present it here, and we are eager to encourage other mother-scholars to consider radically autobiographical and creative forms of documenting what it is to relate as to each other within a matricentric feminist dialogue.

Letter Poems between Mothers

1.

I share my introduction and invite yours
I am teaching this class, a new faculty member, [beginning to own this title] mother-scholar
And upon the mention of my maternal status
I notice your face shift.
You share your own introduction
"Became a mother"
"Birth of my son"
And it begins, you teaching me a bigger class—us teaching each other,
Reciprocal.
It's like
Our bodies recognize it, the feeling on the playground
At the mommy group that meets on Wednesdays
7:30 a.m., for the working mother
Caramelized coffee, Styrofoam chalices
Knowing glances across the circle
("I am hanging on as Mother ... my stunningly beautiful child is Just Average")
While The Room compares
Milestones, millstones.
First it's
Noticing your vibrance, intellect, humour, presence
Recognizing that You are a mother, too
Suddenly it feels like more.
Mother is the most atomic element
Not overshadowing or foreclosing
Instead amplifying, opening, making me the realest I have ever been or could be;

I notice
Recognize
That you are your most Real too.

          2.
Your single, last-surviving, still-flickering brain cell
Nearly snuffed by the impossible reality of working motherhood
          Calls to my own
Like a lighthouse in a sea of uncertainty and shame.
          In my felt inadequacy
Your recognition of the blood, sweat, and breastmilk
          On which my scholarship floats
          Lifts me out from drowning
          Onto your life raft built of the same.
Your outstretched hand welcoming me to a secret club
          That bemoans its own secretiveness.
          Your fierce vulnerability,
A soft challenge to actually do something about the silence,
          Out loud.
          Your truth I hold precious
          As a sister to my own.

3.

This existence

Carving out a warm, nourishing womb-space of my own

Difficult, crushing, the most profound isolation

The academy demands whatever it takes.

Having begun

To create this space

You enter in—

[Holding a flickering lantern to see the crumbling path,

Stones missing,

Do they care if you-in-your-fullness make it to the destination?]

As we welcome each other

Recognition.

The feeling of shoulders curved down

Encircling our meeting spaces

The felt necessity of protecting what we are creating

Attending to

Opening up

Feeding with sunlight and togetherness, the life giving of our generative mother bodies.

4.

A large black coffee.

Earl Grey with a hint of sweet cream.

Hands used most to hold tinier hands

Or worn-down pens

Wrapped around the thinly contained

Warmth of the moment.

Nestled into the corner of a crowded coffee shop,

We sink—

Our obligations heavy

Our histories weighty
Our daydreams grounded
In a demand,
An ache,
For a crumbled path leading to wholeness.
Together we nurture,
Nourish our hopes concurrently.
We are a village.

5.

A man I often see
At our spot
Where we meet to unfurl dreams, plans, hopes—trust
We know each other's orders with an intimacy that feels well worn.
This man has approached me to ask
If I am an editor for a Big Publisher
Or perhaps if that's you
Because he saw us meeting yesterday and noted that
I seem very important,
In the way that I carry my body and expand into space,
And that you, likewise
Seem very important,
And his fantasy was that we are perhaps both in some sort of powerful, creative work.
I realized that it is in the between of us
And certainly not on my own: isolated, singular
That I become both grounded and expansive,
Powerful, creative
That it is what emerges from the between
That makes me more of me and you more of you.

6.

As a girl, I loved to dance
Hidden among dozens
All dressed in sequined skirts and tasseled boots.
Not one girl stood out.
Not for too long.
I often wonder what people think,
Witnessing what emerges between us.
Girls
Women
Mothers
Expanding noticeably
Dancing unapologetically
(To no music apart from the vibration of our bond)
Refusing to be small.
I smirk when others say the shimmy of my shoulders reminds them of yours.
In truth my shoulders,
Which have danced this way
Alone and hidden for so long,
Have found resonance
Recognition
In rhythm with yours.

A Reflection and an Invitation

In reflecting, both alone and in conversation, on the process of writing to each other in this way, surprises emerged, which we offer here. As scholars well trained to comport ourselves in a manner that aligns with the distanced professionalism associated with formal academic mentoring relationships, we already knew that the vulnerability and interpersonal richness of our relationship felt different and nourishing. Yet we both described embodied feelings of genuine surprise: being touched by and seen in our writing to and about each other—about us. Both the process of writing to each other, which called upon us to settle into the sensorial memories associated with our work together, and the process of reading each letter poem, which invited us to receive the care and love radiating from the other, generated a depth of emotional response and resonance, which are truly subversive in academe.

In particular, we notice the ways in which the matricentric nature of our relationship has brought out, nourished, and strengthened our individual—and shared—feminist identities and commitments over time. At the beginning of our relationship, we introduced our mother identities as a matter of fact, without recognizing that those identities would contextualize the whole of our working together ("mother is the most atomic element").

I (Elizabeth) introduced myself to my students with the brief inclusion of my kids: I had, at the time, a newly minted three-year-old and an exclusively nursing baby. I had birthed my son less than three months before that first-class meeting; as an early career academic, I knew well that the only way to cultivate any kind of leave pretenure would be to perfectly time the birth at the beginning of summer. Success. Yet I entered a new job, in a new state, with new colleagues and new students, my breasts full and uneven in my new postpartumness—and I felt unsettled. Perhaps in that newness of transition and maternity, more mother than teacher. I felt tender and fresh, entering this new space knowing that I was very close in age to my students—closer, I have since learned, than most of them guessed or anticipated—and was replacing a beloved maternal presence in the department. I had not before centred my mother identity in my teaching, although for a few years, I had begun to centre mothering in my research. In my class introduction that day, I remember encouraging myself to go for it and thinking that these students are adults and may be curious about having their own children and there may be (maybe?) a parent in the class! I leaned vulnerably into the wobbliness of new motherhood the second time around, and for the first time in my young professional life mentioned my kids as part of my formal introduction.

When I (Rachel) was accepted into the clinical psychology doctoral program, it was the start of a second attempt at a career. As such, I knew that I did not want to put my personal life on hold given that I had been married to my partner for several years, and we both wanted children while we were fairly young. Recognizing that the more my training progressed the more complex the logistics of starting a family would be, I hoped to perfectly time my pregnancy and childbirth for the second semester of my first year (where I could use transfer credits to create a maternity leave). Success. What I did not plan, however, were the complications that came with the global COVID-19 pandemic. My partner had been one of the many people laid off from work due to the pandemic, so we were left with no childcare, and my ability to remain in this unpaid doctoral program was tenuous. Driven by a lack of support and intense postpartum anxiety, I quit the program. Although I returned just as hastily three days later, I continued to wonder if completing my program requirements was even possible as a new mother. During my first week back on campus, I experienced guilt both for leaving my still exclusively nursing child and for not feeling fully present among my peers or in my classes. During my maternity leave, there had been a change in the faculty, so when I returned, I was met with an unfamiliar face at the front of my classroom. I wondered what she might have heard about me, "the mother" in the cohort, from other faculty or students—perhaps that I was less dedicated or more distracted. Before I could fall further into insecurity and self-deprecation, she disclosed her new mother status, and my heart lit up at once I felt stabilized by her bold display of vulnerability. We soon began meeting regularly to talk about our shared interest in researching the maternal experience and, "witnessing what emerges between us," I felt compelled to ask her to be my advisor and dissertation chair, formalizing our existing mentor-mentee relationship.

As we have deepened our relationship, at times unintentionally and at times with great and serious intention situating our maternity and maternal experiences at the centre, we have in our own ways recognized the parallel deepening of what it is and means to be a feminist thinker, psychotherapist, and scholar via the centring of shared maternity. In our letter poems, we write about sisterhood and community ("we are a village"). In reflecting on our experiences of writing to each other, we have noticed the profound consciousness-raising elements of our work. It is in the sitting together, protecting our space, and our truth telling ("we welcomed each other ... recognition ... protecting what we are creating") that we hear our stories in each other and the realities of our matrescence become more real. Indeed, as we have moved through these last nearly two years of mothering together (through a global pandemic no less!), our commitments to the core tenets underlying much of feminist theory have only strengthened: As we have fought for a kind of radical matricentric feminism in our mentoring and friendship, we value even more principles of nonhierarchy. We focus on collaboration and reciprocity in tangible ways. We address, readdress, and eschew power. We hold that—especially for the mother-scholar—the personal is richly and imperatively political.

We hope that our dialogic exchange has touched the reader as well and that you are experiencing the kind of warmth and radical nonhierarchical relating that we lean into cultivating. We also hope for more mentoring relationships, particularly between mother-scholars, to grow in the relational possibilities inherent in upending the traditional mentoring script. A true matricentric feminist mentoring opens worlds for mother-scholars seeking to find place within, and without, these intellectual spaces historically and systemically reserved for not us. Our feminisms and our mothering have indeed come into being via the tenor and affordances of our mentoring relationship; here, we present a welcoming call for other mother-scholars who desire a different kind of academic mentoring.

Works Cited

Adams-Hutcheson, Gail, and Lynda Johnston. "Flourishing in Fragile Academic Work Spaces and Learning Environments: Feminist Geographies of Care and Mentoring." *Gender, Place & Culture*, vol. 26, no. 4, 2019, pp. 451-67.

Anderson, Eugene M., and Anne Lucasse Shannon. "Toward a Conceptualization of Mentoring." *Journal of Teacher Education*, vol. 39, no. 1, 1988, pp. 38-42.

Bozeman, Barry, and Mary K. Feeney. "Toward a Useful Theory of

Mentoring: A Conceptual Analysis and Critique." *Administration & Society*, vol. 39, no. 6, 2007, pp. 719-39.

Jacobi, Maryann. "Mentoring and Undergraduate Academic Success: A Literature Review." *Review of Educational Research*, vol. 61, no. 4, 1991, pp. 505-32.

Levinson, Daniel Jacob. *The Seasons of a Man's Life*. Random House Digital, Inc., 1978.

McGuire, Gail M., and Jo Reger. "Feminist Co-Mentoring: A model for academic professional development." *Feminist Formations*, vol. 15, no. 1, 2003, pp. 54-72.

Merriam, Sharan. "Mentors and Protégés: A Critical Review of the Literature." *Adult Education*, vol. 33, no. 3, 1983, pp. 161-73.

O'Reilly, Andrea. *Matricentric Feminism: Theory, Activism, Practice*. Demeter Press, 2021.

Prouty Lyness, Anne M., and Karen B. Helmeke. "Clinical Mentorship: One More Aspect of Feminist Supervision." *Journal of Feminist Family Therapy*, vol. 20, no. 2, 2008, pp. 166-99.

Wilson, Peter F., and W. Brad Johnson. "Core Virtues for the Practice of Mentoring." *Journal of Psychology and Theology*, vol. 29, no. 2, 2001, pp. 121-30.

Wolgemuth, Jennifer R., and Clifford P. Harbour. "A Man's Academy? The Dissertation Process as Feminist Resistance." *NASPA Journal About Women in Higher Education*, vol. 1, no. 1, 2009, pp. 183-203.

Chapter 19.

The COVID-19 Pandemic as a Catalyst for Feminist Thought

Lisa H. Rosen and Linda J. Rubin

In this chapter, we present findings from a study examining mothers' experiences during the pandemic, and our findings highlight that mothers experienced acute stress and significant duress while trying to balance work and childcare during the pandemic. We—Lisa and Linda—sought to gather qualitative accounts to examine whether experiencing the acute expectations of motherhood during the COVID-19 pandemic could serve as a catalyst for mothers to realize the need for feminism in their lives and the larger society. Scholars, such as Jennifer Borda, view the pandemic optimistically and believe that the postpandemic world will be a world more supportive of mothers and their families. Borda asserts that the pandemic "requires a rededication toward collective feminist politics" and shares her "feminist hope that by building back from the cultural and economic devastation wrought by COVID-19, we may create a new paradigm, inspired by feminist politics and imbued with immanent values of equity, diversity, and inclusion" (84). Our study sought to examine whether working mothers voiced similar sentiments of hope that the challenges brought about by the pandemic would bring greater possibilities of equality and inclusion for them and their daughters.

Indeed, pandemic-related challenges for working mothers abounded, amplifying inequalities, which have led feminist scholars, including Borda, to call for change. In their volume *Mothers, Mothering, and*

COVID-19: Dispatches from the Pandemic, Andrea O'Reilly and Fiona Green highlight the idea that "Many feminist and social justice researchers and activists see the COVID-19 crisis as an opening space for a coalition movement for workplace justice and for the reevaluation of carework as an essential part of an economic agenda" (29). Drawing on this scholarly work, the research findings described in the current chapter examine whether the untenable pressures many mothers face during the pandemic strengthened their hope that society would build back better from the challenges to create a more equitable future for their children.

The working mothers who participated in our study were recruited through Prolific, an online participant recruitment platform. Participation was limited to working mothers currently residing in the United States; however, a diverse sample of mothers was recruited in terms of age, race/ethnicity, marital status, education, income, and field of work. Participants reported demographic information (see Table 1). Many different fields of employment were reported, including agriculture, business management, education, healthcare, hospitality, information technology, manufacturing, marketing, and science/engineering.

Participants reported on their experiences during the pandemic and answered open-ended questions about how the pandemic affected them, their views of feminism, and how the pandemic influenced their views of feminism. We incorporate quotes from this diverse group of mothers in our review of the literature and then devote specific attention to the themes that emerged from these mothers' responses.

Table 1. Participant Demographics

Age Range	18–24 years (3.1%)
	25–34 years (34.4%)
	35–44 years (41.4%)
	45–54 years (18.8%)
	55–64 years (2.5%)
Race/Ethnicity	White (81.3%)
	Black (8.6%)
	Latina (7.0%)
	Asian (1.6%)
Marital Status	Married (56.3%)
	Not Married (43.7%)
Highest Education Level	Some High School (1.6%)
	High School Diploma/GED (14.1%)
	Some College or Two-year Degree (31.3%)
	Four-year College Degree (20.3%)
	Some School Beyond College (3.9%)
	Graduate/Professional Degree (28.9%)
Total Household Income	$10,000–$24,999 (8.6%)
	$25,000–$49,999 (22.7%)
	$50,000–$74,999 (15.6%)
	$75,000–$99,999 (18.8%)
	$100,000–$149,999 (18.8%)
	Over $150,000 (14.8%)

Stress of Mothering during the Pandemic

Undeniably, the challenges of motherhood have been exacerbated by the COVID-19 pandemic (O'Reilly and Green). The disproportionate toll of the pandemic on mothers has received much attention in empirical work across a wide range of disciplines (Connor et al.; Kim and Patterson; O'Reilly; Raile) as well as in the popular press (Dickson; Perelman). The vast majority of mothers assumed more household work and caregiving responsibilities during the pandemic than they had been doing previously, reflecting historic inequalities (Friedman and Satterthwaite). As women took on these additional responsibilities due to school closures and other pandemic-related disruptions, mothers reported being physically and mentally exhausted (Barroso and Horowitz; Igielnik; O'Reilly and Green). Coupled with these increased stressors, mothers often had less support from friends, families, and daycare providers due to pandemic restrictions. For many working mothers, balancing family and work was nearly impossible during the early waves of the pandemic (Cummins and Brannon). The challenge of juggling all these responsibilities is evident in what one mother in our study shared: "Trying to focus on my usual tasks, as well as the extra work stress caused by the pandemic ... was incredibly hard ... it was definitely stressful to try and work, parent, and teach my child at the same time." As a result of these challenges, many mothers reported decreased productivity on the job and, by necessity, reduced work hours (Barroso and Horowitz; Igielnik).

However, not all mothers were able to decrease their work demands because of financial obligations or being an essential frontline worker (Friedman and Satterthwatie). This circumstance was reflected in what was shared by one of the mothers in our study:

> I had to go into work every day. This affected my children because I wasn't home to help with online school, so they ended up not paying attention or just not doing the work. When I got home in the evening, we were trying to play catch up for all the school work that they didn't understand because they could not stay on task for eight hours a day staring at a computer screen. I also put my children at risk of catching COVID-19 by continuing to leave the house and work with the public every day.

Thus, difficulties were associated with working from within or outside the home during the pandemic.

The pressures of the pandemic also took a toll on mothers' mental health and wellbeing (O'Reilly and Green). Mothers reported higher levels of depression and anxiety during the pandemic, and expectant mothers also faced increased stress and mental health concerns with the onset of COVID-19 (Cameron et al.; Davenport et al.; Thapa et al.). The effects of the pandemic may be especially pronounced for vulnerable populations, including BIPOC mothers (Black, Indigenous, and people of colour), working-class mothers, single mothers, and mothers who have children with disabilities or who have a disability themselves (Friedman and Satterthwaite; Gur et al.; Mehta; Yoshikawa et al.).

Child Development during Pandemic Times

The pandemic has both direct as well as indirect effects on child wellbeing through maternal mental health. Allison Hermann and colleagues assert that "Maternal mental health is a bellwether in the COVID-19 pandemic" (124). The amount of time children spent with their mothers during the pandemic might have amplified these effects, especially during periods of school closure. With school and daycare closures and reductions in activities, mothers felt increasingly responsible for their children's development (Staneva). Media attention and scholars were drawing attention to the profound ways that fear of the virus, social isolation, maternal stress, and dramatic changes to day-to-day life could disrupt children's development (De Araújo et al.). This added pressure might have been associated with feelings of guilt for mothers (Whiley et al.), which was the case for one of our study participants who shared the following:

> During the lockdown, I had to make/take phone calls and focus on work tasks on the computer while she [daughter] was around, which was difficult. She was doing her schooling virtually and needed a huge amount of direction, which complicated the matter further. I believe that she felt less important to me than she had in the past because she hadn't been around to see me working previously.

Similar experiences of role overload were shared by mothers across the globe during the pandemic, as mothers tended to their children's development and work simultaneously, which as Dana Malone argues "makes the second shift visible." Even if they wished to do so, many mothers could not hide that they were working while interacting with their children in close proximity, as Zoom meetings and conference calls became the norm. As one of our study participants shared: "I worked from home 100 per cent. It was difficult for my children, as I didn't have a proper work space, so I had to be either in a bedroom or the kitchen table, both places easily accessible to my children. They tend to come to me for all things, so I had a very difficult time staying focused or being present during Zoom meetings and phone calls." For many mothers, children watched their work unfold over Zoom while colleagues were granted a view of what was unfolding at home.

In contrast to past waves of feminism, Malone reflects on Arlie Hochschild's *The Second Shift* and suggests that the landscape is different thirty years later: "Women's shift work is now visible in new ways. In these COVID days, there are no longer first and second shifts; it all bleeds together." As mothers shared their struggles within their community and across the globe, and experiences of role strain were highlighted, mothers might have been more confident in the need for changes to occur and hope that the future would be a more equitable landscape for their children. This need for change is reflected in what was shared by one of our study participants who noted that the pandemic "made it more apparent how much women do for their family and jobs and the importance of our role."

Fostering Feminism at Home

Although much attention has been devoted to negative consequences, the pandemic also had the potential to impact mothers and children in positive ways. For many mothers, the pandemic allowed them to spend greater amounts of time with their children and foster stronger relationships. O'Reilly and Green suggest that the greater time mothers spent engaging with their children allowed for shared activities and discussions, which "offers ways to talk with each other about their relationship and to challenge obligations of mothers and the expectations of patriarchal family structures" (28). This idea was reflected in what one mother in our study shared: "My kids and I have spent a lot of time together. A lot more of our conversations were about world events/politics. I think they became more aware of some of the less good things in society because they were paying more attention to what was happening in the world around them." The stress that mothers endured and the sociopolitical climate during the early waves of the pandemic were topics of discussion for many mothers and their children.

The pandemic highlighted for children the different responsibilities held by their mothers and fathers. Children are quite observant and are aware of the inequity in division of household responsibilities and care-work, and this has the potential to affect children's own aspirations (Croft et al.). For some families, mothers and children specifically discussed this inequity and the immediate resulting impact. One mother in our study reported that she and her daughter "have talked about the sacrifices that women have made because it's important for her to be aware of that." Similarly, another mother reported discussions of gender equality during the pandemic: "Overall, I don't think that women are treated much worse than men, but I am aware that I have internalized messages that make me blind to a lot of the slights and difficulties that women deal with and don't even realize they are a problem. I continue to try to educate myself and my daughter about these issues." Mother-child discussions about gender equality, such as those reported by some mothers in our study, might have led to hopes for a feminist future in which daughters do not need to make the same sacrifices as their mothers had to make during the tumultuous times of the pandemic.

Children also had greater opportunities to observe their mothers' work during the pandemic. Mothers are critical role models for their children and help shape their future aspirations and feminist identity (Croft et al.). The manner in which mothers model and discuss balancing or integrating work and family has the potential to affect their daughters' feminist identification and, in turn, career aspirations (Armstrong; Colaner and Rittenour), and this may be heightened under the pervasive stress of the pandemic. Along these lines, one mother in our study reported having to do substantially more work with the onset of the pandemic but noted a positive in that this enabled her kids to see the importance of this work. Other mothers in our study reported the positive impact on their children of being able to model the practice of balancing multiple roles. One mother in our study shared that her children "see me as a busy mother even though I am so close to them and never too busy for them." She continued: "They see these qualities and aspire to be like their mother when they are grown. Balancing work and raising a family is never easy, but it must be balanced; with my behaviour, I believe I am influencing the future of my children in a positive manner." Another mother in our study suggested that the increased opportunities for her children to observe her working "made them more determined to not give up even if they have to take on extra responsibilities."

Although we included several positive examples from participants, it is important to note that families' experiences varied greatly during the pandemic. In contrast to these positive accounts, one mother in our study shared the following:

> My daughter has made several mentions since the pandemic that "mommy works a lot." In truth, I did have to take up a side assistant job to keep up on the bills, but with being home more often, she sees just how much I'm running around trying to get things done. While I don't think she has much of an opinion on my job itself, she does seem to be influenced by the fact that I'm almost always working, and when I'm not, I'm working on our home life (cleaning, chores, dinner, etc.).

As some mothers dealt with the untenable pressures of balancing it all during the early waves of the pandemic, and their daughters observed them struggle, it is possible that daughters might have considered a different path for themselves and thought of having to make a choice of either work or family. Unfortunately, our study was limited to the accounts of mothers, but future research is needed to better examine the positive and negative effects of children observing mothers adapt to the pandemic.

Lived Experiences during the Pandemic: Catalyst for Feminist Thought

In our study, mothers reflected on how the COVID-19 pandemic has influenced their identification with feminism. Several participant quotes were shared above as the literature on mothers and the pandemic was reviewed. The themes that emerged are discussed in greater depth below, as we considered whether our participants viewed the pandemic as an impetus for feminist thought.

Pandemic Sparks Hope for Greater Equality

Mothers in our study frequently highlighted the uneven division of household labour. One mother shared: "More women have quit their jobs during COVID due to lack of childcare. In a more feminist world, it wouldn't be the 'norm' for women to be the ones expected to always be the parent to take care of the children." Another mother articulated:

"If anything, it [the pandemic] has made me believe in feminism even more since this pandemic has revealed just how much women and femmes need to be heard and seen and our needs to be met." In addressing whether the pandemic influenced her, or her children's, identification with feminism, one mother noted:

> If anything, it's [the pandemic] strengthened my belief in feminism. I've seen women pull off incredible feats of energy and talent to rearrange their lives during this pandemic and ensure that their families' needs are met. I've watched a lot of women walk away from lucrative careers to care for their families—a decision that was made solely on them being the "least valuable" in terms of earnings in their household. Overall, I've seen women make the biggest sacrifices because society leaves them with no choice. I admire their strength, but it makes me angry that we're left figuring it all out, as usual.

Thus, the pandemic seemed to foster feminist thinking in many mothers who shared their experiences.

Beyond the pandemic's direct effects on mothers, some also highlighted its effects on their daughters' hope for a more equitable future. This theme is seen in one mother's words: "I want to make the world a better place for them. I need to make sure my kids know that life isn't fair, and that's okay sometimes, but everyone should get a chance, and there are things we can do to level the playing field." Another mother spoke more directly about advocacy and suggested that the pandemic had changed her daughter in terms of her advocacy: "She is very concerned about the treatment of others and advocates for those who can't advocate for themselves." Thus, the pandemic may also be encouraging some daughters to become feminists.

Continuing the Status Quo

It is important to note that not all mothers described the pandemic as a catalyst for feminist thought for themselves or their children. As one mother said, "My perspective on feminism hasn't really changed since before the pandemic." Likewise, another mother indicated: "My thoughts and opinions on this are the same as before the pandemic." Thus, the mothers in our studies reported diverse responses, and not all viewed the pandemic as a potential impetus for a more feminist future.

Of those who did not believe the pandemic affected their perspective on feminism, some indicated that they already had a strong feminist identity. For instance, one mother shared: "I don't think the pandemic has affected my answers. I identified as a feminist before COVID." Similarly, another mother indicated that the pandemic did not affect her views on feminism because she had always been a feminist and had worked to raise a feminist child. For some mothers, discussions about gender equality occurred both before and during the pandemic, with one mother sharing: "I believe my family has always had an open dialogue about this and many other topics, and this has not changed with the pandemic."

Still, some mothers suggested that they did not previously identify as a feminist and that the pandemic did not shift their thought. A mother shared: "I feel people that identify as feminist have every right to feel and think how they do depending on how they perceive things to be. I do not think there is anything wrong with being a feminist. I just do not personally see myself as one." Of those who believed the pandemic did not influence their perspective on feminism, some shared that they had never viewed themselves as feminists.

Too Overwhelmed to Consider

Throughout our study, mothers reported being incredibly overwhelmed, which might not have allowed them energy to focus beyond their immediate situation. This theme was reflected in a mother who indicated that her thoughts on feminism had not changed: "I feel overworked and tired and as a result, women's rights take on less of a priority." Many mothers in our study highlighted the incredible stress that they experienced during the pandemic, and given this, might not have had the opportunity to think about what a postpandemic world could look like.

Conclusions

The findings of our study shine further light on the acute stress and significant duress many mothers experienced during the pandemic. Mothers reported being overwhelmed at home and work, and some noted that this role strain was not something that their male colleagues experienced or fully grasped. These reported experiences are consistent with past studies as well as articles published in the popular press

(Connor et al.; Dickson; Kim and Patterson; Perelman; Raile). It is not clear whether the attention paid in the popular press to women leaving the workforce, or drastically scaling back work hours to care for children, has been widely conceptualized as a feminist issue. Many of the mothers in this study hoped that the pandemic would bring greater attention to these issues to help create a more equitable future.

The challenges mothers experienced frequently sparked discussions with children. As O'Reilly and Green suggest, mothers had greater opportunities to discuss the historic inequities in childcare and how these inequities were magnified by the pandemic. These mother-child discussions might have encouraged feminist thinking in their daughters.

Mothers reflected on their own careers and thought of their children's futures, which sometimes acted as a further impetus for feminist thinking. In their responses, many mothers shared that they or mothers they knew faced additional challenges at work. At the same time, many mothers felt increased responsibility for their children's development, and some reported that thinking about their children's future furthered their feminist thought. In line with other scholars (e.g., Borda; Malone), some mothers viewed the pandemic as having the potential to promote policies that would benefit mothers and their families. It is important to note that this was not universally expressed by mothers in this study, as some noted that the pandemic had not changed their views.

As these gender inequities became apparent during the pandemic, mothers often believed that these circumstances would help to highlight the needs of working mothers and advance policies to support them. Following the pandemic, attention to these specific gender inequities, in the form of advocacy for the needs of working mothers and an examination of the impact of mothers' work on their children's futures, will deserve to be conceptualized as feminist issues.

Authors' Note

This work was part of a larger project, *Maternal Influences on Daughters' Career Aspirations: Reflections on Working Together during the Pandemic*, supported by the Jane Nelson Institute for Women's Leadership.

Works Cited

Armstrong, Jill. *Like Mother, Like Daughter?: How Career Women Influence Their Daughters' Ambition*. Oxford University Press, 2017.

Barroso, Amanda, and Juliana Menasce Horowitz. "The Pandemic has Highlighted Many Challenges for Mothers, But They Aren't Necessarily New." 17 March 2021, https://www.pewresearch.org/fact-tank/2021/03/17/the-pandemic-has-highlighted-many-challenges-for-mothers-but-they-arent-necessarily-new/. Accessed 8 Apr. 2023.

Borda, Jennifer L. "Workplace and Social Justice: A New Feminist Movement for Labour and Love." *Mothers, Mothering, and COVID-19: Dispatches from the Pandemic*, edited by Andrea O'Reilly and Fiona Joy Green, Demeter Press, 2021, pp. 83-100.

Cameron, Emily E, et al. "Maternal Psychological Distress & Mental Health Service Use during the COVID-19 Pandemic." *Journal of Affective Disorders*, vol. 276, 2020, pp. 765-74.

Colaner, Colleen Warner, and Christine E Rittenour. "'Feminism Begins at Home': The Influence of Mother Gender Socialization on Daughter Career And Motherhood Aspirations as Channeled Through Daughter Feminist Identification." *Communication Quarterly*, vol. 63, no. 1, 2015, pp. 81-98.

Connor, Jade, et al. "Health Risks and Outcomes That Disproportionately Affect Women during the Covid-19 Pandemic: A Review." *Social Science & Medicine* (1982), vol. 266, 2020, pp. 1-7.

Croft, Alyssa, et al. "The Second Shift Reflected in the Second Generation: Do Parents' Gender Roles at Home Predict Children's Aspirations?" *Psychological Science*, vol. 25, no. 7, 2014, pp. 1418-28.

Cummins, Molly Wiant, and Grace Ellen Brannon. "The Balancing Act Is Magnified: U.S. Mothers' Struggles amidst a Pandemic." *Mothers, Mothering, and COVID-19: Dispatches from the Pandemic*, edited by Andrea O'Reilly and Fiona Joy Green, Demeter Press, 2021, pp. 211-20.

Friedman, May, and Emily Satterthwaite. "Same Storm, Different Boats: Some Thoughts on Gender, Race, and Class in the Time of COVID-19." *Mothers, Mothering, and COVID-19: Dispatches from the Pandemic*, edited by Andrea O'Reilly and Fiona Joy Green, Demeter

Press, 2021, pp. 53-64.

Davenport, Margie et al. "Moms Are Not OK: COVID-19 and Maternal Mental Health." *Frontiers in Global Women's Health*, vol. 1, pp. 1-6. 10.3389/fgwh.2020.00001.

De Araújo, Liubiana Arantes et al. "The potential impact of the COVID-19 pandemic on child growth and development: a systematic review." *Jornal de pediatria,* vol. 97, no. 4, 2021, pp. 369-377.

Dickson, E.J. "Coronavirus Is Killing the Working Mother." *Rolling Stone,* July 2020, https://www.rollingstone.com/culture/culture-features/working-motherhood-covid-19-coronavirus-1023609/. Accessed 8 Apr. 2023.

Gur, Raquel, et al. "The Disproportionate Burden of the COVID-19 Pandemic among Pregnant Black Women." *Psychiatry Research,* vol. 293, 2020, pp. 1-8.

Hermann, Allison, et al. "Meeting Maternal Mental Health Needs during the COVID-19 Pandemic". *JAMA Psychiatry,* vol 78, no. 2, 2021, pp. 123-24.

Igielnik, Ruth. *A Rising Share of Parents in the U.S. Say It's Been Difficult to Handle Child Care during the Pandemic.* Pew Research Center. 26 Jan. 2021, https://www.pewresearch.org/fact-tank/2021/01/26/a-rising-share-of-working-parents-in-the-u-s-say-its-been-difficult-to-handle-child-care-during-the-pandemic/#:~:text=Overall%2C%20about%20half%20of%20employed,said%20this%20in%20March%202020. Accessed 8 Apr. 2023.

Kim, Eunji, and Shawn Patterson. "The Pandemic and Gender Inequality in Academia." *Political Science & Politics,* vol. 55, no. 1, 2021, pp. 109-16.

Malone, Dana. "The Pandemic Makes the Second Shift Visible." *Women in Higher Education,* 27 Jan. 2022, https://www.wihe.com/article-details/215/the-pandemic-makes-the-second-shift-visible/. Accessed 8 Apr. 2023.

Mehta, Punam. "Are We Not the Heroes?: Racialized Single Mothers during the COVID-19 Lockdown." *Mothers, Mothering, and COVID-19: Dispatches from the Pandemic,* edited by Andrea O'Reilly and Fiona Joy Green, Demeter Press, 2021, pp. 459-66.

Perelman, Deb. "In the Covid-19 Economy, You Can Have a Kid or a

Job. You Can't Have Both", *New York Times*, July 2020, https://www.nytimes.com/2020/07/02/business/covid-economy-parents-kids-career-homeschooling.html?auth=link-dismiss-googleltap. Accessed 8 Apr. 2023.

O'Reilly, Andrea, and Fiona Joy Green, editors. *Mothers, Mothering, and COVID-19: Dispatches from the Pandemic*. Demeter Press, 2021.

O'Reilly, Andrea. "'Certainly Not an Equal-Opportunity Pandemic': COVID-19 and Its Impact on Mothers' Carework, Health, and Employment." *Mothers, Mothering, and COVID-19*, edited by Andrea O'Reilly and Fiona Joy Green, Demeter Press, 2021, pp. 41-52.

Raile, Amber, et al. "Women and the Weight of a Pandemic: A Survey of Four Western US States Early in the Coronavirus Outbreak." *Gender, Work, & Organization*, vol. 28, 2020, pp. 554-65.

Staneva, Aleksandra. "Mothering during a Pandemic and the Internalization of Blame and Responsibility." *Mothers, Mothering, and COVID-19: Dispatches from the Pandemic*, edited by Andrea O'Reilly and Fiona Joy Green, Demeter Press, 2021, pp. 411-22.

Thapa, Suraj, et al. "Maternal Mental Health in the Time of the COVID-19 Pandemic." *Acta Obstetricia Et Gynecologica Scandinavica*, vol. 99, no. 7, 2020, pp. 817-18.

Whiley, Lilith, et al. "Motherhood and Guilt in a Pandemic: Negotiating the "New" Normal with a Feminist Identity." *Gender, Work & Organization*, vol. 28, pp. 612-19.

Yoshikawa, Hirokazu, et al. "Effects of the Global Coronavirus Disease-2019 Pandemic on Early Childhood Development: Short- and Long-Term Risks and Mitigating Program and Policy Actions." *The Journal of Pediatrics*, vol. 223, 2020, pp. 188-93.

Chapter 20.

Feminist Representations of Maternity in Caryl Churchill's *Top Girls* and Sarah Daniels's *Neaptide*

Tuğrul Can Sümen

Introduction

The history of sexual politics between 1980 and 1990 in the United Kingdom is intertwined with the policies of Margaret Thatcher's administration. Elected as prime minister at the height of the women's liberation movement, the Iron Lady's strategy to revive the economy reserved domestic roles for most women, and negatively affected the unifying efforts of the feminist groups.[1] This chapter briefly examines Thatcher's critical role in influencing and reshaping feminism, and how her political conduct regressed the evolution of parenting for the modern woman, by surveying Thatcher's socio-political position regarding mothers in the 1980s. For this purpose, Caryl Churchill's (1938 –) *Top Girls* (1982) and Sarah Daniels's (1956 –) *Neaptide* (1986) are analyzed by focusing on mother characters to explore how the feminist playwrights protested the effects of Thatcher's anti-feminist stance on women and attempted to reconcile mothers and feminism.

Margaret Thatcher's Political Discourse on Feminism and Maternity in the 1980s

Thatcher is crucial to any discussion about feminism in the 1980s for an important reason: Thatcher's administrations coincided, or perhaps led to, a transition period between the second and third waves of feminism in the United Kingdom. Throughout her time as the prime minister, Thatcher carefully exhibited an assortment of empowering characteristics, which inspired pro-Thatcher feminists, such as Natasha Walter,[2] who claims Thatcher to be not only "'the great unsung heroine of British feminism'" but also a role model for female success: "She allowed British women to celebrate their ability not just to be nurturing or caring or life affirming, but also to be deeply unpleasant, to be cruel, to be death-dealing, to be egotistic. It was cathartic for us to acknowledge those possibilities in the female character writ so large" (qtd. in Aston 24). From a maternal perspective, the emphasis of Walter's remark is on the contrasting adjectives, positioning a binary between the traits regarded as the hallmarks of motherhood and the traits associated with empowerment, materialized through agonistic and self-centred attributes. The fact that traditional motherhood is oppressive and overdemanding to women is expounded by Adrienne Rich, one of the pioneers of the maternal theory. Andrea O'Reilly, in *Matricentric Feminism*, clarifies Rich's distinction between mothering and motherhood; mothering is a more progressive practice of maternity and refers to women's experiences of mothering, whereas motherhood is a mode of patriarchy, male defined, and institutionalized against women (55). Rich shares the viewpoint of third-wave feminists in calling for a shift towards a more empowered femininity and for liberating motherhood from patriarchy. However, it should be noted that instead of opposing maternity altogether, Rich encourages an autonomous and feminist praxis of mothering. In the light of this information, it could have been expected that Thatcher, a mother and a politician, would popularize a more forward-looking and beneficial manner of parenting for women. Nevertheless, the Iron Lady openly expressed her disdain for feminism,[3] and she made no compromises of her antifeminist views, advocating for the preservation of a traditional kind of motherhood.

Thatcher's stance on families, feminism, and maternity was a crucial component of Thatcherism, an ideology referring to the prime minister's distinct set of principles. Nigel Lawson, who served in Thatcher's cabinet, defines Thatcherism as "a mixture of free markets, financial discipline, firm control over public expenditure, tax cuts, nationalism, 'Victorian values' (of the Samuel Smiles self-help variety), privatization and a dash of populism" (64). Thatcherism prioritized economic growth by encouraging free trade and promoting privatization, opposed state interventions, and discouraged social reforms and welfare. The ideology stressed the significance of individual responsibility, as the Iron Lady strongly believed that there was "'no such thing as society, only individual men and women,'" (qtd. in Harvey 23) and for progress "[a]ll forms of social solidarity were to be dissolved in favour of individualism, private property, personal responsibility, and family values" (Harvey 23). True to form, Thatcher did not offer a helping hand to underprivileged women; only the governing elite benefitted from her leadership. For instance, Thatcher did not allow any woman from the House of Commons into her cabinet, but she did allow Baroness Janet Young to be the leader of the House of Lords, only to dismiss her fourteen months later, leaving no female politicians in the cabinet. Similarly, following her election, she turned down Emma Nicholson's (vice chairman of the party) offer of taxing women separately (Nicholson 89). Nicholson stated that "[t]he Conservative Party is now, and has been for a long, long time, an army led from the top" (96). Thatcher's aversion to social solidarity and favouring of the privileged exhibit a bourgeois feminist disposition, which is an inconsistent blend of feminism and liberalism. The incongruity is especially striking regarding maternity. Thatcher suffered hardships in her career due to the burdens of motherhood,[4] meaning she had firsthand experience of the overwhelming nature of parenting for women. The struggle did not alter the Iron Lady's frame of mind towards mothers, however, as through the entirety of her career, Thatcher propagandized for the conservation of regressive family values and the perpetuation of traditional motherhood. Thatcher's emphasis on family values negatively affected the political interest of women, especially feminist mothers. The Iron Lady's anti-progressive definition of family centred around the institution of heterosexual marriage: "Thatcherite rhetoric ... laid stress on the government encouraging the natural values and caring instincts of motherhood and the associated naturalness of patriarchal life" (Winter and Connoly 31). Observing the effects of Thatcherism on women, especially mothers, feminist playwrights Caryl

Churchill and Sarah Daniels questioned the eligibility of Thatcher as a symbol of feminism. The playwrights responded to the prime minister's policies by demonstrating how traditional maternity is inadequate to practise mothering, and by attempting to consolidate feminism and mothers.

The idea that a select group of women can be successful only through conformity is the subject of Churchill's play *The Top Girls*. The play introduces women from diverse fictional and historical backgrounds, exposing the continuity of the institutionalization of motherhood and the existence of class differences, which must be overcome to achieve the unity of women. Churchill is skeptical of Thatcher being a role model for women: "She may be a woman but she isn't a sister, she may be a sister but she isn't a comrade ... Of course, socialism and feminism aren't synonymous, but I feel strongly about both and wouldn't be interested in a form of one that didn't include the other" (*Interviews* 78). Churchill expresses her disapproval of the Iron Lady and Thatcherism through a socialist feminist perspective by "emphasiz[ing] the condition of collectives not individuals in the play" (Ülker 23). Accordingly, her critique concentrates on the situation of mothers and the abandonment of parenting in a competitive business climate. Daniels shares Churchill's skepticism regarding Thatcherism, and she focuses on society's norms of family values and maternity in her play *Neaptide*. In the play, Daniels presents an overview of discrimination and harassment a lesbian mother is subjected to while trying to keep the custody of her daughter. The aim of the playwright is to deconstruct Thatcher's regressive definition of family, making the concept more inclusive and restoring the dignity of nonconformist mothers. Daniels's answer to misogyny in her play relies on radical feminism, as most of the male characters in the play turn out maladapted to queer mothering. Churchill's and Daniels's examinations of the issues challenging women in their plays are different. Regardless, both playwrights offer contrasting yet complementary representations of maternity, as both recognize that eliminating inequalities between women, specifically mothers, can only be accomplished by forming sisterhoods.

Exchange of Maternity and Power in Caryl Churchill's *Top Girls*

The examination of the relation between feminism and maternity in *Top Girls* centres around Marlene, an ambitious and competitive businesswoman, who has recently got a promotion in the Top Girls Agency. The play begins with a celebration dinner in a restaurant and introduces five fictional and historical characters along with Marlene: Dull Gret, Isabella Bird,[5] Lady Nijo, Pope Joan, and Patient Griselda. Churchill's monochromatic depictions of womanhood are conjoined by similarities in each character's narrative. All characters at the table, excluding Dull Gret, have their autonomies, as women and as mothers, controlled and dominated by male-centric hierarchies. Moreover, to survive and advance in their respective social systems in which they are othered, the women internalize the male-centric values and abandon maternity altogether.

The first figure the opening scene focuses on is Lady Nijo—a representation of a historical figure from thirteenth-century Japan. From an early age, Nijo was raised by her father to obey the norms of male dominance. For example, Nijo's father arranges for her to become a concubine to the emperor, and in his dying words he orders Nijo to "'[s]erve His Majesty, be respectful, if you lose his favour enter holy orders'" (Churchill, *Top Girls* 3). Consequently, her identity and her idea of self-worth are defined only through the male authority figures in her social environment. Nijo becomes a concubine to the emperor of Japan when she is fourteen years old. Marlene notices that Nijo's narrative is ambiguous regarding whether the sexual union was consensual or not, and when she asks about it, Nijo replies: "No, of course not, Marlene, I belonged to him, it was what I was brought up for from a baby" (3). Throughout the dinner, Nijo continues narrating her past life, and her traumas resurface when the discussion focuses on being a mother. Although she miscarries her first child with the emperor, Nijo conceives her second child with Akebono, a man she has an affair with. Following childbirth, Akebono severs the umbilical cord with a short sword and takes the baby away. The father severing of the cord with a weapon symbolizes the severing of the bond between mother and child by patriarchy, which is experienced by all of the women at the table, except Isabella. For Nijo, renouncing her daughter and her identity as a mother is the only choice to avoid a political scandal. She has additional third and fourth pregnancies with Ariake, a priest she falls in love with; however, out of her own volition, Nijo abandons her children because the male figures in her environment, whom she relied on for her identity and purpose, disappear. She falls into a deep depression and claims she feels nothing for her child. However, Nijo regrets losing the chance of mothering her children, as during Griselda's story, when Griselda's children are returned to her after they were taken away, she bursts into tears:

NIJO. Did you feel anything for the children?
GRISELDA. Of course, I loved them.
...
NIJO. Nobody gave me back my children.
NIJO *cries. The WAITRESS brings brandies.* (25)

Nijo feels remorse to some degree for abandoning her children, but such a regret is not seen in Joan, a woman who cross-dresses to hide her feminine features and become the pope. Joan concentrates on passing as a man for so long that she becomes alienated from her own body. Her narrative on becoming pregnant and giving birth to her child borders on the bizarre, for she did not even realize that she was pregnant and thought that she was simply gaining weight. Her childbirth occurs during a procession, and she gives birth right in the middle of a parade. When Marlene asks Joan whether she thought of "getting rid of it," Joan answers the question expected of her religious upbringing: "Wouldn't that be a worse sin than having it?" (15). Joan internalizes the codes of patriarchy, similar to Nijo, only she interconnects her expression of self with an androcentric religious doctrine. Following childbirth, the clergymen drag her away from the town and stone her to death. When Nijo asks about the baby's fate, Joan's answer is simple and indifferent:

NIJO. And the child died too?
JOAN. Oh yes, I think so, yes. (17)

Through Nijo's and Joan's narratives, Churchill exemplifies how motherhood and womanhood are controlled by male-dominated hierarchies. However, her exemplification reaches the extreme with Griselda's narrative. Like Nijo's story, what marks the beginning of Griselda's narrative is a union with a male figure with political authority, as she is married to a marquis at the age of fifteen. The similarity continues in the representation of the power dynamics between the dominant male (Walter) and the oppressed woman (Griselda). Walter explains to Griselda's father that should they marry, Griselda "must always obey him in everything" (21). Although Griselda never complains, the social standing she attains comes at the cost of her maternity.

Walter exhibits a tyrannical mentality by controlling Griselda's marital and maternal identities. The authoritarian ruler expects complete subservience from Griselda, and she obeys him without any objections. One day, Walter asks Griselda to abandon her daughter, stating that the source of the unhappiness of the masses lies with their ruler siring a child with a commoner. Griselda does not object, and her daughter is taken from her while she is breastfeeding. Eventually, Walter sends Griselda back to her father's house, only to recall her, so she can organize the household chores. Nevertheless, she completely submits to her husband's every wish, explaining "[b]ut of course a wife must obey her husband. / And of course I must obey the Marquis*" (21). Griselda's story is distinguished from the stories of other women at the table by the happy ending, befitting of a fairy tale. Griselda's children return to her, and she remains with the marquise, rewards for her obedience to Walter. Griselda exhibits an almost comical manner of obedience, submitting to everything that is ever asked of her. Content with the happy conclusion of her story, Griselda has no complaints about the male-dominant hierarchies, given the fact that Walter rewarded her for her absolute loyalty.

As the scene ends, representations of all women at the table, except Dull Gret, criticize Thatcher's liberal feminism in two ways. First, as Michelene Wandor points out, despite suffering abuse by patriarchy, nobody at the table perceives themselves as a victim: "[F]or each, taking responsibility for herself is the central thread" (*Carry On* 172). Griselda, Joan, and Nijo realize early on that the patriarchal system is ever-present and inescapable, and to cope, the three women sacrifice their sense of mothering and children. However, for these three women at the table, the requisite sacrifice is not simply for survival but also for remaining in prestigious social positions: Nijo is held in high regard in the palace, Joan enjoys the prestige of the top of the ecclesiastical hierarchy, and Griselda experiences upward social mobility and rules over the masses.

Even the free spirit of the group, Isabella, made an effort to conform: "I tried to do what my father wanted" (Churchill, *Top Girls* 3). Conforming to patriarchy ensures women develop the necessary adaptation methods in a discriminatory environment, such as internalizing male-centric codes. Even though the cost of their conforming is losing autonomy, no woman at the table complains.

Second, even though all women at the table suffer similar abuse and trauma, especially concerning their maternity, there is no solidarity between them. Churchill hints at the role social class plays in an all-women space through the waitress in the restaurant. The waitress has no lines and only functions by serving the women at the table, creating a hierarchy in an all-women space. Churchill's representation of women draws "attention to the national, ideological, and class differences that must be elided to achieve ... idealized visions of female solidarity" (Cameron 144). All six women present at the table are members of the elite social class of their respective cultures, and as such, they occupy singular positions in which solidarity or sisterhood is not plausible. Consequently, they all exhibit an upper-class disdain towards the lower classes. Griselda would "rather obey the Marquis than a boy from the village" (Churchill, *Top Girls* 27). Joan enjoyed the top of the hierarchy: "I never obeyed anyone. They all obeyed me" (21). The disunity between the women created by the class system grows further with the disjointed dialogue, in which multiple characters speak at once, without listening to each other. The scene ends on a hysterical note, with Nijo crying, Joan puking in the corner, Marlene drinking Isabella's brandy, and Isabella continuing her monologue, now absent of an audience. There is no sisterhood between the women at the table. The hardships each has suffered as a mother cause the group to experience a variety of emotions, with the exception of Isabella, who cannot even try to empathize with the women.

The scene closes with Gret's monologue, in which Gret explains in a mythical fashion how after losing her babies to the Spanish, she united women in her village and descended into hell to fight off demons. The description of hell resembles Gret's village, and she sees a devil, who excretes money from a rooftop to the streets below. Some of the women are led away from the group to collect the money; however, Gret keeps the majority of women from such distractions and leads them to battle. She is represented in full-clad armour and wearing an apron, rendering her a typical representation of both a soldier and a mother. Even though she is intended to be a traditional kind of mother, she empowers all women around her, showing that unification of women can be a solution to oppression. Sharon Ammen claims that "[i]t is the caring for sisters that is the important take-off point for the kind of social feminism that Churchill advocates" (95). The women at the table find no consolation in each other because they refuse to bond. Moreover, the bourgeois feminist mentality is represented as a poor remedy for women's sufferings, who renounce maternity for social standing. Churchill proposes socialist feminism as a guide to forming sisterhoods, which can also provide women with the agency and liberty to practise mothering.

Throughout the first scene, nothing concrete about Marlene is revealed. However, in the first scene of the second act, Marlene's Thatcherite attitude towards maternity draws parallels with the rest of the women, save Gret. Marlene interviews Jeanine, a young secretary, who is looking for a better job. The interview exposes how the business climate during the Thatcher administration became increasingly anti-women:

> JEANINE. I'm saving to get married.
> MARLENE. Does that mean you don't want a long-term job, Jeanine?
> JEANINE. I might do.
> MARLENE. Because where do the prospects come in? No kids for a bit?
> JEANINE. Oh no, not kids, not yet.
> MARLENE. So you won't tell them you're getting married?
> JEANINE. Had I better not?
> MARLENE. It would probably help. (Churchill, *Top Girls* 31)

It could be argued that Marlene's advice to Jeanine reveals that she has found the solution to adapting to the sexism of the workplace by emulating and conforming to masculinist values. Throughout the play, Marlene exhibits a simulacrum of masculinity, which has advanced her career immensely. She advocates against marriage and parenting, perceiving both as hindrances for women in the workplace. Moreover, she disregards the role of sex in the workplace, which allows Marlene to break the glass ceiling, as she is promoted to managing director, surpassing even her male co-worker (Howard). However, the compromise is that she is deprived of the chance to become a wife and a mother. Marlene's Thatcherite attitude towards other women does not result in equality for all but the superiority of the few. Marlene and her assistants (Nell and Win) continue to remain in the office, whereas the applicants (Louise and Shona) remain, respectively, dissatisfied and unemployed.

In the last scene of the play, Marlene visits her sister Joyce, a year prior to the play's initial setting, and the conversation between the sisters brings the play's examination of the relationship between feminism and maternity to the climax. It is revealed that Angie (Marlene's niece) is actually her daughter, and to pursue her ambitions and dreams, Marlene abandoned Angie with Joyce, who could not have a child of her own. In the context of mothering, Joyce and Marlene represent opposing ends of a spectrum, with neither of them shown as an ideal mother. The sisters grew up in an abusive home, with domestic violence occurring frequently. Marlene despises her alcoholic father for abusing her mother and not providing any financial security for them. Joyce sympathizes with him, claiming that the life of the working class made him a bitter man. Joyce views her father in a more positive light because both the father and the daughter are members of the lower social class, working as manual labourers. She channels the same sympathy she feels towards the working class to her father. In contrast, Marlene's contempt towards her father causes her to have antipathy and disdain towards the working class.

Marlene's comment demonstrates her liberal stance regarding working mothers, and she believes the system offers equal advantages for all women: "I know a managing director who's got two children, she breast feeds in the board room, she pays a hundred pounds a week on domestic help alone and she can afford that because she's an extremely high-powered lady earning a great deal of money" (80). For Joyce, who works four different cleaning jobs and has no future prospects, such a position remains out of reach. Since Marlene is a stand-in for Thatcher— through Marlene's inability to empathize with her sister's situation— Churchill criticizes the Iron Lady's hostility towards the working class and unions.

Marlene's past actions convey an aversion to mothering, and her contemporary mentality negates any possibility of unity between mothering and Thatcherism. In a heated argument with Joyce, Marlene confesses to having had two abortions and abandoning Angie. Marlene abandoned her daughter because she feared a child could permanently ensnare her in working-class conditions. Contradicting her own comment, Marlene finds mothering and success incompatible, and she takes contraceptive pills to avoid pregnancy. Advocating for reproductive rights is considered to be a core aspect of second-wave feminism, and although Marlene benefits from the activism of feminist women, she refuses to offer a helping hand to other women, as witnessed in the previous scene, in her dialogue with Jeanine. Marlene's political outlook mimics the prime minister's. Admiring the Iron Lady and Ronald Reagan, Marlene fiercely supports individualism and monetarism. She disregards the determining role of the social classes, claiming anyone, through self-development, can reach a high position in a capitalist system. She detests unions, associating them with the Soviets. Marlene's repetitive emphasis on the role of the individual, combined with her relinquishing of parenting, reveals the improbability of a functional motherhood in the workplace and the need for a more adaptable kind of maternity.

Contrary to Marlene, Joyce represents the domestic space, motherhood, and the working class. Joyce's becoming a surrogate mother for Angie may resemble mothering; however, the relationship between the mother and daughter is represented as unstable. After Angie discovers Marlene is her biological mother, she harbours resentments towards working-class conditions, domestic responsibilities, and motherhood, and her relationship with Joyce deteriorates. However, unlike her biological mother, Angie has no skills or talents, which is confirmed by Marlene. Knowing Angie's inadequacy to survive in the workplace, Joyce attempts to guide her daughter to the domestic sphere, claiming "[Angie's] not going to get a job when jobs are hard to get. I'd be sorry for anyone in charge of her. She'd better get married. I don't know who'd have her, mind. She's one of those girls might never leave home" (43). Joyce's shortcoming is in the discrepancy between her frame of mind and her parenting. She is aware of the disadvantages the younger generation of the working-class faces, and she ideologically opposes them. However, in practice, she offers no resistance. Joyce does not support Angie's ambitions or nurture her daughter's dreams for the future. All Joyce can offer her daughter is discontentment in stasis by confining her to marriage and domestic responsibilities. Moreover, although Joyce contrasts Marlene in perspective, in exercise, she is prone to show sympathy for patriarchy, which is incompatible with feminism. Canan Şavkay argues that regardless of all her self-sacrifice, Joyce's supporting of her father and patriarchy makes her an unacceptable figure to emulate[6] (48).

Both Marlene and Joyce are unsuitable role models for feminist mothers. Marlene's empowering and would-be feminist attitude is self-centred and exclusive, mirroring Thatcher's. Moreover, it requires sacrificing maternity instead of encouraging mothering. For a Thatcherite, such as Marlene, the equality between the sexes can only occur through imitating masculinity, and the reward for it is not uplifting a generation of underprivileged mothers but creating singular positions of power, reserved only for the elite. In contrast, Joyce rejects Marlene's Thatcherite outlook; however, her resistance only remains in language. Churchill hints that the solution to finding an ideal manner of mothering is forming sisterhoods. However, the sisters in the play remain at odds with each other, and the play ends with Angie observing the future as "[f]rightening" (Churchill, *Top Girls* 87). There is no direct reference to Rich's theory of motherhood and mothering in the play, but a safe assumption is that *Top Girls* can be revaluated through Rich's *Of Woman Born*, as the dangers of separating feminism from mothering and the harms to mothers who adhere to the male-centric values are demonstrated in almost all mother characters in the play.

Solidarity of Mothers and Daughters in Sarah Daniels's *Neaptide*

Sharing Churchill's artistic vision, Daniels examines the issues concerning women's economic independence in *Gut Girls* (1988); however, the play that truly complements *Top Girls*, regarding women's experiences as mothers, is *Neaptide*. *Top Girls* is concerned with how motherhood is constituted against the political interests of women, how mothers abandon maternity, and how the disconnection between mothers and daughters hinders the possibility of solidarity. *Neaptide* contrasts with and complements *Top Girls* by demonstrating how mothers and daughters can achieve solidarity through abandoning traditional womanhood and practising mothering. In the play, mothering is represented as a force that sanctifies the bond of mothers and daughters. Following decades of exposure to the male-centric way of thinking, mothers initially find it difficult to adapt and change; however, younger generations inspire older generations to stand against patriarchy.

Neaptide's focus is on Claire and her daughter Poppy, and the narrative is strengthened by Joyce's (Claire's mother) and Val's (Claire's sister) experiences. In the play, Claire, a teacher in an all-girls school, is seen in a legal battle with her ex-husband, Lawrence, to keep the custody of her daughter. Through the legal process, Claire is subjected to psychological violence by her father, by Lawrence, by her co-workers, and by the judicial system due to her nonconformist sexual orientation, especially after coming out. Besides Claire, Diane (Claire's student) and Bea (the headmistress of Claire's school) come out as lesbians as well. Although Bea and Claire are reluctant to come out, Diane's bravery inspires both women to come out and support each other. Three generations of women achieve solidarity through the older generations protecting the younger ones from a homophobic social environment. The legal system fails Claire, however, who flees from the United Kingdom to the United States to live with her daughter, after Lawrence wins the custody of Poppy. This bittersweet ending is only made possible after Joyce arranges a new life for Claire and Poppy in the United States. Joyce's actions create a bond of solidarity with her daughter, removing generation gap as an obstacle to the unification of women and affirming the sanctity of mother-daughter relationships.

The primary conflict between mother and daughter in the play is demonstrated through Claire and Joyce's relationship. Joyce represents traditional and oppressed women. She submits to mistreatment from Sid (her husband) and internalizes the male dominant culture's definitions about mothers: "Me? Me? Picking on you? Huh, I like that. It's usually only drunk and insane mothers who are considered unfit for parental control" (Daniels 248). Moreover, Joyce prefers silence in the face of child abuse. When Sid asks Poppy to sit on his lap, Poppy clearly and firmly refuses, which results in an argument between Claire and Sid, with Sid openly threatening Claire with a beating. Gabriele Griffin states that "[v]iolence against women ... is a persistent topic in Daniels's work, notoriously difficult to deal with since violence against women is such an unequivocally gendered phenomenon, indicting men" (199-200). Contentment for Joyce is to "have a marvellous husband and a lovely family" (Daniels 248). However, Joyce is far from being content with the situation of her family. Val is clinically depressed, and Claire is in a legal dispute with her ex-husband over the custody of her daughter. Her husband, an unemployed docker, is a possible alcoholic, and he makes misogynistic remarks towards Claire. Through Sid's actions, Joyce's frustration is justified, and her powerlessness is revealed: "What else am I supposed to do? What else can I do? Sometimes you forget—" (251), but before she can even finish her sentence, Sid cuts her off.

In this violent atmosphere, mothers are represented as dynamic characters, for they change to protect their daughters from the sexism of different institutions. Joyce realizes the injustices surrounding Claire's case and finds the means for Claire to be with Poppy. Claire realizes she cannot remain silent about her own sexual identity as a lesbian when she sees how bravely Diane comes out. Bea, who is secretly a lesbian, realizes she has been a hypocrite and decides to drop the charges against Diane, who caused a scandal by publicly coming out as a lesbian in an all-girls school. Subsequently, the relationship of Bea and Diane gains a mother-daughter dimension. Following such feminist awakenings, the mother characters abandon traditional womanhood and construct a new one. The mothers embrace feminism to support the members of the younger generations, which can be interpreted as a transition from motherhood to mothering, according to Rich's conceptions of maternity. Moreover, Daniels emphasizes the importance of women accessing scholarly domains, as education is an important part of feminist awakening and one of the causes of the division between Joyce and Claire, Val, and Jean (Claire's flatmate). Joyce could not attend university, but Claire, Val, and Jean received a formal education. Younger generations have more access to education; therefore, they are more aware of their rights regarding their autonomy—something Joyce, a member of an older generation, struggles with.

In *Neaptide*, feminism requires relinquishing the established norms of maternity and womanhood, and through this requirement, Daniels declares her radical feminist stance. Diane S. Hope's research on radical feminism clarifies the tenets of traditional womanhood:

> Contrary to some analyses of the radical feminist movement the emergent victim is not men, although men are clearly seen as the enemy. The real victim is "traditional womanhood" or as another feminist writes, "the enemy ... in your head." The victim is

traditional woman, for it is the "male-identified woman" who was condemned to acquiesce in her own oppression, who was socialized by the male definition of her sexual identity, and identified as an appendage to man. Until this socialized identity was killed off, the new woman could not be born. (qtd. in Brown 12)

Daniels resorts to radical feminism in her survey of the situation of lesbian women, as she explains that "'in its origin feminism had a very radical agenda to do with rights and justice and of course neither of those things have been too popular recently'" (qtd. in Aston 40). In *Neaptide*, traditional family values and womanhood are deconstructed and reconstructed in accordance with the idea of sisterhood. In the play, all women are oppressed by patriarchy to various extents, but Claire suffers double oppression, both as a woman and as a lesbian mother. Dimple Godiwala remarks that there "will always be a struggle for lesbian mothers who are denied control in parenting and the custody of their children (Claire) through mis-representation and lack of understanding" (129).

In this regard, the play brings discrimination against both lesbian women and lesbian mothers to the stage, making the injustices public at a time when such issues were swept under the rug. Daniels's analysis of the troubling situation of queer women is prophetic, as her play seems to predict Thatcher's infamous Section 28 of 1988, which "banned the 'promotion' of homosexuality by local authorities and in Britain's schools" and forced libraries to remove any material that included non-conformist sexual representations (Sommerlad). Incidentally, *Neaptide* is set in an all-girls school, revealing the connection between patriarchy and the institutions, as all institutions in the play serve the patriarchy.

Daniels favours the empowerment of women from all generations; however, she shares the power with all women characters, as no women is left behind in the play. If women agree to support one another, they are liberated from the chains of patriarchy, thus contradicting Thatcherism. The piece written in the school's end-of-term magazine by Diane can be read as a political commentary on how Thatcher's individualism discriminates marginalized women:

MARION (*reads*). It is about time the education system recognised the hypocrisy it transmits while trying to be liberal in its purporting to care for the individual. Its liberalism is total reactionary rubbish and sexist crap. We are not allowed freedom of choice over our sexuality, which if it is different to that as suggested by the hierarchy of this establishment, is evil. We have a right to our identity and we are not going to be silenced by a smack in the gob from this fascist, poxy school. (Daniels 288)

The only exception in this case is women refusing to support other women, such as Marion (Claire's co-worker), who outright dismisses any notion of accepting lesbian women as sisters: "There just isn't anything natural about women kissing each other" (264).

Not only does Daniels find addressing a woman's eligibility as a mother based on her sexual orientation a non sequitur, but she also finds silencing abuse unacceptable. The abuse is most recognizable in Roger's (Claire's co-worker) dialogue with other women. Roger is perhaps the most outspoken misogynist in the play, for he openly sexually harasses Claire and calls Diane "a bit butch" (262). His misogyny is combined with homophobia, and he truly becomes a menace, as demonstrated by his comment on Diane's and Terri's parents: "Can't be very fruitful knowing there are bent genes in the family tree" (265).

Regarding her case on the eligibility of nonconformist women as mothers, the playwright examines Claire's struggles with coming out as a lesbian. Claire's coming out results in her losing custody of Poppy, as Lawrence accuses Claire of immorality during the legal proceedings. Daniels draws attention to public hostility towards feminist and queer mothers through adapting a fertility myth from a radical feminist perspective:

CLAIRE *picks up a book.*

In the beginning, if there ever was such a time, Demeter, the goddess of life, gave birth to four daughters, whom she named Persephone, Psyche, Athena and Artemis. The world's first children were unremarkably happy. To amuse their mother— with whom they were all passionately in love—they invented language, music, laughter—and many more useful and boisterous activities. (238)

The myth of Demeter and her four daughters is narrated by Claire, and it differs from the original myth. In Claire's version, the four daughters were "unremarkably happy" (238). The word "unremarkably" within the context of the play becomes a reference to the lives of the children of the lesbian mothers, which indicates that having a mother with nonconformist sexual orientation is nothing out of the ordinary—removing the stigma towards the lesbian mothers. The joyful atmosphere is broken when Persephone is abducted by Hades, following her menstruation, and the mother and the children "discovered that in shame and sorrow childhood ends, and that nothing remains the same" (238). Upon discovering that her daughter is abducted, Demeter is enraged, and she demands her daughter back: "'Yea, if that be the natural fate of daughters, let all mankind perish. Let there be no crops, no grain, no corn, if this maiden is not returned to me'" (239). Demeter's wish is made manifest, and her daughter returns to her, as she "belonged to her mother" (239). Mothers rescuing daughters from situations in which they endure abuse and violence is a recurring theme of the play. Claire likes the myth better than *Cinderella* or *Sleeping Beauty*, as these fairy tales exempt the relationships between the mothers and the daughters and instead focus on the nuptial bliss of the young women. Poppy wants to listen to more of the myth, but Joyce's arrival prevents Claire from finishing her story, symbolizing the ongoing process of mothers and daughters fighting against patriarchal oppression.

A common motif in Daniels's plays is that male characters remain apathetic to women's grievances, which is seen in *Neaptide*, with the exceptions of Colin (Val's husband) and Cyril (Claire's coworker). Doctors in the hospital maltreat Val with misogynist remarks. Roger makes inappropriate misogynistic and sexual remarks to Claire. Lawrence threatens Claire with humiliating her in a legal battle by exposing her as a lesbian. The offensiveness of men is loudest in the institutions, namely the educational, marital, medical, and legal ones. Hospitals disregard women's mental well-being. Schools discriminate against the sexual other. Traditional marriage is oppressive to women, and the legal system favours men. Only Colin and Cyril support women; Colin supports Val in her battle with depression, and Cyril states Claire is a good teacher, and her sexual orientation should not prevent her from keeping her job.

The playwright's shortcoming in her play is that patriarchy remains unbowed, as the institutions continue to discriminate against women. Wandor criticizes Daniels's pessimism: "[Daniels] tacitly accept[s] that power is held by men and is unchallengeable, for which fact there is neither analysis nor alternative" ("The Impact" 90-91). From this perspective, the happy ending of Claire and Poppy is made bleak by the fact that only escaping to another country could keep the mother and daughter together. However, Daniels concludes the play with a hopeful outlook for the future, as mothers always support their daughters against oppression. In the conclusion, Val takes her mother's hand, and Joyce removes her daughter from the hospital—the same institution that mistreated her daughter. Joyce's saving of Claire, Poppy, and Val from the institutions in which they were imprisoned reconciles women from three generations and abolishes generational differences as obstacles to solidarity between women.

A Comparison of Representations of Maternity in *Top Girls* and *Neaptide*

Churchill and Daniels seem to be of one mind about Thatcher's self-centred and antifeminist rhetoric; both perceive that mothers seem to be receiving the brunt of the regressive effects of Thatcherism. Churchill is skeptical about the possibility of empowerment under a system that discriminates against women and confines mothers to the borders of domestic responsibilities. In such a system, connection between mothers and daughters is nearly impossible, and mothers find it difficult to support their children. Daniels is aware of how male-centric institutions oppress women and attempt to break the sacred bond between mothers and daughters. She argues that more traditional concepts of womanhood must be left behind to practise a more progressive kind of mothering, which includes nonconformist mothering. Both playwrights examine the underprivileged positions mothers find themselves in as a subject and offer a more feminist way of parenting as a solution.

Churchill examines the age-long effects of oppression of women, by showing how women compete for privilege in male-dominated societies and relinquish maternity, as shown in the dinner scene and the confrontation between the sisters. Daniels is more concerned with both the immediate and the aftershocks of violence and oppression enacted by the institutions towards queer mothers, such as Claire's struggles both before and after coming out. Churchill's exclusion of male characters, as well as her using of all-women spaces in her play, highlights the issues standing against the unity of women, namely the social class system and Thatcherism. Daniels employs representations of several stereotypically sexist and violent men within her play and presents them in everyday situations, in which they abuse women psychologically. By blending contemporary life with the reimagination of the myth of Demeter and Persephone, Daniels exposes the timelessness of women's abuse at the hands of patriarchy and reveals the strength of the solidarity between mothers and daughters.

The idea that unifies both plays is that mothers can only practise mothering when women support one another, form sisterhoods, and embrace feminism. The sole prominent distinction between the messages of the playwrights is that for Churchill, only after class differences are eliminated can women form sisterhoods, which necessitates embodying socialist feminism. Daniels agrees with Churchill, and she advocates for the removal of social inequality in her plays, such as in *Gut Girls*; however, in *Neaptide*, she focuses on relinquishing the established norms of womanhood from a radical feminist standpoint. Both playwrights agree that feminism is essential for unifying mothers and daughters against patriarchy, and they advise mothers to change for the better by practising feminist mothering.

Conclusion

Top Girls and *Neaptide* are prominent examples of feminist drama that explores the topic of motherhood. Both plays are political declarations during a time in which feminism was troubled with disorder and disunity. Motherhood and mothering in the plays are presented as part of broader issues, and a solution is offered in each play. Churchill's socialist feminism and Daniels's radical feminism may seem to contrast with each other as answers to the problems mothers experience; however, a unity is achieved through advocating for feminist mothering, forming sisterhoods, and overcoming intergenerational differences. The plays examine the contemporary problems of mothers; nevertheless, both plays transcend the borders of contemporary issues, for the playwrights place the timeless problems concerning motherhood at the centre of the plot and expose them through examining the power relations between characters. In the conclusion of both plays, traditional motherhood is disfavoured, and a more progressive manner of mothering is advocated. The plays and the ageless lessons offered within them remain relevant to feminist mothering today.

Endnotes

1. Sylvia Bashevkin's research reveals that the number of laws supporting women's political interests declined during the Thatcher administration (281-86). Regarding women's liberation, Thatcher asked what the movement "had 'ever done for [her]'" (qtd. in Bashevkin 278).
2. Natasha Walter is a British feminist author of influential works, such as *The New Feminism* (1998), *On the Move: Feminism for a New Generation* (1999), and *Living Dolls: The Return of Sexism* (2008).
3. "'I hate feminism. It is poison'" (qtd. in Petri)
4. "'I did not try for the 1955 election,' she told *Woman's Hour* in 1986. 'I really just felt the twins were ... only two, I really felt that it was too soon. I couldn't do that and so I didn't try for a candidature then'" (qtd. in Campbell 100)
5. Isabella Bird is the only woman at the table who is not a mother. To focus on the relationship between motherhood and patriarchy, Bird's story is excluded.
6. Translated and paraphrased from Turkish to English by the author.

Works Cited

Ammen, Sharon. "Feminist Vision and Audience Response: Tracing the Absent Utopia in Caryl Churchill's *Top Girls*." *Utopian Studies*, vol. 7, no. 1, 1996, pp. 86-102.

Aston, Elaine. *Feminist Views on the English Stage: Women Playwrights, 1990-2000*. Cambridge University Press, 2003.

Bashevkin, Sylvia. "Confronting Neo-conservatism: Anglo-American Women's Movements under Thatcher, Reagan and Mulroney." *International Political Science Review / Revue internationale de science politique*, vol. 15, no. 3, 1994, pp. 275-96.

Brown, Janet. *Feminist Drama: Definition & Critical Analysis*. The Scarecrow Press, 1979.

Cameron, Rebecca. "From *Great Women* to *Top Girls*: Pageants of Sisterhood in British Feminist Theater." *Comparative Drama*, vol. 43, no. 2, 2009, pp. 143-66.

Campbell, John. *Margaret Thatcher Volume One: The Grocer's Daughter.* Pimlico, 2001.

Churchill, Caryl. *Interviews with Contemporary Women Playwrights.* By Kathleen Betsko and Rachel Koenig, Beech Tree, 1987.

Churchill, Caryl. *Top Girls.* Methuen, 2008.

Daniels, Sarah. *Plays: One: Ripen Our Darkness, The Devil's Gateway, Masterpieces, Neaptide, Byrthrite.* Methuen, 1991.

Griffin, Gabriele. "Violence, abuse and gender relations in the plays of Sarah Daniels." *The Cambridge Companion to Modern British Women Playwrights*, edited by Elaine Aston and Janelle Reinelt. Cambridge University Press, 2000, pp. 194-211.

Godiwala, Dimple. *Breaking the Bounds: British Feminist Dramatists Writing in the Mainstream since c. 1980.* Peter Lang Publishing, 2003.

Harvey, David. *A Brief History of Neoliberalism.* Oxford University Press, 2007.

Lawson, Nigel. *The View from No. 11: Memoirs of a Tory Radical.* Bantam, 1992.

Nicholson, Emma. *Secret Society: Inside—and Outside—the Conservative Party.* Indigo, 1996.

O'Reilly, Andrea. *Matricentric Feminism: Theory, Activism, Practice.* 2nd ed. Demeter, 2021.

Petri, Alexandra. "Margaret Thatcher, Iron Lady, unusual feminist suspect." *The Washington Post.* WP Company, 2 Dec. 2021, https://www.washingtonpost.com/blogs/compost/wp/2013/04/08/margaret-thatcher-iron-lady-unusual-feminist-suspect/. Accessed 9 Apr. 2023.

Sommerlad, Joe. "Section 28: What was Margaret Thatcher's controversial law and how did it affect the lives of LGBT+ people?" *Independent.* 25 May 2018, https://www.independent.co.uk/news/uk/politics/section-28-explained-lgbt-education-schools-homosexuality-gay-queer-margaret-thatcher-a8366741.html. Accessed 9 Apr. 2023.

Şavkay, Canan. Caryl Churchill in Top Girls Oyununda Yeni Kadın İmgesi. *Tiyatro Eleştirmenliği ve Dramaturji Bölümü Dergisi (Journal of Theatre Criticism and Dramaturgy)*, no. 4, 2004, pp. 40-54.

Ülker Erkan, Berna Ayça. "A Socialist Feminist Reading of Thatcherite

Women in British Feminist Plays." *SEFAD*, no. 42, 2019, pp. 21-34.

Wandor, Michelene. *Carry on, Understudies: Theatre and Sexual Politics*. Routledge, 1986.

Wandor, Michelene. "The Impact of Feminism on the Theatre." *Feminist Review*, no. 18, 1984, pp. 76-92.

Winter, Karen, and Paul Connolly. "'Keeping It in the Family': Thatcherism and the Children Act 1989." *Thatcher's Children? Politics, Childhood and Society in the 1980s and 1990s*, edited by Jane Pilcher and Stephen Wagg, Falmer, 1996, pp, 29-42.

Notes on Contributors

Jillayna Adamson, MA, LPC, LMHC (pronounced Jill-anna) is a mother, practising psychotherapist, and writer. She loves all things people, connection, and culture and is particularly interested in identity development and mental wellness within the psychosocial implications of the modern Western world. Jillayna's writing often explores the motherhood role, otherhood, and identity. She is a Canadian transplant currently in the US with her partner and kids and is a firm believer in letting your freak flag fly.

Victoria Bailey is currently completing the final year of a PhD by practice in creative writing and has a master's in women's studies, the research for both has focused upon representation of single mothers in written texts. Her nonfiction and creative writing work has been included in a wide range of feminist focused publications, including other Demeter Press anthologies. She is also a feminist mother of three.

Elizabeth A. Bennett, PhD, is an assistant professor of psychology at Point Park University. She is a mother-scholar interested in the use of creative arts in both qualitative research and psychotherapy. Her primary research interests centre maternal trauma and experiences of embodiment as well as the subversive nature of feminist relationships. She is a mama of two (soon to be three!) young children, equal parts precocious and delightful.

Kahaema Byer is a Black feminist mother, activist, scholar, and practitioner from Trinidad and Tobago. Byer has a background in psychology and human development and works at the intersection of gender and trauma. She is deeply committed to racial justice and to a world where all womxn can live with joy and freedom. Kahaema is in the early stages of exploring her Indigenous heritage. She is known by friends for a scandalous laugh and enjoys play and dance.

Tara Carpenter Estrada is an associate professor of art education at Brigham Young University. As a practising artist, she makes mixed-media and ceramic art, which has been shown in national and international juried exhibitions. Her writing and art have been featured in the *Journal of the Motherhood Initiative*, *Visual Inquiry*, and *Art Education*. Tara is also the director of BYU Jumpst(ART), a series of workshops for K-12 students.

Eve Darwood is a final year PhD researcher, teacher of religious studies and philosophy, and mother of three. Her work explores the relationship between the body and self, in response to family breakdown, motherhood, and disability. She has published life-writing relating to depression and trauma and has written articles for *MS Trust*, MS Society, and her own blog. She also writes and performs poetry discussing the themes of the body and the feeling-self.

Heather Dillaway was professor of sociology and associate dean in the College of Liberal Arts and Sciences at Wayne State University in Detroit, Michigan, at the time of writing this article. In July 2022, she transitioned to become dean of the College of Arts and Sciences at Illinois State University in Normal, Illinois. Her research focuses on women's reproductive health, motherhood, aging, and disability experiences. She has two teenagers who participate in, and inform, her pursuit of feminist mothering.

Fiona Joy Green is a cisgender, temporarily able-bodied, feminist mother who believes in the power of revolutionary feminist motherwork. She is a white immigrant and holds the position of professor in the Department of Women's and Gender Studies at the University of Winnipeg, located within Treaty No. 1 Territory, the traditional lands and waters of the Anishinaabe, Ininew, Oji-Cree, Dene, and Dakota and the homeland of the Métis Nation. Dr. Green is the author of *Practicing Feminist Mothering* (ARP) and coeditor of five Demeter Press collections that address evolving feminist parenting practices and maternal pedagogies. Her current interests include exploring parenting and families in relation to the everchanging digital world in her role as coauthor of the blog *Family Blog Lines: Ta[l]king Care*: https://familybloglines.com/blog/.

Zaje A. T. Harrell, PhD, is a health psychologist with a passion for integrating theory and praxis. She holds a joint doctorate in psychology and women's studies with content expertise in coping, mental health, and community change. She descends from the activist, justice-seeking tradition of Black clubwomen. Zaje is a married Black feminist mother of three children, ages twelve, ten, and eight. They live in the greater Baltimore Maryland area.

Renée E. Mazinegiizhigoo-kwe Bédard is of Anishinaabeg (Ojibwe/ Nipissing/ Omàmiwininiwag), Kanien'kehá:ka and French Canadian ancestry. She is a member of Okikendawdt Mnissing (Dokis First Nation). She holds a PhD from Trent University in Indigenous studies. Currently, she is an assistant professor at Western University in the Faculty of Education. Her areas of publication include practices of Anishinaabeg motherhood, maternal philosophy, and spirituality.

Ketoki Mazumdar, M.Sc., MPhil, PhD, is an Assistant Professor of Psychology at the FLAME University, Pune, India. She is also a consultant psychotherapist. Her interest lies at the intersection of gender and mental health, particularly feminist perspectives in the areas of maternal mental health, mothering practices across cultures, parenting, work-family interface, and self-compassion.

Jen McGowan is coming back to her art practice after having and raising small children. She graduated from Concordia University in Montreal in the late 1990s. Although motherhood asks so much, the role of a mother—so fraught and charged—drives her to make art whenever and however she can. Throughout the pandemic, the pressures on mothers (primarily) have increased exponentially, and art has been her lifeline. She uses whatever accessible processes and materials she has on hand to explore her new(ish) identity through a feminist lens. The work she makes reflects her own internal struggle to negotiate the expectations that confine her as a mother. Her work has been included in shows throughout Canada and internationally.

Lianne Milton Lianne Milton is an American journalist, social documentary photographer, and visual artist. Her photographic research investigates the complexities of the maternal experience. She explores interconnecting themes of history, identity, mythology, and human rights. Lianne has photographed throughout Latin America and Southeast Asia, including Brazil where she lived for seven years. While there, her photography for news publications brought international attention to the social impact of the country's health crises, political turmoil, and environmental issues. Lianne is multiple recipient of international reporting grants and fellowships, and her photography is shown in national and international juried exhibitions.

Rachel O'Donnell is an assistant professor of writing at the University of Rochester. Her ongoing work is on feminist critiques of science, colonialism, and biotechnology. She has lived and worked in Latin America, and has previously published on Sor Juana de La Cruz, revolutionary movements, migration, and mothering, as well as works of short fiction. She previously published a piece of creative nonfiction for Demeter's collection, *Interrogating Pregnancy Loss* (2017).

Andrea O'Reilly, PhD, is full professor in the School of Gender, Sexuality and Women's Studies at York University, founder/editor-in-chief of the *Journal of the Motherhood Initiative* and publisher of Demeter Press. She is coeditor/editor of twenty-plus books, including *Feminist Parenting: Perspectives from Africa and Beyond* (2020), *Mothers, Mothering, and COVID-19: Dispatches from a Pandemic* (2021), *Maternal Theory*, 2nd edition (2021), and *Monstrous Mothers; Troubling Tropes* (2021). She is editor of *The Encyclopedia on Motherhood* (2010) and coeditor of *The Routledge Companion to Motherhood* (2019). She is author of *Toni Morrison and Motherhood: A Politics of the Heart* (2004), *Rocking the Cradle: Thoughts on Motherhood, Feminism, and the Possibility of Empowered Mothering* (2006), and *Matricentric Feminism: Theory, Activism, and Practice*, 2nd edition (2021). She is twice the recipient of York University's Professor of the Year Award for teaching excellence and is the 2019 recipient of the Status of Women and Equity Award of Distinction from OCUFA (Ontario Confederation of University Faculty Associations).

Sneha Parekh Gupta, M.Sc., M.Phil, is a clinical psychologist (RCI registered) practising in Kolkata, India. Her areas of interest are positive psychology, specifically, resilience and mindfulness as well as interventions for parents and children.

Emily Rae Robertson is a writer and long-time fan of sci-fi and fantasy. She started writing in kindergarten, when her teacher gave her a Hannah Montana folder and told her to go wild. In her spare time, Emily likes to read, draw, bake, and play video games.

Shruti Raji-Kalyanaraman is a doctoral student in gender, feminist, and women's studies at York University. Her research draws from her life experiences of being a rainbow mother and a first-generation Indian immigrant settler on Turtle Island. She explores racialized mothering in a pandemic through Indigenous-immigrant relationalities as well as race and caste privilege and advocates for reciprocal and non-exploitative relationships in the path towards antiracism. Raji-Kalyanaraman's community activism has been featured in York Region Magazine and the Toronto Star.

Lisa H. Rosen is an associate professor and the director of the Undergraduate Psychology Program at Texas Woman's University. Her research focuses on parent-child communication and exploring ways that parents can best support victimized youth.

Linda J. Rubin is a professor of psychology and licensed psychologist at Texas Woman's University. Her research, clinical, and teaching interests target traumatic stress and violence against women. She has offered empirically based intervention to college students who experience domestic/dating violence, sexual assault/rape, and stalking.

Isha Sen, M.Sc., M.Res. leverages her background in clinical psychology, developmental psychopathology, and neuroscience in her research and clinical endeavours. Along with her interest in maternal mental health, she is also keen on studying the applications of technology-based interventions.

Lili Shi is an associate professor and the director of speech at the Department of Communication and Performing Arts. She grew up in Yunnan, China, and received her PhD at Howard University in 2010. Her teaching and research of intercultural communication focus on issues of gender, space, Asian diasporas, and transnationalism.

Natasha Steer is an educator, traveller, and writer who lives with her son in the Greater Toronto Area. She became a single-lone mother at the age of nineteen and has travelled to over fifty countries with her teenage son. Natasha has a BA in English Literature and a MEd in Social Justice Education. She enjoys writing memoir and personal essays about the intersection of feminism and motherhood, creativity, and travel. You can find her online at www.natashasteer.com.

Rachel E. Stough, MA, MPH, is a mother and a clinical psychology doctoral candidate at Point Park University. Her clinical work is oriented towards feminist, relational, and somatic therapies, with a particular emphasis on the embodiment of trauma. In her research, she is interested in mothering experiences, collective and complex traumas, and healing in community.

Tuğrul Can Sümen is a research assistant in the Department of English Language and Literature at Cappadocia University and an MA student in the Department of English Language and Literature at Hacettepe University. His research paper on feminist theatre, titled "Matricentric Feminism in Charlotte Keatley's *My Mother Said I Never Should*," was the recipient of Best Graduate Paper Award in 15th IDEA (English Language and Literature Research Association of Turkey) Conference. His academic interests are environmental humanities, feminist theory, and the English Renaissance.

Molly Wiant Cummins received her PhD from Southern Illinois University. Currently, she is an Assistant Professor in the Department of Communication at the University of Texas at Arlington. Dr. Wiant Cummins's research converges at the intersections of rhetorical, critical, and feminist methods. Part of her research focuses on critical communication pedagogy and critical/cultural studies, whereas some of her research is centred in (intensive) motherhood and feminism as they relate to pregnancy, birth, and mothering discourses.

Deepest appreciation to
Demeter's monthly Donors

DEMETER

Daughters
Summer Cunningham
Tatjana Takseva
Debbie Byrd
Fiona Green
Tanya Cassidy
Vicki Noble
Myrel Chernick

Sisters
Amber Kinser
Nicole Willey

Grandmother
Tina Powell